1992

104229

OPERATING SYSTEMS
Concepts, Policies, and Mechanisms

JAMES R. PINKERT

California State University, Chico

LARRY L. WEAR

California State University, Chico

PRENTICE HALL, Englewood Cliffs, New Jersey 07632

LIBRARY OF CONGRESS
Library of Congress Cataloging-in-Publication Data

Pinkert, James R.
    Operating systems: concepts, policies, and mechanisms/James R. Pinkert, Larry L. Wear.
        p.   cm.
    Bibliography: p.
    Includes index.
    ISBN 0–13–638073–5
    1. Operating systems (Computers)   I. Wear, Larry L.   II. Title.
QA76.76.O63P56 1988
005.4'3—dc 19   88–345
                                                                           CIP

To Pam Wear and Mom

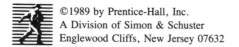
©1989 by Prentice-Hall, Inc.
A Division of Simon & Schuster
Englewood Cliffs, New Jersey 07632

Apple, Macintosh, and LaserWriter are registered trademarks of Apple Computer, Inc. CP/M is a registered trademark of Digital Research, Inc. IBM, IBM 360, IBM/370, MFT, OS/360, PC-DOS, and VM/370 are registered trademarks of International Business Machines Corporation. MS-DOS is a registered trademark of Microsoft Corporation. Norton Utilities is a registered trademark of Peter Norton Computing, Inc. Tandem and Guardian are registered trademarks of Tandem Computers, Inc. Turbo Pascal is a registered trademark of Borland International, Inc. UCSD PASCAL is a registered trademark of the Regents of The University of California. UNIX is a registered trademark of Bell Laboratories.

The authors and publisher of this book have used their best efforts in preparing this book. These efforts include the development, research, and testing of the theories, pseudocode algorithms, and programs to determine their effectiveness. The authors and publisher make no warranty of any kind, expressed or implied, with regard to these algorithms and programs or the documentation contained in this book. The authors and publisher shall not be liable in any event for incidental or consequential damages in connection with, or arising out of, the furnishing, performance, or use of these algorithms or programs.

Printed in the United States of America

10   9   8   7   6   5   4   3   2   1

ISBN 0-13-638073-5

Prentice-Hall International (UK) Limited, *London*
Prentice-Hall of Australia Pty. Limited, *Sydney*
Prentice-Hall Canada Inc., *Toronto*
Prentice-Hall Hispanoamericana, S.A., *Mexico*
Prentice-Hall of India Private Limited, *New Delhi*
Prentice-Hall of Japan, Inc., *Tokyo*
Simon & Schuster Asia Pte. Ltd., *Singapore*
Editora Prentice-Hall do Brasil, Ltda., *Rio de Janeiro*

7-14-92 Published $44.30

Contents

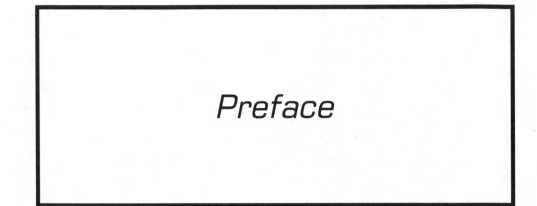

Preface

Operating Systems! The very mention of the class causes some undergraduate computer science students to shudder, and perhaps there is good reason for such trepidation. In many curricula the first course in operating systems is one of the most difficult classes, both to take and to teach. Several factors contribute to this difficulty.

One reason is that the student must be ready to make sophisticated use of concepts he or she has learned only recently in previous computer science courses. Understanding operating systems and implementing operating system programs require a pragmatic, in-depth knowledge of programming languages, design methodologies, and data structures.

Another aspect of the problem is the phenomenal growth of the science of computing. This growth constantly challenges curriculum planners, who must allocate the units of a computer science major among three areas: (1) required computer science core classes that provide the students with a firm foundation in their discipline; (2) required complementary courses in other departments, such as mathematics, physics, and English; (3) electives, so that the student can have a specialization within the major. The result of such curriculum demands is that many computer science majors include only one required courses in operating systems.

Not too long ago one class was reasonable. However, the growth of the science of computing again comes into play. We have gone from "single user" and "batch" to "time sharing," "real time," and "multiprogramming" systems, with all this material often compressed into just one class. A one-semester class in operating systems, as described by the ACM [1978] and the IEEE [1983], is a most challenging class for both students and faculty.

In ten years of trying to meet the challenge of teaching the first course in operating systems, we have seen seven textbook changes. These changes have been made after many long reviews, meetings, and discussions among students and faculty. Changing texts is hard on everyone concerned, and is not done lightly. Furthermore, we are in no way claiming that some of these books are not excellent—it is just that they are not right for a first course in applied operating systems.

Very early in the semester the time and work pressures force students to seek a concise explanation of important concepts directly applicable to operating system programs. Perhaps one might say a "bare bones, nuts and bolts" presentation. That is exactly what we have tried to create with this book.

By "bare bones," we mean that we have not included some topics that are certainly important, but that we just cannot cover in our class—historical development, network operating systems, and case studies, for example. We have pared down topics to what we believe is a minimal complete set.

By "nuts and bolts," we mean that the topics we do cover are covered all the way down to the implementation. In the section on I/O, we do not just discuss I/O at a high level in terms of functional characteristics—we look at bits and bytes and code needed to implement the functions. This is in part a programming class, and we anticipate that a number of our graduates will be directly involved in design and programming, or will have to thoroughly understand these aspects to do their jobs well.

We do not mean to imply by "code" that this text is designed for one machine or one language. Descriptions of programs are given primarily in a block-structured pseudocode. Assignments are designed so that they can be implemented in virtually any language on almost any system. For example, in the last few years we have had our students do assignments in PASCAL, C, FORTRAN, COBOL, SPL, FORTH, and assembly languages on machines such as an HP 1000, an HP 3000, a CDC CYBER, a Data General Eclipse, a PDP-11, an ATT 3B5, an IBM PC, an Apple II, and a MacIntosh.

To increase this flexibility even more, we have provided a selection of assignments from which to choose. Instructors can then tailor the programs to both the material they want emphasized and the hardware and software environment in which the students will be working. Perhaps the term "selection" should be stressed. Even the most rigorous of classes would normally require four of these assignments in any given semester.

In terms of prerequisites, the assignments—and indeed the text itself—assume advanced undergraduate standing. Students should have had one or two semesters of design and high-level programming, a semester of assembly language programming, and a semester of data structures. Some experience in machine architecture, systems programming, discrete mathematics, and statistics is helpful, but not specifically required. For curricula where linkage editing is not covered in a previous systems programming course, we recommend covering the material in the Appendix before Chapter 7. An understanding of relocation will be helpful in understanding some memory management problems.

In closing this preface, we would like to extend a word of encouragement. We think that computer science, particularly operating systems, is special because it is at once so difficult, frustrating, fascinating, simple, and even enjoyable. We hope that we can convey with this book both a knowledge of operating systems and a realization that computers are fun.

Acknowledgments

The authors wish to express their sincere appreciation to Professor Charles Shub of The University of Colorado at Colorado Springs for two very comprehensive reviews. His comments, suggestions, and criticisms evinced a tremendous amount of effort and insight. Professor Shub's contributions played a significant role in the development of this book.

Bill Lane, Ralph Hilzer, Tom Vayda, and Don Vilen of California State University, Chico, Doug McBride and Mike Chiusolo of Hewlett-Packard, and Michele Bailey of NWC, China Lake, reviewed various chapters of the book and made many valuable suggestions.

This book has evolved from ten years of teaching operating systems at California State University, Chico. During that time, our students' comments and questions have helped us clarify ideas, develop programming assignments and review material, and hone presentation techniques. For the past three years, we have used draft versions of the book as a text; our students have provided thorough proofreading that can come only from dedicated individuals in search of knowledge.

Special thanks must go to our copy editor, whose meticulous editing was almost always appreciated and almost always correct. We say "almost always correct" because somewhere around page 200 we found an error in the editing, making the score copy editor 8345, authors 1.

Finally, we must tip our hats to our IBM PCs. Without these wondrous machines the innumerable revisions of this book would have been much more difficult and time-consuming. An Apple Macintosh and LaserWriter were used to generate some figures and textural material; thanks to them also.

Introduction

Before delving into operating system design, we want to provide some motivation for studying the subject, tell you a little about the rest of the book, and discuss some required background material and terminology.

1 GETTING MOTIVATED AND AVOIDING PITFALLS

Some of you are probably looking forward with great enthusiasm to tackling the subject of operating systems and can't wait until you get a chance to actually design and implement one. Others of you may feel that you are about to be force-fed something quite unpalatable that will be of no value to you as an applications programmer or analyst or data-base expert. The first group of you are already motivated to learn the material, and so we will focus on getting the second group interested in operating systems.

First, we will try a scare tactic. Can bad things really happen to you as a user if you are not aware of what the operating system is doing either for or to you? The answer is definitely yes! The following two examples emphasize this. First, suppose you want to write a program that sums the elements of a large two-dimensional array, and this array cannot be kept in main memory all at one time. A possible code segment to accomplish this is as follows:

```
total := 0;
for i := 1 to row_max do
  for j := 1 to column_max do
    total := total + bigarray[i,j];
writeln('The array sum is ',total);
```

Another possible solution could be:

```
total := 0;
for i := 1 to column_max do
  for j := 1 to row_max do
    total := total + bigarray[j,i];
writeln('The array sum is ',total);
```

Your immediate response to this is probably "So what! They both give the answer." And you are correct. However, depending on how arrays are stored and how memory addresses are calculated, one of the methods may take 1000 times longer to produce that answer [McKellar and Coffman, 1969]. We will explore this problem in Chapter 7, Memory Management.

For the second example, consider a greatly simplified version of an automated teller machine (ATM) system. The ATMs will be viewed as asynchronous processes accessing a central computer. They will be able to call two procedures, one for deposits and one for withdrawals.

```
procedure deposit (ACCOUNT_NUMBER, AMOUNT);
  begin

    {  read the current balance from the given account
       in the database  }
    read(ACCOUNT_NUMBER, BALANCE);

    {  add the deposit amount  }
    BALANCE := BALANCE + AMOUNT

    {  write the new balance back to the database  }
    write(ACCOUNT_NUMBER, BALANCE);

  end deposit;

procedure withdrawl (ACCOUNT_NUMBER, AMOUNT);
  begin

    {  read the current balance from the given account
       in the database  }
    read(ACCOUNT_NUMBER, BALANCE);

    {  subtract the withdrawl amount  }
    BALANCE := BALANCE - AMOUNT

    {  write the new balance back to the database  }
    write(ACCOUNT_NUMBER, BALANCE);

  end withdrawl;
```

Could anything be simpler? Perhaps not, but unfortunately if two customers can simultaneously access the same account then this code might not always give the expected results. We will explore these types of problems in Chapters 1 and 2.

Now for some positive incentives. Aside from wanting to make the system do the most at the least cost and give correct, predictable results, another reason for learning how operating systems are built is that you can then avoid making mistakes that have already been made by others. Programmers have all too often not learned from the successes and failures of their predecessors. The situation was summed up quite nicely by a system designer from a large computer manufacturer. He stated that in other fields such as mathematics and physics, scientists make advances by standing on their predecessors' shoulders, whereas programmers seem to make advances by standing on each other's feet.

The history of operating systems seems full of examples of standing on feet. When computers were first making their presence felt in industry, there was no body of knowledge to help programmers develop systems, and progress was rather slow. By the 1960s several organizations had succeeded in creating sophisticated computer systems with interrupt-driven multiprogramming operating systems [Irons, 1965; Howarth et al., 1968; Daley and Dennis, 1968]. About this time other organizations started developing smaller computers, "minis," for smaller tasks. Did the builders of the new minicomputers learn from what had been done with their larger predecessors? Unfortunately, the answer was most often no! Each organization effectively reinvented the wheel and designed its own proprietary operating system. The result was that many of the same mistakes were made over and over again.

Let's be generous and assume that this mistake was an accident. But look at what happened with the next generation of hardware, the microcomputer. Did the builders of microcomputers learn from the mistakes of the mainframe and minicomputer manufacturers? Typically they did not. We now see microcomputers with operating systems as sophisticated as those found on mainframes; many of them went through the same growing pains as earlier systems, and they contain some of the same errrors that were in those minicomputer and mainframe operating systems.

Do not give up. There is hope! We are now beginning to see companies use proven designs in their operating systems. The success of the Bell Laboratories UNIX operating system [Ritchie and Thompson, 1974] and the cost of developing new operating systems over and over again from scratch are probably the primary reasons why companies are now forcing system designers to look at what has been created by others.

The goal of this text is to present ideas that have proved successful in the design of operating systems so that you will be able to stand on shoulders or at least be able to recognize those who are standing on each other's feet!

2 WHAT CONSTITUTES AN OPERATING SYSTEM

Many texts attempt to pin down a precise definition of an operating system. We prefer instead to look at a few things that most people consider an operating system to be. For a concise description of what constitutes an operating system, see Barron [1971].

Many people consider operating systems to be strictly *resource managers*. One can easily take this view in situations where the operating system is allocating resources like printers, disk drives, and other peripherals. And since memory, time, the CPU, and almost everything else can also be viewed as resources, the functions of an operating system can be described in terms of resource management.

A popular term nowadays is interface. An operating system can be considered an *interface* between the user and the hardware [Barron, 1971]. It provides a friendlier environment where users can do things at a "higher level" and not have to worry about low-level hardware operations. For example, the operating system allows the user to perform I/O in a simple way without being concerned about data rates, device characteristics, and the like.

Although the resource manager and interface approaches provide comprehensive descriptions, the operating system is also some more specialized things. For example, the operating system is a *coordinator*. It makes it possible for complex activities to be performed in a predefined order. The operating system is a *guardian*. It sets up access controls to protect files, allows restrictions on the reading, writing, or executing of data and programs, and keeps users out of each other's hair and out of its own. It may even control who can log onto the system.

The operating system is also a *resource utilization maximizer*. Individual users sequentially running programs by themselves on a large machine most likely are not fully utilizing the machine's potential. An operating system, combining some users' inputs, others' data-base accesses, others' computations, others' outputs, and so on, can dramatically increase the utilization of resources. A typical estimate is that going from one user to four or five can increase the utilization from 30 percent to over 90 percent. [Madnick and Donovan, 1974].

In some computer centers there are monetary charges for all resources and services consumed. Other centers might not charge, but will keep track of usage in order to plan for growth. Whatever the case, the operating system is the *accountant*. It keeps track of CPU time, memory usage, I/O calls, disk storage, terminal connect time, and almost any other information you might want to have. Maintaining this type of information makes it possible to bill users accurately and fairly for the services they receive.

As implied above, the operating system is also in some senses a *server*. It provides services users frequently require, either implicitly or explicitly. A fundamentally important example of this is the file access mechanism. In most high-level languages, it is so easy to specify a file access that we tend to forget all that is actually being done.

So far, we have mainly been saying what an operating system is. This might be an appropriate time to look a little at the other side—what it isn't. We mentioned that the operating system itself provides some services. However, there are a number of other services not normally considered part of the operating system. One such group is typically called "utilities"; it includes such operations as sorting, merging, and listing files.

On the other hand, the operating system must provide low-level file access mechanisms. "Low-level" implies that we are not including the data-base managers with which many of us are familiar. The data-base managers are higher-level programs that allow the user to structure data from a logical rather than a physical view. One or more data bases might be provided as part of a software package called the "system support library," which we view as separate from the operating system and will therefore not cover in this text.

The system support library may also include various compilers, assemblers, editors, and word processors. You might extrapolate and assume that these programs are not part of the operating system and therefore will not be topics of this text; you will be correct. Another routine which is usually included in the library is the program linker. The purpose of this routine is to link together separately compiled and assembled programs into an executable module. Although linking is not usually considered part of the operating system proper, we include a description of linking in the Appendix. This was done because linking is an important subject which is related to memory management and might not be covered elsewhere in the curriculum.

We've looked at things an operating system is and isn't. It probably would not surprise you that items we think an operating system *is* are included in the table of contents for this book. The other items we mentioned in this section (that an operating system *isn't*) can be found in books on compilers, data-bases, editors, word processors, and so forth.

To close this section, let us consider something a little different. It used to be a standing joke around computer centers that beginning students were looking for a FORTRAN machine or a BASIC machine, a piece of hardware that ran their programs directly. That notion no longer seems so farfetched. It is conceivable that some parts of a computer system that we have always assumed to be software (such as an operating system) might be implemented directly on a chip. As a matter of fact, a "silicon operating system" is now a definite possibility [Gorsline, 1986; Intel, 1981].

3 SOFTWARE PREREQUISITES

This text is designed for a hands-on programming approach to the subject of operating systems. With this in mind we need to say a few words about the expertise required for the programming assignments.

Probably all programmers have at some time sat down at a keyboard and begun typing in a program without previously designing it. Such an approach to assignments in operating systems may have you sitting there quite a long time.

The assignments for this class are typically 1000 to 2000 lines of high-level-language code that implement sophisticated algorithms. It does not matter how you categorize the design and implementation of such programs, but you must:

1. Subdivide the assignment into an organized group of component parts.
2. Design these components and specify each in pseudocode.

3. Implement and test individual parts independently.

4. Methodically integrate the parts into a working whole.

Only in this way can you expect consistent success in your endeavors.

The emerging field of software engineering has led to the development of several approaches to the design of complex software systems. For a brief introduction to one approach see Parnas [1972a, 1972b]. More complete coverage can be found in texts by DeMarco [1979], Pressman [1982], and Sommerville [1985]. For more about what can go wrong in very large software projects, see Brooks [1982].

In addition to the knowledge of a proper approach to the design of large programming projects, we assume that the reader has a thorough understanding of fundamental software concepts usually covered in a data structures class. These include pointers and indirect addressing, linked lists, and algorithms for basic computing techniques such as sorting and searching.

4 HARDWARE PREREQUISITES

It is not possible to understand the development of operating systems by looking just at software. You must also look at the hardware advances that have made new features in operating systems possible. In this section we will examine a few hardware features that have had significant effects on the design of operating systems.

Early machines forced programmers to do things in a serial manner. If the programmer wanted to read several cards, then process the data from these cards, and finally print out the results, the operations were performed sequentially in that order. It should be obvious that a significant improvement could be made if some of these operations could be done in parallel. It took the invention of *interrupts* to make such parallelism practical in computer systems.

In fact, it is the interrupt feature of modern computers that makes possible much of the sophistication we now design into operating systems. For example, a simple use of the interrupt feature that made timesharing feasible came about when someone attached a counter to an interrupt line so that the processor would be notified after a fixed amount of time had passed. Interrupts are so important that we will return to them in the next section to consider in detail how they work.

High-speed secondary storage devices also play an important part in the design of the operating system. These devices make it possible for the CPU to read and write information at a rate much greater than that available with card readers and line printers. These devices led to the development of spooling and swapping, which will be described later.

Along with interrupts and fast peripherals there came a need to get data into and out of the main memory more quickly than is possible when going through the CPU for each transfer. This need led to the development of direct memory access (DMA) and input-output channels, which decreased the required software intervention [Mano, 1982; Stone, 1982; Gorsline, 1986]. It is important to stress that these devices were actually the first steps toward *multiprocessor* systems, because they could perform I/O operations while the CPU was busy doing something else.

Main memory has been around almost as long as computers; however, the drastic reduction in the cost of memory during the last decade has led to changes in system design. Mini- and microcomputer systems are now designed to use more memory than they can directly address at one time. New applications of main memory, such as RAM disks, have also become commonplace on these systems.

Along with inexpensive memory, very fast memory has also been developed. Unfortunately, such fast memory is not inexpensive, and so its use has to be limited. This memory, called *cache memory* [Mano, 1982], has enabled designers to improve the performance of computer systems by creating hierarchical access techniques that take advantage of smaller but faster memories.

Another type of memory which has influenced the design of the operating system is *associative memory*, or *content-addressable memory* [Mano, 1982]. This type of memory, which is addressed by its contents rather than its physical location, has made it possible to build a very fast table look-up device. This, in turn, has made it possible to build very fast paged memory systems, and paged memory systems have kept designers and researchers busy for years exploring all the possible implementations.

Many other hardware changes, too numerous to mention here, have also affected the design of systems. For example, would interactive systems be so widely used if we still had to communicate with 10 character per second mechanical terminals?

5 SOME INITIAL TERMS AND CONCEPTS

In the previous two sections we looked at general aspects of software and hardware that are important to the study of operating systems. In this section we want to consider two particular topics, interrupts and processes, and define some terms that will be used in the remainder of the text.

For our purposes, an **interrupt** in a computer system is a condition that can cause the normal execution of instructions to be altered. Those not familiar with interrupts will probably want to know what the conditions are. The following is a list of typical conditions that can cause an interrupt:

Completion of an input or output operation
Division by zero
Arithmetic overflow or underflow
Arrival of a message from another system
Passage of an amount of time
Power failure
Memory parity error
Memory protect violation
Signal from another program
Fire in the line printer

When one or more of these conditions become true, an electrical signal (an interrupt request, or IRQ [Stone, 1982]) is sent to the CPU to notify it that something besides the currently running program needs attention.

If the CPU is in the middle of an instruction, it will probably ignore the interrupt request until it has finished executing the instruction. (Note that this could take many microseconds for an instruction such as a floating-point divide.) When the CPU reaches a point where it can easily stop what it is doing, the CPU sends an interrupt acknowledge signal (IAK) to signal that the request has been received and is about to be processed.

When an interrupt is acknowledged, the CPU does not execute the next sequential instruction from the program currently running; instead it fetches and executes one or more instructions in a part of the operating system called the interrupt service routine. The program that was running must relinquish control, and the operating system takes over. These operations are shown in Figure 1.

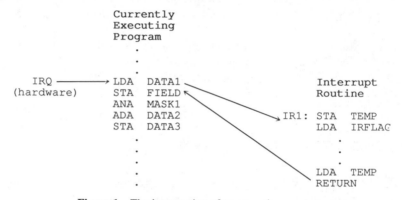

Figure 1   The interruption of an executing program.

When control is transferred to the interrupt service routine, the current state (or context) of the machine must be saved so that the interrupted program can continue execution at a later time. On some systems the status may be saved by the hardware, prior to the time the first instruction is executed from the interrupt service routine. On other machines, the interrupt service routine must explicitly save the status before it can process the interrupt.

A good question to ask at this point is "How does the CPU know where to go to find the instructions in the interrupt service routine?" On some CPUs, the address of the service routine is placed in a specific location in memory and the hardware always looks at that location to find the address of the service routine. On other CPUs, special registers are used to quickly compute the effective address of the service routine.

Nowadays there are usually not just one interrupt and one service routine; most current systems have multiple levels of interrupts and usually have separate service routines for each. On these computers, the hardware is designed to recognize certain sets of interrupt types (or classes). These sets might include input-output completion, machine error, operator request, and program error. As an example, assume that there are eight interrupt classes. Each of the eight classes has an associated hardware interrupt flag in an interrupt pending register. The flag for a given class is set by the IRQ signal when a condition causing that class of interrupt occurs. There is also an 8-bit interrupt mask register with one bit corresponding to each class. This register is used to enable or disable the individual interrupt classes.

Prior to fetching and executing the next instruction in the normal program flow, the hardware checks the interrupt registers to see if there is any interrupt flag set for which the corresponding mask bit is also set. (For those of you with some Boolean algebra background, this operation is ANDing the interrupt flag register with the interrupt mask register and bitwise ORing the result.) Hence, the function of the interrupt mask is to specify which interrupts will be enabled. A graphical description of the operations is shown in Figure 2.

If no interrupts are recognized (either because there are no requests or those that were made are masked out), normal processing continues. If it is possible for more than one interrupt request to be requesting service at any one time, a priority system [Stone, 1982] is typically used to select the one that will be acknowledged first.

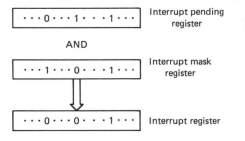

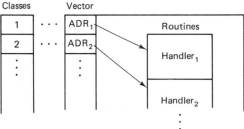

Figure 2   Interrupt recognition.

Figure 3   The relation between interrupts, interrupt vectors, and interrupt handlers.

How does the CPU know which interrupt routine will be used to process a particular interrupt? A memory location can be associated with each interrupt class. This location contains the address of a service routine, sometimes called a **handler,** for the corresponding class. The set of locations containing the addresses of the interrupt handlers is usually called the **interrupt vector,** and it is often located in the very highest or the very lowest part of memory. Figure 3 shows the relation between classes, interrupt vectors, and interrupt handlers.

That was a quick explanation of one way interrupts could work. However, it should be sufficient for you to understand the use of interrupts in this text. For a detailed discussion of interrupt structures, the texts by Mano [1982], Stone [1982], and Gorsline [1986] are good references.

The other concept we introduce in this section is process [Presser, 1975]. In subsequent chapters you will read about a process being scheduled, a process being queued up, a process this, and a process that. What *is* a process?

Unfortunately, process is a word that is easy to talk about but harder to define precisely. Before we explain what processes are within a computer system, consider the following analogy. Suppose you are a building contractor. As a requirement for obtaining your license, you were probably asked to list the set of operations you would follow to construct the foundation for a building. This set of instructions is equivalent to a set of instructions that make up a computer program. After you have passed your contractor's exam you will probably take the set of operations for creating a foundation and store it in a file cabinet. This is equivalent to storing a program on a disk.

Now suppose you get a contract to build a house at 1015 Main. You will go to your file cabinet for your set of operations for constructing a foundation, add to it the specific information about the house at 1015 Main, and start constructing the required foundation. Applying the set of rules to one set of data and thereby constructing the foundation at 1015 Main is equivalent to taking a copy of a program from secondary storage and running it with a specific set of data. The process of constructing a specific foundation is the equivalent of creating a process on a computer system. Stating this another way, in a computer a **process** is the *unique execution of a program with a specific set of data.*

For a computer-related example, consider the PASCAL compiler on your system. The compiler, which resides on disk, is essentially a set of rules for converting source code into object code. On a multiprogramming system there could be several users executing the program known as the PASCAL compiler; each such execution is a separate process in the system. For a program or segment of code to execute, it must first become a process. How does this happen, and who makes it happen?

If you are a user and you want the system to run a program on your behalf, you will usually type somthing like RUN PASCAL MYPROG. Assuming that the system understands RUN, it will probably search the secondary storage for a file PASCAL which contains executable code. When it finds this file, it will copy the code into main memory so that the program can be executed.

There is more work to be done before the program can run. In order to keep track of several programs executing at the same time, the system will create a separate block of information for each which contains information about that program: size, location in memory, priority, time the program has been running, and much more. This information will be kept in a **process control block** (PCB). The combination of the executable code and data along with the PCB makes up a process. (On some systems what we call a process might be referred to as a *task* or *activity*.)

Perhaps we can clarify this a little more by showing you some things a process is not. A user sitting at a terminal is not equivalent to a process; that user could at any one time have many different processes active in the system. Could we say that an individual *job* which the user executes is a process? No, because that job might have several component subjobs, often called *steps* [Presser, 1975]. How about equating these steps with processes? Again no, because even a step could invoke multiple processes—a RUN command may require separate processes for compiling, linking, loading, and execution.

We hope that you now have an idea of what processes are and will not look askance next time you see the word in the text. As you read more about process (especially in Part II), you will see the importance and usefulness of this concept.

In addition to process, there are a number of other terms that we will be using frequently in the next few chapters. These need to be defined before we continue. First, one of the most important terms we will use throughout the text is **concurrency.** When we say that events happen concurrently, we mean that they occur within a small interval $[T, T + t]$. If $t = 0$, then we have simultaneity; this is some-times called **true concurrency.** In computer systems we can have simultaneous op-erations if we have multiple processors. More commonly, however, concurrency refers to situations in which t is small but not equal to zero. This is sometimes called **apparent concurrency.** We see this form of concurrency on single-processor sys-tems where multiple processes will all execute for some time period within the inter-val $[T, T + t]$.

Next, there are a number of terms that have been used to describe either a type of operating system, the method in which the system is accessed, or the hardware upon which the system is based. For the remainder of the text, the following definitions apply:

> **Batch.** Systems that execute programs serially with no direct interaction be-tween the user and the program.
>
> **Timeshare.** Systems that allow multiple users to run concurrently. Early timesharing systems transferred each user's program from disk or drum into memory for execution and transferred the program back when finished. This was called swapping [Irons, 1965].
>
> **Real-time.** Systems designed to input and process data that is created while the system is running. Some authors believe that timesharing systems are a subset of real-time systems, since they must respond in real time to requests for service. Our use of real-time will be more restrictive and not include timesharing systems.
>
> **Foreground-background.** Systems often considered to be the first examples of multiprogramming; they were capable of concurrently operating on two tasks, one a foreground task and the other a background task. Typically, fore-ground implied real-time and background implied batch.
>
> **Multiprogramming or multitasking.** Systems that are designed to concur-rently execute more than one task or process. This is the type of system we will be discussing for most of the remainder of the text.
>
> **Uniprocessor.** Systems that have only one central processing unit. Although they may have hardware capable of executing input-output operations in paral-lel with the main program, only one user or system program can be executed at any instant in time. These are the configurations upon which our discussions of multiprogramming will be based.
>
> **Multiprocessor.** Systems that have two or more CPUs. These are typcally complex systems and beyond the scope of this book.
>
> **Multiprocessing.** Systems that are designed to concurrently execute more than one task or process by utilizing a configuration with two or more CPUs (that is, multiprocéssor).

Two terms that you will see frequently in the following chapters are policy and mechanism [Wulf et al., 1974; Calingaert, 1982]. When we use the term **policy,** we are implying a logical way to solve some problem; when we use **mechanism,** we are describing the way in which a policy is implemented. For example, a grocery store may state that its policy is to guarantee fast checkout for customers who wish to purchase only a few items. Two possible mechanisms that could be used to implement this policy are (1) to set up checkout lines for those who have ten items or less and are paying with cash and (2) to open an additional checkout register any time there are more than two people waiting in line.

Finally, to save a lot of paper and ink, we will abbreviate operating system to OS and input-output to I/O (in most cases).

6 PREVIEW OF WHAT'S TO COME

This book is in a sense a tetralogy. The material falls naturally into four well-delineated parts, parts which complement each other and have strong common threads running through them.

Part I is a discussion of concurrency. We see notions of concurrency every day, from making an airline reservation to building a house or planning a computer science curriculum. What things can be done in parallel? How do we regulate access to shared resources? How can we impose an ordering among the activities? In the first part of the book we consider concurrency in a non–operating systems environment and then relate it to operating systems. We firmly believe that once you understand concurrency, the remaining concepts are an order of magnitude easier.

In Part II we consider the basic components of an operating system. These include process creation and termination, states in which a process can reside, scheduling, memory management, and resource allocation. Notions of concurrency are used frequently in the explanations.

Having considered concurrency and some of the basic components of an operating system, we next look at some functions that make an operating system more useful and efficient. These include I/O systems, spooling, and file systems, which are covered in Part III.

Finally, we take the various pieces and consider them reassembled as a functional whole. In Part IV, we consider the kernel, the heart of the system, and view the organization of an operating system as a layered structure with the kernel at its center. We complete our study of operating systems by looking at some aspects of system security and ways to measure the performance of systems.

One of our goals is to provide the reader with a knowledge of major developments in the history of operating systems. A good way to facilitate this learning is for you to read about some of the important operating systems. We suggest that you look, at least briefly, into the Atlas system [Kilburn et al., 1961a; Kilburn et al., 1961b; Kilburn et al., 1962], the THE system [Dijkstra, 1968], the Multics system [Corbato and Vyssotsky, 1967; Organick, 1972], the RC 4000 system [Brinch Hansen, 1970], the OS 360 system [Madnick and Donovan, 1974], the Venus system [Liskov, 1972], and the UNIX system [Ritchie and Thompson, 1974]. In addition to these papers on specific systems, two texts, by Watson [1970] and Wilkes [1972], provide good coverage of timesharing systems.

As we noted earlier, interrupts have played an essential part in the development of operating systems. With this in mind, we suggest the following additional references on interrupts. In their paper on hardware-software interaction, Hatch and

Geyer [1968] describe how system overhead can be reduced with vectored interrupts. Erwin and Jensen [1970] suggest the use of content-addressable memory to speed up interrupt servicing, and Boardman [1977] shows how microcode can be used to improve speed and guarantee mutual exclusion when processing interrupts.

Finally, since it is still possible that we have not succeeded in motivating everyone to study operating systems, we recommend that you read the paper by P. J. Denning [1982] entitled "Are Operating Systems Obsolete?" Maybe it will help convince you of the need for operating systems and therefore the need to study them.

QUESTIONS AND EXERCISES

1. If you have access to the documentation for a computer system, anything from an Apple to a CRAY, find out where the interrupt vectors are stored and how many there are.
2. For an operating system to which you have access, show how processes are created, executed, and terminated.
3. For the shared-file example in Section 1, try to explain how problems can occur.
4. How could you apply associative memory to a phone directory?
5. Have you encountered instances in which programmers have:
   (a) Repeated costly mistakes?
   (b) Built on the work of others?
6. What are some advantages of having a common operating system such as CP/M, MS-DOS, or UNIX?
7. Give an example from outside the field of computers where going from one user to multiple users of a resource or service can improve the utilization of the resource or server.
8. List some additional functions that are not included in the operating system.
9. Draw a diagram showing the hierarchy of memory devices on a computer system.
10. What information, in addition to that listed in Section 5, would be included in a process control block?
11. List some additional hardware advances that have had a significant effect on the design of operating systems.
12. Why wouldn't something like a data base be part of the OS?
13. List some additional conditions that can cause interrupts to occur.

PART I
Concurrency

Suppose that you saw the following information listed in your college catalog:

> Course description: This course includes a detailed coverage of a concept that can (1) triple CPU utilization, (2) improve peripheral utilization, (3) simplify the design of operating systems and (4) facilitate the implementation of complex application software. We hope that you would find such a concept intriguing.

What is this powerful concept? The answer is concurrency. It has been observed that a system with one user typically runs at 30 percent CPU utilization, whereas a system with multiple users executing programs concurrently typically runs at over 90 percent CPU utilization. Allowing peripherals to run concurrently with each other and with the CPU can greatly increase both peripheral and CPU utilization. In addition to increasing resource utilization, concurrency principles can be the basis for the design of the entire system. Operating systems can be viewed (and written) as a set of cooperating concurrent operations. Applications software, especially real-time software, is much simpler to write when the notions of concurrency are understood and process coordination techniques are applied.

Part I of this book considers concurrency and related aspects. Chapter 1 discusses basic ideas of concurrency, problems associated with it, and solutions to these problems. This discussion is centered on non–operating systems applications, to facilitate your general understanding. Diagrams, generic descriptions, and high-level pseudocode are used to focus on ideas rather than very specific details. Chapter 2 then considers the concepts in a more precise, programming-language style. Two major topics are covered in Chapter 3: (1) the relationship of concurrency, virtual resources, and sharing; and (2) the philosophy of designing an operating system based on the notions of concurrency.

1

An Introduction
to Concurrency

In this chapter we discuss the fundamentally important notion of concurrency, problems associated with it, and solutions to these problems. Once you understand the material in Chapter 1, you will have found the Rosetta stone of modern operating systems.

That understanding might not always come easy. Many people (including the authors) have struggled with the intricacies of seemingly simple, but deceptively complex, problems. Some people who "thought they knew it all" have designed and implemented truly classic faux pas in the history of operating systems. While studying this chapter, you are encouraged to draw diagrams, to chart out timings, and to simulate scenarios with your classmates. Extra work now can greatly reduce the effort required later.

We have tried to facilitate your study of concurrency in this chapter by not using operating systems per se in the descriptions, examples, and analogies. Thus you can focus on the concepts themselves, without the added burden of having to understand associated hardware and software complexities.

Some other educators believe that concurrency should be discussed later, that it's too difficult and should be "worked up to." We lean more toward the Vince Lombardi philosophy—tackle this difficult part first, because once you've mastered it you can approach the rest of the text (and the rest of the course) with confidence.

1.1 THE SCENARIO FOR INTRODUCING CONCURRENCY: TADS

As we mentioned in the introduction to this chapter, our initial study of concurrency will not deal with operating systems per se. Instead, let's consider the following hypothetical scenario involving an increasingly popular computer configuration—a hard disk shared by two or more work stations.

For the first edition of their first book, Larry and Jim used similar work stations and swapped floppy disks. With increased writing commitments this became impractical. Furthermore, there were now voluminous joint financial records to maintain: royalties from book sales, honorariums for speaking engagements, and consulting fees.

Therefore the authors decided to developed a shared hard disk system for their work stations. To facilitate development, they sponsored (and funded) a design contest among their computer engineering students. For reference purposes, the group decided to name the project TADS, for *Two Author Disk System*.

The contest was an enormous success. Many excellent prototypes were built, and the authors got their system. The general structure of the winning entry is shown in Figure 1.1. A commercially available hard disk is augmented by two components. The communications interface provides the electronics necessary for the device to talk to Larry's and Jim's work stations; it will not be described in detail. The command interface is a programmable module which can be set up to accept desired high-level disk access commands. Thus (with appropriate software) Larry and Jim can issue symbolic commands such as READ ROYALTIES_ACCOUNT rather than use primitive disk access commands such as READ TRACK 10 SECTOR 13.

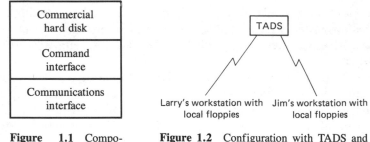

| Commercial hard disk |
| Command interface |
| Communications interface |

Figure 1.1 Components of the shared disk system.

Figure 1.2 Configuration with TADS and work stations.

It is unnecessary to burden you with further internal details of the command interface at this point. However, as you read later chapters (such as Chapter 9, on I/O, and Chapter 10, on files), you will see how it could be designed and implemented.

Larry and Jim debated whether to write the software for the command interface themselves, sponsor another contest, or choose some other alternative. They ended up (for time and financial reasons) contracting out the job to a cut-rate software house. It appeared to be a good decision, since in almost no time at all the package was installed and running.

The simple TADS configuration is shown in Figure 1.2. In a typical situation, one of the authors would retrieve data from TADS, modify it locally at his work station, and then send it back to TADS. Local disk storage facilitated operations such as creation of new data blocks and temporary storage of data for printing.

Although somewhat lengthy to explain, TADS was efficient and easy to use. All were very proud and patted one another on the back for such a simple but elegant system.

1.2 ERRONEOUS RESULTS FROM CONCURRENT ACCESSES

Then disaster struck! It happened one semester when Larry and Jim coincidentally had exactly the same schedule. Suddenly, manuscript revisions were being lost, ledgers didn't balance, and things in general seemed all messed up.

A graduate OS class was hired to help investigate, and it quickly discovered the problem. A typical adverse situation could be described as follows. Larry would receive a check from the publisher, while Jim received a bill from the trucking company. Each would retrieve the current ledger and balance from TADS (say the balance was $200). Larry would add $50 at his work station (giving $250) while Jim subtracted $75 at his work station (giving $125). Next, both would store the updated values in TADS. TADS had to process the requests sequentially, ordering them by time of arrival. If Larry happened to store his value first, the balance would briefly show $250; then Jim would store his, overwriting Larry's value and giving a final value of $125. If Jim happened to store his value first, the reverse would be true and the final value would be $250. Obviously, neither value is the correct one, $200 + $50 − $75 = $175.

To summarize, we can say that the order in which the operations were executed on the shared data was *critical* in determining the final result. This word conveys the concepts so well that it has become a standard term in concurrent programming. **Critical sections** (or **critical regions**) of code are those whose execution must be regulated in order to guarantee predictable results. Alternatively, one could say that critical sections of code are those that operate on critical data, that is, data which must have its accesses regulated.

When the two authors had different schedules, there was an implicit separation of the access and modifications to critical data. Hence the critical operations had (by chance) been properly executed. Having the same schedules resulted in truly concurrent access to shared information, and thus resulted in one of the classic problems of concurrency.

1.3 PROPOSED ALGORITHMIC SOLUTIONS TO CONCURRENCY PROBLEMS

Undaunted, the designers decided to search for an algorithmic solution to the problem. One of the first modifications was to set aside and label a data element in TADS for use as a communication control variable. They called the communication control variable TURN.

The first attempted solution was as follows. Before actually accessing other shared data, Larry would access the turn variable. If it was his turn, he would proceed; if not, he would periodically test TURN until it was his turn. He would then perform the desired update, and after finishing he would set the TURN variable to "Jim." Jim followed a similar pattern, except that he would set TURN to "Larry" when finished.

LARRY'S ALGORITHM

```
while TURN is not equal to "Larry", meditate
access other shared data
TURN := "Jim"
```

This worked very well in terms of preventing problems of concurrent access to shared data. However, Jim almost wore out his fingers testing TURN for a week before someone informed him that Larry had gone to a conference. The unfortunate idiosyncrasy of this solution was that it required Larry and Jim to take turns. Put another way, it required *strict alternation*.

Deciding that strict alternation was not the answer, the duo tried a different approach using two additional communication variables called FLAG_LARRY and FLAG_JIM. Before accessing other shared data, Larry would retrieve Jim's flag, FLAG_JIM. If it was false, Larry would proceed; otherwise he would keep testing it until it became false. Larry would then set his flag, FLAG_LARRY, to true and access the data. When finished, he would set his flag back to false. Jim would follow an anlogous procedure.

LARRY'S NEW ALGORITHM

```
while FLAG_JIM is true, meditate
FLAG_LARRY := true
access other shared data
FLAG_LARRY := false
```

Alas and alack, this great idea went down to defeat also. The graduate OS class was called in again, and again they found the problem. Immediately after Larry retrieved Jim's flag in the "while" statement, Jim retrieved Larry's flag in his corresponding "while" statement. Both found the other's flag to be false, so both proceeded to set their flags to true and access the data. Disaster!

A correction seemed obvious—set your flag before testing the other person's. Hence Larry would set his flag to true and then keep testing Jim's flag until it went to false. Jim would do likewise.

LARRY'S NEW NEW ALGORITHM

```
FLAG_LARRY := true
while FLAG_JIM is true, meditate
access other shared data
FLAG_LARRY := false
```

This seemed to be working, but then everything ground to a halt—no updates were occurring. Guess who came to the rescue. The class found Larry and Jim in their offices, aimlessly testing flags and wondering why they ever decided to work together in the first place. An analysis showed that Larry and Jim had each set their flags to true before the other had been able to do a test. Hence both flags were true and both tests would go on forever—neither person could complete a data access and clear his flag.

This sad tale could go on for many iterations. Suffice it to say that Larry and Jim discovered that the problem was not as easy as it first appeared.

1.4 CORRECT ALGORITHMIC SOLUTIONS TO CONCURRENCY PROBLEMS

Impossible as it may seem at this point, there are solutions. The first was developed by a mathematician named T. J. Dekker. (See question 10 at the end of this chapter for Dekker's algorithm.) In 1965 Dijkstra published papers that extended Dekker's work [Dijkstra, 1965a and 1965b]. Peterson developed a correct solution that is both more elegant and easier to understand than Dekker's solution, and thus will be illustrated here [Peterson, 1981; Peterson and Silberschatz, 1983]. Peterson's solution has the same TURN and FLAG variables that the previous solutions employed without success.

Using Peterson's algorithm, when Larry wants to access some shared data he sets his flag to true, then sets the TURN variable to "Jim." Next, Larry enters a test loop. He repeatedly checks whether Jim's flag is true and whether TURN is equal to "Jim." When one of these conditions becomes false, Larry accesses the desired shared data. After finishing, he sets his flag back to false.

LARRY'S CORRECT ALGORITHM

```
FLAG_LARRY := true
TURN := "Jim"
while FLAG_JIM is true and
      TURN is equal to "Jim", meditate
access other shared data
FLAG_LARRY := false
```

Study carefully how this solution works. Strict alternation is avoided because of the check on the flag. If Jim does not want access, then Larry will find Jim's flag false each time he checks, and Larry can get as many accesses as he needs. If both want access, then the TURN variable provides arbitration.

To see how, assume that Larry has executed FLAG_LARRY := true and TURN := "Jim." He is now about to test FLAG_JIM, and there are two possible situations. If Jim has not yet set FLAG_JIM := true, then Larry will find FLAG_JIM false and will access the shared data. Jim will have to meditate, because he will subsequently set TURN := "Larry" and hence his "while" statement will find both conditions satisfied: FLAG_LARRY is true and TURN is equal to "Larry."

Now consider the other possibility: Jim has set FLAG_JIM := true before Larry tests it. In this case Larry will move on and test TURN, and there are three potential timing sequences. If Jim has not yet set TURN := "Larry," then Larry will find TURN equal to "Jim," and so he will begin meditating. However, when Jim subsequently sets TURN := "Larry," then Larry will move on and access the shared data while Jim meditates. In the second case, if Jim sets TURN := "Larry" after Larry sets TURN := "Jim" but before Larry executes his while statement, then Larry will find TURN not equal to "Jim." Again, Larry moves on while Jim meditates. Finally, if Jim sets TURN := "Larry" before Larry sets TURN := "Jim," then Larry will find both conditions in his while statement true and he will meditate; Jim will find TURN not equal to "Larry," and so he will move on and access the shared data.

We realize that this has been a long explanation, and it may be tricky to follow. However, we think it is important for two reasons: to show you how this elegant algorithm works, and to show you the complexities involved in regulating concurrent access to shared data.

1.5 PROBLEMS WITH THE ALGORITHMIC SOLUTIONS

There are three major difficulties with the type of solution just discussed, even though it definitely does work. First, there is a great deal of overhead. Accessing a single shared data element such as an account balance requires a minimum of two reads and three writes—400 percent overhead. Second, the person waiting for an access must constantly be testing the variables, when he or she could be doing other work. Such testing is called a **busy wait** loop, and in computer systems it can waste a great deal of valuable CPU time. Finally, in the above examples we have been concerned with only two users. The solution can be expanded to work on a system for an entire community of authors, but at a considerable cost in increased complexity and overhead. (See Exercise 2 at the end of this chapter.) In the following sections we will look at some alternative solutions which avoid the overhead and complexity problems.

1.6 NEW APPROACHES TO THE PROBLEMS OF CONCURRENCY

We are now ready for a "quantum leap" in the history of operating systems—the development of tools to facilitate implementation of concurrent programs. There have been two major approaches to that development, one based on the concept of *semaphores*, the other on the concept of *monitors*.

The name "semaphore" [Dijkstra, 1965a] suggests an excellent noncomputer analogy to explain the concept—semaphores, or flags, on a railway system. Just as computer programs can run into trouble sharing data and resources, trains traveling in opposite directions can run into trouble sharing the same piece of track [Holt et al., 1978].

Railway semaphores used to be brightly painted pieces of metal, in the days before signals were electrified; the position of the semaphore conveyed a message to the engineer. Nowadays semaphores usually convey their messages by combinations of the painted metal and electric lights. An engineer approaching a shared resource, such as a bridge used by two lines, can check the semaphore. If it indicates "go," the train can proceed, and when it proceeds the semaphore will change to indicate that the bridge is now in use. If the semaphore indicates "stop," the engineer will stop the train and wait. When the train currently using the bridge has cleared it, the semaphore will be changed and the waiting train will proceed.

The formal computer concept of semaphores will be presented in great detail in Chapter 2. However, in order to illustrate the application of semaphores to TADS, we will introduce the notions here.

Essentially, a **semaphore** is a protected binary variable whose value can be changed only in certain predefined ways, and only by an indivisible sequence of operations. Requiring an indivisible sequence of operations when modifying a semaphore prevents interleaved access problems which plagued our initial versions of TADS.

To illustrate the importance of the *atomicity* of a sequence of operations on a semaphore, consider a flag used to indicate whether or not a certain resource is available. If this flag is an ordinary shared variable, then the following sequence can take place:

1. User A reads the flag, which indicates "available."
2. User B reads the flag, which indicates "available."
3. User A writes to the flag a value indicating "unavailable."
4. User B writes to the flag a value indicating "unavailable."
5. Both A and B attempt to use the resource simultaneously, resulting in chaos.

If the ordinary shared variable is replaced by a semaphore, then potential simultaneous access to the semaphore would proceed as follows:

1. User A requests allocation of the resource by performing the appropriate operation on the semaphore; execution of that operation begins.
2. User B *tries* to request allocation of the resource by *attempting* to perform the appropriate operation on the semaphore; execution of that operation is delayed because A has not yet finished accessing the resource.

Note the important difference. Since the control variable is a semaphore, A's access must be *completed* before B's can begin. This precludes the previous problem of interleaved accesses to the flag, and it is the fundamental reason that semaphores work as a tool to implement concurrent programs.

Before moving on, we should discuss briefly some ways to guarantee atomicity of a sequence of operations. One of the oldest techniques is to disable interrupts before executing the sequence, and then to enable interrupts after completion. This is simple and requires no special hardware; however, such use of interrupts necessitates that the OS be involved in all semaphore operations. It is generally not considered a good idea to allow users to control interrupt disable and enable. On some machines, such as the IBM 360 [Madnick and Donovan, 1974], a special op-code was created which guaranteed that a memory location could be read from and then written to in a single, uninterruptible machine instruction. On the 360 this instruction was called **test-and-set.**

The problem of guaranteeing atomicity for a sequence of operations on a system with multiple CPUs is more complex. Questions at the end of the chapter allow you to explore this problem.

The other major tool to facilitate implementation of concurrent programs is the monitor [Brinch Hansen, 1973b; Hoare, 1974]. A **monitor** is perhaps best likened to a fence surrounding a restricted region [Hold et al., 1978]. The essential characteristic of the structure is that at most one process at a time may be inside the fence.

This characteristic facilitates implementation of concurrent programs by imposing a fundamental restriction—once a process begins executing a critical section of code (that is, code protected by the monitor), that process will be allowed to execute until it relinquishes control of the monitor. Until such relinquishment, no other process can intervene and execute any part of the protected code within the monitor. Again we see the notion of atomicity of operations, although with monitors the indivisible execution applies to an arbitrary section of code rather than the limited set of functions related to a semaphore.

In order to create an illustration of a monitor, let's refer back to our example of the automated teller machine (ATM) system in the Introduction. We begin by placing a fence around the deposit and withdrawal procedures, and the accounts database, as shown in Figure 1.3.

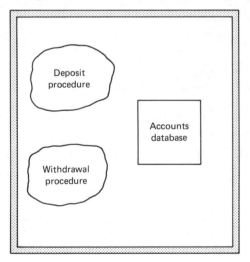

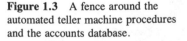

Figure 1.3   A fence around the automated teller machine procedures and the accounts database.

A process initially enters a monitor by calling one of the procedures (entry points) in that monitor. These entry points can be likened to gates in the fence, each of which corresponds to a different operation that will be performed within the restricted area.

We can incorporate this idea into our automated teller machine system by adding two gates to the fence. One corresponds to the deposit procedure and one to the withdrawal procedure, as shown in Figure 1.4.

Often, during execution of a critical section, a process will need to check

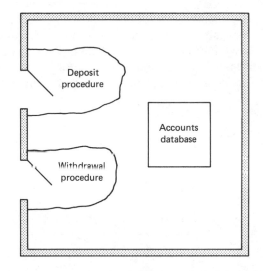

Figure 1.4 Adding gates (entry points) to the automated teller machine monitor.

whether or not some condition is satisfied (such as whether a resource is available). If the condition is not satisfied, we have two design choices: force the process to check again later, or "hold up" the process until the condition *is* satisfied. The first choice leads us back to the busy waits discussed earlier, and so we select the second choice. We add holding areas (typically queues) immediately adjacent to the fence but outside it. These holding areas allow the currently executing process to temporarily leave the restricted area and wait for the given condition to be satisfied. The importance of having the holding areas outside the fence is that when a process leaves the restricted area and enters the holding area, the monitor can allow another process into the restricted area.

Our automated teller machine system has an immediate application for holding areas. If someone attempts to withdraw more money than there is in the account, then he or she could be forced to wait in a holding area for sufficient deposits to cover the withdrawal. Figure 1.5 shows the ATM monitor with holding areas.

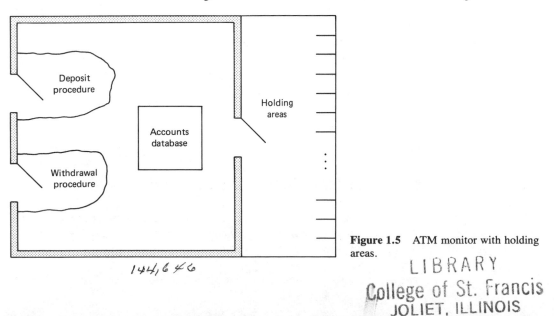

Figure 1.5 ATM monitor with holding areas.

144,646

As a second example of monitors, consider a simple computerized system for a small trading company. Let's again envision the code and data for this system in a physical environment, as shown in Figure 1.6. There might be two data areas, one for messages and one for inventory information. The monitor can then be viewed as a fence surrounding these data areas and restricting access to them.

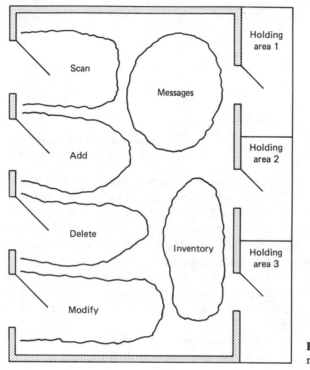

Figure 1.6 A graphical description of a monitor.

There will also be shared procedures to perform operations such as scanning messages and inventories, adding and deleting messages, and modifying inventory. Again, the "fence" surrounds these procedures and regulates access to them. The entry points of the procedures can be viewed as gates in this fence.

Finally, we have the holding areas. Often a trader will want to just enter the monitor, perform some operation, and leave (for example, to update inventory to show the result of a transaction just completed). In some cases, however, the trader might want to actually wait for a condition, such as the arrival of a crucial message. In this case, the process would be moved to the appropriate holding area and "put to sleep" until the message arrived.

1.7 APPLYING THE NEW APPROACHES TO CONCURRENCY

Having looked at the concepts of semaphores and monitors, let us turn now to their application. In this section we return to TADS; in the remainder of the book we will see numerous applications in operating systems.

Recall from Section 1.1 that with TADS our problems developed when Larry and Jim were accessing a given data element in an interleaved sequence of reads and writes. Either semaphores or a monitor can be used to eliminate the problems.

With semaphores, the most straightforward approach would probably be to place a semaphore on each data element in TADS. This semaphore can be envisioned as a "record lock" on the data element, allowing only one user at a time to access that particular data element.

Commands are sent to TADS just as they were previously. If the referenced data element is available (that is, not locked), then the command is processed. If another user already has access to the data element, the new requestor is sent a message and put on hold. In this latter case, when the first user is finished, the one on hold will be notified and his or her command processing can then begin. In either case, after any user has finished with a data element, he or she notifies TADS to clear its semaphore (that is, to unlock the element) and allow someone else waiting to access the element to proceed.

Some early file systems used record or file locks, which we now see as semaphores. However, when they were designed the notion of semaphores had not yet been introduced, and hence people didn't view the approach in that light. Designers solved specific concurrency problems in ways that today we might call semaphores—it's just that they had not yet abstracted, generalized, and named the concept. (Such situations have actually happened quite often in the history of operating systems.)

You might also notice how easy it is to add other authors to TADS. Additional users test, set, and clear semaphores—that is all they worry about. The complexity changes little with 2 or 20 users. Of course, the waiting time to access a specific data element can increase greatly. Furthermore, we will have to establish a policy for selecting the next author when more than one are waiting.

Our second tool for solving concurrency problems is a monitor. Again, there are several ways to approach the problem with TADS, but a simple implementation in this type of situation would be as follows. Modify the software in the command interface to essentially create a fence around all code that accesses shared data elements. This monitor guarding the critical code will have a single gate (entry point) called ACCESS in Figure 1.7.

Commands are issued exactly as before. If no one else is in the monitor, the new requestor is granted exclusive access to it (that is, is allowed to enter the moni-

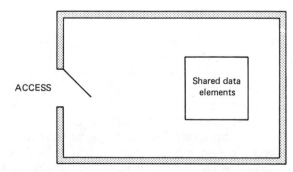

Figure 1.7 A simple monitor for TADS.

tor). If someone else is already in the monitor, the new requestor is sent a message and put on hold. In this latter case, when the first user is finished, the one on hold will be notified and his or her command processing can begin. In either case, any user who has finished notifies TADS that he or she is leaving the fenced area. This allows a user who is waiting at the gate to enter the monitor.

We hope that a modification won't make things too confusing, but to show you the variety of approaches available let's consider a second monitor for TADS. This monitor will have two entries, ACQUIRE and RELEASE.

A user sends a request for a given data element and awaits entrance into the monitor via the ACQUIRE entry. Once he or she is allowed entrance, the system checks the status indicator of the desired data element. If it shows "available," the user is granted access permission and the status is changed to "in use." He or she then leaves the monitor, performing the actual data access outside of the monitor. If the data element status indicator shows "in use," then the user is placed in a holding area (outside of the monitor), to wait for the desired element to become available. When that element does become available, he or she will be signaled, will reenter the monitor, will be granted access permission, and will leave the monitor to access the data.

In either case, after gaining access permission, leaving the monitor, and completing an update of the desired data element, the user sends a message releasing that element. Again, it is necessary to await entrance into the monitor, this time via the RELEASE entry. Once the user is allowed entrance, the element is released by changing the corresponding status indicator, anyone awaiting it is notified, and the user leaves the monitor. (See Figures 1.8 through 1.10.)

Because there are two possible waits with this implementation, we want two distinct WAIT messages. One indicates that the user is waiting to get into the monitor. The other indicates that the user is waiting for a specific condition—the availability of a data element. With the first version of a monitor for TADS, the only possible wait was to get into the monitor. Gaining such entrance implicitly granted access to *all* data elements.

There is an important reason for structuring the system this second way. With the first version, everyone else would have to wait at the ACCESS gate while each user did his or her entire update, even if different users were accessing different data elements. In our ACQUIRE/RELEASE version, the other users have to wait only while the user currently in the monitor receives or releases a specific data element—not while he or she does the actual update.

A general rule of thumb for monitors is, in and out as quickly as possible, doing only what is absolutely necessary inside the monitor. As a simple example, consider a queue shared among several users. In one implementation, the monitor controlling access to the queue is used only to add or delete a node; in another implementation the actual computation performed on the data in the node is done inside the monitor. The second implementation could result in long, unnecessary delays for many other processes while the executing process works inside the monitor.

Perhaps at this point we should make a few comparative comments. Semaphores and monitors are in essence the same, since each can be used to build the other [Hoare, 1974]. Semaphores are a more basic structure, and so in a sense they are like individual circuit elements as opposed to an integrated circuit. In TADS,

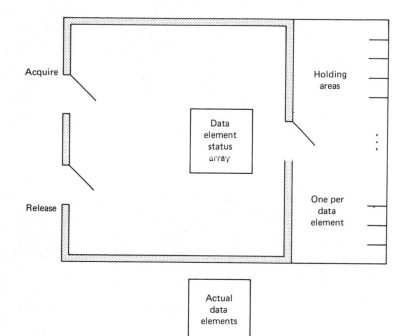

Figure 1.8   A second monitor for TADS.

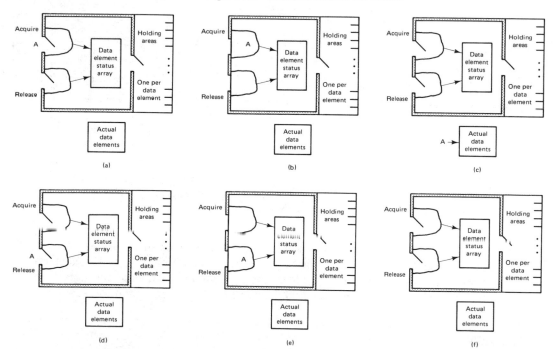

Figure 1.9   (a) Sending request. (b) Entering monitor and receiving access permission. (c) Leaving monitor to access data. (d) Sending release. (e) Entering monitor and releasing element. (f) Leaving monitor.

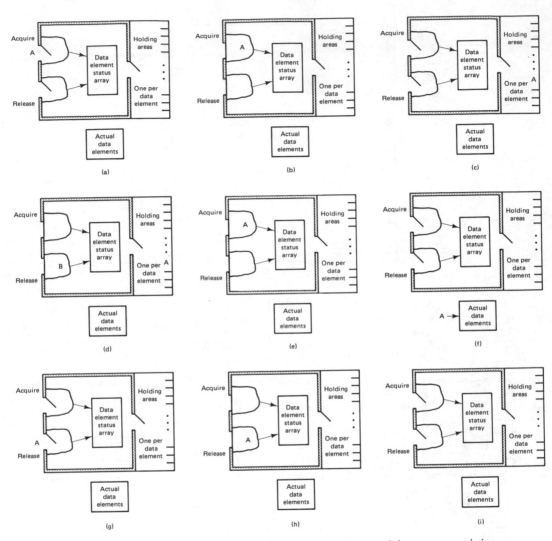

Figure 1.10 (a) Sending request. (b) Entering monitor and not receiving access permission. (c) Being forced to wait. (d) Someone else releasing element. (e) Entering monitor and receiving permission. (f) Leaving monitor to access data. (g) Sending release. (h) Entering monitor and releasing element. (i) Leaving monitor.

and in other applications such as guaranteeing that a set of programs execute in a certain order, all we need is the basic control structure, and hence semaphores are appropriate. In other applications, such as a complex resource manager, we can make good use of the more powerful structure inherent in a monitor.

1.8 SUMMARY

In this chapter we have looked at concurrency from a conceptual standpoint. We examined some unsuccessful software solutions to the problems of concurrent accesses, and we then looked at a successful solution. Finally, we turned our attention to semaphores and monitors, the mechanisms by which concurrency is usually implemented in operating systems. We are now ready to see how concurrency is specified and used in a programming environment.

Hoare's paper on monitors [1974] is mandatory reading for students who want to learn more about concurrency. Interesting, informative, and readable, this paper is especially important to understanding the use of monitors for resource control, and the equivalent power of semaphores and monitors.

Serious students would also be remiss in not looking at Dijkstra's works. Two pertinent references for this chapter are his classic foundation effort [1965b] and his solution for N-process mutual exclusion [1965a].

Dijkstra's N-process work was followed by Knuth [1966], who eliminated the problem of indefinite postponement, and deBruijn [1967], who reduced the maximum waiting time for a process. A new approach to N-process mutual exclusion was presented by Lamport [1974]; it was called the "bakery algorithm," since its operation was similar to customers' taking numbers for service as they enter a bakery.

Two early general articles on concurrency are Brinch Hansen [1972] and Brinch Hansen [1973b]. A look at the classic readers and writers problem is given in Courtois et al. [1971].

Semaphores and monitors are not the only possible tools for concurrent programming. Message passing is described in Habermann [1972], input-output in Hoare [1978], and eventcounts in Reed and Kanodia [1979].

Hoare challenged his readers to find proofs of correctness for the monitors he described. Since that time, there has been considerable interest in this area; as an example, see Howard [1976].

Most of the above references have been to journal articles. An extremely informative and thoroughly enjoyable book on the subject is Holt et al. [1978]. This text is especially well written, and presents some lighthearted but highly educational examples of concurrency problems (for example, the Peru-Bolivian train problem).

Another good book focusing on concurrency is Ben-Ari [1982]. More general OS books with substantial emphasis on concurrency are Brinch Hansen [1973a] and Habermann [1976].

QUESTIONS AND EXERCISES

1. Select a number of different timing sequences, and carefully work through the algorithm in Section 1.4. Show how it responds to the various situations.
2. Expand that algorithm in Section 1.4 to allow an arbitrary number of users.
3. Consider a queue data structure that is being accessed by several users. Show how interleaved adds and deletes can totally destroy this structure.
4. List at least four additional examples of concurrent access to shared resources in everyday life.
5. Define the following:
   (a) Semaphore
   (b) Monitor

6. Give an example where strict alternation would be an acceptable way to restrict access to a shared response.

7. Give a general approach that could be used to determine whether a proposed algorithm to solve the concurrent access problem works properly.

8. What effects could a power failure at one of the author's work stations have on TADS if Peterson's algorithm were being used to regulate access to critical data?

9. The following is a proposed algorithm to solve the concurrent access problem. We assume that the given code is for Larry; Jim's would be analogous. Does this algorithm work properly?

```
LARRY: while TURN is not equal to "neither", meditate
       TURN := "Larry"
       if TURN is not equal to "Larry" then goto LARRY
       if FLAG is equal to "busy"
           then go to LARRY
           else FLAG := "busy"
       access other shared data
       TURN := "neither"
       FLAG := "not busy"
```

10. The following is Dekker's algorithm using our variables. Explain how it works.

```
FLAG_LARRY := true
while FLAG_JIM is true do
       if TURN = "Jim" then
           begin
                   FLAG_LARRY := false
                   while TURN = "Jim", meditate
                   FLAG_LARRY :_ true
           end
access other shared data
TURN := "Jim"
FLAG_LARRY := false
```

11. Discuss why disabling interrupts and creating test-and-set type instructions are not sufficient to guarantee atomicity on multi-CPU systems.

12. What mechanisms can be used to guarantee atomicity on multi-CPU systems? (*Hint*: Look at the Intel 8086 processor.)

PROGRAMMING ASSIGNMENTS

1. Work with a partner to test the algorithms in Chapter 1. In order to make the assignment doable on many systems, and to avoid the necessity of learning a new concurrent programming language, use files for your shared elements.

For each variable name allocate an individual file. Set up this file so that it can be accessed by multiple users. (For example, put the file in a group PUB account, or release it to other users, depending on your system.)

To emulate normal variables, specify that the file can be open and accessible by more than one person at a time. (Usually this is done by giving it the attribute SHARE or something similar.) To emulate semaphores, restrict the access to one user at a time.

(Usually this is done by giving it the attribute EXCLUSIVE, NOSHARE, or something similar.)

To test the algorithms, write a menu-driven program which will allow the user to select and perform specified operations, such as FLAG_LARRY := false. Working with your partner, generate sequences that cause the dismissed algorithms to fail. Also try sequences to see why the selected algorithms work.

Required output for the assignment will be logs listing each operation, the time it was done, and the value of the quantity referenced (if any). Use these logs to illustrate the success or failure of each algorithm.

2. Implement a game called "put and take." The game starts out with some number, say n, of bits in a central bit bucket. Each player also has his or her own bit bucket, initially empty. A player is allowed to execute one of two commands:

Put m: Move m bits from player's bucket to central bucket.

Take m: Move m bits from central bucket to player's bucket.

In most versions of the game, the number of bits moved by one command is limited to some maximum, say M. In any case, the number moved must be limited to the number available—if I say "Put 7" and I have only 5, then 5 will be moved. The loser of the game is the player who takes the last bit from the central bit bucket (that is, whose "take" command drops the number of bits in the central bit bucket to 0). The winner of the game is the player who executes the last "take" command before the loser executes the "take" command that takes the last bit.

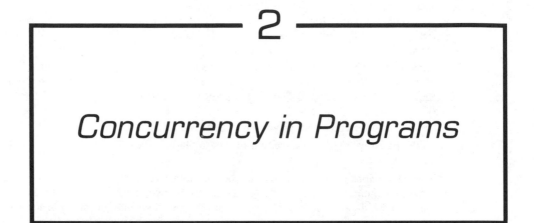

2

Concurrency in Programs

In Chapter 1 we discussed semaphores and monitors in terms of the shared disk scenario. Let us now turn to these constructs as they appear in an actual programming environment. We will consider their definition and specification in this environment, and examine some typical applications.

2.1 SEMAPHORES

In its most elementary form, a semaphore is a protected binary variable whose value can be changed only in specific, predefined ways, and only by an uninterruptible (indivisible) sequence of machine instructions [Dijkstra, 1965b]. A user can specify the initial value of a semaphore, and then must access it via two system calls—P and V; these are the only valid operations that can be performed on a semaphore.

The P and V operations are called **wait** and **signal,** respectively. The use of the letters P and V stems from the original work by Dijkstra; they are the first letters of the Dutch words for wait and signal. We stress this not only for historical reasons, but also because the wait and signal used in monitors have slightly different definitions from those of P and V.

In the previous chapter we discussed the P and V operations in very general terms. The corresponding code that precisely defines these operations could be something such as the following:

```
P(S):       if S = 0

                    then put calling process on a waiting
                         queue for semaphore S

                         {The calling process will be
                          removed from the waiting queue at
                          some later time after a V(S) from
                          another process.}

                    else reset the semaphore, S := 0, and
                         allow the calling process to continue

V(S):       if waiting queue for S is not empty

                    then remove a process from the waiting
                         queue for semaphore S and put it on
                         the active queue

                         {The calling process and the process
                          removed from the waiting queue will
                          now be scheduled for execution by
                          the OS.}

                    else set the semaphore, S := 1, and
                         allow the calling process to continue
```

In the above definitions we have attempted to be both precise and complete, encompassing the semaphore, the processes, and the queues. However, the reader is cautioned not to infer more than what is stated. The definitions do not restrict this powerful concept only to a set of cooperating processes using semaphores to lock themselves into a rigid execution pattern. The processes might simply be communicating, or even competing (for example, in resource allocation). They might use a semaphore at only one coordination point, and execute independently for the vast majority of the time. The applications of semaphores are many and varied.

We stress again that the block of code for each of these operations must be uninterruptible. To see why, consider for example the "if $S = 0$" in the P(S) code. Suppose process A executed this test and found $S = 1$ and then was interrupted. Before process A executes $S := 0$, process B could perform the same "if" test and find the same result. So much for semaphores!

Usually, languages which support semaphores have them declared just as you would declare integers, reals, and other variables. For example, one might say

```
INTEGER I,J;
REAL X;
SEMAPHORE BUSY,AVAIL;
```

The compiler can then check for valid operations on the semaphores (initialize, P, and V) and can generate the appropriate code. To guarantee their integrity, the semaphores themselves are stored in an area of memory which can be accessed only by the OS.

In Chapter 1 we briefly discussed two ways to guarantee the atomicity of the code for the P and V operations. One is by using special machine instructions such as test-and-set, the other by disabling interrupts.

Some form of test-and-set instruction is found on a number of machines [Mano, 1982]. Essentially this instruction does just what its name implies. In one uninterruptible operation it *tests* the contents of a memory location and *sets* the contents to some value. The test-and-set does what we would normally consider two instructions in *one indivisible* operation.

An example of an assembly statement might be

```
                        TSTSET  7,FLAG,#0;
```

which moves the contents of FLAG to register 7 and then sets FLAG to a 0 (all in a single, uninterruptible instruction cycle).

It is easy to use this instruction for guaranteeing that a block of code will be uninterruptible. We initialize FLAG to 1; then any process wanting to execute the block must use the following:

```
    LOOP:   TSTSET      7,FLAG,#0;
            JMPZERO     7,LOOP;
            {block of code to access critical data}
            MOVE        FLAG,#1;
```

The first process to find FLAG equal to 1 gets to execute the block; everyone else trying to execute the block has to "idle" until the executing process sets FLAG. The importance of testing and setting in an indivisible operation is that only one process can test FLAG and find it 1 before it is set to 0.

Unfortunately, there are still two drawbacks. First, you obviously need hardware or microcoded instructions to perform the test-and-set. Second, even if you have the instruction, this implementation uses the busy wait loop we encountered in Chapter 1; a great deal of CPU time could be used up in the TSTSET–JMPZERO loop. For these reasons we consider an alternative approach, disabling interrupts.

One way to implement this second approach is to have a user access a semaphore by generating an interrupt which invokes the OS. The system's ability to disable the interrupts allows it to control access to the semaphore. As a simple hypothetical example, suppose a user put the following command into a high-level-language program:

```
                        P(JOB);
```

This might be translated into the assembly language statement

```
                    SYSCALL #7,"P","JOB";
```

where SYSCALL specifies a user-generated interrupt to the OS, the 7 indicates that it is an operation on a semaphore, the P says it is a wait, and JOB specifies the name of the semaphore.

When the instruction is executed, an interrupt will be generated. It might be recognized immediately, or delayed while some other operations are completed. When the interrupt is recognized, the system will execute the code for P(JOB) (as described previously). While this code is being executed, the system can disable interrupts to ensure that no other user is allowed to access semaphore JOB until the current access is completed.

Let us turn now from implementations to an example of the use of semaphores. Consider a set of concurrent processes, one that deletes, or consumes, items from a queue, and a number of others that add, or produce, items into the queue. This is a very practical example, since queues are used so frequently in operating systems and since the results of interleaved concurrent operation on a queue data structure can be so disastrous. (See Exercise 3 at the end of Chapter 1.) Furthermore, this example is such a common problem that it has been given its own name: the producer-consumer problem.

Our example will use the semaphore "access_queue" to maintain the integrity of the queue. The queue itself will consist of cells with a link field and a data field. There will be two special cells: queue_head, whose link field points to the first cell on the queue; and queue_tail, whose link field points to the last cell. An empty queue will have queue_head^.link = NIL and queue_tail^.link = queue_head.

The code for this example will be presented in two phases. First, we will show you the necessary data declarations, specify the required initializations, and define three operations on queues. Second, we will introduce the semaphore, showing the three queue operations as blocks rather than actual code. This will allow us to keep the discussion at the programming language level, but it will not detract from your study of semaphores by giving queue manipulation details.

Our data declarations are as follows:

```
cell              : a structure made up of
                        link: pointer to a cell;
                        name: name of person waiting
                              to buy this book;
                    end cell;
cell_removed  :   pointer to a cell;
cell_added    :   pointer to a cell;
queue_head    :   pointer to a cell;
queue_tail    :   pointer to a cell;
access_queue  :   semaphore initialized to 1;
```

The semaphore is initialized in the data declaration. The remainder of the initialization code creates the special head and tail cells and sets the pointers in these cells to indicate that the queue is empty:

```
queue_head := new(cell);
queue_tail := new(cell);
queue_head^.link := NIL;
```

```
queue_head^.name  := "head cell";
queue_tail^.link  :=  queue_head;
queue_tail^.name  := "tail cell";
```

The three queue operations and their definitions are as follows:

| queue is empty |

```
queue_head^.link = NIL
```

| remove cell from nonempty queue | ;

```
cell_removed := queue_head^.link;
queue_head^.link := cell_removed^.link;
if queue_head^.link = NIL
   then queue_tail^.link := queue_head;
```

| add cell to queue | ;

```
(queue_tail^.link)^.link := cell_added;
queue_tail^.link := cell_added;
cell_added^.link := NIL;
```

We now introduce the semaphore "access_queue" to guarantee the integrity of the queue when it is used by multiple concurrent processes. The code to delete (or consume) a cell from the queue is

```
P(access_queue);
```

if | queue is empty | then cell_removed := NIL

     else | remove cell from nonempty queue | ;

```
V(access_queue);
```

The code to add (or produce) items into the queue is then

```
P(access_queue);
```

| add cell to queue | ;

```
V(access_queue);
```

Study the above code carefully. That imperative is not directed toward our version of queue manipulation, but rather toward the beauty, simplicity, and power of semaphores. With a few small strokes of the keyboard one can coordinate 20, 40, or 100 processes.

We can extend the use of semaphores in this example. The above implementation assumes that an attempt by the consumer to delete an item from an empty queue will simply return NIL. If the consumer process has other activities and only occasionally checks the queue, then this might be acceptable.

If, on the other hand, the consumer process is in a tight loop waiting for a non-NIL pointer, then the above implementation will result in a busy wait loop and will not be efficient. We will waste a great deal of CPU time with the constant testing. A different approach would be to add another semaphore, "item_in_queue," and have the consumer process execute a P(item_in_queue) if the queue is empty.

Initially, we might attempt a very straightforward implementation with this second semaphore. The added data declaration is as follows:

```
item_in_queue  :  semaphore initialized to 0;
```

The new code for the consumer is

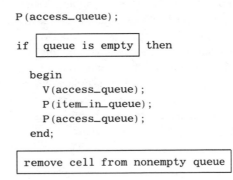

```
P(access_queue);

if  queue is empty  then

  begin
    V(access_queue);
    P(item_in_queue);
    P(access_queue);
  end;

remove cell from nonempty queue  ;

V(access_queue);
```

The corresponding producer code would be

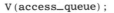

```
P(access_queue);

if  queue is empty  then

    begin

      add cell to queue  ;

      V(item_in_queue);
    end

else  add cell to queue  ;

V(access_queue);
```

Let us consider this code in more detail. Semaphores give us a simple and powerful tool, but concurrent programming can still be tricky.

Suppose the consumer process has just taken the last item, has signaled "access_queue," and is now waiting while a producer process accesses the queue. The producer process adds an item, signals "item_in_queue," and signals "access_queue." Now suppose the consumer process executes twice before another producer process is ready. The first time, it finds the queue not empty, and so it does not execute P(item_in_queue). The second time, the consumer process does find the queue empty, and so it executes P(item_in_queue). However, "item_in_queue" is still set, and so the P operation does not cause a wait—the consumer process goes right on and crashes as it attempts to delete from an empty queue.

An immediate response might be to remove the "if" test and always wait on "item_in_queue." Unfortunately this has problems too; suppose two producer processes were executed and were followed by two executions of the consumer process. The first time through, the consumer process would not wait, since "item_in_queue" had been signaled. The second time, however, "item_in_queue" would be 0 and so the consumer process would be waiting when it shouldn't.

This example is not as simple as it first appears. If you do not understand it completely, step through the code line by line, draw diagrams, and (if all else fails) ask for help!

There are several approaches to developing a correct solution for this application. Question 4 at the end of the chapter suggests an elegant one involving the use of a *counting semaphore* rather than a binary semaphore. Here we will illustrate a solution which retains the binary semaphores, but adds an auxiliary variable.

The auxiliary variable, "yearning," will indicate that the consumer process has found an empty queue and is eagerly awaiting a cell. The data declarations are as follows:

```
yearning       :  integer initialized to 0;
item_in_queue  :  semaphore initialized to 0;
```

The new code for the consumer is then

```
P(access_queue);

if  │ queue is empty │  then

    begin
      yearning := yearning + 1;
      V(access_queue);
      P(item_in_queue);
      yearning := yearning − 1
    end;

    │ remove cell from nonempty queue │  ;

V(access_queue);
```

The new code for the producer then becomes

```
P(access_queue);
```

add cell to queue   ;

```
if yearning > 0 then V(item_in_queue)
         else V(access_queue);
```

We hope that the philosophy behind this approach is straightforward, given the discussion of problems with the previous incorrect "solutions." However, you should still go through various timings to satisfy yourself that these algorithms do work, and to see the potential difficulties that can arise when multiple semaphores are in use.

We could continue, discussing additional interesting variations of this algorithm and related ones. Furthermore, different types of semaphores and semaphore operations have been designed to help alleviate various problems encountered in the diverse applications of concurrent programming. However, instead of continuing along these lines, we will look at two additional general applications of semaphores—resource control and program synchronization—and then move on to monitors.

Semaphores can naturally be associated with resources. The 1 and 0 states correspond to "available" and "not available" states of a resource. Requesting a resource can be equivalent to executing a wait operation on a semaphore which controls access to that resource. Being on a waiting queue for the semaphore is then equivalent to waiting for the resource. When a process finishes with a resource, it signals the appropriate semaphore to allow some other process to access that resource.

Semaphores can also be used for synchronizing concurrent processes. Let us explore this application with a simple example. Suppose that processes B and C cannot execute until process A has completed, and process D cannot execute until both B and C have finished. Graphically, we could show this as illustrated in Figure 2.1.

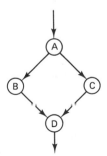

Figure 2.1 Required order of execution for processes A, B, C, and D.

We can synchronize these processes by declaring four semaphores corresponding to the four arrows. We will name the semaphores AB, AC, BD, and CD, corresponding to the nodes at the tails and heads of the arrows. These semaphores are initialized to 0, indicating that no one has finished. The four processes are then

Code for process A with synchronization added	$\left\{\begin{array}{l}\texttt{original code for process A}\\\texttt{V (AB) ;}\\\texttt{V (AC) ;}\end{array}\right.$
Code for process B with synchronization added	$\left\{\begin{array}{l}\texttt{P (AB) ;}\\\texttt{original code for process B}\\\texttt{V (BD) ;}\end{array}\right.$
Code for process C with synchronization added	$\left\{\begin{array}{l}\texttt{P (AC) ;}\\\texttt{original code for process C}\\\texttt{V (CD) ;}\end{array}\right.$
Code for process D with synchronization added	$\left\{\begin{array}{l}\texttt{P (BD) ;}\\\texttt{P (CD) ;}\\\texttt{original code for process D}\end{array}\right.$

Figure 2.2   Code to provide synchronization for processes as shown in Figure 2.1.

modified as shown in Figure 2.2. This forces the desired order of execution as described in Figure 2.1.

Semaphores are one tool for concurrency. We now continue on to the other, monitors.

2.2 MONITORS

A semaphore is a variable and can therefore be incorporated into programs just as other variables are. A monitor is a structure, and so its declaration and use are a little more involved.

In most languages a monitor is defined in a manner similar to a subprogram or procedure. As we proceed, the reader might wish to refer back to our descriptive analogy of a monitor and observe the correspondence between components in that analogy and their specification in the programming environment.

Our monitor specifications will follow those of Holt et al. [1978] and Ben-Ari [1982]. However, precise syntax is not the primary goal; we are more interested in general structure and philosophy.

We begin by defining the overall construct as follows:

```
MONITOR name
    {code to be discussed later}
END name;
```

Within this construct we then specify variables local to the monitor, in the usual fashion. However, we also declare the condition variables (holding areas) for our monitor, such as

```
count       : integer;
in_use      : boolean;
buffer_full : condition;
```

When the monitor is started up, initialization of some of these variables is often required. This is usually specified in code immediately following the declarations:

```
MONITOR name

{declaration of local variables}

     count        :  integer;
     in_use       :  boolean;
     buffer_full  :  condition;

{initialization code}

     count := 0;
     in_use := false;
             .
             .
             .

{other monitor code}
             .
             .
             .

END name;
```

Alternatively, there might be a special entry in the monitor which is called for initialization.

Now we come to the gates from our analogy. In programming terms, these are called entry points, and they lead to blocks of code that will be executed within the monitor. Sometimes users will need to pass information to or from the monitor, and so these entry points can have a parameter list. The following is an example:

```
ENTRY add_cell(user_number: integer, cost: real)
   {code for this entry}
END add_cell;
```

The complete form of a monitor is then

```
MONITOR name

{local variables}
         .
         .
         .
{initialization code}
         .
         .
         .
{entry gate 1}
         .
         .
         .
{code for gate 1}
         .
```

```
                    .
         {entry gate n}
                    .

                    .
         {code for gate n}
                    .

                    .
         END name;
```

Those of you who have used systems which allow subprograms with multiple entry points probably see a structural similarity here. However, you must be very careful not to infer too much functional similarity.

In the subprogram case, there is usually a declaration for the entire block, and the name used there is also the primary entry point. Code immediately following that declaration is executed when the primary entry point is used. In a monitor, the name used in the MONITOR declaration is not an entry point. Code following that declaration is executed only when the monitor is initialized. (Some PASCAL compilers, UCSD, for instance, allow this with procedures [Softech, 1983].)

In a multiuser system, it is possible that several processes could be executing a subprogram block concurrently. They would have individual copies of private data; they could also have shared data if the sharing did not result in concurrency problems (for example, they could share read-only access to a tax rate table). In a monitor it is mandatory that at most one process be in the monitor at any given instant of time. We assume that there is shared data or a shared resource which requires access control—that is why the monitor is being used.

We will not go into detail on the actual OS implementation of monitors. Suffice it to say that, in a manner similar to the case for semaphores, we could again use special instructions or the interrupt system to guarantee that only one process at a time is in the monitor.

Monitors, like semaphores, are used for a variety of purposes in concurrent programming. They are especially convenient for ensuring mutually exclusive access to shared information structures. Since the monitor itself provides the mutual exclusion, we do not need to declare and manipulate a semaphore for this purpose. Monitors can also be used for resource control, as described in a landmark paper by C. A. R. Hoare [1974]. Each resource has a corresponding monitor containing one boolean variable, one condition variable, and two entry points: release and acquire. The boolean variable indicates whether the resource is busy or not; it is set or tested according to which entry point was used. The condition variable is used to manage processes which try to acquire the resource when it is busy.

A similar approach can be used to coordinate processes with a monitor. In the previous section we employed semaphores AB, AC, BD, and CD to coordinate processes A, B, C, and D. With monitors, we can set up one boolean variable and one condition variable for each of these semaphores. The boolean variable would be initialized to false, and it would be set to true when the corresponding process was completed. The condition queue would be used to hold a process which tested a variable and found it false. The monitor would have two entry points: (1) an entry for setting the Boolean variable that indicates process completion and signaling the corresponding condition if a process is waiting, and (2) an entry for testing the Boolean

```
MONITOR coordinate_ABCD;
{local variables}
   declare booleans    AB_bool, AC_bool, BD_bool, CD_bool;
   declare conditions AB_con, AC_con, BD_con, CD_con;
{initialization code}
   set booleans to false;

{entry gate 1}
ENTRY process_completed(process_name);
   case process_name of
   "A":  begin
         if AB_con is empty then set AB_bool to true
                            else signal AB_con;
         if AC_con is empty then set AC_bool to true
                            else signal AC_con;
         end;
   "B":  if BD_con is empty then set BD_bool to true
                            else signal BD_con;
   "C":  if CD_con is empty then set CD_bool to true
                            else signal CD_con;
   end;
END process_completed;

{entry gate 2}
ENTRY permission_to_execute(process_name);
   case process_name of
   "B":  if AB_bool is true then set AB_bool to false
                            else wait(AB_con);
   "C":  if AC_bool is true then set AC_bool to false
                            else wait(AC_con);
   "D":  begin
         if BD_bool is true then set BD_bool to false
                            else wait(BD_con);
         if CD_bool is true then set CD_bool to false
                            else wait(CD_con);
         end;
   end;
END permission_to_execute;

END coordinate_ABCD;
```

Figure 2.3 Informal monitor for the process coordination requirements shown in Figure 2.1.

variable and waiting if it is false. These entry points would be used for indicating process completion and for requesting permission to begin, respectively. A pseudocode definition of this monitor is shown in Figure 2.3.

Often semaphores rather than monitors are used for process coordination if the requirement is strictly for proper sequencing of the processes. (Compare Figures 2.2 and 2.3.) Monitors, on the other hand, are more useful when there is process coordination along with concurrent access to shared information structures.

A good example of coordination involving shared information structures is the queue manipulation example presented earlier in the discussion of semaphores. We now consider a monitor for that same example. The value passed to and from the monitor will be the name of the person waiting to buy this book. The code for this monitor is shown in Figures 2.4 and 2.5.

Some of the complexity of our semaphore version is eliminated by the structure of the monitor. There is no need to have a semaphore for queue access, since the monitor itself restricts access. A signal in a monitor signals a condition and does not cause a variable to be set; therefore, if no process is waiting for the signal, there

```
{ The following is an illustration of a monitor.  It controls additions
  and deletions of a queue.  The general structure is shown in this
  figure, and the entry points are detailed in Figure 2.5.              }

monitor waiting_list;

   {local declarations}

   cell                          :   a structure consisting of
                                            link : pointer to a cell;
                                            name : name of a person;
                                     end cell;
   cell_added, cell_removed      :   pointer to a cell;
   queue_head, queue_tail        :   pointer to a cell;
   item_in_queue                 :   condition;

begin                      {initialization code}

   create new cells pointed to by queue_head and queue_tail;
   queue_head^.link := NIL;
   queue_head^.name := "head cell";
   queue_tail^.link := queue_head;
   queue_tail^.name := "tail cell";

end;


entry delete(person:a name of a person);

   { Code for this entry is shown in Figure 2.5. }


entry add(person:a name of a person);

   { Code for this entry is shown in Figure 2.5. }


end waiting_list;
```

Figure 2.4   Monitor for controlling queue manipulations.

is no effect. (The signal falls into the bit bucket.) For this reason we do not have to worry if the "add" process signals and no "delete" process is waiting. An initial add followed by two deletes would not cause a problem—the process attempting the second delete would find an empty queue and would be forced to wait for "item_in_queue" to be signaled at some later time.

We close this section with a few assorted comments about monitors. First, processes on a condition queue are normally signaled on a first come, first served (FCFS) basis. However, they could also be signaled in some other sequence. A simple scheme would be to order the waiting queue according to priority values specified when the processes enter the queue. These values could be specified in a modified wait statement, WAIT(condition,priority).

Before a signaled process can enter the monitor, the process which executed the SIGNAL must leave. If the system allows a SIGNAL operation anyplace in the monitor code for a given entry point, then the usual approach is to place the signaler on a special "waiting signaler" queue and reschedule it later. Alternatively, some systems require that the SIGNAL be the last statement executed in the code for a given entry point. In this case the signaling process just exits the monitor.

```
entry delete(person:a name of a person);

{  Called by             : person managing the book sales
     Procedures called    : none
     Parameters passed    : none
     Parameters returned  : next person on the queue
     Entry conditions     : someone wants the book
     Exit conditions      : return the name of the lucky person

begin

   if  queue is empty  then wait(item_in_queue);

   remove cell from non-empty queue   ;

   person := cell_removed^.name;
   return cell_removed to system;

end delete;



entry add(person:a name of a person);

{ Called by               : a person who wants the book
    Procedures called     : none
    Parameters passed     : name of person
    Parameters returned   : none
    Entry conditions      : person wants the book
    Exit conditions       : name of person added to queue

begin

   create a new cell pointed to by cell_added;
   cell_added^.name := person;

    add cell to queue   ;

   if queue_head^.link = cell_added then signal(item_in_queue);

end add;
```

Figure 2.5 Code for the entries in Figure 2.4.

Finally, some status changes might occur in the system while a process is waiting on a condition queue. For example, the process which is supposed to signal the condition might be terminated. We know of no standard syntax to specify desired actions, or even of any standard approaches to follow in such situations.

2.3 DEADLOCK AND STARVATION

There are two problems that are constant sources of concern, even in concurrent applications which might be called technically correct. Because of the significance of these problems we have set apart this distinct section to describe them, rather than including them with the previous discussion. Furthermore, for the sake of continuity, we will only introduce them here; additional detailed study will be postponed until Chapter 8.

Suppose that when Jim was typing in the semaphore programs of Section 2.1 he accidentally switched lines 5 and 6 and keyed in the following:

```
P(access_queue);

if │ queue is empty │ then
    begin
      yearning := yearning + 1;
      P(item_in_queue);
      V(access_queue);
      yearning := yearning - 1
    end;

│ remove cell from nonempty queue; │

V(access_queue);
```

The first time the consumer process found an empty queue, the system would grind to a halt. The consumer process would be waiting for an item, but none of the producer processes could provide one—they would all be waiting for access to the queue, and the consumer process would be blocking that access. This situation is called *deadlock* or *deadly embrace*, and it can be a serious problem in operating systems.

The above deadlock is caused by a typo; however, we stress what we said in the opening of this section—even correct concurrent processes can run into deadlock problems. For example, suppose two concurrent processes which each need three tape drives are running on a system which has a total of four drives. Process A requests and receives two, and then process B does the same. After executing for a while, process A requests its third drive, but no more are available and so it is queued up waiting for a tape drive. Assume that process B now requests its third drive and is similarly queued up waiting for a tape drive. In this case neither process can continue unless a tape drive is released, and a tape drive cannot be released until one of the processes finishes.

A deadlock, as the name implies, locks up a system or a subset of processes on a system. The second important problem situation occurs when one subset of the system is running but another subset is inordinately delayed—that is, starved. This situation is called *indefinite postponement* or *starvation*.

As an example of starvation, consider four processes on a system with four tape drives. Suppose each of processes A, B, and C frequently requires two tape drives; the fourth process, D, needs three drives.

In a typical scenario, A and B would be using the four drives while C and D are waiting. Now one of the processes, say A, surrenders two drives. The system could give D two drives, but D would still not be able to execute, since it needs three drives. The other process, C, could execute if given two drives. Assume that in the interest of better resource utilization the system gives the drives to C.

It should be easy to extrapolate. Processes A, B, and C continually trade off pairs of drives. Process D waits forever—that is, process D starves.

2.4 SUMMARY

This chapter has offered a brief introduction to programming with semaphores and monitors (it is truly brief, given the amount that could be said on the subject). Part of what was not discussed you might study in other classes; part of it is probably best left to learning by experience.

An extensive look at various classes of semaphores can be found in Henderson and Zalcstein [1980]. Among these classes are "chunk," in which the semaphore can be incremented and decremented by values other than 1; "multiple," in which each wait and signal can refer to more than one semaphore; and "general," in which each wait and signal can refer to more than one semaphore and semaphores can be incremented and decremented by values other than 1.

Trade-offs between semaphores and monitors are discussed in Lampson and Redell [1980]. This paper also points out some potential problems which are often ignored, such as the aborting of a process while it is in a monitor.

Those of you familiar with PASCAL can see the concurrent version of the language in Brinch Hansen [1975]. The addition of monitors to MESA is described in Lampson and Redell [1980]. New language constructs for implementing capability mechanisms and controlling access to shared objects are introduced in Kieburtz and Silberschatz [1978] and McGraw and Andrews [1979].

A number of authors have described implementations of concurrency support on specific machines, and introduced efficiency considerations in concurrency tools. Among these are Atwood [1976], Schmid [1976], and Kessels [1977].

QUESTIONS AND EXERCISES

1. In the second algorithm of Section 2.1, we used the variable called "yearning." Why do we increment or decrement that variable, rather than just setting it to 1 or 0?
2. Show that semaphores are as powerful as monitors.
3. Show that monitors are as powerful as semaphores.
4. A counting semaphore is a semaphore whose value can go from 0 to n, where $n > 1$. Discuss its usefulness.
5. Show how a counting semaphore could be used to control allocation of the four tape drives discussed at the end of Section 2.3.
6. In Section 2.1, when a process signals and the wait queue is *not* empty, which process should execute—the signaler or the waiter?
7. Use a semaphore to guarantee correct operation of the data-base example in the Introduction.
8. Repeat Exercise 7, but with a monitor.
9. Discuss the relationship among mutual exclusion, test-and-set, semaphores, and monitors.
10. If you were designing an application that required synchronization of processes but no sharing of resources, would you use semaphores or monitors? Why?
11. If you were designing an application that required sharing of resources among processes, would you use semaphores or monitors? Why?

12. If signalers are not forced to exit the monitor and wait for the process being signaled to continue, a potential problem can develop. What is it?

13. The following version of the second algorithm in Section 2.1 seems more straightforward. Why didn't we use it?

<u>producer</u>
```
P(access_queue);
```

```
add cell to queue;
```

```
if yearning > 0 then V(item_in_queue);
V(access_queue);
```

<u>consumer</u>
```
P(access_queue);
```

```
if  queue is empty  then
    begin
    yearning := yearning + 1;
    V(access_queue);
    P(item_in_queue);
    P(access_queue);
    yearning := yearning − 1;
    end;
```

```
remove cell from nonempty queue;
```

```
V(access_queue);
```

3

Concurrency in Operating Systems

In Chapters 1 and 2, concurrency was considered in a somewhat isolated sense. Now let's put it into an OS environment. First, we will look at concurrency as it relates to the crucially important notions of virtual resources and sharing. Then we will see how an OS can be organized on the basis of concurrency.

3.1 CONCURRENCY, VIRTUAL RESOURCES, AND SHARING

There are three interrelated concepts that you will see constantly in your study of operating systems: concurrency, virtual resources, and sharing. We have already looked at the fundamental idea of concurrency; in this section we will see how it relates to the other two concepts.

3.1.1 Basic Concepts

Essentially, the term **virtual** conveys the idea that what appears to us in one way is in reality quite different. We must be careful, though, to distinguish it from the connotations of "mirage," "dream," "vision," and similar ideas. The important difference is that in the context of operating systems virtual means the appearance is functional, whereas the other terms imply that it is purely hallucinatory.

As an example, Joe, a student who has a huge OS assignment due the next day, might have a vision of a lavish computer room with his own personal LEP 9000 supercomputer. However, when he gets to the supposed computer room and opens the door the system is not there.

On the other hand, suppose the university has a LEP 9000 which, for all intents and purposes, Joe can think of as his personal supercomputer. He can apparently use all of available memory, access all registers and flags, do direct I/O to any device, stop and start the machine at will—everything one would ever need for the OS assignment. Functionally, then, this student does have a personal LEP 9000. Actually (unless the university is wealthy beyond imagination) Joe is one of many people using a virtual machine.

In this example, then, virtual is being used to mean that a resource actually does exist but each individual only *appears* to have direct, exclusive, continuous possession of it. As a simple noncomputer analogy, consider a large stenographic pool. Nancy S., a field salesperson, might be told to address all stenographic work to a specific desk in the main office, and she might think that she has a private executive secretary—especially when the work is done quickly and accurately. In reality, her correspondence could be checked for various kinds of errors, collected together temporarily, and then sent to the next available employee in the pool. Ms S. then has a virtual executive secretary.

This example also points out the idea of sharing. The stenographic pool is a resource shared among many salespeople, just as the LEP 9000 is a resource shared among many students.

3.1.2 Explicit Computer Applications

Conceivably, one could have concurrency in a computer system without sharing and without virtual resources. However, it would probably be rare; usually concurrency implies the other two concepts.

Consider a standard timesharing system with many users working concurrently. Each user has exclusive use of a terminal, but other resources (as the name timesharing implies) are shared. Individual users are allocated the CPU for remarkably brief periods, even though it appears to all concerned that each one has his or her own dedicated CPU.

Users of timesharing systems frequently store items on and retrieve them from a disk. It is obvious that they share space on that disk, but normally not so obvious that they are also sharing thousands of interleaved accesses to the disk.

On most timesharing systems, the amount of memory a user is allocated at any given time can change, as can its physical location. Hence the users are sharing that very important resource main memory. Furthermore, each of their programs might be referencing more memory than it has been allocated or, as a matter of fact, more than even exists in the entire system. Therefore these programs are using virtual memory, which is in reality part main memory and part secondary storage.

We should stress immediately that memory is not the only shared resource and not the only virtual resource. However, most people immediately associate these ideas with memory, so let's use memory to look more closely at the concept of virtual resources.

On many early systems, users had to consciously work within the constraints of main memory. If program code was too large, there were two standard approaches. The program could be split up and run using overlays (sequential parts each written over the top of the previous one) [Kurzban et al., 1975]. Alternatively, the program could be organized as a set of load-on-call subprograms (subprograms brought in only when called, usually to a single, designated area of memory) [Calingaert, 1982]. If arrays were too big, they had to be stored in files, and elements had to be specifically read as needed.

On a more modern system with virtual memory, there can appear to be orders of magnitude more main memory than there actually is. A user can write a program which is 10 times larger than the system's actual main memory but write it as though it executed in one unit. That same user can have an array 100 times larger than main memory but access it using normal subscripts.

How can this be? The OS performs the transfers between main memory and external storage without any need for the user to worry about it. We will consider specific techniques for memory management in Chapter 7; for now just concentrate on the basic concept.

3.1.3 Other Examples of Virtual Resources

Virtual memory is now a commonly used technique. In this section we will consider two other important examples of virtual devices: spooling, and privileged instructions.

Spooling seems to be a term that is used a great deal but often not really understood. It is a simple concept, once you know about virtual resources and sharing. A multiprogramming system typically has many users and not so many printers; hence the printers have to be shared. If such sharing were implemented by having everyone just write directly to the line printer, then the outputs from all the users would be interleaved. The computer center would have to hire people to cut the listings apart and paste each user's output back together as one unit. With spooling, the users execute code which appears to write to the line printer; actually, it is writing to a mass storage device such as a disk or a drum. Later, when a given user's process has finished and the line printer is available, the OS will print all of the output from that process as one unit.

The second example we will consider involves the use of privileged instructions, that is, instructions reserved for execution by the OS. In most early systems the only way a user could execute such instructions was indirectly, by making an OS call and requesting that the privileged operation be executed. In current virtual machines, the user writes code in which the privileged instructions are *in-line,* and they appear to be executed just as normal instructions. What actually happens is that the attempt to execute a privileged instruction causes an interrupt which invokes the virtual machine's control program. This control program checks out what the user is trying to do and, if it is valid, allows the instruction to be executed.

At first glance this might seem silly, but it definitely is not. Recall our previous example of the student with the OS assignment on a LEP 9000. Using a virtual machine, he can write and debug an OS as though he were the only user, running on the "bare machine." Actually, he is just one of many users, running under complete control of the operating system of the LEP 9000. With the virtual machine technique, a single computer can be running several different operating systems at the same time. (A common situation is to have one OS tailored for timesharing and one for batch.) Security is increased, since each virtual machine is a self-contained entity; even if the OS for one element crashes, other elements are unaffected.

3.2 CONCURRENCY AS THE BASIS OF AN OPERATING SYSTEM

In this section, we will present an overview of an OS organized on the basis of concurrency. Chapters 5 through 11 will then elaborate on the component parts of such an OS. In Chapters 12 and 13 we will reconsider this organization in a much more detailed and technical manner.

3.2.1 Early Operating Systems

Early operating systems were small and simple because they had little to do. Programs were executed sequentially; only a single program at a time was actually in the system, and it had to finish completely before the next one was loaded. Input-output devices were slow, and they were under the direct control of the CPU; the entire system had to wait for the completion of every I/O request.

As machines grew in power and complexity, more and more demands were placed on the OS. Many designers responded by making the OS larger and more complex, while attempting to keep it one all-inclusive functional unit. (You might hear the term **monolithic monitor** [Holt et al., 1978] applied to these systems, since they were constructed as a single entity.)

Usually the results of this approach did not meet the expectations of either users or designers. Hundreds of person-years were involved in the development of an OS, and even after all of this effort there were long sequences of versions and subversions attesting to the necessity of seemingly endless revisions [Brooks, 1982].

We recall two graphic illustrations of the size of these projects. At a time when very large memories were still measured in K-bytes, a computer salesperson was heard to remark that 256K was the recommended minimum configuration because the OS itself needed more than half of that to run efficiently. In the second case, the card backup for the source code of an operating system was being moved into a computer center. A rough count of the cabinets indicated that over 1000 boxes (that is, over 2 million cards) were involved.

Besides sheer memory requirements, the size of these systems often led to other problems. Debugging such an OS was frequently difficult, as evidenced by the long sequences of "fixes" that became commonplace. Most modifications or additions were inordinately time-consuming because they had to be embedded into such a complex environment. Furthermore, performance often suffered severely as the overhead in this environment seemed to increase exponentially with the number of users.

3.2.2 Managing Large Projects: An Analogy

The change in OS design philosophy (away from what was just described) sometimes seems difficult for students to really grasp. The idea has so many direct equivalences in other areas that an analogy might help. Let's consider the Wear-Pinkert Construction Company, WEPICCO.

When the firm started out, it did everything itself. All phases of bidding, permits, materials, construction, and so forth, were entirely a one-company operation. As the number and size of the projects grew, so did the company. More and more employees were hired, more and more equipment purchased.

Unfortunately, problems developed. Expensive, specialized equipment was often underutilized. Because of improper scheduling and planning, employees were assigned to tasks that were totally outside their area of expertise, or they just sat around idle. Materials were ordered too late and held up progress, or too early and got in the way. Through it all Larry and Jim slowly buckled under the increasing demands.

Now let's go back in time and take a different approach. As the volume of business grew, WEPICCO did not hire more employees and purchase more equipment. Instead, Larry and Jim developed a small, constant-size group of talented individuals. This "nucleus" handled only the fundamental company operations—the rest was subcontracted.

The subcontractors could be very specialized, with highly skilled employees and expensive equipment. They could keep abreast of technological changes in their areas. They could obtain their own supplies.

The company nucleus still had to do coordination, but only a limited amount and only on the macro level (only the coordination of subcontractors)—they never worked at the detail level, and often the subcontractors even handled their own coordination at the macro level. Several benefits accrued with this approach. First, the company could take on additional projects without increasing the size of its nucleus. Second, efficiency was maintained, even with an increased workload. Finally, customers also benefited because of reduced overhead, which led to lower costs.

Assuming you believe that the second approach is better, you might still wonder how the techniques of concurrency are applied. The answer is that they are applied in order to control access to shared data and to coordinate system processes.

With the first (monolithic) approach, Larry and Jim did all of the bookkeeping themselves, so there were no problems with multiple simultaneous data accesses. Larry and Jim directly controlled operations, so there were no problems of multiple independent processes (subcontractors) trying to coordinate their activities.

With the second approach, the multiple simultaneous operations can result in problems. Imagine the roofers scheduling their materials shipments and work force for a certain day and then arriving and finding that the framers hadn't put up the walls yet. Or consider two subcontractors, each needing 100 sheets of plywood, simultaneously checking a supplier data base and seeing that 101 sheets are on hand. Then, thinking they're in fine shape, they arrive at the yard and find out the sad news.

These potential problems illustrate the fundamental need for concurrency tools in the second approach. Without tools that make it possible to coordinate concurrent operations and regulate sharing of data, our nucleus and subcontractor approach would encounter as many problems as the monolithic monitor.

3.2.3 Building Large Operating Systems

In the previous section we discussed two approaches to managing large projects. In this section we will apply the second and hopefully better approach to the design of operating systems.

The heart of the OS is often called the **kernel** or **nucleus** [Brinch Hansen, 1970]. It is a small block of code which performs the minimum set of operations necessary to interface the hardware to the outside world. Often it is written in assembly language and possibly also microcode, since it works directly with the basic hardware.

The kernel oversees the operation of the system, but like the supervisors in our analogy, it does only a minimum amount of the actual detail work. The bulk of this detail work is done by procedures—the subcontractors—invoked from the kernel.

Let's consider a typical example. Suppose we have a computer which runs large batch programs. These programs are initiated by an operator at the system console. The operator types in a program request, including parameters such as the name(s) of the data file(s) to be used.

When the operator presses ENTER, an interrupt occurs, which invokes the kernel. The kernel does not itself analyze the operator's request. Instead, the kernel recognizes that an operator request has occurred and invokes a command line interpreter—a subcontractor—to analyze the input.

When this interpreter is executed, it analyzes the operator's request, determining what the request is and what resources are needed. It constructs a run request entry, which is passed to a scheduler and added to the queue of pending run requests.

This queue is protected by a monitor. Hence the scheduler must itself invoke the kernel, asking permission to enter the monitor and modify the queue. The kernel checks whether the monitor is occupied, and either allows the scheduler to enter or forces it to wait. When the scheduler enters the monitor it adds the new run request to the queue. If the queue has been empty up to this point, the scheduler will SIGNAL an initiator to say that a new run request is available. If the queue already has jobs on it, then the scheduler will just leave, assuming that the initiator is "in progress." Note, as in our contractor analogy, the importance of data control (for access to the queue) and process coordination (among the command interpreter, scheduler, and initiator).

The initiator might evaluate a variety of parameters, such as main memory needed and CPU time requested. However, its overall task will be to get the newcomer into the **mix**—the set of processes currently executing in the machine. While doing this it will probably communicate several times with the kernal via service requests.

During the execution of user processes, we again see the subcontractors at work. If the currently executing process exhausts its allocated CPU time slice, a clock interrupt will occur. The kernel will invoke another scheduler, this time to decide which process in the mix will be the next to get the CPU. Once it has decided, another module, called a dispatcher, will set the environment and start the new process executing.

During execution, our sample process will most probably request I/O. Again we will see the use of interrupts, monitors, and subcontractors such as device allocation modules and channel programs. Here also we see the need for data control and process coordination.

It may be that our sample process will not be loaded into main memory all at once. An attempt to access something not currently in main memory will alert the kernel, which will invoke a memory manager to allocate or deallocate space.

Some programs encounter errors during execution. Overflow, illegal operations, invalid memory accesses, and other errors will cause interrupts, and the kernel will invoke the appropriate error handlers, which again act as subcontractors that deal with a specific job.

3.2.1 Rationale for Applying Concurrency to Operating Systems

We realize that many concepts were introduced briefly in the previous section. The intent *is not* to try to teach you all about operating systems with one example on a few pages. The true intent *is* to have you see the overall structure and appreciate the elegant simplicity in this approach to OS organization. The kernel can be carefully coded and thoroughly checked out. (There is research going on at present to actually prove mathematically that the kernel is correct [Karp, 1983].) The subcontractors can be written and tested individually. New ones can be added easily, and modifications can be made in a small local environment rather than in a large overall operating system.

Beginning with Chapter 5, we will look at the various components individually and thoroughly. For now, concentrate on the overall picture and the role that concurrency plays in it.

3.3 SUMMARY

In this chapter we attempted to bridge the gap between the notions of concurrency covered in Chapters 1 and 2 and their relation to operating systems. We considered concurrency and two other important OS ideas, virtual resources and sharing, and then saw how the fundamental design philosophy of an OS could be based on concurrency. We are now ready to go into into the components of an operating system in detail.

The use of semaphores in constructing a large OS is described in Lauesen [1975]. The books cited in Chapters 1 and 2 are also appropriate here.

Distributed systems are receiving much attention nowadays. Programming and modeling such systems are discussed in Brinch Hansen [1978] and Witt [1985].

QUESTIONS AND EXERCISES

1. We have discussed many disadvantages of the monolithic approach to operating systems. What are the advantages, if any, of this approach?
2. List the functions you think the kernel performs directly (without calling on subcontractors).

3. Write the pseudocode for the monitor that controls the execute queue. Be sure to show all gates and condition queues.

4. List all the virtual resources you think would be found on a computer system.

5. Some resources, such as the CPU, can be shared easily; others, such as the line printer, cannot. List several system resources that fall into each of these categories. Can you define what it is that determines in which category a resource will be placed?

6. Where did the name LEP come from?

7. On some very large operating systems, the number of "bug fixes" per release becomes relatively constant. Could you think of a reason for this?

8. Try to give an example of a case where a virtual device does not exist physically.

9. Why is virtual memory more useful than a management scheme based on overlays?

10. What are some examples of privileged instructions? Why are they privileged?

PART 2
Process and Resource Management

The first part of this book, we hope, has given you a good understanding of the concepts of concurrency, sharing, and virtual resources. In the second part, we will use these concepts to illustrate and explain how the parts of an operating system work.

We will start in Chapter 4 with a description of process creation within the system. Next, we will define the possible states in which a process can reside within the system. The conditions that cause a process to change states will also be discussed. Finally, we will describe how a process leaves the system. This includes a discussion of normal process completion and an explanation of the problems caused when a process is forced to terminate because of some anomalous condition.

Chapter 5 describes how processes are chosen to enter the system. The rationale for limiting the number of processes contending for resources will be presented along with methods for doing so. The portion of the system that has the responsibility for controlling the number of processes on the system is the long-term scheduler.

In Chapter 6 we will see the way one process is selected to execute on the CPU. Various methods of scheduling processes for the CPU will be presented and analyzed in terms of several performance metrics. The CPU scheduler, or short-term scheduler, is a highly visible part of the system, since it, in large part, determines how well the system responds to various types of users' needs.

Memory management, one of the most analyzed subjects in operating systems, is the topic of Chapter 7. The historical development of memory management is discussed, and we show how memory management has changed as memory size and speed have changed. We then survey and analyze memory management techniques used in current systems.

Chapter 8, the final chapter in this part, presents problems associated with allocating resources (other than memory and the CPU) among competing processes. The concepts of static and dynamic resource allocation are discussed. The two methods are contrasted in terms of resource utilization, system overhead, and potential problems.

The last four chapters in this part present a major part of the operating system. In order to facilitate your understanding of the concepts upon which these components are designed, we will include the pseudocode that could be used to implement the individual functions. When examining the pseudocode, remember that it is not intended to represent a syntactically correct program. Its purpose is to describe the important features of a program or procedure and to show how the program is accessed by other routines and which routines it accesses.

4

A State Space Description of the Operating System

In the Introduction we described what a process is and when it is created. In this chapter we will first look at what happens to a process while it is in the system. We will then see how a process is created and how it is removed from the system. To make the descriptions of process creation and removal complete, we will describe the pseudocode used to implement each.

4.1 STATES IN WHICH A PROCESS CAN RESIDE: THE SNAIL DIAGRAM

On some systems, when you are sitting at the terminal waiting for a prompt that will let you continue, it seems to take an eternity before the cursor appears. You might almost feel that it is a snail that's inside the machine shoving bits around rather than state-of-the-art integrated circuit chips. Examination of the state diagram for processes within the computer might further enhance that image.

Figure 4.1 shows what happens to a process within a system. The image of a snail dragging processes around within the system had a strong influence on the physical layout of the diagram. In the remainder of the text, we will refer to Figure 4.1 as the SNAIL diagram to remind us of those long nights of sitting in front of a terminal and waiting for the system to respond to our request.

The diagram contains four ellipses; these represent the states in which a process may reside: active, execute, suspend, and blocked. (In some texts you will see

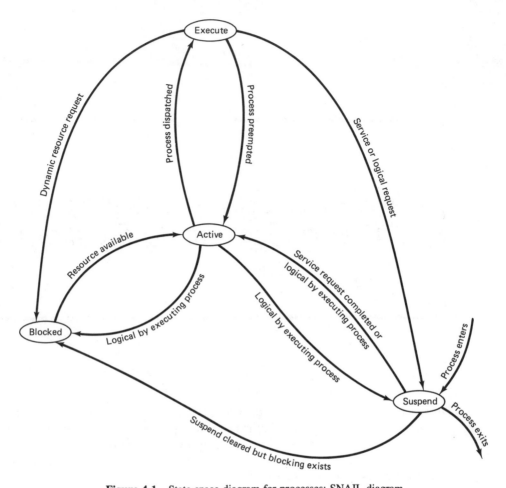

Figure 4.1   State space diagram for processes: SNAIL diagram.

the active state called the ready state and the execute state called the run state. Other authors will also lump the suspend and blocked states together [Lampson, 1968; Presser, 1975; and Nehmer, 1975].) The **active state** is a queue of process control blocks (PCBs) for processes that have all the resources they need to execute except the CPU. The **execute state** is where the PCB for the currently executing process (the process that *has* the CPU) is found. On a multiprocessor system there can be more than one process executing at any time and therefore multiple PCBs on the execute queue. The **suspend state** is primarily for processes that are waiting for completion of an I/O operation on a resource that they already control. The **blocked state** is for processes that must wait because they have tried to acquire the use of some resource and that resource is not available.

Many texts on operating systems will contain a diagram that is similar to our SNAIL diagram [Madnick and Donovan, 1974; Deitel, 1984]; however, nearly every author will have his or her own terminology to describe the states and the reasons for moving from state to state. As we describe the diagram in detail in the following sections, we will include alternative terminology so that you will be able to relate the material in this book to corresponding presentations in other books and papers.

Examination of the SNAIL shows that it has two lines which are connected to the suspend state at one end but dangle off into space at the other end. The one that points to the suspend state represents the path taken by a process at the time it is created. At that time, a PCB is created and the process is given a name or some form of identification. Deciding when new processes should be created is the responsibility of the long-term scheduler, which is described in the next chapter.

Once the PCB has been created, the process becomes the responsibility of the operating system. Before the process can execute on the CPU, however, it must have its code and data loaded into memory from secondary storage. For now, let's assume we can move the process to the suspend state while it is waiting for this transfer.

What do we mean when we say "move the process to the suspend state"? Do we imply that the code and data associated with the process are physically transferred from one area to another? No, this would be a waste of time. All that the system needs to do is to make a note to itself that the process is in a different state. There are two simple ways to accomplish this: (1) add a field to the PCB which contains the current state of the process, or (2) place the PCB on a list that holds the PCBs for all processes in a given state. We will use a combination of the two.

The second dangling line on the diagram points away from the suspend state. This line indicates the path taken by a process which is being removed from the system. When a process is removed, all of the resources it has claimed are returned to the system and the PCB is eliminated. At that time the process ceases to exist even though the original program file still resides somewhere in secondary storage.

This concludes our introduction to entering and leaving the system, and to the creation and deletion of processes. The remainder of the section describes the states in which a process can reside while in the system, and what causes the transitions between the states.

4.1.1 Suspend State

The suspend state, sometimes called the wait state, is for processes that are waiting for an event to occur. There are many possible events for which a process can be waiting, but we will discuss just a few. One of the most common reasons that a process is placed in the suspend state is so that it can wait for an I/O operation to be completed. This is because (in most cases) a process is not allowed to continue executing after it has made a request for input or output.

Processes can also be placed on the suspend queue while they are waiting for a particular time of day. Some processes need to run at a specific time each day, and the suspend queue is where they wait. There are also instances in which a process needs to wait for another process to send it a message so that it can continue. Again, the suspend queue can be where such a process waits.

The time a process spends waiting depends on something external to the process: completion of an I/O operation, passage of time, or a message from another process. It is probably apparent that there is no guarantee that a process will ever be removed from the suspend state once it has been placed there. In a case such as this, the operator may have to abort a process that has been waiting too long.

4.1.2 Active State

After a process has acquired all but one of the resources it needs and is finished waiting for I/O, it is transferred to the active, or ready, state. The one important additional resource a process in this state needs is the CPU. It needs to have the program counter (or instruction pointer, if you prefer) set to the address of the next instruction it wants executed. Furthermore, it must have access to the CPU's other registers and facilities.

There are usually several processes in the active state at one time. All of them are available for execution. The number of processes in the active state is sometimes referred to as the **degree of multiprogramming.** In Chapter 6, which describes the short term schedulers, we will discuss some of the methods the system uses to choose which process on the active queue will be selected for execution.

4.1.3 Execute State

After the system has selected a process for execution, only one operation needs to be done before the process runs. This operation, which we will call dispatching, stores into the registers of the CPU all the values that must be there for the selected process to execute correctly. As you might guess, the last register to be set by the dispatcher is the program counter. When it is set, the CPU begins executing the code that belongs to the process. The dispatching operation, shown on the SNAIL diagram by the line from active to execute, is described in Chapter 12.

A reasonable question to ask at this point is, "How long does the process continue to execute?" Unfortunately, there is no simple answer, but we will look at several possible answers in Chapter 6. As an example, one of the scheduling methods we will discuss there is round robin. With this method, a process is allowed to execute only for a predefined amount of time. If in that time it has not finished, it is removed from the execute state and placed back into the active state. The operation that accomplishes this state change is **preemption** and is shown on the SNAIL diagram by the line pointing from execute to active.

If the executing process requests an input or output operation, it is usually forced to give up the CPU. Then another process on the active queue can execute while the one requesting I/O waits for its I/O operation to be completed. This is shown on the SNAIL diagram by the line from execute to suspend. What happens in the suspend state and how I/O operations are performed are discussed in Chapter 9.

There is one other path leaving the execute state, the one going to the blocked state. A process leaves the execute state and is placed in the blocked state when it asks the system for access to a resource and that resource is not available. If, for example, the process needed more memory before it could continue executing and there were no more available memory at the time of the request, the system would place the process in the blocked state.

In our earlier discussion of semaphores and monitors we saw other examples in which processes were blocked. In those cases, the processes requesting access to critical regions were denied access if another process had already been given access to the region. Processes not allowed to continue were placed on blocked queues associated with the semaphore or monitor.

4.1.4 Blocked State

As we stated above, processes typically end up in the blocked state because they have requested access to a resource that is not available. This form of request, which is made after the process has started executing, is called a dynamic resource request. It should be noted that not all systems allow dynamic resource allocation and therefore on some systems the blocked state does not exist. On these systems all resources must be allocated before the process is allowed to start executing.

In most cases, after the process has waited in the blocked state for a while, the requested resource will become available and be allocated to the process and the process will then be transferred to the active state. However, there are some instances when processes end up waiting indefinitely for a resource. This indefinite wait can result from hardware failure. It can also result when another process keeps the requested resource indefinitely, a situation that is described in Chapter 8.

Two additional paths also lead to the blocked state. These paths exist because a resource could be taken away from a process after it has requested and been granted the resource. If a process in the active state has a resource taken away, it no longer has everything it needs to move to the execute state and therefore must be transferred to the blocked state. When we take a resource from a process before it is finished with that resource, we call the operation **resource preemption.** Resources can also be preempted from processes that are in the suspend state waiting for an event; that is why we also show the path from the suspend state to the blocked state.

One last comment about suspend and blocked states should be made here. Some readers are confused by these two states and feel that they should be lumped together as one; in fact, on some systems they are. We will use the following example to try to clarify the difference.

Suppose a process has been executing for a while and needs an additional magnetic tape drive so that it can write out a temporary file. Before it can initiate a write to a tape, it must be given permission to use one of the drives. When it makes its request a tape drive might not be available, and if that is the case, the process will be placed in the blocked state. At some point we assume the system will allocate the tape drive to the process; at that time the process will be moved back to the active state. When the process is placed into the execute state again it will request a write operation to its newly acquired tape drive. At this point, the process will be moved to the suspend state, where it waits for the completion of the write on the tape drive that it now owns. The difference between the two states can be summarized as follows: A process is blocked if it is waiting for permission to use a resource, and it is suspended if it is waiting for an operation to be completed on a resource it has already acquired.

4.2 THE DETAILS OF PROCESS CREATION

In this section we will look at the details of process creation in a simple system and develop *pseudocode* that accomplishes the task. (In the remainder of the text we will use pseudocode to represent the programs and procedures we discuss. For those unfamiliar with the concept, a description can be found in Bailey and Lundgaard [1983].) For many application programs, we are not even aware that processes are being created and run on our behalf. At other times we may need to create our own processes and coordinate their activities. In both of these situations, we will need the create procedure.

4.2.1 Creating a Process Control Block

The first step in creating a process is to generate a PCB; if this can't be done, the appropriate status, "Unable to create PCB," is returned to the parent process. The parent process can then either terminate or retry the creation request later. If the PCB is created successfully, information about the new process is stored into the PCB. As can be seen in Figure 4.2, one of the fields in the PCB contains a pointer to the PCB of the process that requested the creation, the parent process. This field is needed so that status information, such as termination conditions, can be returned to the parent.

```
pointer to next PCB
process identification
process state
pointer to PCB of parent
starting memory address
memory size
program counter
register 0
      *
      *
      *
register n
child list pointer
child status
file list pointer
resource list pointer
accounting information
```

Figure 4.2 Process control block (PCB) information.

4.2.2 Finding the Program and Allocating Memory

After the PCB has been created, the system looks for the code the new process will execute. This code is stored in secondary memory, typically a disk file. If this search is not successful, the PCB is deleted and the parent process is notified of the error, "Unable to find code for the process."

Before the request is made to read the program into memory, the newly created PCB is placed onto the execute queue so that it appears as though the new process had requested the read. As a result of the disk read, the PCB is moved to the I/O suspend queue. An error in reading the code file will cause the process to be terminated. After the disk read, if no errors have occurred in the reading of the program, the PCB is then transferred from the I/O suspend queue to the active queue, where it waits for the CPU.

At this time, the process has been created. There is a PCB for it and the executable program has been loaded into main memory. The process is now ready to compete with other active processes for use of the CPU. The operations described above are shown as pseudocode in Figure 4.3 The pseudocode is meant only to show

```
procedure CREATE_PROCESS(name,file name,priority,status);

{ This procedure creates a process when called.  It requests a new PCB
  and inserts the appropriate information, requests memory, puts the new
  PCB onto the execute queue, and initiates the program load.          }

{ Called by          : executing system or user process
  Procedures called  : FILE_MGR, CREATE_PCB, DELETE_PCB, MEMORY_MGR,
                       MOVE_PCB, ADD_PCB, INITIALIZE_NEW_PROCESS
  Parameters passed  : name, file_name, priority
  Parameters returned: status of creation request
  Entry conditions   : PCB of requesting process on execute queue
  Exit conditions    : new process created and its execution started   }

begin
{ Generate a PCB for the process or return an error status.           }

   CREATE_PCB(new_pcb,result);
   if result<>ok then return error status;

{ Search the directory for the program that is to be run. If the file is
  not found, the PCB is deleted and appropriate status is returned.    }

   FILE_MGR(search,,,file_name,fcb_ptr,,,,size,strt_adr,true,result);
   if result<>ok then DELETE_PCB(new_pcb) and return error status;

{ Insert information into the newly generated PCB.                     }

   with new_pcb insert name, parent_ptr, priority;
                set child_ptr, resource_list_ptr to nil;
                set file_list_ptr to fcb_ptr;

{ Request memory on behalf of the process.  If the request cannot be
  satisfied, the new pcb is deleted and the program file is closed.    }

   MEMORY_MGR(allocate,size,location,result);
   if result<>ok then begin
                      DELETE_PCB(new_pcb);
                      FILE_MGR(close,,,file_name,,,,,,,);
                   end; {memory not allocated}

{ Initialize acquired memory and new pcb so that new process can execute
     INVOKEFM: FILE_MGR(programread,location,size,file_name,,,,,,,,);
               goto start_of_new_process;                             }

   INITIALIZE_NEW_PROCESS(new_pcb,location,size,file_name,strt_adr);

{ Move requesting process to active and new process to execute.       }

   MOVE_PCB(execute_queue,active_queue,restart=address(RTRN));
   ADD_PCB(new_pcb,execute_queue,start=address(INVOKEFM in new area));
   RTRN: return;
end; {process creation}
```

Figure 4.3 Process creation pseudocode.

the logical flow of events. Because of the interaction of the release routine and other system operations, the actual implementation given in the next chapter will be slightly different.

You might be wondering who the parent of the parent is, and how it was created. On many systems there is one special process created when the system is initialized. This process, which is described in Chapter 3, is the progenitor of all other processes on the system and can never be terminated. After much meditation and discussion, we came up with the name "universal process progenitor," or UPP, for this process. (Based on your gender and religion you may select your own appellation.)

4.3 THE DETAILS OF PROCESS REMOVAL

When talking about people, we are accustomed to saying that a death was, or was not, due to natural causes. When we discuss operating systems, we differentiate the analogous situations by saying that a process either terminated normally or aborted. In this section, we will consider both types of termination.

4.3.1 The Termination Call

Some high-level languages have a specific command to indicate to the compiler that at a certain point the programmer wants to terminate execution of the program. Not unexpectedly, the command is typically called STOP.

Obviously, we would not want to literally stop the system, and so a more appropriate command might be CALL EXIT. This command is actually implemented on at least one system used by the authors early in their careers. It causes a jump to the special EXIT subprogram and, in so doing, informs the OS that the calling process is ready to terminate.

Some languages do not have an explicit termination command. However, it is assumed that when you leave the outermost block, finish the outermost function call, and so on, you are implicitly executing such a command. Therefore, the situation is in reality the same.

Whether implicit or explicit, the STOP, CALL EXIT, BYE BYE, or whatever it is called in a particular system, results in a normal termination. The process is telling the system that, of its own free will, it wants to terminate execution and be removed from the system.

4.3.2 Abort Processing

The other kind of termination, the abort, is not a normal termination. It is forced upon the process by the operating system because some unusual situation has occurred.

There are myriad circumstances that could cause a process to abort. The following are some of the most often encountered:

Time limit exceeded	The process has run longer than the specified time limit.
Memory unavailable	The process requests more memory than the system can provide.
Bounds violation	The process tries to access a memory location that it is not allowed to access.
Protection error	The process attempts to use a resource or a file that it is not allowed to use, or it tries to use it in an improper fashion, such as writing to a read-only file.
Arithmetic error	The process tries computations such as division by zero, or tries to store numbers larger than the hardware can accommodate.
Time out	The process has waited longer than a specified maximum for a certain event to occur.
I/O failure	An error occurs in input or output, such as inability to find a file, failure to read or write after n tries (when, for example, a defective area is encountered on a tape), or invalid operation (such as reading from the line printer).
Invalid instruction	The process attempts to execute a nonexistent instruction (often as a result of branching into a data area and attempting to execute the data).
Privileged instruction	The process attempts to use an instruction reserved for the OS.
Data misuse	A piece of data is of the wrong type, or is not initialized.
Operator intervention	For some reason the operator has terminated the process (for example, if a deadlock exists).

And finally, one system on which we worked gave a long error number, something like M123456789, which, when you looked it up in the operations manual, was defined as "probable programmer or execution error."

In some systems a user process is allowed to intervene in potentially fatal situations and hence avoid the abort. For example, the user process might be trying to open a certain file and read from it. If the file does not exist, the simple thing for the system to do is to let the process abort and leave the user wondering what happened. A more friendly approach would be to detect the error condition (file name not found), notify the user of the error, and allow him or her to take the appropriate corrective action.

Some versions of BASIC and PASCAL offer examples of statements that allow the user process to interpret its own errors and take corrective action for them. The "ON ERROR nn" statement in BASIC causes the program to transfer to statement "nn" if an error is detected. UCSD and Turbo PASCAL have a compiler option that prevents the system from checking for errors in an I/O operation and make it the responsibility of the user [Softech, 1983; Borland, 1983]. The user can check the system variable "ioresult" to see what status was returned after the last I/O operation. On most systems, the user will be allowed to intervene in only a specified subset of the abort cases. Some errors *will always* cause an abort.

Many of the aborts are invoked via interrupts. The offending action will cause an interrupt, control will transfer from the user process to the OS, the operating system will see what has happened, and it will abort the user process. In other cases the OS will discover the problem directly; for example, prior to initiating a system function on behalf of a user process, the OS might check the parameters in the user's subprogram call and find them invalid.

Whether a process terminates normally or aborts, it will no longer be using the resources it was allocated; this brings us to the topic of releasing resources.

4.3.3 Releasing Resources and Picking Up Loose Ends

One of the first actions the operating system will perform when terminating a process is to find out what resources the process has and to return them to the list of available resources. In some cases the reallocation might be very easy (for example, in reallocating the CPU). In others, the operating system might have to do some "cleaning up" first (a tape might need to be rewound or a disk buffer area written out).

There are often other details that need to be resolved. When a process is aborted on some systems, information that explains the reason for termination is added to the output listing or the system log. This information might include register contents, some or all of memory, cross-references, or an explanation of the error and the location at which it was detected, for example.

Another example of a loose end is in file maintenance. Files opened by the process but not closed will have to be closed. Scratch (temporary) files will need to be deleted. Output listings or spool files will need to be closed and sent to the system process that transfers them to the printer.

A special situation occurs if the application uses checkpointing. With **checkpointing,** the system keeps track of enough of the process's environment to guarantee that the process can be restarted from the last of several specified points, called checkpoints. For example, a user updating 10 million records would want this. If the update process were aborted 90 percent of the way through, it would not be acceptable to have to rerun the program from the beginning. Rerunning might involve even more than just the time factor. For example, it may be impossible to verify which cumulative totals have or haven't been updated. To implement checkpointing, the OS needs to ensure that the environment is properly stored and that information is recorded to indicate exactly where everything was before the disaster struck. The Tandem Guardian operating system [Bartlett, 1978] supports the type of checkpointing described above.

When one process leaves, there might be room for one or more additional processes to enter. This means that the termination routine will have to notify the long-term scheduler to check for new processes that are waiting to enter the mix. If the installation is keeping accounting information [McKell et al., 1979], the termination routine will want to record required metrics from the PCB. These could include CPU time, memory used, I/O calls, lines printed, and terminal connect time.

There might be other activities that a particular system does at process termination time, but we have looked at most of the standard ones. We say *most* because there is one final detail: filicide.

4.3.4 The Details of Eliminating Offspring Processes

In biological systems it is normal for the offspring of each generation to continue on after the parent has passed away. In computer systems (which as far as we know are not yet biological), this is sometimes the case; for example, in successive file updates we normally delete the oldest version when we retain the newer one. In process termination, however, the situation is often quite the opposite; when the parent terminates, all of the offspring must also terminate. The termination procedure we describe in this chapter will force all offspring processes to abort.

To see the rationale for this, consider the following. A given process, P, can spawn other processes so that it can complete a set of disjoint operations in an optimal fashion. A process could spawn offspring processes to perform a set of arithmetic operations that could be executed in parallel. Another common example is to create a set of offspring processes to perform I/O. Now, given this situation, what should happen to an offspring when the parent terminates abnormally? The *raison d'être* of the offspring processes is to help P complete; and if P terminates, this reason no longer exists and therefore the offspring should also terminate. One of the questions at the end of the chapter asks you to give an example of when it would be desirable not to terminate offspring processes.

If P can spawn processes, then these offspring probably can also spawn processes themselves, which could result in a family tree. The OS must keep track of the lineage in this tree, and at any point if a given process terminates, then the OS must ensure that all descendants are properly handled.

Perhaps we should comment at this point that termination of offspring by the OS is in a sense often a last resort, such as in abort processing. One would assume that in many cases the offspring have completed their tasks and terminated themselves or were terminated by their parent. (In some systems this latter case is graphically carried out when the parent issues a KILL command.)

We close by relating an incident that happened to us while teaching operating systems one semester. Through an unusual combination of programmer errors and system flaws, offspring processes on the machine we were using were not being terminated. Eventually the system came to an odd kind of halt—nothing would run, but nothing seemed wrong. It turned out that these unterminated but parentless processes had used up all of the valid process control blocks and nobody could do anything because no more processes could be created. The operator could not even intervene, because, alas, operator intervention required creation of a process.

4.3.5 The Details of Process Termination

In this section we will look at all the steps involved in termination processing. The code for these steps, which will be used by the long-term scheduler, will manage normal terminations in addition to the abnormal ones.

Figure 4.4 contains the pseudocode for the termination operation. First, the memory acquired by the process is returned to the memory manager. Next, the termination routine checks to see whether any resource control blocks have been ac-

```
procedure TERMINATE_PROCESS(pcb);

{ This code is responsible for terminating a process.  The major
  operations are: release resources, pass the output spool file to
  OUTSPOOL, initiate termination of offspring, and notify the parent
  process of the termination of the child.                              }

{ Called by          : cleanup process
  Procedures called  : FILE_MGR, DELETE_PCB, MEMORY_MGR, RESOURCE_MGR
  Parameters passed  : pcb
  Parameters returned: none
  Entry conditions   : interrupts disabled,
                       executing process is terminating
  Exit conditions    : resources released, offspring set to
                       terminate, parent notified of termination        }

begin

{ Return any resources the process has claimed.                         }

  while the resource list is not nil
    remove an rcb;
    RESOURCE_MGR(release,,rcb,);
  end while;

{ If the process has any files remaining open, close them.              }

  while the open file queue is not nil
    remove an fcb;
    FILE_MGR(close,,,,fcb,,keep,,,,true,);
  end while;

 { If the process has any child processes, set them to terminate
   the next time they execute.                                          }

  for each process in child_list set terminate flag to true;

{ Notify the parent that the process has terminated, close spool
  file, release all main memory the process has claimed, and
  finally, delete the PCB for the process.                              }

  set child terminated status in parent pcb and signal parent;
  if output spool file open then close file and signal OUTSPOOL;
  MEMORY_MGR(deallocate,starting_address,size,status);
  DELETE_PCB(pcb);

end; {process termination}
```

Figure 4.4 Process termination pseudocode.

quired by the process and returns them to the resource manager. It then checks to see whether any file control blocks are still attached to the PCB. If there are any, the files are closed. A check is then made to see whether the process has any active offspring. If there are any, their termination flags are set so that they will be forced to terminate the next time they try to execute. Finally, the PCB is deleted. When the PCB has been deleted, termination is complete.

In our example, the pseudocode knows how to properly return all resources used by the process. However, the termination procedure need not know the details of returning specific resources. Instead each device driver could have an entry point, such as RESTORE, which, when called by the termination routine, would take care of the details of returning a resource to the system so that it might be allocated to another process.

The pseudocode shown in Figure 4.4 is meant only to show the logical flow of events. The actual implementation given in the next chapter will be slightly different, because of the need to coordinate use of the memory allocation and release routines.

4.4 SUMMARY

In this chapter we have defined the states in which a process can exist within the OS. Each of the four states—active, execute, suspend, and blocked—contains one or more lists of processes within it. The details of how processes are created and how they are removed from the system were also presented, and sample pseudocode to accomplish these tasks was given.

Starting with Chapter 5, Long-Term Scheduling, we will look at several of the individual components that make up the operating system. We will study their functions to see how they interact with processes in the system and with each other. Throughout the discussions we will refer to the SNAIL diagram in this chapter to see how all of the components fit together.

Most texts on operating systems include a section on processes, sometimes called tasks, and what causes them to change states. The texts by Madnick and Donovan [1974] and Deitel [1984] cover this material quite well. The paper by Nehmer [1975] also gives a good description of states and state transition.

QUESTIONS AND EXERCISES

1. Draw a state diagram for a system that does not allow dynamic resource allocation.
2. Does the SNAIL diagram need to be modified for a multiprocessor OS? If yes, why?
3. What additional information could be stored in a process control block?
4. On some systems there are many separate suspend and blocked queues. Why? What are the advantages and disadvantages of this approach?
5. In Section 4.1 we mentioned two ways to indicate the current state of a process: put an appropriate field in its PCB, or put its PCB on a linked list of processes in the same state. Discuss the advantages and disadvantages of each method. Would there be any reason to use both?

6. In the process creation routine there is an error exit if no PCB can be allocated. Why would this happen? What should the parent do in this case?

7. We indicated that a process could wait in the suspend queue forever. What difficulties could this cause? Why is it difficult for the OS to just discard some process when it "gets sick of waiting"?

8. A resource can be taken away from a process in the suspend state; hence, the arrow from suspend to blocked. Why is there no arrow from blocked to suspend?

9. Should the routines that move processes among states in the SNAIL diagram be processes themselves? If so, who schedules the scheduler and who dispatches the dispatcher?

10. What conditions, other than those listed, could cause a process to terminate abnormally?

11. There is a potential problem with the exit procedure in Figure 4.4 when a process's children can have children. What is it? How can it be overcome?

12. Files are a special type of resource that may belong to a process. What should be done with files that are opened at the time a process terminates?

13. Modify the termination routine to make it take care of open files. Be sure to show any modifications that need to be made to the common data structures such as the PCB record.

14. If a process has started outputting to a virtual printer (that is, a spool file), what should be done with the spool file when the process is aborted?

15. The create routine in Section 4.2.4 places the priority that it was passed into the new PCB. What checks would you perform on that priority value before storing it?

16. What, if any, limits should be placed on a user's ability to create new processes? Why?

17. Give an example that justifies not terminating all offspring processes when the parent terminates.

18. How should the termination routine be modified to allow offspring processes to continue after a parent terminates?

19. If parent and child process share a resource, such as memory, a problem can occur with termination. What happens when either process terminates (prematurely) and releases the shared resource before the other process is finished using it?

20. On some systems a child is given access to all the resources held by the parent. How could the termination procedure be modified to accommodate this situation?

5

Long-Term Scheduling

Before any process can start executing, we have to decide which processes will get into the system. The SNAIL diagram in Section 4.1, shown here as Figure 5.1, has an arrow coming out of nowhere and into the suspend state. We described that arrow in terms of a PCB that was created for a process and was entered into the suspend queue. However, we did not consider decisions about which request for a process would get a PCB. We will now look at the decision maker: the long-term scheduler.

In the following discussion we assume that *all* process creation requests go through the formal long-term scheduling sequence. On some systems, certain process creation requests can bypass significant portions of the long-term scheduler. For example, a process in execution might "fork" into multiple subprocesses sharing a common set of resources; this new set of process might be created directly, without passing through the long-term scheduler's request queue. (For an explanation of the fork operation, see Shaw 1974.)

5.1 THE NEED FOR LONG-TERM SCHEDULING

Have you ever gone into a bakery, been given a number, and watched as the number of the customer being served moved toward your number? Or have you attempted to log onto a system and been told "No more sessions being initiated at this time" or

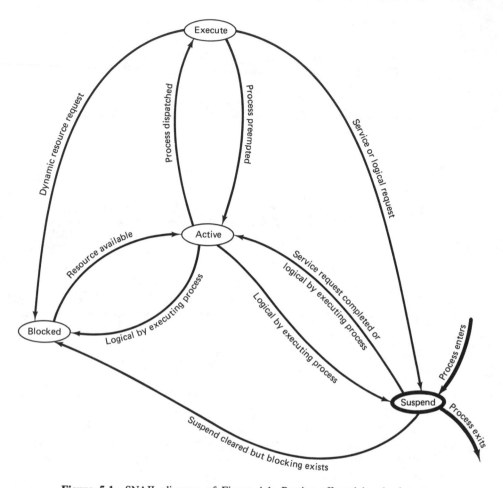

Figure 5.1 SNAIL diagram of Figure 4.1. Portion affected by the long-term scheduler is drawn bold.

"You are number 7 on the queue"? In these situations you have met some long-term schedulers.

If we all had all of the resources we would ever desire, then there would be no need for long-term schedulers. If architects could build an infinite stadium or concert hall (in which you could still see and hear from the last row), then any number of people could attend every event. If computers had an infinite number of CPUs, memory locations, ports, and terminals, then any number of users could log on and run any number of programs.

However, they don't, so we can't. Current stadiums and halls have a limited number of seats. Current computers have limited resources, and this implies a limited number of PCBs in the system at one time. Because of these limitations, we need long-term schedulers to act as "keepers" and regulate admissions.

5.2 SCHEDULING BY SEQUENTIAL INPUT DEVICES OR AN I/O WINDOW

In the early days of computing, when jobs were punched on cards or paper tape, the long-term scheduler was quite simple. Users lined up at the system's single input device, and the jobs were entered and run one at a time, in sequence.

Soon it became evident that both users and the system might be better served if a mediator arranged and ran the jobs, rather than having the users themselves run their jobs. Based on this premise, systems evolved to a situation in which long-term scheduling took place at the "I/O window." Users would submit their input at this window, and the I/O clerk would enter and run these jobs.

5.2.1 The Price for Fast Response

One important aspect that came into consideration on these systems was economics: users could select a class in which their jobs would be run. The higher the class, the quicker the turnaround, and the higher the cost. Our input device could still be a single card reader, but the I/O clerk would put jobs into different trays and read the trays in a certain order. The clerk was in essence the job scheduler for the system.

Typical environments in which the authors have worked have implemented the following job classes (listed in order of decreasing priority):

Emergency

Express

Standard

Deferred

Weekend

Student

Faculty

Emergency jobs were taken to the reader and entered as soon as the current input had cleared. "Express" was grouped and read in periodically, prior to "Standard." Deferred jobs normally were run on the graveyard shift, unless by a series of coincidences the center became completely "inactive." (Even in this case some centers did not run deferred jobs; they could be very long and hold up higher-class jobs that arrived after the deferred job began executing.) Determining the scheduling times for "Weekend," "Student," and "Faculty" is left as an exercise for the student.

There was another class that was sometimes used. Although it did not fit neatly into the previous schema, it was important and is sometimes still used—"deadline" scheduling. As the name implies, with deadline scheduling a user would submit a job and specify that it *must* be done by a certain time. It was then the long-term scheduler's (that is, the operator's) responsibility to ensure that the job was run by the stated deadline.

5.2.2 Keeping the System Busy

As computer hardware advanced and became more expensive, another aspect of scheduling came into play: system utilization. Users were required to put various parameters on their job cards, such as CPU time, amount of memory, number of lines printed, and any other resources required. Overall system utilization became an important consideration for long-term scheduling. The scheduler attempted to optimize that utilization on the basis of user-specified job parameters. For example, we might try to mix a high-CPU-time, low-output job with a low-CPU-time, high-output job, and we would avoid grouping together several jobs that all required the one slow plotter on the system.

5.3 LETTING THE SYSTEM MAKE THE CHOICE

Unfortunately, this was not always effective. In some cases, users simply were unable to make good estimates. In other cases, they tried to cheat to get better response times. However, even these imprecise metrics gave better utilization than sequential scheduling. By having users specify all such parameters, the potential for automatically scheduling jobs materialized.

The next step in the evolution of the long-term scheduler came about when sequential job input devices (card readers and tape drives) were replaced by direct-access devices (disks and drums). This change made it possible to automate scheduling on the basis of user-specified job parameters. When a current job exited, the scheduler would check the list of waiting jobs, decide whether one (or more) of them could be started, and, if so, select the one(s).

Before continuing, we should make a small aside and consider again the idea of process. At first, job and process were synonymous—a user submitted a job, and the job created a process. Soon, however, it became possible for one job to create several processes [Presser, 1975], and we had to consider these individual processes rather than the job as a whole. Hence, from now on we will be talking about the long-term scheduler with respect to *processes*, not jobs.

The long-term scheduler fits nicely into our SNAIL diagram. We establish a list of waiting requests, each of which is intended to create a process that enters the system via the dangling arrow going into the suspend state. When the system can accommodate another process, the long-term scheduler selects a request from this waiting list. A PCB is created and entered onto the suspend queue, thus *creating* the corresponding process.

5.3.1 Decision Criteria

In order to automate our long-term scheduler, we need to consider various criteria on which to base decisions. Two of the more obvious candidates are shown:

Arrival time }
Predefined priorities }   Measured

We have also mentioned some others:

$$
\left.
\begin{array}{l}
\text{CPU time, } C \\
\text{Memory, } M \\
\text{Lines of output, } L \\
\text{Other resources required}
\end{array}
\right\} \quad \text{Estimated}
$$

For the present time, let us eliminate one entry: other resources required. This is obviously an important criterion, but there are two mitigating factors to consider. First, many resources we commonly deal with are **serially reusable** [Shaw, 1974]. This term means that the system can preempt a resource from a process, use it elsewhere, give it back later, and start executing again with *no adverse effects*. (Common examples would be the CPU and a random-access device.) In such a situation, the "other resources required" are not so important in long-term scheduling. Second, dealing with non–serially reusable resources (resources which cannot be easily preempted, such as a tape drive and plotter) is a difficult problem, so we prefer to devote an entire chapter (Chapter 8) to it. For now, let's ignore it and concentrate on the other criteria.

There is an important difference between the two groups of scheduling criteria listed above. The first group consists of known quantities, and the second consists of estimates. As illustrations of the difference, the system can *record* the arrival time, but often the user can only *estimate* CPU time and lines of output. Also, the first group is applicable to all processes, but the second is normally applicable only to batch-oriented systems. The system can reasonably expect a user to place some estimate on CPU time for a batch submittal, but how does a user estimate anything when sitting down to log onto a timesharing system? We will want to keep these differences in mind as we consider scheduling policies.

5.3.2 Decision Policies

A simple batch scheduling policy is to take the processes in the order they arrive. The long-term scheduler in this case uses first come, first served, or FCFS, and the scheduling criterion is based strictly on arrival time. A problem with this can be demonstrated with an example and a little analysis.

Suppose four process creation requests arrive at approximately the same wall clock time. Assume (1) that the long-term scheduler takes these requests one at a time, using FCFS, and (2) that the resulting processes run as follows:

```
#1      spent 2 minutes in system
#2      spent 60 minutes in system
#3      spent 2 minutes in system
#4      spent 2 minutes in system
```

Furthermore, assume that time in the system is directly proportional to CPU time used. The ratio of elapsed wall clock time to time in the system, and hence to CPU time used, is then as follows:

```
#1      2/2
#2      62/60
#3      64/2
#4      66/2
```

The long process has a ratio of about 1 to 1, while the short processes have an average ratio of about 22 to 1. From these ratios we can observe the general principle that FCFS tends to favor the long processes.

We can obviously favor the short processes by always scheduling the shortest of the remaining processes next. This does not seem to penalize long processes significantly. Under the terms of the previous scenario, the short processes would have an average ratio of $(\frac{2}{2} + \frac{4}{2} + \frac{6}{2})/3 = 2$ to 1, while the long process still has a ratio only a little over 1 to 1.

Of course, the ratio for long processes would become worse as the relative lengths of the long processes and the short processes shrunk. (A "long" process of 4 instead of 60 would have a ratio of 10 to 4.) Perhaps an even more critical problem occurs when many requests for short processes are entering the system while one or more requests for long process are waiting. The requests for long processes keep getting pushed back and might have to wait forever.

In an attempt to be more universally fair, we turn to what might be called hybrid policies. These policies will consider more than one criterion, or one criterion but with some tempering factors. Before analyzing these policies, however, we must stress an important point. It is absolutely impossible to be completely fair. Anything done for the benefit of some subset of the processes will adversely affect some other subset.

One of the tempering factors alluded to above could be to limit the number of times a request for long process is pushed back (or bypassed) by requests for shorter processes. When the limit is reached, that request for the long process retains its place in line regardless of subsequent arrivals of requests for shorter processes. This policy is often referred to as **shortest process next with bypass and freeze**.

Another tempering factor employed in some policies is called **aging**. As a request for a process waits, the scheduling metrics are modified by some function of the wait time. As a simple illustration, we might define

$$C' = \frac{\text{estimated CPU time}}{1 + (\text{wait time})/k} \qquad (5.1)$$

and apply a shortest process next to this new value C' rather than just the estimated CPU time. (In this case, k gives a relative measure of importance to the wait time.) Using our previous numerical example and a k of 2, Equation (5.1) shows that the request for the 60-minute process would have the same C' after waiting 58 minutes as a newly arrived request for a 2-minute process.

This last technique seems quite appealing and fair. It has been used with various modifications in a number of operating systems. Names incorporating phrases such as *response ratio* and *penalty ratio* have been given to these schedulers [Brinch Hansen, 1971].

You might have noticed that up to this point we have discussed only batch scheduling. The reason was implied previously; there is little to go by with interactive users except arrival time and priority. Therefore, instead of considering this special case of scheduling interactive users, let's develop a generalized model for long-term scheduling. This generalization will be applicable to any situation.

We have repeatedly spoken of estimated CPU time, but we could also consider parameters like estimated memory usage. We have previously elaborated on several "hybridizations," but they could be considered particular elements of a set of possible modifications to the basic scheduling parameters. Furthermore, the entire long-term scheduling function could be viewed as starting with an initial scheduling value $S(0)$ and then developing subsequent scheduling values $S(t)$ modifications of $S(0)$ as time passes. The parameter C' in Equation (5.1) is an example of such a scheduling value.

The point in bringing up this idea of generalization is to suggest to you that you might benefit from viewing a given long-term scheduler as simply a specific implementation of a general class of functions. Using our previous examples, we could have initial parameters

A	arrival time
P	predefined priority
C	estimated CPU time
M	estimated memory usage
L	estimated lines of output

and modifications

$B(t)$	number of times pushed back by other requests
$W(t)$	wait time

Our initial value is

$$S(0) = f(A, P, C, M, L, B(0), W(0)) \tag{5.2}$$

where $B(0) = 0$ and $W(0) = 0$. Our subsequent values are

$$S(t) = f(A, P, C, M, L, B(t), W(t)) \tag{5.3}$$

In the next two sections we will consider specific examples of this general policy.

5.4 DESIGNING A LONG-TERM SCHEDULER

Having decided to implement a long-term scheduler, one might begin by equating certain quantities in terms of scheduling import. For instance, we could assume

$$1 \text{ cpu second} = 10K \text{ memory} = 1K \text{ lines of output}$$

Using the variable names introduced in the previous section, and assuming units of milliseconds (ms), bytes, and lines for C, M, and L, respectively, we can compute an overall "size" of a process as follows:

$$\frac{C}{1000} + \frac{M}{10,000} + \frac{L}{1000}$$

For this scheduler we might consider everyone to be "created equal," and so there will be no initial priority assignments. Assuming an elapsed time in milliseconds and a wait time factor $k = 2$, the aging algorithm described by Equation (5.1) becomes

$$N(t) = \frac{2(C/1000 + M/10,000 + L/1000)}{2 + t} \tag{5.4}$$

Just to facilitate computations, we can make a few observations and simplifications. Instead of keeping track of elapsed time for a given process, we will use the current system clock value T and substitute $T - A$ for t (recall that A is the arrival time):

$$N(T) = \frac{2(C/1000 + M/10,000 + L/1000)}{2 + T - A} \tag{5.5}$$

Next, note that the numerator in the equation is a constant for each process request; let's call this constant $1/R$. With this substitution, Equation (5.5) becomes

$$N(T) = \frac{1/R}{2 + T - A} = \frac{1}{R(2 + T - A)} \tag{5.6}$$

We have not specified whether low numbers or high numbers have a higher priority, and so we will arbitrarily invert the equation, defining a new scheduling metric $S(T) = 1/N(T)$, and specify that higher values of $S(T)$ imply higher priorities. These manipulations give

$$S(T) = \frac{1}{N(T)} = R(2 + T - A)$$
$$= RT - R(A - 2) \tag{5.7}$$

The second term in Equation (5.7), $R(A - 2)$, is a constant; it is determined when the process request is first recognized. Let us call it Q. We then have

$$S(T) = RT - Q \tag{5.8}$$

Finally, we will put an identifier in so we can speak of all process requests being considered; call the identifier j. Then, at any time T the scheduling priority number for process request j is

$$S_j(T) = TR_j - Q_j \tag{5.9}$$

Before continuing with development of the scheduler per se, it might be helpful to comment briefly on our scheduling equation. Recall that R is a metric which varies inversely with the amount of resources requested; the more the resources a process request specifies, the smaller the R it will receive. The value of R serves as a coefficient applied to the request's wait time. Therefore, as the request waits in the scheduler, its priority will always increase, but at a rate determined by R. The more resources requested, the slower the priority will increase for a given interval of wait time. Conversely, the fewer resources requested, the faster the priority will increase.

This situation is shown graphically in Figure 5.2. Process requests A, B, and C have R values of 0.5, 1, and 2, respectively. Request B enters the system 20 time units after A, and request C enters 20 units after B. Note how the priorities of the requests with lower resource requirements catch up to requests that have been waiting longer but have higher resource requirements.

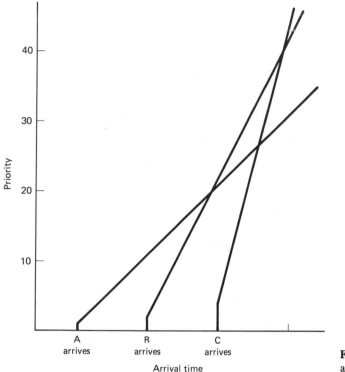

Figure 5.2 Process request priorities as a function of time and resources required.

Equation (5.9) represents the mathematical design of a scheduling policy. We will turn now to the description of a scheduler based on a mechanism implementing that policy.

We will use an array structure for our scheduler. The elements in this array will contain the following fields:

```
request_identifier j
size_ratio Rⱼ
normalizing_constant Qⱼ
scheduling_number Sⱼ(T)
```

We might keep the array elements ordered on $S_j(T)$, or we could just select the largest value whenever we want to create a new process. For this implementation we choose use the second approach; we leave the first as an exercise for the student.

At this point we have defined a data structure and an equation for selecting the next process to enter the system. Now we must determine

1. Who will add requests for process initiation to the waiting list,
2. When the list will be evaluated to see whether one or more requests can be removed,
3. What criteria will be used to decide whether a request can be removed, and
4. How concurrent access to the waiting list will be regulated.

In Chapter 4 we implied that a process was created as soon as a user told the system to run his or her program. In reality, the RUN command just places a request for a new process on the long-term scheduler's waiting list. Hence, the command interpreter will be one source of requests.

Another source of requests for new processes is the currently executing user or system process. That process might issue explicit requests, with the execution of a command such as CREATE or FORK to create a new process. It might also issue implicit requests, with the execution of commands such as READ and WRITE. This explains who adds requests to the waiting list. Now we need to look at removal operations.

The long-term scheduler is responsible for managing the mix of processes in the system. It removes requests from the waiting list, on the basis of the scheduling number described in Equation (5.9), and creates the corresponding process. The question still remains, When should the long-term scheduler check the list to see whether a request should be removed? The answer is that requests are evaluated whenever any resources become available.

Of course, if the system is currently underutilized, we can create a new process and put it into the mix when the request for the process is made. This implies that any time we add a request to the waiting list, the long-term scheduler should check to see whether the corresponding process can be created immediately.

By definition, any time a current process terminates, resources are freed. (At a minimum, process termination would free up some portion of memory.) Therefore, the waiting list should also be evaluated after process termination.

Another time the long-term scheduler needs to check whether a new process should be created is when one of the currently executing processes releases non−serially reuseable resources. On systems with dynamic allocation and deallocation, this implies that the resource manager should call the long-term scheduler after it has completed a dynamic deallocation request. On systems with static allocation and deallocation, the long-term scheduler should be called after the non−serially reusable resources of a terminated process have been released.

The overall flow described above is shown graphically in Figure 5.3. Paths have been labeled with a general description of the action (for example, Process exits system) and a sample command which would cause that action (for example, CALL EXIT).

Entry 3 in the previous list is to determine how the long-term scheduler decides whether or not to remove one or more requests from the waiting list and create the corresponding process. One criterion should be allocation of non−serially

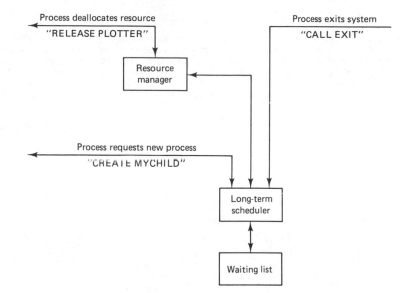

Figure 5.3   Flow involving long-term scheduler and its waiting list.

reusable resources; as mentioned earlier, this will be considered in detail in Chapter 8. Another criterion should be an evaluation of the current system mix, and the projected effects the new process will have on that mix. Unfortunately, these are very subjective judgments, and appropriate metrics are difficult to establish. Metrics which might be used include the following:

Current system response time to a simple terminal command like TIME_OF_DAY
Current number of disk access per unit time
Current ratio of process execution time to total time in the system
Currrent percentage of spool space in use
Current percentage of CPU time the idle process is using

Finally, the last design aspect for our long-term scheduler is to specify how additions to and removals from the waiting list will be regulated. Since there are independent, asynchronous accesses to the list, we will use a monitor for guaranteeing mutual exclusion.

Our scheduling monitor will have three entry points. There will be one for adding a new request to the waiting list, and another for selecting the next creation request to be considered. There will also be a "housekeeping" entry for returning memory and signaling the selection process. The pseudocode for our monitor is shown in Figures 5.4 through 5.7.

When a process wants to add a request, it must first obtain a place in the request data structure. Once this is done, the scheduling metrics described earlier are entered into the allocated request element. The process then signals the initiator, in case the system is underutilized and the request can be satisfied immediately. If the

```
monitor WAITING_LIST;

{ This monitor regulates access to the long-term scheduler's waiting
  list.  It has four main sections, including three entry points.  The
  first section initializes the scheduling array. The second section is
  the entry point for adding a new request to the waiting list.  The
  third section is the entry point for selecting the next request from
  those waiting. The fourth section is the entry used to return memory.}

constant
    max_requests            : integer; {maximum requests allowed}

definition
    info                    : record
                                max_time            : integer;
                                max_lines           : integer;
                                max_memory          : integer;
                                scheduling_metric : integer;
                              end record;
variables
        element_used        : array[1..max_requests] of boolean;
        element_selected    : array[1..max_requests] of boolean;
        request_pending     : condition;
        memory              : condition;
        parent_waiting      : array[1..max_requests] of condition;
        element_available   : condition;
        info_nodes          : array[1..max_requests] of info;
        memory_allocated    : array[1..max_requests] of integers;


{ Initialization code which is executed when the monitor is created.
  It sets all the entries in the element_used and element_selected
  arrays to false.                                                              }

begin
    set element_used[1..max_requests] := false;
    set element_selected[1..max_requests] := false;
end; {initialization}

entry add_request(memory,cpu,lines,start_address);
    { Code for entry add_request is shown in Figure 5.5. }

entry select_request;
    { Code for entry select_request is shown in Figure 5.6. }

entry return_memory(size,start_address);
    { Code for entry return_memory is shown in Figure 5.7. }


end; {monitor WAITING_LIST}
```

Figure 5.4   WAITING_LIST monitor declarations and initializations.

request is not selected, the parent process (the one making the request) puts itself to
sleep on its assigned condition variable. In either case, this request will (it is hoped)
be selected at some time. Control will then return to the long-term scheduler to
complete the creation of the offspring.

The "select" entry is called by the system process initiator from the long-term
scheduler. It first checks whether any requests are waiting; if not, it goes to sleep.
When one or more requests are present, it picks the one having the highest priority.

```
entry add_request(memory,cpu,lines,start_address);
```

{ This entry gate is used to add a process creation request to the
  waiting list. It is called from the long-term scheduler on behalf of
  any process (system or user) which wants to create an offspring
  process. The parameters passed are the metrics used for scheduling;
  the beginning address of assigned memory is returned.   }

```
{ Called by                 : long-term scheduler
  Procedures called         : scheduling function
  Parameters passed         : memory, amount of memory process needs
                            : cpu, estimated execution time
                            : lines, estimated lines of output
  Parameters returned       : start_address, address of allocated memory
  Entry conditions          : parent wants offspring created
  Exit conditions           : offspring request added to list           }

begin

{ Find place to add the request; wait if none available.                }

    if element_used[1..max_requests] = true then
      wait(element_available);
    j := available element in element_used;

{ Add the request and signal the process initiator.  If the request
  is not satisfied, the requesting parent process must wait.            }

    element_used[j] := true;
    element_selected[j] := false;
    info_nodes[j].scheduling_metric :=
        scheduling_function(memory,cpu,lines);
    signal(request_pending);
    if element_selected[j] = false then wait(parent_waiting[j]);

{ After the request has been selected, get memory and free up the
  request element.  Signal any process waiting to add a request.        }

    start_address := memory_allocated[j];
    element_used[j] := false;
    element_selected[j] := false;
    signal(element_available);

end; {add_request}
```

Figure 5.5   WAITING_LIST entry for adding process creation requests to the list.

The next step is to see whether the highest-priority request can be satisfied. If not, the process initiator must wait for more resources. When sufficient resources become available, the process initiator can satisfy the request and return control to the waiting parent process that placed the selected request on the list.

The "return memory" entry is used when memory is released. It simply returns the memory to the system and then alerts the process initiator that this memory is now available.

The long-term scheduler itself is shown in Figures 5.8 through 5.13. Its primary function is to accept requests for new processes, order them, and create new processes according to the ordering, the resources available, and the process mix.

```
entry select_request;

{ This entry point is used by the process initiator, a system process
  which runs forever attempting to create new processes.  For
  consistency, the call goes through the long-term scheduler using
  the "initiate" command.  The code for the process initiator is:

              program INITIATOR;
                begin
                  do forever LONG_TERM_SCHEDULER(initiate,,,,,,,,,);
                end;                                                          }

{ Called by              : process initiator
  Procedures called      : none
  Parameters passed      : none
  Parameters returned    : none
  Entry conditions       : initiator is trying to satisfy requests
  Exit conditions        : a request has been satisfied                     }

begin

{ Select highest priority request; if none are available, wait.             }

    if no requests are pending then wait(request_pending);
    select j such that info_nodes[j].scheduling_metric >
      info_nodes[i].scheduling_number for all i<>j;

{ Try to acquire memory for the new process.  If sufficient memory is
  not available, wait.  When memory is available assign it and signal
  the waiting parent process.                                               }

    repeat
      MEMORY_MGR(allocate,block_size,first_location,status);
      if status <> OK then wait(memory);
    until status = ok;
    memory_allocated[j] := first_location;
    entry_selected[j] := true;
    signal(parent_waiting[j]);

end; {select_request}
```

Figure 5.6 WAITING_LIST entry for selecting a request from the list.

```
entry return_memory(size,start_address);

{ This entry is used by the removal process.  It returns the  memory
  which the terminating process had, and signals the process initiator
  that more resources have become available.                               }

{ Called by              : removal process
  Procedures called      : none
  Parameters passed      : size, size of memory block released
                         : start_address, first location in memory block
  Parameters returned    : none
  Entry conditions       : none
  Exit conditions        : initiator process was signalled                 }

begin

{ Release memory and let initiator know if it's waiting.                    }

    MEMORY_MGR(deallocate,size,start_address,status);
    signal(memory);

end; {release_memory}
```

Figure 5.7 WAITING_LIST entry for returning the memory freed when a process terminates.

```
procedure LONG_TERM_SCHEDULER(command,device:prog.file,name,pri,cpu,
        lines,wait_nowait,pcb_ptr,user_error,status);

{ This is the long-term scheduler, a procedure responsible for
  the following operations:
            creation of a process
            termination of a process
            initiation of a process                                          }

{ Called by                     : user or system process
                                : initiator process
                                : removal process
  Procedures called             : WAITING LIST monitor, CREATE PROCESS,
                                : SHORT_TERM_SCHEDULER, TERMINATE_PROCESS
  Parameters passed             : command, operation to be performed
                                : device:prog.file, location of program file
                                : name, identification for new process
                                : pri,cpu,lines, scheduling metrics
                                : wait_nowait, flag causing parent to wait
                                    on termination of the offspring
                                : pcb_ptr, pointer to process's pcb
                                : user_error, allows the creating process to
                                    test for errors
  Parameters returned           : status, the error condition
  Entry conditions              : none
  Exit conditions               : process created or terminated             }

global variables
    memory_available            : integer; {maximum memory request}

variables
    termination_ptr             : pcb pointer; {list of pcb's for termination}
    removal_ptr                 : pcb pointer; {pcb of removal process}

begin

  case command of

      create      :   CREATE_CODE;
      terminate   :   TERMINATE_CODE;
      initiate    :   INITIATE_CODE;
      exit        :   EXIT_CODE;
      otherwise   :   ERROR_EXIT(invalid_command);

  end;


      {  The code for these procedures is shown in figures 5.9
         through 5.13.  We assume they are defined within the
         long-term scheduler, but show them as separate figures
         to facilitate presentation.                                         }

end; {long-term scheduler}
```

Figure 5.8   Long-term scheduler.

However, it also includes the code for process termination and the resulting resource returns.

The steps in the "create" portion (detailed in Figure 4.3) are as follows:

Create a PCB.

Find the specified program file.

```
procedure CREATE_CODE;

{ This section is used by a process to request creation of an
  offspring process.                                                    }

  begin
    CREATE_PROCESS(name,device:prog.file,pri,cpu,lines,
                   start_address,cr_status);

            {IMPORTANT! The code in Chapter 4 for CREATE_PROCESS
             must be modified slightly to work within our monitor
             structure.  Instead of calling the memory manager
             directly, we must call WAITING_LIST.add_request.          }

    if cr_status <> ok then ERROR_EXIT(cr_status);
    if wait_nowait = wait then block parent;

  end; {create}
```

Figure 5.9 Procedure for process creation.

```
procedure TERMINATE_CODE;

{ This section is used by the removal process.  It calls a
  procedure to return resources held by the terminated process,
  notify the parent that its offspring has terminated, close the
  corresponding spool file, and signal the spooler that another
  spool file is ready to be printed.  Finally, since memory has
  been released, the appropriate condition is signalled.  The
  code for the process using this entry is:

            program REMOVAL_PROCESS;
            begin
            execution_priority := very_high;
            do forever
                LONG_TERM_SCHEDULER(terminate,,,,,,,pcb_ptr,,);
            end;                                                        }

  begin

{ In the following code, interrupts are disabled to ensure that
  there will not be problems caused by simultaneous accesses to the
  termination list.  We did not use a monitor because the other
  access to this list is from the short-term scheduler.  Also, if
  the termination list is empty, execute_queue and removal_ptr
  must be modified without interruption.                               }

    disable interrupts;
    if termination list is empty then
      begin
        remove pcb from execute_queue and point removal_ptr to it;
        SHORT_TERM_SCHEDULER;
      end
    else
      begin
        remove pcb from termination list;
        enable interrupts;
        TERMINATE_PROCESS(pcb);
      end;

            {IMPORTANT! The code in Chapter 4 for TERMINATE_PROCESS
             must be modified slightly to work within our monitor
             structure.  Instead of calling the memory manager
             directly, we must call WAITING_LIST.return_memory.        }

  end; {terminate}
```

Figure 5.10 Procedure for process termination.

```
procedure INITIATE_CODE;

{ This section is used by the process initiator.  It is only one
  line, but is included so that everything related to process
  creation, initiation, and termination will go through the long-term
  scheduler.  The code for the process initiator is:

          program INITIATOR;
            begin
              do forever LONG_TERM_SCHEDULER(initiate,,,,,,,,,);
            end;                                                          }

  begin
    WAITING_LIST.select request;
  end;  {initiate}
```

Figure 5.11 Procedure for process initiation.

```
procedure EXIT_CODE;

{ This section is used by a process which wants to terminate itself.
  Again, the code itself is short but for consistency it is included
  in the long-term scheduler.                                           }

  begin
    execute_queue^.terminate_flag := true;
    SHORT_TERM_SCHEDULER;
  end;  {exit}
```

Figure 5.12 Procedure for exiting the system.

```
procedure ERROR_EXIT(error_type);

{ Error exit procedure for long-term scheduler. }

  begin
    if user_error = true then
      begin
        status := error_type
        return;
      end {if user handles errors}
    else
      begin
        set parent process's termination flag to true;
        SHORT_TERM_SCHEDULER;
      end; {if user does not handle errors}
  end; {error exit}
```

Figure 5.13 Error exit procedure for long-term scheduler.

Put the necessary information into the PCB.

Wait for memory.

Read in the program file.

Move the newly created process into the mix.

If errors occur at any step, then either the parent process is terminated or it is notified of the error, depending on whether or not it set the user_error flag to true.

The termination section of the long-term scheduler is used by the system removal process, which is initiated whenever a PCB is encountered with its termination flag set. This section returns the resources held by the terminated process, notifies the parent that its offspring has terminated, closes the corresponding spool file, and signals the spooler that another spool file is ready to be printed. Pseudocode for these operations was shown in Figure 4.4.

The "initiate" entry is used by the system initiation process. This process runs forever, its sole purpose in life being to attempt to initiate processes from requests on the long-term scheduler's waiting list.

Finally, we have the "exit" entry. When a process wants to terminate itself, it does a STOP, CALL EXIT, BYE BYE, or something similar. This is translated into a call to the long-term scheduler specifying the EXIT command. The exit section does nothing more than set the termination flag in the process's PCB to true and then call the short-term scheduler to get a new process into the execute state. The interaction of processes, the long-term scheduler, and the scheduler's monitor is shown in Figure 5.14.

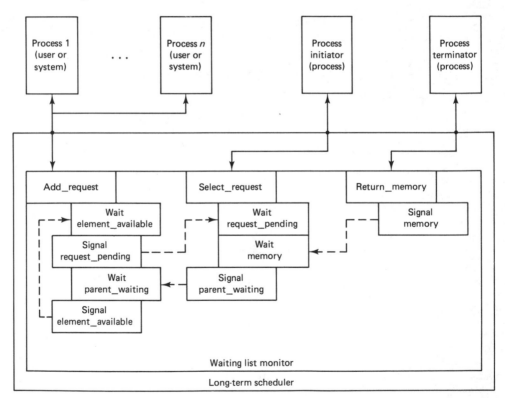

Figure 5.14 Processes accessing the long-term scheduler.

5.5 SUMMARY

So much for long-term schedulers. Our OS is now able to select process creation requests on the basis of specified scheduling metrics, create the corresponding processes, and enter them into the system mix. It is also able to terminate processes and to return the resources held by the terminated processes.

In addition to explaining what long-term scheduling is and how it can be implemented, we have seen how the OS itself is in part made up of cooperating concurrent processes. The initiation and termination processes are system processes which run concurrently with other processes on the system. They are examples of the subcontractors we described in Chapter 3. They are highly specialized entities that operate essentially independently, with a little coordination from their supervisor, the long-term scheduler.

In Chapter 6 we will turn to the short-term scheduler. That scheduler moves processes between the active and the execute nodes of the SNAIL.

For an excellent overview of a wide variety of scheduling policies, see Coffman and Kleinrock [1968]. This article includes nearly all the standard schedulers, and many variations of them. It also describes how a user can get better performance, given a certain policy.

Another comprehensive description of scheduling is Bunt [1976]. Job and process scheduling are differentiated, and all standard types of scheduling are covered. There are brief overviews of scheduling in several popular operating systems. Discussions refer to a diagram similar to our SNAIL diagram.

Specific schedulers are described in Doherty [1970] and Abell et al. [1970]. The first article also includes a good discussion of responsiveness and why it is important, and a description of tools used to gather data for evaluating scheduling policies. The second article shows how a scheduler can be parameterized, and thus adjusted for various process mixes.

Considerable work has been put into the analysis of scheduling policies and mechanisms. Two examples are Ruschitzka and Fabry [1977], which describes a general approach to analyzing a variety of schedulers, and Conway et al. [1967], which gives an elegant, highly mathematical analysis of scheduling.

QUESTIONS AND EXERCISES

1. What are some examples of scheduling policies and mechanisms used in applications other than computer systems?

2. With I/O window scheduling, some users would actually try to cheat by stating that the jobs they were submitting were shorter than they really were. What could be done to prevent this?

3. Create a scheduling function like the one shown in Section 5.4 that operates as a deadline scheduler, that is, gives low priority to a process until it approaches its deadline.

4. Create a scheduling function that gives high priority to the following:
   (a) Lots of I/O and little memory or CPU time
   (b) Compute bound
   (c) Short CPU time

5. Explain the rationale for selecting (a), (b), or (c) in Exercise 4.

6. Modify the scheduling function so that a process's priority is lowered when it requests a resource like a plotter.

7. Why do we wait until we select a request to compute priorities? Couldn't we keep the list ordered as we add new requests?

8. Why complicate life by making the denominator of Equation (5.1) 1 + (wait time)/k instead of just (wait time)/k?

9. Could we have different priority levels for the long-term scheduler? How would you implement them? Who would assign them?

10. Develop an equation like Equation (5.4) but incorporating all of the factors in Equation (5.3).

PROGRAMMING ASSIGNMENTS

Referring to Equation (5.3) for long-term scheduling, assume that a given group of jobs are disk updates with minimal-line printer output. We could define a scheduling metric $S(T)$ as follows:

$$R = \frac{10,000}{(10C + M)}$$

$$S(T) = R(1 + T - A)^k$$

$$= R(T - Q)^k$$

where

C = estimated execution time, ms

M = estimated core required, bytes

T = current system clock time

A = system clock time at which process arrives

k = relative importance of wait time

R = priority change ratio based on estimated CPU usage and estimated core required

Q = constant determined by time at which process arrives

Many references choose not to separate the size of a job into memory and CPU, but rather incorporate both of them into one term. This would simply mean that we rewrite our above definition of R as

$$R = \frac{10,000}{X}$$

and speak of a combined size value X instead of individual C and M values.

You are to write a program which implements the above scheduling algorithm and tests it for various values of k and various distributions of X. There will be one set of output for each value of k, giving the average wait time as a function of size X.

You need not use a simulation language for this assignment—it can be done on almost any system using almost any language. The only different aspect is the use of generated random data rather than preassigned instructor data (which you are probably more used to).

In real-life situations, random quantities often behave in a *normal* fashion, that is, according to the familiar bell-shaped distribution curve. Many computer systems do not have a generator for such normal variables, but they do have a uniform generator over the range [0, 1]. You can approximate a normal variable by summing a sequence of such uniform random variables.

For this program, compute a sequence of normal random variables G by summing 12 sequential uniform random variables over [0, 1]. Convert these variables G to scheduling size values X by using

$$X = (10,000 + WG) \text{ rounded to a multiple of } 10,000$$

where W is a weighting function which establishes the distribution parameters. Set up your program to run for specified input values of k and W. You should experiment with the values $k = 0.5$, 1, and 2 and $W = 5000$, 10,000, and 15,000.

Besides job size, another important factor is arrival times of the jobs. For this program, assume a very simple case. The system starts at time 0 with 10 jobs in the queue, and a new job arrives every i milliseconds. The system selects the first job at time i and then selects subsequent jobs after an interval I defined by

$$I = \frac{X + 6(15,000 - W)}{10,000} \qquad \text{ms}$$

where X is the scheduling size value of the last job selected.

Your first task for each value of k and W will be to adjust i to get a "steady state"—a state in which the number of jobs in the queue remains approximately constant. Keep printing the last 10 queue lengths and adjusting i until this is achieved.

Once the steady state is established, start keeping statistics of average wait time as a function of size X. The number of trials will depend on the speed of the machine you're using—run each case for a "reasonable" time.

Plot the results. You need not use a computer plotting package, although you certainly can if one is available and you know how to use it.

6

Short-Term Scheduling

In Chapter 5, we looked at the problem of how the long-term scheduler selects the next request to create a process. In this chapter we investigate the problem of how the CPU is allocated among the processes that are ready to run. The system routine that performs this task is called the short-term scheduler, the CPU scheduler, or sometimes just the scheduler. We will present several different scheduling policies and mechanisms and then analyze their performance.

6.1 THE DISTINCTION BETWEEN SCHEDULING AND DISPATCHING

There is definitely a difference of opinion among authors when it comes to defining the terms scheduler and dispatcher. We will try to be precise and consistent in our use of these terms. For our text, the term **dispatcher** will be applied to the low-level system routine that just moves the process at the head of the active queue onto the execute queue. It is a relatively simple operation.

In this chapter we will reserve the term **scheduler** for the system function that determines the order of processes on the active queue. After the scheduler has ordered the active queue, the dispatcher is called to place the top process on that queue into execution. The scheduler may be a very sophisticated routine that keeps track of scheduling metrics, examines process histories, evaluates priorities, and arranges several different queues. Figure 6.1 shows the portions of the SNAIL diagram affected by the dispatcher and the short-term scheduler.

When you read other books and papers on operating systems you might see the authors use dispatcher to refer to both the dispatching and scheduling functions described above. If they use this definition, they will probably use scheduler to refer to the long-term scheduling described in Chapter 5. Other authors may just reverse the definitions given in the previous paragraph. The terms themselves are not terribly important, as long as the author tells you ahead of time how he or she is using them, and as long as you understand the differences.

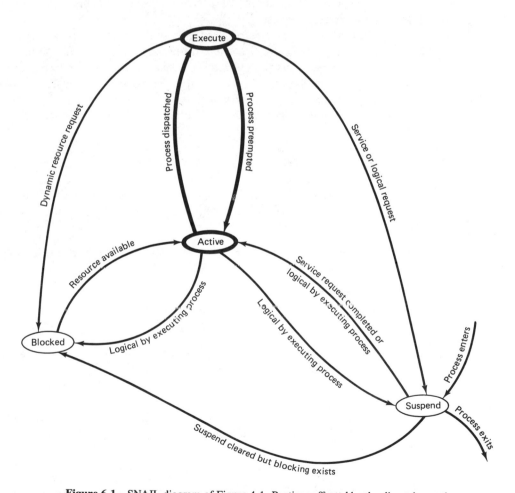

Figure 6.1 SNAIL diagram of Figure 4.1. Portions affected by the dispatcher and the short-term scheduler are drawn bold.

6.2 FIRST-COME–FIRST-SERVED: KEEPING IT SIMPLE

The first scheduling policy we will examine is the first method we examined in the previous chapter, *first come, first served,* or FCFS. Another name given to this policy is FIFO, for *first in, first out*. This is the basic policy chosen to provide service in many applications besides CPU scheduling.

6.2.1 Why Use FCFS?

There are several reasons one might select FCFS as the scheduling policy for the CPU. First, it is simple; this means that a scheduler using an FCFS policy could be fast and efficient. Besides being efficient in terms of execution time, the policy requires very little information about the processes being scheduled. Also, it seems like a *fair* way to service requests.

It is appropriate to note the difference between a policy and a mechanism again. The scheduling policy that we select in this section is FCFS. The mechanism we will use to implement this policy is an ordered linked list. Processes that enter the active queue will be placed at the rear of the queue. By doing this, we are ordering the active queue on the basis of arrival time and accomplishing our goal of FCFS ordering of processes. As you can see, this policy leads to a very simple short-term scheduler.

6.2.2 An Analysis of FCFS

If this policy is so good, why even bother looking at other policies? We might find the answer if we examine the following statistics for processes in the active and execute states:

Response time	Time spent in the active state waiting for the first chance to execute
Wait time	Total time spent in the active state
Execution time	Total time spent in the execute state
Completion time	The sum of the wait time and the execution time

Before deriving equations for these times, we need to make several simplifying assumptions:

1. Once a process has been placed into execution, it remains there until it has completed.
2. There are *n* processes in the system when a new process arrives in the active queue.
3. The average execution time for a process is T seconds.

The first assumption deserves some explanation. Normally, a process will not execute to completion when it is first placed into execution; it will request I/O and spend some time in the I/O suspend queue. However, if the active queue is always ordered on the basis of the time at which the processes first enter the active queue, early-arriving processes will always be placed ahead of those arriving at a later time. Therefore, on the average, the system will serve processes on an FCFS basis.

With these assumptions, we can now derive equations for the times defined above. The length of time a newly arriving process must wait to receive service is

$$\text{Response time} = nT \tag{6.1}$$

The number given by this equation is a worst-case value. Defining how closely the equation approximates the actual response time is left as an exercise.

A newly arriving process will have to wait for all of the processes ahead of it to complete before it executes. Therefore, the total wait time for a new process is

$$\text{Wait time} = nT \tag{6.2}$$

Just to differentiate the execution time of the newly arriving process from the execution times of those already in the queue, assume the new process's execution time is simply t.

$$\text{Execute time} = t \tag{6.3}$$

To calculate completion time, we add execution time to wait time:

$$\text{Completion time} = nT + t \tag{6.4}$$

Note that this definition ignores the fact that a process may have to spend time in the I/O suspend or blocked queue.

From Equations (6.1) and (6.2) we see that response time and wait time for an FCFS system are equal. We also observe that wait time is not dependent on t, the execution time for the new process.

We now ask the question, "Is this a good scheduling policy?" Before you answer, think about the application of this policy at the grocery store. Assume that you are the newly arriving customer at the checkout register and there are n customers ahead of you. They are average customers; that is, each has a cart filled with $100 worth of everything from apricots to zucchini. Now if all you want to buy is a box of cookies and a diet soda, and if you are already late turning in your computer science OS assignment, you probably will not think the scheduling policy is acceptable. In fact, customer dissatisfaction with FCFS is what led to a change of scheduling policies at grocery stores. The *policy* chosen was to give preferential service to customers making only a few purchases. The *mechanism* used was the express checkout line you now find in most larger grocery stores.

If we want our CPU to provide fast service to short processes, the next step seems obvious: install the equivalent of an express line.

6.3 ROUND ROBIN: SCHEDULING FOR TIMESHARING SYSTEMS

Most of us have had the unpleasant experience of waiting for what seemed like a very long time to get a simple carriage return or line feed response from a timesharing system. As timesharing systems came into general use, a new scheduling policy was needed to reduce, if not eliminate, this problem. The method most often chosen was to force a long process to go through the active and execute queues repeatedly, limiting the amount of time it could spend in the execute state on each cycle. If a process failed to complete its work in one of those fixed amounts of time, it was forcibly removed, **preempted,** from the execute state and placed on the end of the active queue. It then had to work its way around to the head of that queue again before it was allowed to execute. This method is called **round robin** (RR) scheduling; it is shown graphically in Figure 6.2.

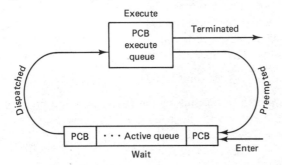

Figure 6.2   Process flow with a round robin scheduler.

6.3.1 Reasons for Using Round Robin

The reasons given for using the FCFS scheduling policy were related to simplicity, efficiency, and fairness. The reasons for using RR scheduling are more subjective. The primary reason is that users are happier and more productive if they get fast responses to their simple requests [Thadhani, 1981, 1984; Lambert, 1984]. They may even pay more money to use a system if they are guaranteed a fast response every time they input a line into the editor or BASIC interpreter.

6.3.2 An Analysis of RR

In an attempt to see what RR does both for us and to us, we will look again at response time, wait time, and completion time. We will have to make more assumptions than with FCFS, because the problem is a little more complex.

In the discussion above we stated that a process would be forcibly removed from the execute state if it did not complete its work in a fixed amount of time; this time, q, is called the **time quantum** given each process. (Typical values for q range from 1 ms to 2 s.) We can now redefine what we mean by an average process: an average process is one that requires T seconds of CPU time:

$$T = mq \tag{6.5}$$

The number m is a measure of how many times the process must enter the execute state before it receives all the CPU time it needs. Now we want to look at what happens to a process that enters the active queue when there are n processes ahead of it.

We next ask the question, "How much time does a process spend in the active queue before it receives its first service?" It must wait until all n processes ahead of it have been serviced, which will be at most

$$\text{Response time} = nq \tag{6.6}$$

as compared to

$$\text{Response time} = nT \tag{6.1}$$

for the FCFS scheduler. What have we gained over FCFS? To answer that, we need values for q and T. If they are the same, or if $q > T$, we have gained nothing. If, on the other hand, $q < T$, we will have improved the response time. You might well ask now, "What value should q be?" If our goal is to just reduce response time, we would be tempted to pick a value of q close to zero. Unfortunately, this usually has drawbacks.

To find out why q should not be made too small, consider what happens each time we remove a process from the execute queue before it has completed its work. We will look at the grocery store again for an analogy. One mechanism that could be used to implement an RR policy for the grocery checkout counter would be to let the checker ring up a fixed number of items, save the total for those items, clear the counter, and move on to the next customer. The checker would obviously spend a lot of time saving subtotals and changing from one customer to another. The same types of operations are required in switching from one process to another in a computer system.

Every time we preempt a process, we must save its current status (context) in the PCB and then dispatch a new process. This requires restoring all register values from the PCB to the CPU registers. Some processors have been designed so that these operations can be executed very expeditiously, but they still take some amount of time. Is the processor accomplishing anything useful during the time it is swapping registers and memory values? We claim that it is not. We will call this time that does not contribute to the execution of a process **overhead time.** As with most any system, from the grocery store to the computer, we try to reduce or eliminate overhead time. Figure 6.3 shows the steps involved in switching from one process to another and where overhead is incurred.

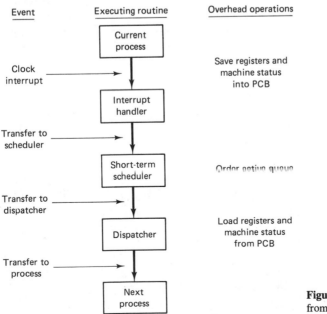

Figure 6.3   Context switching: changing from one process to another.

Let us turn our attention now to wait time. Assume again that a new process arrives at the end of the active queue and we want to calculate the total time it will spend waiting for service. If the process is short, that is, if it can complete in q seconds or less, the total wait time is the time it waits to first reach the execute state. That time is the same as the response time calculated above:

$$\text{Wait time} = nq \tag{6.7}$$

Suppose now that the newly arriving process is a long one, that is, it requires $t >> q$ seconds of CPU time. For this case, assume that

$$t = mq \tag{6.8}$$

What is the total time this process will spend waiting before it has received t seconds of CPU time? Since it must pass through the active queue m times and each time through it waits nq seconds, the total wait time is as follows:

$$\text{Wait time} = m(nq)$$

$$= \frac{t}{q}(nq) \tag{6.9}$$

$$= nt$$

where t is the execution time for the *individual* process. We recall that wait time for an FCFS scheduler is

$$\text{Wait time} = nT \tag{6.2}$$

where T is the execution time for the *average* process.

Although these calculations are correct only if there are always n processes ahead of the process each time it enters the active state, they show the relative bias of each policy. The equations for wait time tell us that for a round robin scheduling policy, the wait time for any process is proportional to *its* length and the number of processes in the active queue. However, for FCFS scheduling, the wait time is proportional to the average wait time for *other* processes.

If all processes in the queue are the same length, the wait time is the same as it was for the FCFS scheduler, and all that RR scheduling has done is to reduce the efficiency of the system with the overhead added by swapping processes in and out of the execute state. If there is a mix of processes of different lengths, however, the short processes will receive preferential service, since their wait is proportional to their shorter length.

Finally, we need to calculate the completion time for a process under RR scheduling. This time is the sum of the wait time and the execute time:

$$\text{Completion time} = \text{wait time} + \text{execute time}$$

$$\text{Completion time}_{\text{short process}} = nq + q$$

$$= (n + 1)q \tag{6.10}$$

$$\text{Completion time}_{\text{long process}} = tn + t$$

$$= (n + 1)t \tag{6.11}$$

If you are one of the system users whose processes are mostly short, you will probably be satisfied with this policy as long as q is small enough. On the other hand, if you have just submitted a process that will calculate the next Mersenne prime number and print it, you will be very displeased with the performance of the system. What are the implications? You probably cannot make everyone happy with one scheduling policy. Because short processes get better service than long ones, RR scheduling is often described as being unfair to long processes. In the next section we will look at some modifications to the basic RR scheduler that attempt to make it less unfair to long processes.

6.3.3 Modifications to the Basic RR Scheduler

In an attempt to have their cake and eat it too, designers have modified the RR scheduler so that it is more fair to long processes [Shemer, 1967]. What they typically do is to change the time quantum given to long processes. One of the mechanisms that have been suggested for implementing a more fair policy for long processes is to double the time quantum given a process each time it has passed through the active queue. For the **modified round robin** (MRR) the execution time received by a process is

$$\text{Execution time} = q + 2q + 4q + \cdots \qquad (6.12)$$

So that we can compare the results of this mechanism with those of the others, we will derive the equations for response, wait, and completion time.

The first value we look at is the response time. You may be tempted to use the equation we found for the basic RR:

$$\text{Response time} = nq$$

Unfortunately, this will be correct for only one case. If there are n processes in the active queue when a new process arrives, the response time of the new process will be nq seconds only if all the processes ahead of it receive just q seconds of service; this is equivalent to saying that they have also just arrived for their first time in the active queue. If there are processes in the active queue that have already passed through several times, they will receive more than just q seconds of CPU time when they reach the execute state. This will increase the response time for our newly arrived process. Therefore, we may give the response time for the modified round robin as

$$\text{Response time} \geq nq \qquad (6.13)$$

To mathematically analyze the other times in which we are interested, assume that there are always n short processes in the active queue whenever our long process is placed at the end of the queue. This assumption may appear too restrictive; however, it occurs often in timesharing systems that have only an occasional long process. In this case the time spent waiting on each pass through the active queue is nq.

Now we will calculate the total wait time for a long process. To do this we must determine how many passes the process makes through the active queue. If the process requires t seconds of CPU time, then

$$t \leq q + 2q + 4q + \cdots + 2^i q$$
$$= 2^0 q + 2^1 q + \cdots + 2^i q \tag{6.14}$$

for some value of i. We will choose the smallest integer i that satisfies the inequality. For this choice, $i + 1$ represents the total number of times the process passes through the active queue. Now all we need is a value for i. Rewriting the equation above, we see that

$$t \leq q(1 + 2 + 4 + \cdots + 2^i)$$
$$= q \sum_{k=0}^{i} 2^k \tag{6.15}$$

If it is not obvious to you how to calculate this sum, add the terms together for $i = 2$, 3, and 4. You should recognize those numbers and see a pattern. The sum can be written as

$$t \leq q(2^{i+1} - 1)$$
$$\approx q(2^{i+1}) \tag{6.16}$$

We now solve for i:

$$2^{i+1} \approx \frac{t}{q}$$
$$i + 1 \approx \log_2 \frac{t}{q} \tag{6.17}$$

This approximation gives us the number of times the long process goes through the active queue. Each time, there will be n short processes ahead of it, and so we can write the equation for the total wait time for the MRR as

$$\text{Wait time} \leq (nq)(i + 1)$$
$$\approx (nq) \log_2 \frac{t}{q} \tag{6.18}$$

as compared to

$$\text{Wait time} \leq nq \frac{t}{q} \tag{6.9}$$

for the basic RR scheduler. We see that wait time grows in proportion to $\log_2 (t/q)$ rather than in proportion to t/q. For large ratios of t/q you can see that this scheduler will reduce the wait times for long processes significantly.

The completion time for the process is

$$\text{Completion time} = \text{wait time} + \text{execute time}$$
$$\approx nq \log_2 \frac{t}{q} + t \tag{6.19}$$

What we have done by modifying the RR scheduler is to reduce the wait time for a long process when it is competing for service with a number of short processes.

To accomplish this, we were forced to accept longer response times for the short processes. Whether or not this is a good trade-off depends on the way the system is being used. Consider the case in which one long process is in the active queue with $n - 1$ short processes and a new short process arrives. If the long process is in its last pass through the active queue, the response time for the newly arriving process will be as follows:

$$
\begin{aligned}
\text{Response time} &= (n - 1)q + 2^i q \\
&= (n - 1 + 2^i)q
\end{aligned}
\tag{6.20}
$$

which can obviously be much longer than nq. In situations in which users require a maximum response time, the modified RR will not be acceptable.

We need to make a comment on the usefulness of the analytical methods used in the preceding sections. By making a number of simplifying assumptions, we were able to calculate some performance measures for FCFS, RR, and MRR schedulers. These performance measures enabled us to say quantitatively why one scheduling mechanism was better for a given application or set of users than another mechanism. There has been a great deal of interesting analysis performed on queueing systems such as those found within operating systems. Three good references to this work are texts by Kleinrock [1975], Lavenberg [1983], and Lazowska [1984].

Unfortunately, the more complex schedulers that will be described in the following sections cannot be as easily analyzed, even with simplifying assumptions. Simulation is a technique that is often used to evaluate system performance when it is not possible to use analytic methods [Conti et al., 1968; Lavenberg, 1983]. The program at the end of the chapter suggests how simulation can be used to analyze the performance of schedulers.

6.4 MULTILEVEL PRIORITY QUEUES: A REAL SCHEDULER

The scheduling policies discussed so far have been relatively simple. Processes enter at the rear of the active queue and work their way to the front; then they are allowed to execute for some amount of time. When they finish executing, they either leave the system or are again placed on the active queue. No attempt is made to show any preference for one process over another. In the real world, there are often times when it is desirable, if not mandatory, to give some processes priority over others. In Section 6.2 we discussed how an express checkout line gave priority to customers with only a few items in their baskets. In this section we will discuss some of the reasons for giving high priority to some processes and then show an example of a scheduler that uses priority to order the active queue.

6.4.1 Why Use More Complicated Schedulers?

As we observed in Section 6.3, going away from a simple FCFS scheduler increases overhead in the system. The schedulers we will look at in this section will be more complex and will potentially add even more overhead to the system. A valid question then is, "Why complicate the scheduler if you are going to make some things worse?" We hope we can answer that question to your satisfaction.

Suppose we are designing the scheduler for a system that is controlling a nuclear reactor. In addition to controlling the rate of the reaction, the system also prints out reports on various parameters that it is monitoring and allows the operator to request the status of various parts of the system. If you were living downwind from the reactor, you would most likely feel that it is more important for the system to control the reaction than print a monthly report for management. When making this judgment, you are in fact assigning a higher priority to the reaction control process and a lower one to the report generator process. In this case, safety has determined that one process should receive priority over another. When we make this decision, we are implying that timely report generation is not the most important measure of goodness for this system and that we are willing to accept the fact that time will be wasted by preempting some processes in order to guarantee that other processes receive prompt service.

The object of this discussion is to point out that sometimes we are quite willing to sacrifice overall system efficiency if it gives us better performance with respect to some other parameter, such as safety.

6.4.2 Methods for Assigning Priority

In the previous section we suggested that safety could be a reason to assign higher priority to a process. There are many other reasons also. By looking at a system that serves both interactive and batch users, we hope to point out some of these reasons. Interactive (terminal) users are characterized by their need for fast response to terminal input. These users typically place the greatest demands on the system from 9:00 A.M. until 6:00 P.M. Batch users are often more interested in the cost of running some job and might be willing to accept overnight turnaround if it costs less. During the normal working hours it would seem reasonable to assign higher priority to timesharing users than batch users, and then to switch the priority after 6:00 P.M.

On many systems, some of the functions you associate with the system itself are just processes that compete for the CPU with users' processes. A routine that reads batch jobs from the card reader, for instance, may be one of the competing processes. If this is the case, does it make sense to have a user process, which may need the card images, run at the same priority or a higher priority than the process reading the cards? Usually it does not. Hence, most systems will automatically give system processes higher priority than user processes. This implies that no user processes will execute until all high-priority system processes that are ready have executed.

Some users are willing to pay more money if they are given priority over others. Therefore, in some cases we may assign priority on the basis of how much users are willing to pay [McKell et al., 1979].

It has also been suggested that the priority of a process should be increased as the process waits longer for service, no matter what type of user the process represents. We saw in Chapter 5 how this concept, aging, was used in long-term schedulers.

Another possibility is to give high priority to a process that has acquired a large number of system resources. The justification is that these resources will remain idle if the process is not allowed to execute and the cost of having these resources idle is too high. In the final section of this chapter, we will briefly discuss some other policies that use different methods to determine priority.

6.4.3 An Example of a Comprehensive Short-Term Scheduler

There is no such thing as a standard scheduler; however, in this section we will present a scheduler that is typical of schedulers on moderate to large uniprocessor systems. For discussion's sake, assume that our system will have six different priority levels, with level 0 the highest and level 5 the lowest. The scheduler will arrange the active queue in priority order. The dispatcher simply takes the process with the highest priority and places it into execution.

For our system we assume that some OS routines run as processes on the system. To ensure that these processes receive quick response, we will allocate priority level 0 to OS processes exclusively. If there is never more than one process in the system at one priority level, our scheduler will have no problems. What will we do if there are multiple processes at one level? Two solutions should come to mind: use FCFS or RR. We will assume that system processes running at priority level 0 are short and therefore there is no need to swap these processes in and out of the execute state. Because of this, we will let all processes on level 0 run on an FCFS basis.

We now turn our attention to user processes to see how they should be scheduled. To give our system a high degree of flexibility, we will allocate priority level 1, immediately below the system priority level, to selected user processes. This will allow programmers to designate critical portions of their applications as high-priority processes. For the same reasons given above, we will designate level 1 as FCFS.

We are now ready to specify the policy that will be used for typical user processes. Assume that our system will be accessed, in part, by terminal users. This means that fast response is important, and as we found earlier in this chapter, an RR scheduler gives good response to short timesharing-type processes. Therefore, we will allocate priority level 2 for a simple RR queue. Since our system must meet the needs of not just timesharing users, we should make some provision to let longer processes run without being preempted as often as they would in the RR queues. To meet these requirements, we will allocate priority level 3 as an RR queue with a time quantum 4 times that allocated to the processes at priority level 2.

About the only users we have not taken care of are those who want to run batch jobs, those that do not require any specific response time. When running these processes, we want to get the maximum efficiency from the system. To do this, we go back to the reliable FCFS for priority level 4. Finally, we will add a priority level 5 for the **idle process,** a system process that executes when no other processes are on the active queue. In Figure 6.4, we show how the active queue is arranged for our scheduler.

You might now be wondering how priorities are assigned to processes as they enter the system. Users on many systems do not even know at which priority level

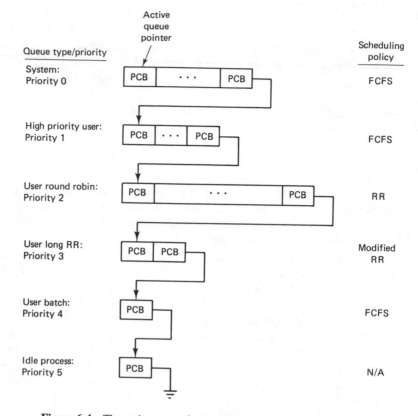

Figure 6.4   The active queue for a priority-based short-term scheduler.

they are operating. For our system, the long-term scheduler will assign a priority of 2, which is on the RR queue, to new processes unless there is a special request for some other priority. Some users may be given permission by the system manager to assign a priority to their processes above level 2, but this will not be the case for the average terminal user.

As stated above, when the long-term scheduler creates a process it normally assumes that the process will be a short one. What happens if the process turns out to be a long, CPU-intensive process that executes for many, many time quanta? A possibility is to let the process continue running at level 2, where it competes with the processes that are short ones. If enough long processes do this, the response time for the timesharing users will be degraded. To avoid this situation we can move the long process off the level 2 queue. Our scheduler will therefore move any process that has executed more than 8 time quanta at level 2 down to level 3, where it will get a larger block of time whenever it executes. What can we do if the process turns out to be a real hog and is still not finished after executing 8 times on the level 3 queue? We can send it to the batch queue, where it can be put on hold until three o'clock in the morning, if necessary.

This may seem a little unfair, especially if the system is heavily loaded and processes below level 2 seldom if ever execute. To eliminate this indefinite wait problem, we will add a type of "aging" to our scheduler. With this aging, if a process at level 3 waits for more than one minute and receives no CPU time, it will be moved up to level 2, and one waiting at level 4 for more than 2 minutes will be moved up to level 3. This means that even the lowliest batch process will get to execute once in a while.

We have embedded the ideas discussed above into our sample scheduler. To keep track of all the information needed by this relatively comprehensive but straightforward scheduler, we had to add additional fields to the PCB. The PCB used for this system is shown in Figure 6.5, and the scheduler itself is shown in Figures 6.6 and 6.7. The need for some of the fields in the PCB will be explained in later chapters

```
next PCB pointer
process identifier
process state
termination flag
pointer to PCB of parent
starting memory address
memory size
program counter
register 0
        *
        *
        *
register n
child list pointer
child status
file list pointer
resource list pointer
accounting information
priority
pass count
last execution time
number of logical units
logical unit number
driver address
logical unit number
driver address
logical unit number
driver address
logical unit number
driver address
```

Figure 6.5 A detailed PCB for the short-term scheduler.

The first thing our short-term scheduler does is to disable interrupts so that all the system queues can be accessed without using monitors. If a PCB is passed as a parameter to the scheduler, it places that PCB on the appropriate active queue. It then removes the executing process and places it onto the active queue at the correct priority level.

The scheduler next checks to see whether any processes have executed the maximum number of times on the round robin queue at level 2, and it moves any that have down to level 3. It then moves processes that have executed too long on the long round robin queue down to the batch queue and moves processes that have waited too long on the long round robin queue up to the round robin queue.

Next, the scheduler checks to see whether any processes have been forced to wait in the batch queue a long time without receiving CPU time, and it moves any

```
procedure SHORT_TERM_SCHEDULER(new_pcb);

{ This procedure is responsible for ordering the active queue.  It
  is called whenever an interrupt has occurred that may require
  reordering the active queue, such as at the end of a time quantum and
  when a process starts or completes an I/O operation. The long-term
  scheduler also calls it during process addition and deletion.

  If there is a pcb on the execute queue when the scheduler is called,
  or a pcb is passed to the scheduler, that pcb is placed back on the
  active queue before the active queue is ordered.                      }

{ Called by              : IOCS, LONG_TERM_SCHEDULER
  Procedures called      : DISPATCHER, ORDER_QUEUES
  Parameters passed      : new_pcb
  Parameters returned    : none
  Entry conditions       : none
  Exit conditions        : the active queue is reordered              }

global variables
      system_queue, user_hipri_queue, user_rr_queue  : pcb pointer;
      user_longrr_queue, user_batch_queue,           : pcb pointer;
      removal_ptr, termination_queue                 : pcb pointer;

local variables
      temp_pointer, remember_pointer : pcb pointer;

begin

{ Disable the interrupt system, move the new pcb (if one is passed) to
  the active queue, and move executing process to active.              }

    disable interrupts;
    if new_pcb <> nil then move new_pcb to active queue;
    if execute_queue <> nil then move executing pcb to active queue;

    ORDER_QUEUES;

{ Check the termination flag of the highest priority process.  If set,
  the process is placed on the termination queue and the removal
  process is placed at the head of the system queue if it is idle.
  The removal process then deletes the process from the system.        }

    repeat
      find highest priority process;
      if termination flag set then move pcb to termination queue;
      if removal_ptr <> nil then
         move pcb of removal process to head of system queue;
    until termination flag not set;

    DISPATCHER;

end; {SHORT_TERM_SCHEDULER}
```

Figure 6.6   A multi level queue-based short-term scheduler.

that have exceeded their wait time up to the long round robin queue. The final operation performed by the scheduler before transferring to the dispatcher is to find the
highest-priority process on the active queue; if that process has its termination flag
set, the scheduler swaps it and the termination process. The termination routine,
which was described in Chapter 4, will then remove that process from the system.

```
procedure ORDER_QUEUES;
{ This procedure is defined within the scope of the short term
  scheduler and therefore has access to the variables defined within
  the scheduler.

  It first checks all of the processes below level 2 to see if any
  need to be moved up.  It also checks to see if any processes at
  level 2 or level 3 need to be moved.                                 }

begin
{ Move processes out of the rr (level 2) queue if they have executed
  8 times without completing; place them on the long rr queue.         }

  for all pcbs on user_rr_queue
    if pcb.pass_count = 8 then
      begin
        move pcb from user_rr_queue to user_longrr_queue;
        pcb.pass_count := 0;
      end; {if pass_count = 8}

{ Move process out of the longrr (level 3) queue if they have
  executed 8 times.                                                     }

  for all pcbs on user_longrr_queue
    if pcb.pass_count = 8 then
      begin
        move pcb from user_longrr_queue to user_batch_queue;
        pcb.pass_count := 0;
      end; {if pass_count = 8}

{ Move processes up to the rr queue from longrr queue if they have
  received no service in the past minute.                              }

  for all pcbs on user_longrr_queue
    if current_time > pcb.last_run+1 then
      begin
        move pcb from user_longrr_queue to user_rr_queue;
        pcb.last_run := current_time;
      end; {if no execution in last minute}

{ Move processes up from the batch queue to the longrr queue if
  they have waited 2 minutes without receiving service.  The last_run
  variable is set to the current time so that the process will have
  to wait another minute before it can move onto the RR queue.         }

  for all pcbs on user_batch_queue
    if current_time > pcb.last_run+2 then
      begin
        move pcb from user_batch_queue to user_longrr_queue;
        pcb.last_run := current_time;
      end; {if no execution in last 2 minutes}
```

Figure 6.7   Queue ordering procedure for the short-term scheduler.

6.5 OTHER SCHEDULING POLICIES

The scheduler described in the previous section is obviously just one possible implementation. In the limited space here we cannot possibly describe all of the scheduling policies that have been used on computers, but we will briefly describe a few.

One interesting scheduler, called a **deadline scheduler** [Kleinrock, 1970; Haber-mann, 1976], was developed to provide some percentage of CPU time to different types of users. The systems that use this scheduler typically have three types of users: real-time (process control), timesharing, and batch. This scheduler guarantees a minimum amount of service to each class of user. A possible allocation of time is shown in Figure 6.8. This scheduler requires that the various types of users make their needs known at the beginning of the specified time period. Note that the response time may suffer in the last minute of a 10-minute period if the batch processes have been delayed.

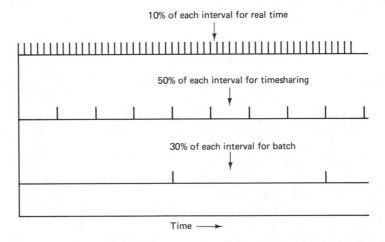

Figure 6.8 Time allocation for types of users in a system with deadline scheduling.

There have been many more modifications to the basic RR scheduler than were discussed earlier. One popular variation combines both short-term and long-term scheduling in one routine. With this method, called **selfish round robin,** or SRR [Kleinrock, 1970; Habermann, 1976], not all processes on the active queue are allowed to compete for the CPU. A delay queue is created for processes that have just entered the system. Processes in this queue are forced to wait until their priority reaches that of the processes in the active portion of the queue. The priority of these processes increases at a rate a as shown in Figure 6.9. Once the priority of a process

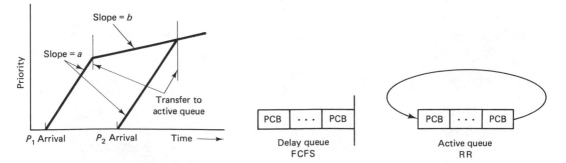

Figure 6.9 Priorities and queues for selfish round robin scheduler.

has increased enough, it can be moved to the active queue, where its priority increases at a rate b. In the questions at the end of the chapter, you are asked to explain how the scheduler performs for the cases

$$b > a$$

$$b = a$$

$$b < a$$

There is another class of scheduling policies, one that was designed to increase the throughput of the system (the number of processes completed per unit time). The philosophy behind these schedulers is to pick a process from the active queue that will finish in the shortest amount of time. By allowing this process to execute, resources, such as memory, are freed up as soon as possible and this enables more processes to enter the system. The **shortest process next,** often called the **shortest job next** (SJN), is one of the schedulers. The policy does just as the name implies; it picks the process or job requiring the shortest amount of CPU time to place at the front of the active queue.

Your first question about this scheduler is probably, "How does it determine the time a process will need?" This problem was discussed in the previous chapter in relation to long-term scheduling. One solution is to have the user specify the maximum amount of time the process will need. This information is stored in the PCB and used by the scheduler to order the active queue.

A related policy that has the same goals is the **shortest time remaining** (STR). To determine where to place a process on the queue, this policy uses not only the information provided initially by the user, but also the amount of time the process has already received. It takes the maximum time needed and subtracts the time already used. The process with the smallest difference is placed at the front of the active queue. This method will enable a long process that has gradually received some time on the execute queue to get to the point where it becomes the one with the shortest time remaining and will therefore be allowed to execute.

Both the SJN and STR give very poor service to long processes. Because of this, Brinch Hansen [1971] proposed a policy that takes into account the time a process has spent waiting. The response ratio for a process is defined as follows:

$$\text{Response ratio} = \frac{\text{waiting time} + \text{service time}}{\text{service time}}$$

After this ratio is calculated for each process, the process with the highest response ratio is moved to the front of the active queue. The method is called **highest response ratio next** (HRN). The overhead associated with this policy can be quite high, since the scheduler must calculate the response ratio for every process before it can order the active queue.

Before leaving the topic of short-term scheduling, it is important to observe that the user's perception of how well a computer system works is very directly affected by the design of the scheduler. For this reason, many different schedulers have been built and tested. One very practical way of testing a variety of scheduling policies is to simulate their operation. This gives a good way to predict how the system will respond before delivering it to an unsuspecting customer. The programming assignment for this chapter suggests a simulation that could be used to evaluate scheduler performance.

6.6 SUMMARY

In this chapter we have looked at two problems of scheduling: which process in the active state should be allowed to move to the execute state, and how a process is preempted from the execute state. The other operation introduced in this chapter, dispatching, is described in more detail in Chapter 12.

Choosing which process to move to the execute state can be a simple or a complicated operation, depending on the policy and mechanism that are used to select the process. We examined several different types of schedulers, from the simple FCFS to complicated multilevel priority-based methods. In order to compare the different scheduling algorithms, we looked at several measures of performance, such as response time, wait time, and turnaround time. We discussed alternative ways of evaluating schedulers, including analytical methods and simulation, and gave some advantages of each approach.

To show the details of implementation, we gave the pseudocode for a rather sophisticated scheduler with multiple priority levels. In this scheduler we showed how aging can be used to prevent starvation and how short processes can be given high priority.

In this chapter we assumed that processes had all the memory they needed to execute. In the next chapter we will look in detail at what happens when a process needs more memory than it has been allocated.

Two researchers who have contributed significantly to the analysis of scheduling algorithms are Coffman and Kleinrock. In addition to references cited earlier in the chapter, the following are recommended for your examination: Kleinrock [1967], Coffman and Kleinrock [1968], and Coffman [1968]. A brief, well-written introduction to the analysis of timesharing systems that summarizes many of the results obtained by Coffman, Kleinrock, and others can be found in McKinney [1969].

QUESTIONS AND EXERCISES

1. Sometimes a process is added to the front of an active queue and other times to the end. What are the reasons for choosing one method over the other?

2. What is the worst-case response time for the MRR described in Section 6.3.3?

3. Often a process on a system with an RR scheduler will not receive its full quantum before it is forced to the suspend state for an I/O operation. What should be done with such a process when it returns from suspend [Oppenheimer and Weizer, 1968]?

4. Suppose that you must design an RR scheduler that guarantees a worst-case response time of RT seconds. Assume that there are a maximum of n processes on the active queue. Taking into account swap time S, what should the time quantum be? Discuss your answer.

5. When would the scheduler described in Section 6.4.3 be called without being passed a pointer to a PCB?

6. We discussed the importance of giving processes that control real-time events a high priority. What happens to a lower-priority process that has just started execution when it is preempted by the reactor control process?

7. In Section 6.5 we introduced the concept of a delay queue. Recall that the priority of processes in this queue increased at a rate a while priorities of processes in the active queue increased at a rate b. Discuss the effects of the three possibilities

$$b > a$$

$$b = a$$

$$b < a$$

8. There are many possible ways to modify the time quantum allocated to a process on an RR queue. Calculate the wait, response, and total times for the following cases:
   (a) The time quantum is increased by 1 on each pass through the active queue.
   (b) Same as (a), but the quantum remains constant after reaching a value of Q_{max}.
   (c) The quantum allocated to a process follows the pattern

$$q, 2q, 4q, 8q, q, 2q, 4q, 8q, q, \ldots$$

9. The scheduler in Figures 6.6 and 6.7 is not very efficient in the way it selects processes that need to be moved down a level. Write an improved version.

10. Why is it stated in Section 6.3.2 that the response time is *at most nq*?

11. Equation (6.1) was described as being a worst-case condition. What factors determine how closely this equation describes the actual response time?

PROGRAMMING ASSIGNMENT

You have just been told that you will be interviewed by a group that is responsible for the development of a new operating system. In order to prepare yourself for the interview you have decided to write a program that simulates the operation of three different schedulers. To be really prepared for the interview you will create a set of graphs that display the performance of the schedulers.

Your simulation will calculate the time spent waiting for service with FCFS, RR, and MRR schedulers. The MRR scheduler will double the time quantum given a process each time the process is dispatched. To perform the simulation it will be necessary to create a stream of processes as input. The input process stream will contain 95 percent short processes and 5 percent long processes. Short processes have execution times that are uniformly distributed between $0.5q$ and $1.5q$. Long processes have execution times uniformly distributed between $4q$ and $96q$. Assume that the processes have a Poisson arrival distribution with $\lambda = 1/(3.46q)$. You will use a random number generator to create the process stream. Be sure to use the same input data stream for each scheduler.

The data gathered from a simulation can be misleading if the model has not reached steady state. To determine that the model has reached steady state, measure the length of the active queue and start gathering data only when steady state has been reached. Plot the length of the active queue as a function of time to show when steady state has been reached.

The other graphs that you plot will show wait time in the system as a function of process length. To simplify gathering data and plotting it, group processes together in the following manner: $0-4q$, $4.001-8q$, $8.001-12q$, . . . , $88.001-92q$, $92.001-96q$. Run the simulation until there are at least 50 sample points in each group.

Turn in with your graphs an analysis explaining how the simulation results compare with predicted results. You must also hand in your design with your listings and output.

Extra credit: Create computer-generated graphs.

7

Memory Management

In the previous two chapters we discussed long- and short-term schedulers. From the point of view of a process P, those schedulers are essentially the components of the OS that ultimately decide when P will be created and when it can execute.

However, there is another component of the OS which is inseparably involved in the scheduling sequence: the memory manager. It is certainly possible to imagine a process executing without being allocated a line printer or a tape drive, but not without being allocated memory. Therfore the next topic we will cover is memory management.

The memory manager is one of the parts of the system that affect which processes will be placed on the blocked queue. When a process requests memory and sufficient memory is not available, the requesting process will be placed on the blocked queue. Figure 7.1 again shows the SNAIL diagram, with the portion affected by the memory manager highlighted.

Probably no other topic in the study of operating systems (with the possible exception of scheduling) has received as much attention as memory management. That attention is understandable, given the importance of memory management. On the other hand, because this is an introductory text on operating systems, we do not want to get bogged down in special cases or extensive variations on a single theme.

We will use a historical framework for presentation in this chapter, since many of the developments followed a chronological sequence which parallels our discussion. It is interesting to note, however, that some early systems such as Atlas

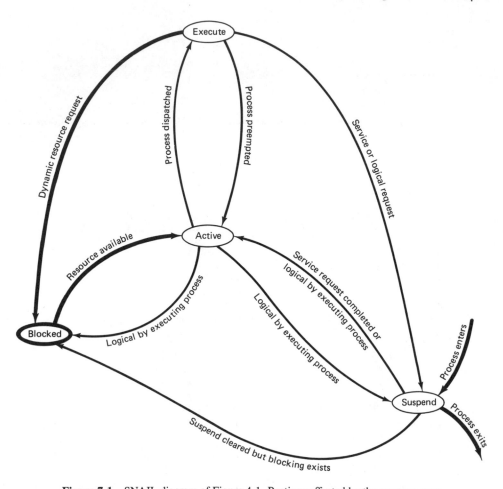

Figure 7.1   SNAIL diagram of Figure 4.1. Portions affected by the memory manager are drawn bold.

[Kilburn et al., 1961a; Kilburn et al., 1961b] implemented remarkably advanced ideas in their memory managers, considering the state of the art at the time.

In keeping with the objectives of this text, we will try to explain only the major techniques, but explain them thoroughly and show you how to implement them. Related topics will be left for other courses, other texts, and experience.

7.1 MEMORY MANAGEMENT IN A SINGLE-USER SYSTEM

On early systems, each user had the machine to himself or herself for the duration of the execution of his or her program. Memory management consisted of nothing more than implicitly allocating all of memory to the next job. "All" included the part of memory containing the OS. This allowed a user's run-time error (such as that caused by storing into a nonexistent array element) to crash the OS.

Such a crash was perhaps best described as an inconvenience. The OS had to be reloaded, but that wasusually a simple matter of a card, or of a tape bootstrap to bring in a small set of system routines from tape. There were no concurrent jobs whose execution could be affected. Files were normally kept on cards or tapes, with access regulated manually by the user or an operator, not the OS. Accounting information was minimal and was maintained on a console typewriter or a tape. All of these aspects reiterate our previous assertion. The crash of the OS was typically not a major problem.

7.2 SEPARATING THE USER AND THE SYSTEM MEMORY

As computer systems evolved, it became necessary to guard the integrity of the OS. There was still only a single job at a time on the system, and so concurrent jobs could not be directly affected. However, it became possible for that single job to affect other users and the system itself *indirectly*.

For example, files had migrated from off-line card and tape storage to on-line disks and were therefore accessible without operator intervention; failure of the OS could leave these files open to accidental or intentional penetration by an unauthorized user. Since many computer centers began imposing monetary charges for use of system resources, and since such charges depended on accurately recording and maintaining utilization records by the OS, crashes could cause the loss of valuable accounting information.

These and other factors resulted in the development of OS protection hardware. A number of different approaches have been used to protect portions of memory from accidental or intentional modification [Saltzer and Schroeder, 1975]. The three early methods that we will describe here are automatic address modification, Page 0–Page 1 addressing, and limit registers.

With **automatic address modification,** the OS was put into either low or high main memory. User references were then modified to make certain they could not access the memory assigned to the system. For example, in a 12K memory with the OS occupying the upper 4K, we could take every user memory reference R and actually address (R mod 8K). Any attempt to reference the OS directly would "wrap around on itself." Alternatively, if the OS were in the lower 4K, we could give the user a 13-bit address space and add 4K to every memory reference. Figure 7.2(a) shows these two address modification techniques.

There are many variations of the above technique, and we need not discuss all of them. However, there is one which should be discussed. If we give the user and the OS each one-half of memory, then they can be separated simply by concatenating a 1 to the beginning of every user-generated address (see Figure 7.2(b)). In reference to this technique, people would describe the OS as being in **Page 0** and the user job as being in **Page 1.** (In this case, Page is used to designate one-half the available main memory.)

All of the previous techniques require that the sizes of the user and system areas be predetermined. Such restrictions were eliminated by having a **limit,** or **fence, register** separate the two areas. The limit register could then be changed when the relative sizes of the areas were modified. Of course, this approach also increased

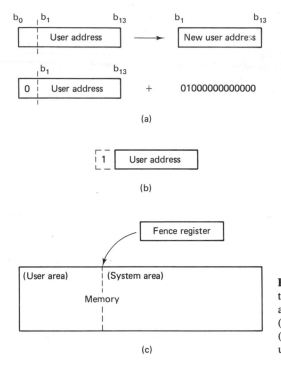

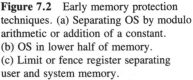

Figure 7.2 Early memory protection techniques. (a) Separating OS by modulo arithmetic or addition of a constant. (b) OS in lower half of memory. (c) Limit or fence register separating user and system memory.

overhead, since every user memory access now required a full comparison rather than one of the faster modifications discussed previously. Figure 7.2(c) shows this method, which was used on numerous machines, including the Hewlett-Packard 2116 family of minicomputers [Hewlett-Packard, 1969].

In closing this section we note that a user job could not be totally isolated from the OS. It would sometimes have to communicate with the OS (for example, for file access), and to accomplish this some form of system call operation had to be available. This communication mechanism could be an actual supervisor call op-code, or it could be a normal op-code used in a special way. As an example of the second case, the system could have a set of special locations in its protected area. To communicate with the OS, the user job would execute a subroutine call to one of those designated locations. This would cause a protection violation, which would in turn call the OS. On the basis of the interrupt, op-code, instruction address, and target address, the OS would service the user's request, if valid, or abort the program, if the request were not valid [Hewlett-Packard, 1969].

7.3 MULTIPLE USERS: FIRST VERSIONS OF MEMORY MANAGEMENT

Memory management took on a whole new dimension with the advent of multiuser systems. Decisions had to be made about how to divide up memory, how to allocate the resulting regions, and how to protect each user's processes (and the system) from other users' processes.

Before proceeding, we need to clarify some terminology. A number of authors refer to a section of memory as a partition. We prefer to call the section of memory a **region,** and the division between two such regions a **boundary.** The act of splitting up memory into regions will be called **partitioning.**

Another concept, which has uniform usage but which might be unfamiliar, is contiguity. If a process or data area is stored **contiguously,** then the entire entity is stored as one unit in successive memory locations. If something is stored noncontiguously, then one portion of it would be in one region and one or more other portions would be in separate, disjoint regions.

7.3.1 Managing Fixed Boundaries

If you were to transport yourself back in time, then your first idea for multiuser memory management might be to simply split up memory into pieces of arbitrary size when the system was initialized or "booted." Each user would then be allocated one of these pieces [Dennis, 1965; P. J. Denning, 1970].

Going back to our discussion of terminology, we might say more precisely that we would partition memory into regions of fixed size with fixed boundaries. Users would then be allocated separate regions. The notion of two boundaries determining the user's area also suggests a first idea for protection. When a given user was executing, the locations of his or her two boundaries would be placed into two limit registers. Normal memory accesses could then be confined by requiring them to lie between the limit register values, as shown in Figure 7.3(a). References beyond either

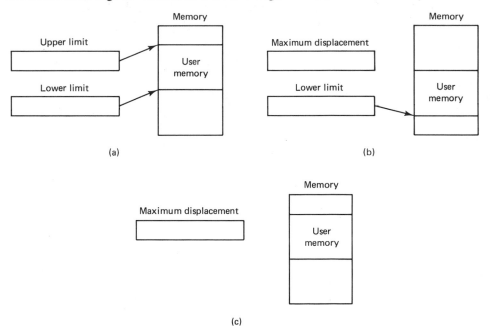

Figure 7.3 Memory protection techniques for multiuser systems (a) Upper and lower limit registers. (b) Lower limit and maximum displacement. (c) Maximum displacement register.

limit register would cause an interrupt called a **memory protection violation** [Saltzer and Schroeder, 1975].

This technique could be modified slightly if the hardware used a displacement form of addressing (that is, if addresses were offsets from some starting point). If negative displacements were allowed, then instead of two limit registers you would keep a lower limit register and a maximum displacement value. If only positive displacements were implemented, then you would need only the maximum displacement. These two modifications are shown in Figure 7.3(b) and (c).

So far in this discussion of fixed boundaries, we have ignored one very important point. How many regions should we have, and what sizes should they be?

It is tempting to respond by saying that we'll put off the decisions and establish boundaries and region sizes dynamically, depending on the process mix. Remember, however, that we are putting ourselves back in time. Given the state of technology at the time we are recalling, many designers believed that the overhead involved in such a dynamic scheme would be prohibitive. The memory manager would not be the only module involved, since any component of the OS dealing with individual processes would have to allow arbitrary numbers of such processes rather than a known maximum (the number of available regions). Furthermore, it would be necessary to develop a decision algorithm for dynamic partitioning that achieved demonstrably better results than simple predefinition.

For these reasons, most systems did not use dynamic partitioning. Some established the regions at system generation time [Madnick and Donovan, 1974; Watson, 1970]. [Others did it at boot time by having the operator specify the number and size of the regions [Madnick and Donovan, 1974].] An illustration of fixed partitioning is shown in Figure 7.4.

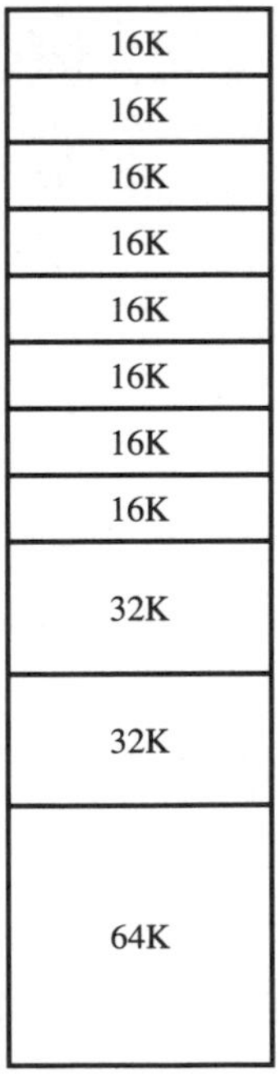

Figure 7.4 Example of fixed partitioning.

Of course, if the regions were established at boot time, then the OS could be rebooted and the parameters changed. This was often done for late shifts and weekends, when different process mixes were run. A well-known example of this technique was IBM's operating system called MFT [Madnick and Donovan, 1974; Tsichritzis and Bernstein, 1974].

We still haven't quite specified all of the decisions related to memory management. For these early multiuser systems, the size of the process was determined at the time the long-term scheduler analyzed the process creation request. What should happen when the only processes waiting had small memory requirements? It might be that such processes could run in a size x region but none were available. Should the memory manager select a size $y >> x$ region and waste the remainder of the size y region, or should it make the small processes wait? (The problem of wasted areas within regions of memory that were allocated to processes was called **internal fragmentation**: the memory was said to be fragmented into used and unused portions, and the unused fragments in this case were inside the allocated regions [Randell, 1969].)

7.3.2 Movable Boundaries and a Variable Number of Processes

It is probably apparent that the next logical step would be to allow movable boundaries [Coffman and Ryan, 1972]. With movable boundaries, should we fix the number of regions, or should we allow it to be variable? To examine this important difference, consider a system with a 256K-byte memory. In the first case, we might specify eight regions when we boot the system. Since the regions are variable in size, we have shown them in Figure 7.5(a) as question marks. Assume that at some later time, after the system has been running for a while, 192K is allocated to seven processes and 64K remains, as shown in Figure 7.5(b). Now two processes, P and Q, are ready to execute, and they each need 32K. We have enough memory, but we don't have enough regions. Only one process, say P, can be allowed to execute (Figure 7.5(c)).

With a variable number of regions, our corresponding diagrams are as shown in Figure 7.6. Initially, memory is one large question mark, since no regions have been established. Given the same later configuration as in Figure 7.5 (Figure 7.6(b)), we can create two regions out of the 64K so that both P and Q can run (Figure 7.6(c)).

Assuming that the system has movable boundaries, our memory allocation problem will be as follows. There are a sequence of memory blocks, some in use and some available. The memory manager has to place new processes into available blocks, and any leftover memory in a block becomes available for other processes.

In this situation there are three rather obvious methods which could be used to select a region for a process. The placement algorithms are (1) put the job in the block with the least leftover memory **(best fit)**; (2) use the largest remaining block **(worst fit)**; and (3) go sequentially through the blocks and take the first one large enough **(first fit)** [Shore, 1975; Bays, 1977]. These algorithms are illustrated in Fig-

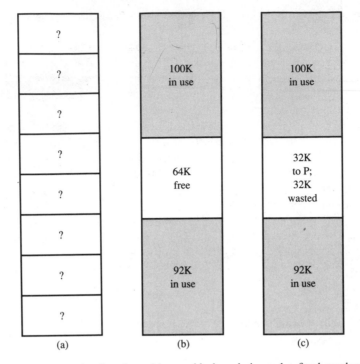

Figure 7.5 Sample allocation with movable boundaries and a fixed number of regions.

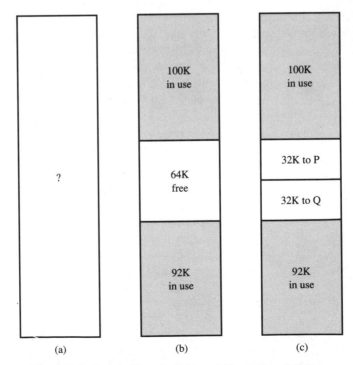

Figure 7.6 Sample allocation with variable number of regions.

ure 7.8, assuming the initial availability shown in Figure 7.7 and assuming that a process P needing 14K arrives, followed by a process Q needing 20K.

By definition, best fit gives the smallest unused region at each allocation. However, over the long run it might leave many "holes" that are too small to be useful. Worst fit leaves the largest space at each allocation, but tends to scatter the unused portions over noncontiguous areas of memory and thus might make it more difficult to fit in larger jobs. First fit tends to average out best and worst fits, with the added characteristic that empty spaces tend to migrate toward lower memory. Furthermore, with first fit the free areas can be kept in some arbitrary order based on the return strategy, rather than being sorted by size, as they typically would be with best and worst fits [Shore, 1975; Bays, 1977].

With all of these approaches, it is necessary to keep a list, called the **free list,** of the available blocks and their sizes. Rather than using extra separate memory, many systems used the free memory itself for the list. The first and last words in each block of free memory contained such things as the links and the size of the block.

In closing this section, we note two important facts. First, when a released block is returned to the free list, the memory manager should not just directly put the block into its proper place. Rather, it should check the blocks on either side to see whether the new free block can be combined with either or both of them, creating a larger free block. Second, you might wonder why there was worry about unusable holes in memory; couldn't processes just be moved around to eliminate such holes? For the period of time we are considering the answer was no; the hardware was such that once a process began executing in a certain set of memory locations, it had to remain in those locations.

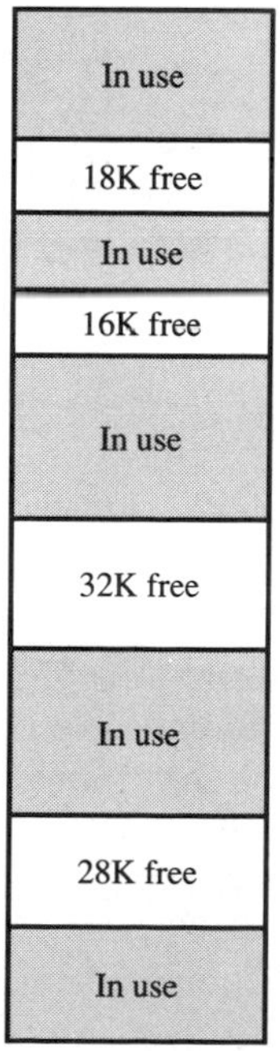

Figure 7.7   Initial free areas of memory.

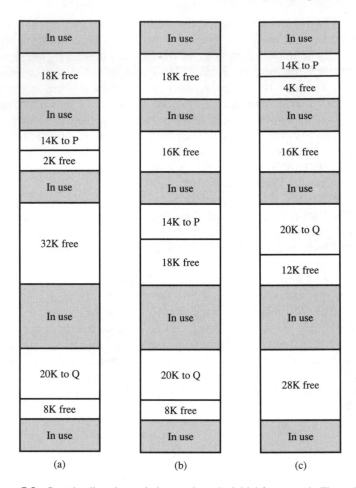

Figure 7.8 Sample allocation techniques, given the initial free areas in Figure 7.7 and the arrival of a 14K process P followed by a 20K process Q. (a) Best fit. (b) Worst fit. (c) First fit.

7.4 MULTIPLE USERS: A NEW IDEA FOR MEMORY MANAGEMENT

With steady increases in the number of users on a system and in the rate at which region contents had to be replaced, the restriction of "nonmovable processes" became a serious bottleneck. Regardless of the memory management algorithm, there was too much space wasted in unusable holes between used regions. (This problem is called **external fragmentation**: available memory was again fragmented into used and unused portions, and the unused fragments this time were *between* occupied regions; that is, they were external to these regions [Randell, 1969].) The net effect of this problem, of course, was that system efficiency suffered. There was often enough memory available to run additional processes, but that memory was fragmented and therefore not usable.

This caused system designers to look toward ways to allow processes to be moved to arbitrary regions in memory. In our view the most interesting and generally applicable technique was the relocation register [Dennis, 1965].

The problem in movable versus nonmovable processes was the ability of users to directly access specific main memory locations. For example, if a programmer used

```
LOADADDRESS 7,X {Place address of X into R7};
```

then at some point the system would replace X by an actual physical address which had been generated for it, and execution of this command would enter that address into register 7. Subsequent execution of

```
STORE 7,ADDRESS_OF_X {Store R7 into ADDRESS_OF_X};
```

would then store that address. If the process were moved to a different region at some later time, that address would no longer be valid. We wanted ADDRESS_OF_X to be some form of logical address, independent of process location. Instead it was an actual memory location, and was therefore completely dependent on process location.

Now suppose that when we compiled or assembled our program we did not replace X by an actual physical address. Instead, we left it as a displacement relative to the starting point of the program, and thus it remained a logical address. When the program was loaded, we recorded the point at which the loading began. When the program was executed, that starting point was entered into a special register called a "relocation register." Furthermore, instead of the standard address mapping

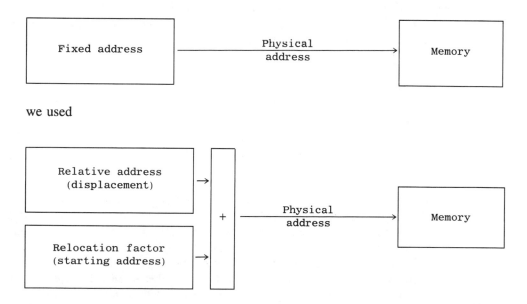

we used

This approach facilitated loading, since address fields could be left as displacements rather than changed to actual memory addresses. Furthermore, and of great importance to our current discussion, it allowed a process to be moved, since after the move the system could replace the relocation register with the new starting point. The contents of a variable like ADDRESS__OF__X were still valid, since its position relative to the start of the program remained the same; all that changed was the starting location.

Given the ability to move processes, which we call **dynamic relocation,** the system could often eliminate the loss of memory due to external fragmentation. One had to be careful, though, since moving a set of processes was a time-consuming task. Systems did not usually do the move every time a new job was loaded, but instead waited until some decision algorithm determined that the amount of memory wasted in holes had become too large. Then the system would move one or more processes to eliminate these holes, using an operation known by a variety of names, such as *garbage collection* or (our favorite) *burping* memory.

We close this section with the introduction of a term you will hear very often in memory management: **mapping.** We have just seen how a logical address can be converted to a physical address by using the contents of the relocation register. Recalling the idea of functions from mathematics, one can say that the logical address is mapped to the physical address. In the following sections we will use this term often, while considering different ways in which such a mapping could be accomplished.

7.5 DIFFERENT APPROACHES TO MEMORY PARTITIONING

Even with relocatable processes, there were an increasing number of problems with delays and overhead. One had to either put up with inefficient use of memory caused by holes (and hence the difficulty in finding appropriately sized regions), or one had to tolerate the time necessary to burp memory.

The crucial problem with all of the techniques we've discussed so far is the requirement that a program be loaded *contiguously*. That is, the entire program had to be loaded as one unit into one region of consecutive memory locations.

A new approach, then, would be to allow the process to be divided into pieces and allow these pieces to be loaded individually into different regions of main memory. The question is, "How?" Designers had to develop a technique whereby the language translators could generate valid addresses within each piece, even though the pieces would later go into disjoint regions of main memory. Furthermore, since main memory would now be a patchwork of pieces of processes, the technique had to include a way to protect the users and the system from other users.

Thinking back to the concept of a system with a relocation register, addresses are generated as offsets from the start of the program. Later, during execution, these offsets are applied to the main memory location of the process's starting point.

Suppose this technique were used on a finer scale. Addresses within each piece of a process would be generated as offsets from the start of the piece. As with the original version, a given piece could be loaded anywhere in main memory.

What about the protection? The idea of limit registers could be used, but that would involve a considerable number of extraneous operations. An address A is specified first of all by the piece it is in, say P. The system would then need a table giving the two limits for each piece, and it would load that register with the entries corresponding to P. Then it would combine the offset portion of address A and the starting point of P to give the final address, which would then be compared with the limit registers.

See the redundancy? It would seem more reasonable to combine some of the look-up and checking operations. We will now consider two possibilities for accomplishing this.

We could arbitrarily set the size of the pieces and have the compilers or assemblers divide up the user's program. We would then have a table for each user giving the starting point of each of his or her program pieces. We would not have to worry about limit registers, because intentionally or unintentionally attempting to go outside of a given piece P would simply result in a reference to an earlier or later piece, say Q. This would occur before the user's mapping table was referenced and hence would simply map to Q in the user's table, not to some other user's region in memory.

To illustrate this, suppose that Jim is running a process with two data areas, one in piece 3 and one in piece 4. Further, suppose part of memory is currently allocated as shown in Figure 7.9.

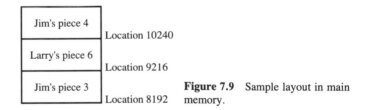

Figure 7.9   Sample layout in main memory.

Now Jim attempts to access the array in piece 3, but makes a mistake and generates a subscript pointing 1536 beyond the base address of piece 3, into the middle of the next piece and apparently into the middle of Larry's piece 6.

Remember, however, that user addresses are *logical*, and remain so until the mapping by the OS just prior to memory reference. The system would *not* generate

$$8192 + 1536 = 9728 = \text{Larry's area}$$

Instead, it would generate

	Piece Number	Displacement
Base address	000011	0000000000
Subscript offset	000001	1000000000
Resulting reference = base + offset	000100	1000000000

Then it would go through Jim's mapping function, find that his piece 4 started at 10240, and access physical address

$$10240 + 512 = 10752 = \text{Jim's area}$$

Although this is not what Jim intended, his mistake is confined to his process and does not affect Larry's or anyone else's.

Another approach to combine look-up and checking would be to allow the user to define the numbers and sizes of the pieces, then incorporate this information into the mapping table. Let's take our previous example of address A consisting of offset D within piece P. When this address was referenced during execution, the system would look up P in the user's mapping table. One field in the table entry for P would be a maximum allowable offset, say M, and the system could check that $O \le D \le M$. If D were valid, then the system would take the starting point of P, add in D, and have the memory location.

We have judiciously used the generic term "piece" because we wanted to explain ideas before going to well-known and sometimes misunderstood terms. However, you might already have anticipated us. The first idea we discussed is *paging,* and the second is *segmentation* [Dennis, 1965; Randell and Kuehner, 1968; Wilkes, 1973; Saltzer and Schroeder, 1975].

7.6 PAGING

Having introduced the general idea of paging in the previous section, we now turn to the details. With paging, the system divides the user's process into pieces of arbitrary size called pages. On most systems that "arbitrary size" is a permanently fixed quantity in the OS. The size of a page could be variable, but that would bring us back to many of the same memory management problems we discussed earlier in this chapter. Furthermore, even systems with variable page sizes [Randell, 1969] usually restricted the selection to a small number of sizes, typically powers of 2. (For example, 256, 512, or 1024 was a common set.) In this text we will discuss only pages of fixed size.

Assuming that the page size is fixed, what size should the page be? One initial factor in such a decision should be the hardware radix of addressing. To see why, suppose we have a binary machine and decide to use a page size of 600. First off, the compiler or assembler will have to do extra decision logic to recognize when it has advanced to the next page. Second, the displacement field will have to be 10 bits, but only about half the possible values will ever be used. Now suppose we used a page size of 1024 instead. No special logic is necessary to increment the page counter, and all displacements in the 10-bit field are possible. The following illustration shows how the instruction counter automatically increments from page 12, displacement 1022, to page 13, displacement 2, just by using a normal binary counter as shown by the following table.

16-Bit Address		Instruction
001100	1111111110	LDA 7,W
001100	1111111111	ADDA 7,X
001101	0000000000	ADDA 7,Y
001101	0000000001	SUBA 7,Z
001101	0000000010	STA 7,W
6-bit	10-bit	
page	displacement	
number		

There are other factors important in determining a good page size. For example, it is often coordinated with the physical record size on the system disk or drum. Otherwise, storage space and transfer time will be wasted because of the unused "fractional pages." Larger pages tend to waste some space because programs do not usually fit precisely into a certain number of pages. (This is another example of internal fragmentation.) However, smaller pages tend to require more bookkeeping, since on the average there will be more pages per process. We cannot detail all of the other considerations, but to give you a guideline, many systems use page sizes of 256 through 2048.

Assuming that we have established our page size, we must now decide how to map our user's logical address to an actual physical memory location. As mentioned earlier, this is usually done via a table, appropriately called a **page map table,** or PMT. Let's illustrate a PMT with the simplest (and also probably most impractical) version of paging. We assume that all of a process's pages must be loaded into memory prior to execution. Furthermore, at completion, all of these pages are written back out to secondary storage (since their contents might have changed). If our sample process had five pages, then its PMT might be:

Page Number	Physical Location
0	10240
1	51200
2	61440
3	20480
4	30720
	PMT

Suppose that the assembler had placed variable X in page 3 at displacement 150. Then, during execution, a reference to X would be mapped to

$$\begin{array}{lr} \text{Start of page 3} & 20480 \\ \text{Displacement of } X & +\underline{150} \\ & 20630 \end{array}$$

(This example uses normal addition, for simplicity. For speed, the actual operation would probably be an OR or a CONCATENATION.)

Even this simple case should raise an immediate question. Where do we keep this PMT? If it's all in main memory, then every user memory reference is effectively two references; one would be required to get the page location, and one to do the actual user reference. If we provide enough registers to hold any PMT, the CPU is more expensive to build and more overhead time is required to change environments during process swapping. We can compromise by keeping part of the PMT in registers and part in main memory, or even introduce high-speed cache memory as an intermediary between registers and main memory. Finally, a good idea would be to use associative or content-addressable memory [Mano, 1982]; we would find the starting address of a page by accessing associative memory with the page number. An extensive analysis of these and other possibilities is beyond the scope of this text.

Another question about our first version might be, "Why rewrite all the pages when the process terminates?" Good question! We should add a bit to each PMT entry to indicate whether the page has been modified or not. Only the modified pages need to be written to disk. (Such a bit is often called a "dirty bit.")

A third question, which seems simple but opens up a whole new world, is "Why require all the pages to be loaded prior to execution?" Any instruction or data address can map through only one page per cycle. In the extreme case, then, you would actually need only that one page in memory, with the remainder on secondary storage.

Normally, keeping just one page per process is unreasonable, because it would cause heavy traffic between the system disk and main memory. However, it is certainly reasonable to keep only a subset of the process's pages in memory. This approach, usually called **demand paging,** forms the basis of modern multiuser systems [Brinch Hansen, 1973].

Demand paging also graphically illustrates the idea of "virtual memory" which we introduced briefly in Chapter 3. The user sees his or her process as one contiguous unit always in memory. In reality, it is probably many noncontiguous pages, only a fraction of which are in main memory at any given time.

An initial consideration with demand paging is how many pages to keep in memory for each process. Should this number be fixed or variable, and if variable, what factors should be used in determining the allocation of pages to a process? Does more memory always improve system performance? [Belady et al., 1969]? We cannot pursue all such considerations further in this text, but in general (1) the number is variable, and (2) a crucial factor in determining the allocation to a given process is that process's pattern of memory references. These ideas are frequently embodied in a term known as the **working set** [P. J. Denning, 1968; 1980].

Look back at some of the large programming assignments you've written (or consider the array summation programs given in the Introduction), and imagine them divided up into pages. If you were to emulate a computer and start executing these programs, you would observe that for a given period of time from T to $T + t$ there are only a certain set of pages that are accessed. For example, one part of one of your programs might be a loop which takes data from two arrays, does some computations with that data, and uses the results to update a third array. Let us say that the code for these operations is contained in two pages, and each of the arrays is in another separate page. During that phase of execution, then, you are concentrating on those find pages.

Now consider what would happen if the example described above were actually executing on a multiuser system with paging. If the system allowed your process to have five pages in main memory, you would be happy. If it allocated seven pages to your process, there would be little if any improvement. On the other hand, if it gave your process only four then there could be a drastic degradation in performance. You might find 20 percent of your references going to a page not in main memory.

The group of five pages we've been discussing is called the working set of your process at that specific period of time in its overall execution. We reiterate immediately: The working set varies not only with the process being executed, but also with time for a given process, perhaps with the particular data set being used, and perhaps with many other factors. The working set is very important, because giving a process more pages than its working set size, say S, is usually unproductive, and giving it fewer than S usually degrades performance.

As a simple example of demand paging using working sets, suppose that we have a system which determines working sets on the basis of intervals of 12,000 memory references. That is, we define the current working set as those pages accessed during the last 12,000 memory references. Consider a process which requires 10 pages, numbered 0 through 9, and which accesses these pages as shown in the first two columns of Figure 7.10. In the example, the first 10,000 memory references are to pages 1, 2, and 3. The next 4000 are to pages 1, 4, and 5, and so on.

The third column of Figure 7.10 shows the sequence of working sets for the access pattern specified in columns 1 and 2. For example, pages 1, 2, and 3 make up the working set for the first 10,000 references; pages 1 through 5 for the next 4000 references; and so on. It is vitally important to stress that in this figure we are assuming sufficient available memory to simply bring in additional pages as we need them; modifications when this is not the case will be discussed later.

The next column shows the points at which the working sets are changed. Thus, the example begins with references to pages 1, 2, and 3, and so these constitute the initial working set. After 10,000 references, pages 4 and 5 are accessed, and so they are added to the working set at this point. During references 14,001 through 22,000 the process accesses pages 4, 5, and 6, but during references 10,001 through 22,000 it does not access page 2 or page 3. These events cause us to add page 6 to the working set after reference 14,000, and (since our "window" is 12,000 references) to remove pages 2 and 3 after reference 22,000.

The last column in Figure 7.10, column 5, shows the pages we mark as "no longer in the current working set," that is, "unused." As explained in the previous paragraph, pages 2 and 3 are removed from the working set after reference 22,000, and so at that point they are shown in column 5. Pages in this column may or may not be left in memory, depending on the number of pages needed by the example process and other processes in the system. For our illustration, we simply ignore them and assume that they are removed.

You can see that our example process is relatively well behaved. The working

Memory references (in 1000s)	Pages referenced	Working set	Points at which working set changes	Pages marked as unused
00			←	
	123	123		
	123	123		
	123	123		
	123	123		
10	123	123	←	
	145	12345		
14	145	12345	←	
	456	123456		
	456	123456		
	456	123456		
22	456	123456	←	
24	1	1456	←	23
26	174	14567		
	176	14567		
	176	14567		
32	176	14567	←	
	18	145678	←	
	18	14678		5
38	18	14678	←	
	178	1678		4
	178	1678		
	178	1678	←	
46	178	178	←	6
48	90	17890		

Figure 7.10   Working sets as a function of memory references.

set varies in size only from three through six pages, and the actual pages in the set change slowly. Of course, not all processes will be this nice. Sometimes, working sets will grow rapidly, memory will become overcommitted, and not all pages required by current processes can be accommodated. The system might temporarily suspend one or more processes and use their space. More likely, it will replace some existing pages, and this is the subject we now consider.

The philosophy of the working set seems intuitively appealing, but you might wonder whether a system can efficiently maintain the necessary reference information. One straightforward technique for doing this employs a set of special hardware counters.

When a page is added to the working set, it is associated with one of these counters. The counter is initialized to the desired window size, such as the 12,000 references in our example. Every time that the page is subsequently referenced, its associated counter is reset to that same initial value.

At the end of each instruction cycle, all of the counters currently associated with a page in the working set are decremented by 1. If any of the counters go negative, then an OS interrupt is generated. The appropriate page or pages are removed from the working set.

A demand paging system might use the idea of working sets, or it might use some other algorithm to decide how many pages to allocate to each process (for example, a fixed number, or a fraction of those available). In any case, we could encounter the situation in which a process needs a new page and the system cannot just allocate additional memory. Which page do we replace? This question has been, and continues to be, a major research topic. Obviously, a crucial factor in system performance will be how well the page replacement algorithm infers user reference patterns, and hence how much or how little time is spent on the overhead of page swapping. Some of you have probably at one time or another been on a system which was bogged down in excessive page replacement, a situation called **thrashing** [Alderson et al., 1972; P. J. Denning, 1970]

Some of our initial ideas for page replacement algorithms encounter immediate problems. We might suggest replacing the oldest page (this would be a FIFO algorithm). The problem here is that this page might *be* the oldest because it contains an important routine which has been controlling the rest of the process. Replacing the newest page (a LIFO method) does not seem like a very good idea. If we've just referenced the page for the first time, we will probably be referencing it again very soon.

Just to check your understanding at this point, let's suppose that processes are allocated three pages in main memory, and that our process references pages as follows:

0011122222333344333555533336663333444333555533336677788888

The sequences of pages in main memory for LIFO and FIFO are shown in Figure 7.11. That figure also shows what the sequence resulting from the optimum replacement would be, if we had a crystal ball. It also shows that FIFO causes fewer page replacements than LIFO, but you must remember that this is based on one short page reference string.

FIFO	LIFO	OPTIMUM
0	0	0
01	01	01
012	012	012
312	013	312
342	014	342
345	013	345
645	015	346
635	013	356
634	016	376
534	013	378
564	014	
567	013	
867	015	
	013	
	016	
	017	
	018	

Figure 7.11 Pages in memory as a result of using different replacement selection algorithms.

After deciding against LIFO and FIFO, we might say, "Isn't it logical to replace the page that has been referenced the least number of times since the last replacement?" A method that does so is called LFU, or **least frequently used.** That is a good idea, but it raises the problem of keeping a counter for each page, updating the appropriate counter at each reference, and sorting or searching to find the page to replace.

That last observation also rules out what is probably your next idea, replacing the page that was referenced the longest time ago (an LRU method, or **least recently used**). We won't yet give up on this idea, though. It is possible to come up with a good compromise that approximates LRU.

Suppose we are allocated n pages, PMT entries PMT[0] through PMT[$n - 1$]. We associate with each of these pages a "use bit," U[i], for the page corresponding to PMT [i]. When we first load our process's pages we initialize each of the use bits to 0 and initialize a counter K to 0. Every time a page is referenced we set the corresponding use bit to 1. (Note, of course, that an oft-used page might have its bit set over and over again—but that's all right.) When a new page needs to be brought into memory, we execute the following algorithm:

```
looking := true;
while looking do
    begin
    if U[K] = 0 then
        begin;
            looking := false;
            U[K] := 1;
            replace page referenced by PMT[K];
        end;
        else U[K] := 0;
    K := (K+1) mod n;
    end;
```

Starting with the current counter K (whatever it might be), we scan the table looking for a use bit of 0. Each use bit with a 1 which we pass over is changed to 0. When we find the first use bit of 0, we replace that page, set the use bit to 1, and advance the counter (so that we don't bother this page for one cycle).

Note a few things about the algorithm. It replaces a page which has not been referenced since the last time we scanned its PMT entry. This selection might be called a first-order approximation of LRU, but not precisely LRU, since (1) the frame of reference is the last few replacements, not the entire life of the process, and (2) even within this frame we might not be using strict LRU: the first U[K] = 0 is selected, and a later U[L] = 0 might have been last referenced longer ago.

However, the algorithm is still appealing from both an intuitive and an implementation standpoint. In most cases the page replaced has not been referenced as recently as others in the group and seems to be a good selection. The only thing that must be done when a page is referenced is to set a bit, and finding the first U[K] = 0 is faster and simpler than keeping the PMT sorted or having to search it entirely before every replacement. (For those of you with a hardware background, it is interesting to observe that one could reasonably consider adding a circuit which selected the appropriate $U[K] = 0$ and did the other operations directly, rather than having the OS scan the table via a software instruction loop.) For the above reasons this algorithm and its variations are popular. It is known as a **modified least recently used** or, more concisely, an MLRU.

An interesting replacement algorithm called the **second-chance** algorithm combines FIFO with a flavor of MLRU. The pages are kept in FIFO order, but each page also has a reference bit. All reference bits are cleared to 0 when the process is initially loaded and whenever a page is replaced; each time a page is referenced the corresponding bit is set to 1. The page selected for replacement is the oldest page whose reference bit is currently 0. The notion of second chance comes from the fact that the oldest page is not replaced if it has been referenced since the last replacement. Of course, we need to have some technique (such as random selection) if all reference bits have been set to 1.

So far we have assumed that page replacement algorithms are applied to each individual process when that process needs another page and none are available. Such is not always the case. For example, in some systems using working sets, whenever *any* process needs another page and none are available, the page replacement algorithm is applied to the process with the lowest priority. Hence all processes keep taking pages from the lowest-priority process until that lowest-priority process loses its last page and is suspended. (Of course, when this happens, some other process then becomes the lowest-priority process.)

We have considered the basic mechanical techniques in paging. Let's look now at two other aspects: virtual versus physical address space and code sharing.

We have repeatedly differentiated the address of a variable X as the user sees it from the actual location of X in main memory at some point in time. We also said that with demand paging the logical address of X can be considered the virtual address of X. How could the number of pages which can be referenced in a virtual address, V, compare with the number which are actually in main memory, P?

V could equal P, in which case a user address space is the same as the main memory size. This was how most early mainframe computers and first-generation minicomputers were designed. Of course, this does not mean that all of the user's pages will always be in memory. It simply means that the field length for a virtual and a physical address are the same.

V could also be much larger than P, a common situation on machines with a large word size. This is how many current CPUs are designed. It allows the user to address much (maybe much, much) more main memory than the machine could actually store even if the user were the only one on the system. It is handy, for example, to treat a large data area as one array, or to write a tremendously large program without having to worry about executing it in separate sections. Virtual memory is often praised with this relationship of V and P implicitly in mind.

Finally, V could be smaller than P. For example, a minicomputer or microcomputer might have a 16-bit virtual address space, but actually have 1 megabyte of main memory. The mapping we've described allows a process to access any 64K-byte block within the 1M-byte main memory.

The relationship $V < P$ is sometimes used as a convenient metric for no-swapping multiuser systems. Given our 16-bit address and 1 megabyte of main memory, we could simply declare that our system will support 16 processes, with each process limited to 64K. Also, on microcomputer systems with $V < P$, additional physical memory is often used to create high-speed-printer buffers and "RAM disks." (With a RAM disk, files that are frequently referenced are loaded into RAM, where they can subsequently be accessed at memory speeds rather than disk speeds.)

Our second topic has to do with sharing on a paged system. Observe how easy it would be for Larry and Jim to share a system routine such as the editor. Both of their PMTs have pointers to the same physical area of memory, the location of the editor. Each of their PMTs also has a pointer to a separate, individual data area. When Larry is executing, he uses the one copy of the editor, and it references his data area through his PMT. When Jim is executing, he uses the same copy of the editor, but now memory references go through his PMT and hence access his data area. (For this to work, the editor must be **reentrant,** that is, it must not contain any self-modifying code.)

Unfortunately, sharing arbitrary code or data sections is not always easy in a paged system [Dennis, 1965]. For example, suppose both Larry and Jim declare 10,240-byte arrays called BOOK in their programs. They plan to run these programs concurrently and to share data by having their separately declared arrays map to the same physical locations. This seems easy, since we could have two user PMT entries point to the same physical page.

The problem is that logical page addresses are determined by relative location in the program. Hence Larry's declaration of his array might put that array in his page 5, offset 200, through his page 15, offset 199. Jim's declaration might put the array in his page 11, offset 0, through page 20, offset 1023. This illustrates the difficulty of getting Larry's reference to a given array element mapped to the same memory locations as Jim's reference to that element.

This closes our discussion of paging. We hope that we have conveyed an understanding of the basic ideas, and we regret having to slight some more advanced topics. Perhaps introducing those topics will pique your interest, however, and you will study them more thoroughly at some later time.

7.7 SEGMENTATION

Paging is interesting and important, but we can perceive some weaknesses. In general, they can be traced back to the arbitrary physical division of a process by the system, rather than a logical division by the designer. We will consider two implications of such physical division which could cause problems.

First, there is the enforcement of access restrictions. Suppose we have designed a system for other departments in our company and we want some data areas to have unlimited access while others are to be read only. This might not be an easy task with paging. We have to split up the data areas and make sure that they are physically arranged to go on pages with the proper access restrictions.

Second, we are not fully utilizing what could be an important factor in system efficiency: the user's knowledge about his or her own program's structure and performance patterns. In paging we normally have only our replacement algorithm's attempts at inferring such factors.

This brings us to the other technique we introduced in Section 7.5: segmentation. The main difference between it and paging is that the user separates and identifies logical components of programs rather than having the system divide out arbitrary physical components. For example, a user might specify that there are three code segments, INPUT, SORT, and ANALYZE, and two data segments, PREVIOUS and TRANSACTIONS.

With segmentation, symbolic addresses consist of a segment name and of a statement label or variable name within the designated segment. These are normally translated to a segment number and a displacement within the segment. We might have an instruction such as

MOVE 7, PERMANENT/GROSS_PAY;

That is, we might want to move the variable named GROSS_PAY within the segment named PERMANENT into register 7. The address portion of this instruction might be translated as follows:

0010110   01001010100011

segment	displacement
number	within segment

Of course, there are conventions to make life easier on the user. If no segment is specified, then the current code and data segments are implied. (It would be very boring to have to attach a segment name to every variable in your program!)

We can think again of a table to implement the mappings. Instead of a PMT with the starting points of pages, we can use a **segment map table,** or SMT. Each entry in the SMT could consist of fields such as those shown in Figure 7.12.

```
segment name
maximum displacement within segment
access rights of this user to this segment
is the segment currently in main memory
if it is in main memory, what is the starting address
```

Figure 7.12   Typical fields in a segment map table entry.

A maximum displacement field is kept in the SMT because, unlike pages, our segments can have different lengths. Note the ease with which one of our paging problems is solved: the third field shown in Figure 7.12 specifies the access rights of the user, such as read-only or execute-only. The fourth field in that figure is included because, as with paging, we will assume **demand segmenting** and not go into a detailed consideration of "static segmenting" (in which all segments would have to be loaded prior to execution).

In the previous section we discussed how paging facilitates the use of shared code with individual data areas. Segmentation has that same desirable characteristic. For example, consider a compiler. Two (or more) users would have an entry in their SMT for that compiler, both (or all) pointing to the same physical region of memory. Each user would have his or her own compiler data areas containing source code and object code; for illustration, we will call them simply SOURCE and OB-JECT. When Larry is using the compiler, his SMT is active. Any time the compiler references SOURCE or OBJECT it will be referencing his individual copies of those areas, since the mapping goes through his SMT. When Larry's time quantum is finished and Jim begins executing, he will be using the same copy of the compiler code. However, it will now be referencing *his* data areas through *his* SMT.

As a matter of fact, segmenting might do even more to facilitate sharing on a finer level. In Section 7.6, Paging, Larry and Jim wanted to share a data array called BOOK, and there was a problem with addressing. With segmenting, they each have the segment name BOOK placed into their SMT, with both entries pointing to the same memory location. By declaring BOOK as a separate logical entity (segment), they avoid the problem of making sure that page boundaries line up the same. Fur-thermore, it is easy for the system to keep a master SMT, with information about all currently active segments, who is using them, and which are or are not in main memory.

We will not repeat the discussion of mapping or the considerations of how to store and use the SMT. Both should follow directly from our previous presentations with paging and the PMT.

We do want to stress the difference between segmentation and paging in terms of placing the unit (page or segment) into memory. With this version of segmenta-tion we are again dealing with variable-size regions, because of the variable-size of segments. Hence we *might* get ready to look back at the early sections of this chapter to review such algorithms as first fit and best fit. We say *might* because there is an immediate modification that should be obvious.

7.8 SEGMENTATION WITH PAGING

Segments are separate logical entities. This allows the modification we implied at the end of the previous section, which is, as you have probably guessed, to use pag-ing on each of the segments [Daley and Dennis, 1968; Randell, 1969; P. J. Denning, 1970; Bensoussan et al., 1972].

Before you throw your arms up in dismay, let's go through an example. It is really not difficult if you follow the mapping step by step. Suppose we have the in-struction

MOVE 0, BOOK/AUTHORS;

This references a location AUTHORS in a segment BOOK. It would be translated to a segment number and a displacement within the segment:

010010	001010011101010011
segment number	displacement within segment

However, let's not just use that displacement as is; let's consider it a page number and a displacement within the page. With a page size of 1024, we would have

010010   00101001   1101010011

segment	page	displacement
number	number	within page

When this address is referenced, the system goes to the SMT. After checking access rights, it next goes to the field we called "location" in our previous version of segmentation. However, in this version the location is not the start of the *segment* in main memory, but rather a reference to the *PMT* for that segment. Once the system has this PMT, it applies the mapping techniques of paging, as we described them in Section 7.6.

We thus have the advantages of segmentation while avoiding the hassles of memory management with variable-size regions. One might object that there is a great deal of overhead involved in the mapping process. True. Therefore, systems that use this full segment and page approach usually have much of the mapping done directly by hardware [Daley and Dennis, 1968].

This concludes our descriptions of many, varied approaches to memory management. Let us turn now to an implementation of one of these approaches.

7.9 A SAMPLE MEMORY MANAGER

In this section we will look at the pseudocode for a very simple memory management procedure. You might already have seen this approach, or something similar to it, in your data structures class. However, our goal is to include a complete procedure, suitable for use with the long-term scheduler in Chapter 5. We have purposely chosen a simple memory manager because we do not want to risk obscuring the overall picture by implementing a more complex scheme.

We will assume that a process must be allocated all required memory prior to entering the system, that a process cannot be moved once it has been loaded, that the allocated memory must be in one contiguous block, and that lower and upper limit registers provide memory protection. A first-fit allocation technique will be used, with available blocks kept in order of increasing memory address.

Each memory block will contain six information fields. The structure for an available block is shown in Figure 7.13(a), for an allocated block in Figure 7.13(b).

```
FREE                                      ALLOCATED
Size of block                             Size of block
Pointer to next available block           Pointer to end of this block
Pointer to previous available block       Unused

┌                                         ┌
│ rest of block                           │ rest of block
└                                         └

Pointer to start of this block            Pointer to start of this block
FREE                                      ALLOCATED
        (a)                                        (b)
```

Figure 7.13   Structure of blocks in memory. (a) Structure of an available block of memory. (b) Structure of an allocated block of memory.

The information fields in the blocks facilitate memory allocation and deallocation. The next pointers and the previous pointers in the available block are used to
form the chain of available memory. The FREE and ALLOCATED indicators are
used to simplify deallocation. They make it possible to quickly check the blocks immediately before and after the block that is being deallocated. This permits adjacent
available blocks to be collapsed into larger contiguous available areas. These indicators are also used, together with the start and end pointers in allocated blocks, to locate the proper place in the available memory chain for a deallocated block if it cannot be collapsed with adjacent blocks.

A process is actually allocated an entire block, including the information
fields. However, the limit registers for the process would be set so as to exclude
those information fields, and hence to protect them from modification by the process. In terms of Figure 7.13(b), the limit registers would be set to the beginning
and end of the area labeled "rest of block."

When a block is deallocated and adjacent blocks are not available, the memory
management procedure must essentially search a structure from the middle out to
find the proper place to insert this block. Such an operation can be complicated considerably by checks for the beginning and ending of user memory. To avoid such

```
FREE
0
Pointer to first available block
nil
Pointer to start of this block
FREE


ALLOCATED
0
Pointer to end of this block
nil
Pointer to start of this block
ALLOCATED



 ⌈
 |
 |   rest of user memory
 |
 ⌊



ALLOCATED
0
Pointer to end of this block
nil
Pointer to start of this block
ALLOCATED


FREE
0
nil
Pointer to last available block
Pointer to start of this block
FREE
```

Figure 7.14 Four dummy blocks used
to simplify deallocation.

```
procedure MEMORY_MGR(command,size,start_address,status);

{ This is the procedure responsible for allocating and deallocating
  blocks of memory.  It is called from the long term scheduler's
  WAITING_LIST monitor during process creation and termination.

  The first fit method is used for allocation.  If the selected
  block is large enough, a new free block is created; otherwise the
  entire block is given to the requestor.  During deallocation,
  adjacent free blocks are collapsed; this makes the largest possible
  contiguous free areas available.                                        }

{ Called by            : LONG_TERM_SCHEDULER
  Procedures called    : none
  Parameters passed    : command, either allocate or deallocate
                         size, the size of the block requested
                         start_address, the start of block
  Parameters returned: start_address, the start of block
                         status, whether or not a block was found
  Entry conditions     : none
  Exit conditions      : memory allocated or deallocated               }

declaration
    block                   : record
                                status_beg   : allocated, free;
                                size         : integer;
                                end_next_ptr : address pointer;
                                previous_ptr : address pointer;
                                mem_block    : array [1..size-6] of memory;
                                start_ptr    : address pointer;
                                status_end   : allocated, free;
                              end; {memory block}

global variables
    first_available_block   : integer; {address of first free block}
    minimum_block_size      : integer;

local variables
    selected_block          : block;
    next_block              : block;
    search_block            : block;
    previous_block          : block;
    following_block         : block;
    previous_available_block : block;
    following_available_block: block;

begin
  case command of
    allocate    :  ALLOCATE_CODE;
    deallocate  :  DEALLOCATE_CODE;
    otherwise   :  status := invalid_request;
  end;
end; {MEMORY_MGR}
```

Figure 7.15 A simple memory manager.

checks, we will assume four dummy blocks, two at the start of user memory and
two at the end. These blocks are shown in Figure 7.14.

Given the structures as described, the pseudocode for the memory management procedure is concise and straightforward. It is shown in Figures 7.15 through
7.17.

The sample memory manager is a procedure, and it modifies a system data
structure. One must therefore be very careful to guard against problems of concur-

```
procedure ALLOCATE_CODE;

{ This section tries to allocate memory to a process.  It first
  checks to see whether there is a block large enough to satisfy the
  request.                                                              }

    begin
      search list of available blocks;
      if search_block >= size then select_block := search_block
      else if no block >= size then
        begin
          status := failure;
          return;
        end; {no block big enough}


{ Remove the selected block and see whether the "leftovers" are large
  enough to form a new block.  If not, just allocate the entire
  (oversized) block.                                                    }

      delete select_block from list of available blocks;
      if select_block.size - size > minimum_block_size  then
        begin
          new_block.size := selected_block.size - size;
          insert new_block into list of available blocks;
        end; {make new block}


{ Change the block from "available" to "allocated" and return
  it to the calling process.                                           }

      new_block.status := allocated;
      starting_address := address of selected_block;
      status := success;

    end; {allocate block}
```

Figure 7.16 Allocation procedure for memory manager.

```
procedure DEALLOCATE_CODE;

{ Deallocation portion.  First see whether there is a free block on
  either side of the returned block.  If so, collapse the
  adjacent free blocks into one larger block.                          }

  begin
    find following_block;
    if following_block.status = available then
      combine returned_block and following_block;
    find previous_block;
    if previous_block.status = available then
      combine returned_block and previous_block;

{ If there is no available block on either side of the returned
  block, then we must find the proper place to put it.                 }

    if neither adjacent block was available then
      begin
        find previous_available_block;
        link returned_block into previous_available_block;
        find following_available_block;
        link returned_block into following_available_block;
        returned_block.status := available;
      end; {returned block linked to list}

  end; {deallocate}
```

Figure 7.17 Deallocation procedure for memory manager.

rent access. The long-term scheduler in Chapter 5 enforces mutual exclusion by calling the memory manager only from within the long-term scheduler's monitor.

7.10 SUMMARY

Memory management is an interesting and important topic. This chapter has been long, and even at that we have only touched on some topics and have described genral approaches without detailing the many possible variations. Furthermore, some questions have not been completely answered; that is because OS designers don't have all the answers yet. Memory management is a good example of a case in which Implementations are often still art rather than science, and one in which there are still innumerable opportunities for further research.

The Atlas computer has been a focus of study for 25 years. One aspect of special interest is its virtual memory system, described in the classic paper Kilburn et al. [1962].

A general article on virtual memory is Doran [1976]. This article includes descriptions of some implementations of VM systems.

We mentioned the use of the cache in memory management systems. Two articles describing the cache and its implementation in a high-speed computer are Padegs [1968] and Conti et al. [1968].

There have been many mathematical analyses and experimental studies of memory management systems. Aho et al. [1971] is a mathematical look at paging, especially the least recently used and working set approaches. Batson et al. [1970] is an empirical study of segment size in typical systems.

First fit and best fit are only two of several possible allocation techniques. "Release match" and "age match" techniques are discussed in Beck [1982].

QUESTIONS AND EXERCISES

1. In Section 7.2 we discussed using MOD and ADD to implement automatic address modification. However, using the actual arithmetic operations would be time-consuming. Discuss better ways of achieving the desired results.

2. A "tagged architecture" attaches to each memory location and registers a bit pattern identifying the type of information currently being stored. For example, a simple scheme would be "tag = 0" for data and "tag = 1" for instructions. How could such an architecture be used to facilitate moving regions of main memory?

3. Illustrate how portions of available memory blocks could be used to store the pointers, counters, and so on, necessary to implement first-fit, best-fit, and worst-fit memory management algorithms.

4. Show how first-fit allocations tends to move available blocks toward one end of memory.

5. Why would one want to have variable-size pages?

6. What happens in MLRU if every page currently in a user's memory space has been accessed since the last replacement (that is, if all of the use bits are set)?

7. Illustrate how the page replaced by MLRU might not actually be the one which was referenced least recently.

8. Why wasn't it possible to dynamically change relative sizes in the automatic address modification technique?

9. What factors would be used to determine the sizes of regions in a fixed boundary system?

10. We discussed advantages of movable boundaries over fixed. What are some disadvantages?

11. We said that burping memory could be a long operation. Estimate the time on a system for which you can obtain cycle speeds.

12. Can you think of a better algorithm for burping than just arbitrarily moving everything to one end of memory?

13. In the Introduction, we discussed associative memory. Illustrate its use in paging and segmenting systems.

14. We described a situation in which we had multiple pages in a segment. What about the other way—multiple segments in a page?

15. Construct a sequence of page references which shows that allocating more pages to a process does not guarantee fewer page faults.

16. A modification to first fit, called next fit, has been proposed. The difference is that the search starts at the entry in the free list immediately following the one last allocated, rather than always restarting at the beginning of the free list. How do you think it would perform compared with first fit?

17. Why would it be advisable not to immediately swap out pages no longer included in a working set?

18. How could you accomplish the sharing of Larry and Jim's array discussed in Section 7.6?

PROGRAMMING ASSIGNMENT

This assignment is a simulation to compare various memory management techniques. We will be interested in both user satisfaction (in terms of wait time) and system utilization.

Input to this program will be job descriptors produced by a random generator. Each such descriptor has a job identifier and a set of job parameters, in the following format:

```
ID   ARRIV   MEM_TIME_REQ   MEM_REQD
```

where

ARRIV	arrival time, relative to the arrival of the last job
MEM_TIME_REQ	time that the job is in memory
MEM_REQD	amount of memory required, in KBytes

You are to simulate the performance of various memory managers operating with this job stream. These memory managers have a variable number of variable size, non-movable regions; they use a highest-response-ratio-next service algorithm. The only variation among the managers is their placement algorithm—best fit, worst fit, first fit, next fit, and a comparison standard. The comparison standard shows what would happen if regions were movable and memory could be instantaneously burped at the termination of each job.

One output for each placement algorithm will be a partial trace to show us that your system is working properly. At an arbitrarily selected point in your simulation, trace 10 jobs as they are taken from the wait queue and loaded into memory. Show the wait queue just prior to each selection, and the memory map before and after the selected job is loaded.

The other output for each algorithm will be a set of statistics gathered with the simulation in a steady state. The required statistics are minimum, maximum, and average queue length and memory utilized, and average wait time as a function of memory required.

Run all simulations with the same set of data. This means that you use a random generator which can be restarted with the same seed value, or generate the job stream once and store it on a file.

Memory size should be a parameter which can be specified at the beginning of your simulation. All job parameters should be normally distributed about the centers of their respective ranges (as described in the programming assignment for Chapter 5):

ARRIV   4 to 96 time units
MEM_TIME_REQD   4 to 96 time units
MEM_REQD   4K to 60K bytes

Select jobs from the wait queue on an HRRN basis, using S(wait time) = (wait time)/(memory required), with a bypass-three-times-and-freeze restriction.

8

Resources and the Blocked Queue

"A horse! a horse! my kingdom for a horse!" Shakespeare's character Richard III was concerned about resource allocation when he spoke that famous line. The allocation of resources, including the CPU and memory, is the main function of an operating system. Because of the importance of this function, resource allocation and the blocked queue are the subjects of this chapter.

You have probably observed that we already discussed resource allocation in the previous two chapters. However, our discussions were limited to two special resources: the CPU and memory. So much research has gone into the methods and problems associated with CPU and memory allocation that separate chapters were devoted to them. In this chapter we will consider allocation problems of resources other than those two. Let us now discuss the different types of resources that are found in a computer system.

In the previous chapter we stated that memory management affected the blocked queue. The resource manager described in this chapter will also affect that queue. When a process requests a resource and the resource is not available, the resource manager places the requesting process on the blocked queue. Figure 8.1 shows the portions of the SNAIL diagram affected by the resource manager.

We will first look at the different types of resources that are found in a computer system. Then we will consider two quite different approaches to the task of allocation. **Static allocation** implies that a process must specify and receive all the resources it will ever need before it begins execution; **dynamic allocation** allows the process to ask for and receive resources during execution. We have already seen in

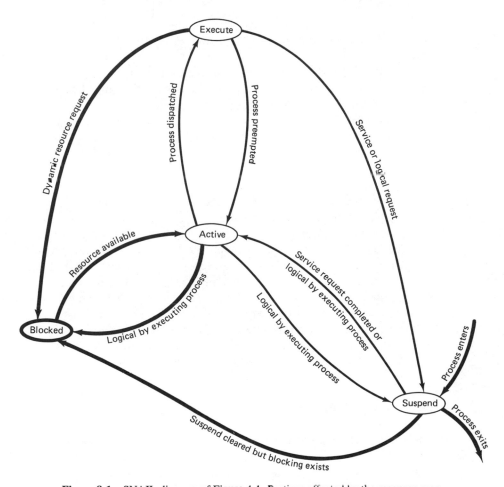

Figure 8.1   SNAIL diagram of Figure 4.1. Portions affected by the resource manager are drawn bold.

Chapter 2 that resource allocation, if not managed correctly, can lead to starvation and deadlock. Later in this chapter we will look at those two problems in depth and see how to deal with them.

Finally, if a process (or a king) needs a resource to continue but that resource is currently not available, then it's off to the blocked queue. Managing the blocked queue is the subject of the last section of this chapter.

8.1 RESOURCE CLASSIFICATION

For our purposes, we will place resources into one of two categories: serially reusable and non–serially resusable. Reviewing our definitions, with one class—serially reusable, or sharable—the resource can be taken away from a process temporarily before that process has finished using it. (The term "serially reusable" has a different meaning when applied to code. For an explanation of the term in that context, see

Calingaert [1979].) With the other class, non–serially reusable, or nonsharable—a process must be allowed to keep the resource continuously until that process has finished using it.

We hope that some examples will clarify the distinction between these two types. One of the resources on a uniprocessor system that must be shared by all processes is the CPU. On a multiuser system we allow processes to use the CPU for some period of time and then we take the CPU away (preempt it) and allocate it to another process. As long as all of the CPU's registers and its internal status are saved and restored correctly, this causes no problems other than slowing individual processes down. Because the CPU can be shared in this serial fashion, the CPU is classified as a serially reusable resource.

Now consider one of the system's other resources, the line printer. Suppose two processes are trying to share the printer in the same way they share the CPU. One process will send output to the printer and then the printer will be preempted. When the second process sends its output to the printer, you can probably imagine what will happen: the output from the process will be interleaved and therefore useless. This means that the printer, when allocated, must remain allocated to one process until that process is finished with it. Because the printer cannot be shared between processes, it is classified as a non–serially reusable resource.

Managing serially reusable resources is generally an easier task than managing non–serially reusable resources. In the remainder of this chapter we will examine the methods used to allocate non–serially reusable resources within the system.

8.2 STATIC RESOURCE ALLOCATION

We haven't used a noncomputer analogy for a while, so let's consider one of the author's passionate loves: classical guitar music. Before indulging himself in the manner to which he is accustomed, the author must acquire the necessary resources. With static allocation, he would generate a single composite request for all resources required or potentially required to relax and enjoy a musical interlude. For this author these resources include the following:

> The on/off switch for the TV
>
> A record album
>
> The console stereo
>
> The portable compact disk player with headphones (in case the console stereo fails)
>
> A compact disk
>
> A comfortable seat in front of the stereo
>
> A pitcher of his favorite beverage
>
> A log for the fireplace

If he were unable to acquire any one of these resources, a static allocation scheme would deny him permission to start listening.

8.2.1 A Formal Description of Static Allocation

The computer version of static allocation is similar. Before a process can be considered for scheduling, it must specify and acquire all of the resources it might possibly require during its life in the system. This must be a worst-case specification—if a process *might* need three or five tape drives, depending on the data, it must request and be allocated all five before it can proceed. The request must also be completely comprehensive; if the process plans on graphically displaying one curve after several hours of computation, it must still request and be allocated the plotter before it can initiate the first calculation

We saw in Chapter 5, Long Term Scheduling, that the resources needed before a process can be created can affect priority and therefore the time spent waiting to enter the system. We also observed that the scheduler had to eventually start denying resource requests which it could actually fulfill so that resources could be accumulated to satisfy an earlier request. Such a situation emphasizes the fact that the method of resource allocation influences the time on the long-term scheduler's waiting list and the efficiency of the system as a whole.

We will close this section by observing that the long-term scheduler is responsible for static resource allocation. To illustrate this, consider the following scheduling function:

$$N(T) = \frac{2(C/1000 + M/10,000 + L/1000)}{2 + t}$$
$$+ \frac{2(100\text{TD} + 500\text{PL} + 200\text{CR})}{2 + t} \tag{8.1}$$

where TD is the number of magnetic tape drives required, PL is the number of plotters required, and CR is the number of optical character recognition units required. In comparing Equation (8.1) with Equation (5.4), we see that the need for additional resources greatly increases $N(t)$ and therefore lowers the priority of the process creation request.

Equation (8.1) determines a priority value, but it *does not* take into consideration whether the resources are currently available. As discussed earlier, part of the long-term scheduler's function is to decide which of these resource requests shall be fulfilled. This also explains why the long-term scheduler must freeze requests on certain resources, in order to satisfy the needs of a high-priority request which has been waiting for those resources.

8.2.2 Advantages and Disadvantages of Static Allocation

Static allocation is a safe and a simple approach to resource allocation. Both the process, P, and the operating system can be assured that, once P begins execution, there will be no case where P has to wait because some other process has a resource needed by P. This is probably the major advantage of static allocation.

Static allocation also simplifies some scheduling problems. Once a process has been granted its resource requests, the OS has much less work to do in terms of resource allocation decisions or scheduling decisions involving resource allocation. We will see later in this chapter that the dynamic allocation approach can require tremendous overhead to constantly guarantee that allocations granted now do not result in problems later.

The complexity of the initial decision algorithm in the long-term scheduler, and therefore also the potential for inequities, can be a disadvantage of static allocation. Imagine that you are the equipment checkout clerk in a highly specialized repair shop with a large set of "one of a kind" test instruments. The owner requires static allocation of the equipment. How do you decide what to do when one technician wants units A, B, C, and D, another B, D, F, and G, another A, C, F, and G, and so on?

This repair shop scenario also illustrates what is probably the greatest problem with static allocation: inefficiency. The inefficiency actually shows up in two ways. First, a technician will be forced to wait if some other process has acquired one of the resources he or she needs. Taken to the extreme, this could mean that only one technician at a time would be able to acquire all the resources needed to start a job and the repair shop would end up operating as a one-man shop. If we equate a technician with a process and apply this logic to a computer system, we can observe that static allocation tends to reduce the degree of multiprogramming and therefore to increase the time during which the CPU will have no processes available to execute. In addition to inefficient utilization of the CPU, static allocation leads to inefficient use of other resources. While a process is holding a resource, that resource can't be used by another process even though the second process might be able to use and return the resource before the first process ever needs it.

At this point, a casual observer might be upset. Why have we spent an entire section on something that does not seem to be an effective approach? Even though the disadvantages seem to far outweigh the advantages, many systems have been designed to use static allocation, primarily because of its simplicity. This is especially true of less expensive minicomputer systems.

8.3 DYNAMIC RESOURCE ALLOCATION

To start our investigation into dynamic resource allocation, recall the guitar music analogy. Using static allocation, all eight resources had to be acquired before listening could begin. From the author's point of view, there are actually only five resources that are essential to start:

The on/off switch for the TV
A record album
The console stereo
A pitcher of his favorite beverage
A comfortable seat in front of the stereo

The remaining resources,

> The portable compact disk player with headphones
> A compact disk
> A log for the fireplace

are needed only when special conditions occur during the concert. In Chico, California, it is never necessary to have a log for the fireplace between May and October, and the portable compact disk player and compact disk itself are needed only if there is a power failure or the stereo fails for some other reason.

8.3.1 A Formal Description of Dynamic Allocation

Given our analogy and the discussions in the previous section, an extensive description of dynamic allocation in operating systems is probably unnecessary. Resources are requested chronologically as they are needed. If a resource only *might* be needed, it is not requested until it actually *is* required at some later time. If a process might need three or five tape drives, depending on the data, it requests three as they are needed and only requests the other two when they are needed. If a resource is not needed to start execution, that resource can be requested later when it is needed.

As with static allocation, there are scheduling decisions for resources themselves and scheduling decisions in which resource considerations are a component. However, with dynamic allocation, the decisions are made throughout the life of the process in the system, rather than once when the process first enters the system.

8.3.2 Advantages and Disadvantages of Dynamic Allocation

One can see immediately that resource utilization and the degree of multiprogramming should be higher with dynamic allocation. The long idle periods during allocation, usage, and release are no longer necessary. Furthermore, because the available resources are better utilized, overall turnaround time should decrease. Each process in the mix can go as far as possible with the resources it currently has; it doesn't have to wait to get everything before it starts.

One reason we said "should" in the previous paragraphs is that users can obviously thwart the approach by requesting resources at the start of their processes and releasing them at the end, regardless of usage patterns. However, this would normally have negative effects on their scheduling, would be costly with respect to resource charges, and would raise the ire of operators, system administrators, and other users.

Another reason for saying "should" is probably of much greater concern. Dynamic allocation can have two serious pitfalls, and these in turn can be disastrous for the system. These pitfalls are starvation and deadlock. They are such important issues that we devote the bulk of this chapter to them.

8.4 DEADLOCKED PROCESSES

Before we start our discussion of deadlocks, we need to briefly describe a condition that is sometimes confused with deadlock; it is starvation, or indefinite postponement. **Starvation** is a situation that occurs when a process is continually denied access to a resource that it needs in order to proceed.

There are several possible reasons for starvation. Probably the most common one is that the starving process has low priority and processes with higher priority keep entering the system and taking the resource that the starving process needs. There can also be an element of luck involved. If two processes of equal priority are sharing a resource, one of them might always just happen to request the resource immediately after it has been allocated to the other process. When this occurs, the unlucky process might have to wait indefinitely.

Fortunately, there are ways to prevent starvation. If it is caused by the timing of requests, a simple queueing of requests for the resource and granting of the requests in first come, first served order will eliminate the starvation. If starvation results because higher-priority processes are always given the required resource, we can use a simple procedure that causes the priority of the starved process to increase as it waits longer. (Note that this was done in the CPU scheduler described in Chapter 6.) In some applications, such as real-time data acquisition, the priority of processes cannot be modified without creating the possibility that data could be lost. In such a case there may only be two choices: lose data, or let the low-priority process starve. Starvation may happen to more than one process, but most of the time it involves just one. Remember this as we discuss deadlock.

Deadlock is a situation that occurs when two or more processes each hold a resource that the other processes need to continue. For example, assume we have a system with four tape drives and process A has requested and received two of the drives and process B has also requested and received two drives. So far there is no problem; both processes can go on. However, what will happen if process A requests another tape drive? Process A will have to wait for a drive to become available. Now suppose that process B also requests another tape drive. At this point we have a deadlock, since each process is waiting for the other to yield a tape drive, neither is willing to give up a tape drive, the system cannot take one away, and no other tape drives are available (assuming that we do not add another to the system). Two processes are blocking each other, and there is no way either can proceed unless there is some intervention.

We will now look at this example of deadlock a little more closely and try to generalize from it to find out just what causes the problem. First, we can observe that the resources involved, magnetic tape drives, like printers and plotters, are non–serially reusable. They are resources of the type that, once allocated, must remain the exclusive property of the requesting process until it releases them. Second, once one of the processes in our example has claimed a resource, it holds onto that resource while waiting for additional resources. Third, resources in this example cannot be temporarily preempted from a process once it has claimed them. Finally, there must be at least two processes involved and they must each have a resource that the other needs before it can continue.

The conditions were summarized by Coffman, Elphick, and Shoshani as follows:

> This deadlock situation has arisen only because all of the following general conditions were operative:
>
> 1. Tasks claim exclusive control of the resources they require ("mutual exclusion" condition).
> 2. Tasks hold resources already allocated to them while waiting for additional resources ("wait for" condition).
> 3. Resources cannot be forcibly removed from the task holding them until the resources are used to completion ("no preemption" condition).
> 4. A circular chain of tasks exists, such that each task holds one or more resources that are being requested by the next task in the chain ("circular wait" condition).
>
> The existence of these conditions effectively defines a state of deadlock. [Coffman et al., 1971]

(Note that those authors use task where we use process.)

In a text published two years later, Coffman and Denning state the following:

> ". . . Three conditions are necessary for the unsafe region to exist:
>
> 1. **Mutual exclusion.** Each task system claims exclusive control of the resources it uses.
> 2. **Nonpreemption.** A task system does not release resources it holds until it completes its use of them.
> 3. **Resource waiting.** Each task system holds resources while waiting for others to release resources.
>
> The deadlock itself is defined by an unresolvable circular wait condition, the unresolvability being guaranteed by the mutual exclusion and nonpremption conditions. [Coffman and Denning 1973]

At first glance it would appear that these two definitions are in conflict. However, we see that in the second case, the authors are first defining an *unsafe region*, one that can lead to a deadlock and then adding another condition, circular wait, which completes the definition of a deadlock situation.

Two additional comments on these conditions are in order. The four conditions are necessary and sufficient to guarantee that a deadlock exists when there is only one resource of each type involved in the circular wait loop. In the next section we will see that when there are multiple instances of each resource, the conditions are still necessary but not sufficient to guarantee that a deadlock exists.

Now that we know what deadlocks are and what causes them, we have several options available:

1. Try to prevent them.

2. Try to avoid them.

3. Try to detect them.

4. Ignore them.

The next four sections will explore these possibilities.

8.4.1 Preventing Deadlocks

In theory, *deadlock prevention* is simple. All we have to do is to eliminate any one of the four conditions that are necessary for deadlocks to occur. We will now examine the conditions one by one and see what can be done.

The "mutual exclusion" condition could be eliminated if all resources were sharable. Unfortunately we cannot just make an edict that says henceforth all resources will be sharable; sharing is what caused interleaved output on the line printer. Suppose, however, that we let processes have access only to virtual devices rather than to the actual devices. In the case of the line printer, a process would be given access to a disk file rather than the actual printer. The disk file would be the apparent, or virtual, device that the process uses and when the process has completed all of its output, a system process that had exclusive access to the printer would dump the disk file to the printer. This is such a common operation that it has been given its own name: output spooling. We will discuss spooling in more detail in Chapter 11.

Unfortunately, it is not possible to apply this technique to all resources (consider for instance, the case in which the resource in contention *is* a disk file). Even if it were possible to create virtual devices for all resources, we could still create another deadlock situation involving disk space [Holt, 1972]. This problem is also addressed in Chapter 11.

As the discussion above indicates, it is nearly impossible to make all resources serially reusable. Therefore some researchers have directed their attention to finding ways to eliminate the other three conditions necessary for deadlock. The following approaches to eliminate the "no preemption," "wait for," and "circular wait" conditions were developed by Havender [1968].

The "no preemption" condition is difficult to eliminate. We could make all resources preemptable but if resources such as printers, plotters, and tapes can be preempted at any time, the old interleaving problem will occur.

The "wait for" condition can be eliminated by forcing every process to release any resource it has already acquired before it can request additional resources. This is probably not practical if a process is holding some of those non–serially reusable resources.

As stated above, eliminating the "wait for" condition is probably not reasonable. However, the "circular wait" condition is amenable to elimination. To get rid of this condition we will first order all of the resources on the system. A sample of the ordered list of resources for a system is shown in Figure 8.2. We will next require that processes request resources in the order that they are shown in the list. This means that if a process has received a resource from level i in the list of resources, it can request only those resources that are at a level j where $j > i$.

Level	Resource
1	Terminal
2	Card reader
3	Array processor
4	Magnetic tape
5	Plotter
6	Printer

Figure 8.2   Ordered list of system resources.

It we apply this method to our example above with two processes vying for the magnetic tape drives, neither process would be permitted to request an additional tape drive, since it already had a resource at that level. The only way a process can request an additional resource from the same level or a higher level is to release all resources it currently holds at or below the level of the resource that is to be requested.

Of the methods described above, having processes release resources while waiting and making resources preemptable are probably of little practical use. That leaves us with either creating virtual devices to replace nonsharable devices or ordering resources as possible ways to prevent deadlocks. In most cases, when we create a virtual device we do it by using a disk file to replace the actual device. This causes performance problems if the disk is heavily used. It can also decrease system throughput, since an extra operation is needed to transfer information from the virtual device to the physical device.

At this point it looks as if ordering the resources and forcing processes to request them in order could be the best solution. There are, however, some disadvantages to this solution also. The primary drawback is that processes are forced to request resources in a predefined order, and this may or may not correspond to the order in which they will be used by the process. This can lead to the inefficient use of resources. Back to square one! It may be possible to come up with an intelligent ordering of the resources that will reduce the inefficiency, but we cannot guarantee maximum resource utilization with this method.

Since none of the methods for preventing deadlocks is perfect, people have looked for other ways around deadlock. In the next section we will examine some methods that have been proposed to avoid deadlocks.

8.4.2 Avoiding Deadlocks

First, let's clarify the distinction between prevention and avoidance. When we prevent deadlocks, we do it by eliminating one of the four conditions necessary for deadlocks to exist. However, deadlock *avoidance* implies that we leave all four conditions intact but that we cleverly allocate resources so that we never let the system get into a deadlock situation.

The first method we will examine for avoiding deadlocks has an analogy in the banking industry and was hence given the name *banker's algorithm* [Dijkstra, 1965a]. The scenario is as follows. Assume that we are on the board of directors of the bank and we have a number of customers each of whom has a guaranteed line of credit from our bank. By "lines of credit," we mean that we have promised each of the customers some maximum amount of money that we will loan. We assume that they are not deadbeats and they will all pay back whatever money they have borrowed. We also assume that we know the maximum amount of money in the bank's loan fund before any loans are made.

At any time, we can examine our books to find out

How much money we currently have in the loan fund,

How much each customer's maximum loan will be, and

How much each customer currently has on loan.

What we must be able to guarantee is that we will not reach a point where we can fully satisfy *none* of our customers' maximum loan needs. This would cause a run on the bank and put a crimp into our retirement plans.

The examle in Figure 8.3(a) shows that we have four customers with total current loans of $12,000, and remaining cash on hand of $1000. As resource man-

Customer	Current Loan	Maximum Loan	Remaining Cash
1	$2000	$6000	
2	$4000	$6000	
3	$1000	$2500	
4	$5000	$6000	
			$1000

(a)

Customer	Current Loan	Maximum Loan	Remaining Cash
1	$2000	$6000	
2	$4200	$6000	
3	$1000	$2500	
4	$5000	$6000	
			$800

(b)

Customer	Current Loan	Maximum Loan	Remaining Cash
1	$2000	$6000	
2	$4000	$6000	
3	$1000	$2500	
4	$6000	$6000	
			$0

(c)

Figure 8.3 Resource allocation in a banking example. (a) Present status. (b) Status after loan of $200 to customer 2. (c) Status after loan of $1000 to customer 4.

agers, we must decide whenever a customer asks for a loan whether to grant the loan immediately or tell the customer to wait a while. In the example shown, suppose that customer 2 comes in and asks for an additional $200. Should we make the loan? Figure 8.3(b) shows what the situation would be if we made the $200 loan. As you can see, we are now in the position we were trying to avoid. There is not enough remaining cash to guarantee that we can fully satisfy any of our customer's maximum needs, and deadlock will occur if all the customers now request their maximum loan.

Now let us assume that customer 4 comes in and asks for $1000. If we grant the loan, the situation will be as shown in Figure 8.3(c). Although we have no remaining cash, we are not in trouble; this is because customer 4 will pay back the resulting $6000. When this is done, we will be able to meet at least one of the other commitments. This in turn will free up more cash and allow all needs to be satisfied.

The banker's algorithm can now be stated rather simply. Assume that any resource request which is made is granted, but then check to see if the assumed allocation leads to an unsafe state. By unsafe state we mean a state where we cannot guarantee that all requests made by the customers will eventually be granted.

If granting the resource request would result in an unsafe state, the requesting process must be placed on the blocked queue until a later time when the request can be granted without creating an unsafe state. The resource manager, which is discussed in Section 8.5, is responsible for blocking processes. The pseudocode for the banker's algorithm is shown in Figures 8.4 and 8.5.

The procedure, BANKER, if called before every resource request is granted, will make sure that deadlocks are avoided. However, several comments need to be made about the procedure. First, as written, it will check the allocation for only one resource. To work with multiple resources, the data structures would have to be expanded to accommodate entries for each resource. Also, since the number of processes in the system is constantly changing, provisions must be made to dynamically change the size of each array.

The problems of multiple resources and dynamic arrays certainly can be solved [Habermann, 1969; Tanenbaum, 1987]; however, there are other, more important drawbacks to the banker's algorithm. If such a procedure were used to avoid deadlocks, it could add considerably to the overhead of the system. Each request requires a complete analysis of the current allocations. With a large number of processes in the system, this can be very time-consuming. Also, there is no guarantee that all of the pending requests for resources will be satisfied in a reasonable length of time. Because of these problems, the banker's algorithm is not practical for real systems.

In the search to find a better solution to the deadlock problem, a number of researchers have applied some techniques from graph theory to the problem [Holt, 1972; Lomet, 1980]. The basic method is to create a directed graph (one which has direction associated with the edges) that describes the current allocation of resources in the system. Such a graph is shown in Figure 8.6. In the graph, circles are nodes of the graph that represent processes, and rectangles are nodes that represent individual types of resources. The edges of the graph represent either resource requests or allocations. If the edge is directed toward a resource, it represents a request. Conversely, if the edge is directed toward a process, it represents an allocation to that

```
procedure BANKER(cus_num,units_requested,grant_request);

{ This procedure is responsible for checking to see whether a resource
  request should be granted.  It first assumes that the allocation can
  be made; then it checks to see whether the allocation results in a
  safe state.  If the state is safe, the allocation is made; if not,
  the request is denied.                                              }

{ Called by            : resource manager
  Function called      : SAFE_STATE;
  Parameters passed    : cus_num, units_requested
  Parameters returned: grant_request, true or false                  }

global variables
    customer_has     : array[1..max_customers] of integer;
    units_remaining  : integer;

local variables
    temp_units_rem        : integer;
    customer_has_temp     : array[1..max_customers] of integer;

begin
{ Set the return status to false, request denied.  Check to see if
  there are sufficient units to satisfy the request.  If not, return;
  if there are, make a working copy of the current customer
  allocations and then use the SAFE_STATE function to determine
  whether the allocation can be made.                                }

    grant_request := false;
    if units_requested > units_remaining then exit;
    copy customer_has to customer_has_temp;
    customer_has_temp[cus_num] := customer_has_temp[cus_num] +
                         units_requested;
    temp_units_rem := units_remaining - units_requested;

    if SAFE_STATE(temp_units_rem,customer_has_temp,units_requested) then
      begin
        customer_has[cus_num] := customer_has[cus_num]
                         + units_requested;
        units_remaining := units_remaining - units_requested;
        grant_request := true;
      end; {safe to allocate resources}

end; {BANKER}
```

Figure 8.4   The banker's algorithm.

process. If an algorithm can be found that evaluates an allocation graph as the banker's algorithm evaluates the allocation matrix, that algorithm could be the core of a deadlock avoidance routine.

Graphical techniques have to this point met with only limited success. It has been shown that a deadlock exists when the resource graph has a cycle and there is only one resource in each box. A cycle in a directed graph occurs when there is a path from a node through at least one other node and back to the original node. Unfortunately, in graphs where the nodes contain more than one resource, there can be cycles even though no deadlocks are present. For this and other reasons, graphical techniques have not yet proved to be of great practical value in helping avoid deadlocks.

```
function SAFE_STATE(temp_units_rem,customer_has_temp,units_requested);
{ This function checks the state created by making an allocation to
  see if it is safe.                                                   }

{ Called by             : BANKER
  Procedures called     : none
  Parameters passed     : temp_units_rem, customer_has_temp,
                          units_requested
  Function returned     : true or false                               }

global variables
  finished      : array[1..max_customers] of boolean;
  customer_max  : array[1..max_customers] of integer;

local variables
  no_change      : boolean;
  finished_temp  : array[1..max_customers] of boolean;

begin
{ Make a working copy of the finished array.                          }

  copy finished to finished_temp;

{ This section checks to see if the state created by making the
  allocation above is safe.  It does this by checking to see if there
  is a way that all users can eventually receive their maximum
  requested resources.                                                }

  repeat
    no_change := true;

    for i := 1 to max_customers do begin
      if not(finished_temp[i]) and
        ((customer_max[i]-customer_has_temp[i])< temp_units_rem) then
        begin
          finished_temp[i] := true;
          temp_units_rem := temp_units_rem + customer_has_temp[i];
          no_change := false;
        end; {if customer need can be satisfied}

    end; {for each customer}

  until all finished_temp[i] = true or no_change;

{ If the state is safe, then all customers will be able to finish.
  If that is the case, then SAFE_STATE is set true.                   }

  if all finished_temp[i] = true then SAFE_STATE := true
  else SAFE_STATE := false;

end; {SAFE_STATE check}
```

Figure 8.5   The SAFE_STATE check for the banker's algorithm.

8.4.3 Deadlock Detection and Recovery

Before anything can be done to eliminate the effects of deadlocks, the presence of the deadlock must be detected. In the previous section, we described a technique for detecting deadlocks that analyzes a resource allocation graph. The method, unfortunately, has limited usefulness.

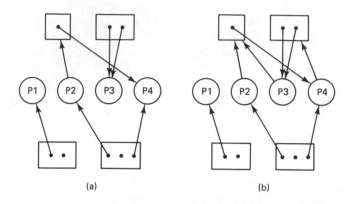

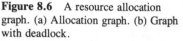

Figure 8.6   A resource allocation graph. (a) Allocation graph. (b) Graph with deadlock.

One of the simplest methods of detecting deadlocks involves no programming at all! Let the system operator be responsible for detecting deadlocks. He or she would do this by observing whether two or more processes remained in the blocked state for an extended period of time. Obviously, this is an imprecise method, but it has the advantage of contributing nothing to system overhead. Although this method is not very scientific, it has been used on many systems because the alternatives are not very attractive. This method does require that an operator be on duty whenever the system is running.

An algorithm that creates allocation and requests matrices and then searches for possible allocation patterns that will satisfy all requests without creating a deadlock is described in Coffman et al. [1971]. The algorithm is quite simple and straightforward. Unfortunately, the execution time of the algorithm is proportional to the square of the number of processes in the system. Using the algorithm could add an excessive amount of overhead to the system.

After a deadlock has been detected, something must be done to break the deadlock. This requires that a decision be made about which process should have its resources preempted and then be aborted. We might invoke a system process to make the decision, or we might let the operator make the decision. In either case, we would need criteria upon which to base the decision. The following are six criteria that have been used:

The CPU time consumed by each process
The lines of output created by each process
Time remaining for each process
Total resources consumed
Priority of the process
The relative abrasiveness of the programmers who initiated the processes

On a given system, some of the criteria listed are easy to measure, and some, such as time remaining, are difficult if not impossible to measure. When the operator is the one making the decision, the criteria are usually kept simple: execution time and output generated, priority, or programmer abrasiveness. If a system process is available to evaluate the criteria, more complex and less subjective methods are used.

The problem of choosing a process to abort gets more complicated when more than two processes are involved in the deadlock. It is possible that simply aborting one of the processes will not free up enough resources to break the deadlock. If this is the case, the operator, or program, must keep aborting processes until the deadlock is eliminated.

8.4.4 The Cost of Deadlocks

No matter what method we choose to eliminate the effects of deadlocks on the system, there are costs that must be considered. If we choose to implement a deadlock prevention method on a system, we risk lower resource utilization or increased system overhead. If we decide to avoid deadlocks, we will definitely increase the overhead associated with resource allocation. Depending on the method used, we may also have less than optimal resource utilization. On the other hand, if we choose to ignore the problem, we will end up wasting CPU time and other resource time whenever we have to abort a process to break a deadlock. Our decision about which approach to take depends on which method will cost the least. In early systems, the responsibility was often given to the operator to detect and correct the problem. As systems became more complex, this choice seemed less and less desirable. There is currently extensive research in the areas of deadlock avoidance, detection and recovery. We can hope that that research will lead to improved techniques for solving the problem.

So far in this chapter we have looked at resources, their allocation, and problems which can occur in allocation. In the final section of this chapter we will discuss what is done with processes that are blocked while waiting for resources. The PCBs for these processes must be kept somewhere in the system, because information in the PCBs will be used to make decisions about resource scheduling.

8.5 MANAGING THE BLOCKED QUEUE

From the SNAIL diagram, we saw that the blocked queue is where processes are placed if they make a dynamic resource request and the resource is not available. The singular "queue" made sense for the purposes of the diagram, and it is conceivable that an operating system might have just one queue for all blocked processes. However, it is also possible that the OS actually keeps one queue for *each type* of resource (one for tape drives, one for disk drives with removable packs, and so on). Such an arrangement reduces overhead when a released resource is being reallocated.

Blocked queues might be accessed concurrently; if they are, we need a monitor or semaphore to protect the critical regions involved. The methods used to allocate the individual resources can be tailored for each resource. Some resources may be allocated on a first come, first served basis; others, on a priority basis; and others, on the basis of some deadlock avoidance technique.

For resources allocated on a priority basis, the routines that allocate and return resources can be quite simple. If the queue is maintained in priority order, the allocation routine can simply (and quickly) allocate the returned resource to the first process on the list. Managing of resources allocated on an FCFS basis is equally easy.

Our final blocked queue list is shown in Figure 8.7. When a process requests a resource which is not available, it is moved from execute to the blocked queue for that resource. When a resource is released, the associated routine goes to the appropriate blocked queue and allocates the returned resource to the process whose PCB is the first on the queue.

In order to keep track of all the resources on the system, we need a new data structure: a **resource control block,** or RCB. Just as we need a place to hold information about a process, we need a like place for resource information. Fortunately, we usually do not need to store as much information about resources as we do for processes. We will create one RCB for each resource on the system. Figure 8.8 shows a sample RCB.

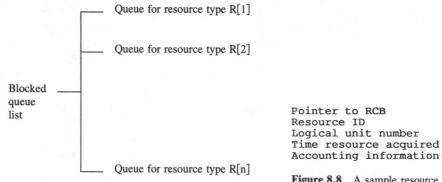

Queue for resource type R[1]

Queue for resource type R[2]

Blocked queue list

```
Pointer to RCB
Resource ID
Logical unit number
Time resource acquired
Accounting information
```

Queue for resource type R[n]

Figure 8.7 The blocked queue list.

Figure 8.8 A sample resource control block (RCB).

In the RCB shown, there are a pointer, a resource identifier, a logical unit number, and resource acquisition information. The pointer is used to link the RCB to other RCBs that are on a process's resource list. We store the resource identification so that we can easily find out which resources a process holds by examining all the RCBs on its resource list. The logical unit number is the means by which the process will reference the resource. By keeping the time the resource was acquired and other accounting information in the RCB, we can accurately charge users for all resources they use when their processes terminate. Figure 8.9 shows a PCB with its associated RCBs.

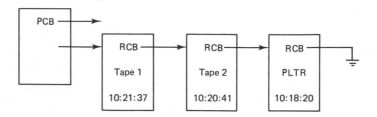

Figure 8.9 PCB with associate RCBs.

8.6 A SIMPLE RESOURCE MANAGER

The code for a simple resource manager is shown in Figures 8.10 through 8.12. For this manager we have assumed that the system supports dynamic allocation and that a process can request only one resource at a time. If a process needs three magnetic tape drives, it will make three requests.

When the resource manager receives a request for a resource, it first checks to see whether a valid resource type has been requested; the status "invalid resource" is returned if no such resource exists. Next, the resource array is checked to see whether a resource of the type requested is available. If a resource is available, it is

```
procedure RESOURCE_MGR(command,resource_type,rcb_pointer,status);

{ This is the procedure that is responsible for allocating resources
  to the executing process.  It accesses the blocked queues of the
  system via monitor calls.  When it is called by the executing
  process it check to see if the requested resource is available.  If
  the resource is  available and its allocation will not result in a
  deadlock, it is allocated to the process and the process continues.
  If the resource cannot be allocated, the process is placed on the
  blocked queue for that resource and the short-term scheduler is
  activated.                                                           }

{ Called by           : executing process
  Procedures called   : DEADLOCK, SHORT_TERM_SCHEDULER, MOVE_PCB,
                        ADD_PCB, REMOVE_PCB
  Parameters passed   : command, request or return
                      : resource_type, type of resource requested
                      : rcb_pointer, pointer to returned rcb
  Parameters returned: status
  Entry conditions    : executing process requested/returned resource
  Exit conditions     : resource allocated/returned, calling process
                        is blocked if necessary.                       }

global variables
  resource_array      : array[1..max_resources,1..2]
                            of RCB_pointer, PCB_pointer;
  execute_queue       : pcb pointer;
  active_queue        : pcb pointer;
  blocked_queue       : array [1..number of resources] of pcb pointer;

local variables
  temp_rcb            : rcb pointer;
  unblocked_pcb       : pcb_pointer;

begin
{ This is the mainline code for the RESOURCE_MGR.  The procedures
  REQUEST_RESOURCE and RETURN_RESOURCE that follow are defined within
  the scope of this procedure and therefore have access to all the
  variables defined within RESOURCE_MGR.                              }

  case command of
    request   : REQUEST_RESOURCE;
    return    : RETURN_RESOURCE;
    otherwise : status := invalid request;
  end;

end; {RESOURCE_MGR}
```

Figure 8.10   Variable definition and mainline for resource manager.

```
procedure REQUEST_RESOURCE;

begin
{ This procedure handles resource requests.  It first checks whether
  the resource type is valid.  If not, it returns status to the caller.}

   if resource_type not valid then
     begin
       status := invalid_resource;
       return;
     end; {if invalid resource type}

{ Check to see whether the requested resource is available and if it
  is, temporarily allocate it to the process.                          }

   if resource_array[resource_type,1]<> nil then
     begin
       move rcb from available list to temp_rcb;
       temp_rcb.allocation_time := current_time;

{ Check for deadlock.  If there is no deadlock return.                 }

        if not DEADLOCK then
          begin
            add new logical unit number to pcb on execute_queue;
            insert logical unit number into temp_rcb;
            add temp_rcb to resource_list of pcb on execute_queue;
            return; {return to process}
          end {if no deadlock}

{ If DEADLOCK then block the calling process.                          }

        else
          begin
            return rcb to available list;
            delete temp_rcb;
            MOVE_PCB(execute queue,blocked queue for resource_type,);
            SHORT_TERM_SCHEDULER;
          end; {deadlock detected after attempted allocation}

     end {if resource is available}

{ The resource was not available so block the calling process and
  goto the short-term scheduler.                                       }

   else {resource is not available}
     begin
       MOVE_PCB(execute queue,blocked queue for resource_type,);
       SHORT_TERM_SCHEDULER;
     end; {resource not available}

end; {resource request}
```

Figure 8.11 The resource allocation portion of the resource manager.

allocated to the end of the resource list for the process. If the resource is not available, the process is placed on the blocked queue. The deadlock routine is called to check whether the allocation will result in a deadlock. If a deadlock would exist, the resource is taken away from the process, the process's PCB is placed on the blocked queue for the resource, and the short-term scheduler is called. The requesting process is also blocked if there are insufficient resources available to satisfy the request.

```
procedure RETURN_RESOURCE;
{ This procedure handles resource returns.  It first checks whether
  the resource type is valid.  If not, return status to the caller.       }

begin
   if resource_type not valid then
      begin
         status := invalid_resource;
         return;
      end; {if invalid resource type}

{ Calculate the charges for using the resource, update accounting
  information, and remove rcb from the returning pcb.                      }

   calculate charges and update resource accounting information;
   delete logical unit number from pcb on execute_queue;
   remove returned rcb from resource_list of pcb on execute queue;

{ Enter the blocked queue monitor and remove a waiting pcb if there
  is one.  Set the current time into the rcb.                             }

   REMOVE_PCB(blocked queue for resource_type,unblocked_pcb,);
   if unblocked_pcb = nil then
      begin
         add returned rcb to resource_array[resource_type,1];
         return;
      end;   {no process waiting for resource}
   temp_rcb.allocation_time := current_time;

{ If there is a deadlock then take the resource away.  If there is
  no deadlock then move the process to the active queue.                  }

   if not DEADLOCK then
      begin
         add new logical unit number to unblocked_pcb;
         insert logical unit number into temp_rcb;
         add temp_rcb to unblocked_pcb.resource_list;
         SHORT_TERM_SCHEDULER(unblocked_pcb);
      end {if no deadlock}

{ If DEADLOCK then block the process again.                               }

   else
      begin
         return rcb to available queue;
         dclete temp_rcb;
         ADD_PCB(unblocked_pcb,blocked queue for resource_type,);
         SHORT_TERM_SCHEDULER;
      end; {deadlock detected after attempted allocation}

end; {RETURN_RESOURCE}
```

Figure 8.12   The resource return portion of the resource manager.

If the allocation request does not cause the process to be blocked, the resource manager returns to the calling process and it continues to execute.

When a resource is released by a process, after it is verified that the resource type is valid, charges for its use are calculated and added to the user's account. The resource manager then checks the blocked queue to see whether a process is waiting for the resource. If there is a process waiting, the manager allocates the resource to the first one on the list. It then checks to see whether that allocation causes a deadlock. If a deadlock exists, the resource is taken away from the process and control is returned to the process that released the resource. If the resource can be allocated to a process, that process is removed from the blocked queue and placed on the active queue, and the "time allocated" field in the RCB is set. The short-term scheduler is then called to reorder the active queue.

There are several comments that must be made about the resource manager. First, it uses a monitor to protect the blocked queue. Second, it assumes the existence of the procedure DEADLOCK to check for a deadlock condition after each allocation. Third, it is not very sophisticated; it only tries to allocate a returned resource to the first process on the blocked queue. If that allocation cannot be made because of a deadlock, no other blocked process is given a chance; in other words, it allows no bypass.

For the resource manager described above, we have purposely kept the design simple and left out any details of how deadlocks would be detected. Even with these restrictions, the resource manager is not trivial. Perhaps you can see why more research is needed in this area.

8.7 SUMMARY

This chapter has dealt with a subject that is still in the development stage. Efficient resource management will become an even more important topic as operating systems become more complex and multiprocessor and distributed systems become more commonly used. In the future you can expect to see advances in techniques used to eliminate the effects of deadlocks on operating systems. The new methods will have to overcome the inefficiency of current methods.

Problems associated with deadlock have often led to interesting discussions between researchers. The series of articles by Habermann [1969], Holt [1972], and Parnas and Habermann [1972] demonstrate this. In his 1973 paper, Frailey gave a good overview of previous work and discussed the need for an efficient solution to the problem. Another, more recent overview with an emphasis on data bases and distributed data bases can be found in Isloor and Marsland [1980]. Kameda [1980] wrote an excellent paper that described when a system can deadlock and which resources will be involved if it does. Three other papers describe some interesting approaches to the problem that were not presented in this chapter [Howard, 1973; Devillers, 1977; Minoura, 1982].

QUESTIONS AND EXERCISES

1. List all of the resources on your computer system and classify them as either serially reusable or non–serially reusable.
2. Why can cycles exist in a resource allocation graph even if there is no deadlock?
3. What are some additional criteria that could be used to select a process to be aborted in order to eliminate a deadlock?
4. Discuss the merits of the various criteria you listed in your answer to question 3.

5. Modify the BANKER procedure of Section 8.4.2 so that it accommodates *n* resources.

6. Some people have confused the terms "starvation" and "deadlock." Why do you think this has happened?

7. An example of a deadlock from the traffic engineering field is shown in the accompanying illustration. Identify the resources that cause the problem, the processes, and a solution to this gridlock problem.

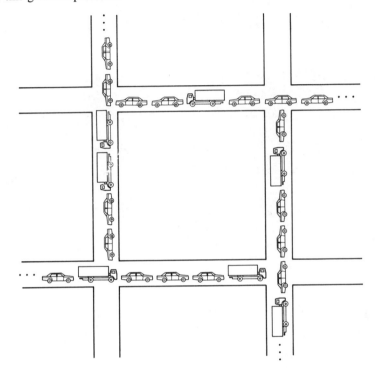

8. How could the resource manager and data structures described in Section 8.5 be modified to allow for multiple resource requests from a process?

9. It has been suggested that the banker's algorithm could be used to detect deadlocks. What is your opinion?

10. How do detection and avoidance differ?

PART 3
Input/Output Operations and Data Storage

The first two parts of the book described some basic concepts and several types of resource allocation and management operations that are performed by the system. We will now direct our attention to some functions that are essential for efficient operation of the system but are not directly associated with resource allocation and management.

Chapter 9 presents the details of input and output operations. It includes a description of the system routines that are responsible for servicing a user program's request for I/O, and a discussion of what the process does while waiting for an I/O operation to be completed.

Devices that store multiple files of information, such as disks and magnetic tapes, require additional study. Chapter 10 contains a detailed analysis of files systems. This includes storage allocation techniques and directory structures.

In Chapter 11, spooling is described in detail. First, the evolution of spooling from early tape systems to modern mainframes is examined. We then discuss how the concept is being applied to current microcomputer systems.

9

Input and Output
Operations

One of the primary services provided for the user by the OS is the ability to access input and output devices in a simple, consistent manner. In this chapter we discuss the routines and structures within the OS that give us this capability.

Few OS books cover the I/O area in any detail. This is probably because it is a complicated part of the system and also one that is very system-dependent. (Our experience has shown that no two operating systems have the same I/O structure.) In order to emphasize the basic concepts that are generally applicable, we have combined features from several different systems without trying to tie the discussion to any one system.

When a process makes a request for I/O service, the process is usually placed on a suspend queue while waiting for the request to be serviced. After I/O completion, the process is typically placed back onto the active queue. Figure 9.1 shows the portions of the SNAIL diagram affected by I/O operations.

9.1 THE STEPS IN PROCESSING A REQUEST FOR INPUT OR OUTPUT

In this chapter we will follow an I/O request, once it begins in a user process, through the input-output control system (IOCS) and then to the device driver; we will see how the user process resumes after the I/O operation is completed. Figure 9.2 shows the steps involved and the operations which allow them to be taken.

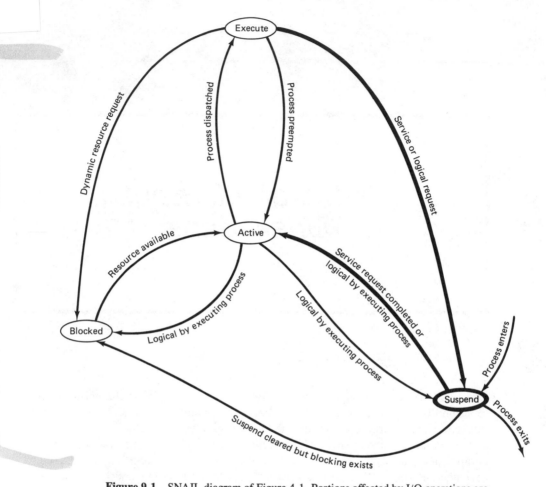

Figure 9.1   SNAIL diagram of Figure 4.1. Portions affected by I/O operations are drawn bold.

9.1.1 I/O Requests from a User Process

The following two statements are from PASCAL and FORTRAN programs, respectively:

```
readln(input,buffer);     (PASCAL)
READ(5,99) BUFFR          (FORTRAN)
```

These statements provide the compilers with information necessary to generate code that will request input from the system.

What information is contained in these statements? First, both statements use keywords to tell the compiler that an input operation is needed: readln or READ. Both statements specify the device from which information will be read: input or 5.

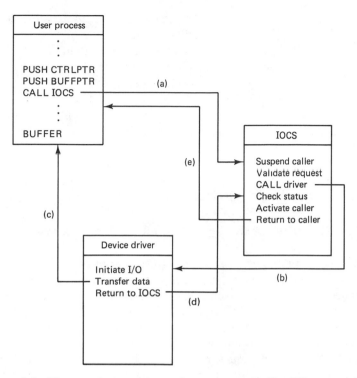

Figure 9.2 The steps in processing an input request: (a) User I/O request; (b) Driver request; (c) Data transfer; (d) Status return; (e) Resumption of user process.

Both also tell the compiler where the incoming information should be stored: in buffer or BUFFR. The FORTRAN statement has an additional piece of information, 99, which tells the compiler where format information for the data can be found. In the case of the PASCAL statement, the format is implied by the type of variables into which the information will be stored. It is the compiler's responsibility to convert source code into an input request that can be processed by the OS.

9.1.2 Calls to the Supervisor or Executive

To accomplish the input operation, the compiler converts the source statement into a call to the OS, which on some systems will take one of the following forms:

$$
\left.\begin{array}{l} \text{CALL IOCS} \\ \text{ADR CONTRL} \\ \text{ADR BUFFER} \end{array}\right\} \quad \text{or} \quad \left\{\begin{array}{l} \text{PUSH CTRLPTR} \\ \text{PUSH BUFFPTR} \\ \text{CALL IOCS} \end{array}\right.
$$

where

      ADR CONTRL   the address of the control information which will tell the

I/O system that a read is requested from one of the specified devices

ADR BUFFER   the address of the data buffer

IOCS   an address within the OS where the routine is found that processes I/O requests

The code on the left assumes a convention in which information is passed via addresses following the CALL statement. The code on the right is for a stack-oriented machine, in which control and buffer information is pushed onto the stack before control is transferred to the I/O routines. In either case, when the code is executed, control is passed to the part of the OS that performs input and output operations. This is seen as step (a) in Figure 9.2.

9.1.3 Overview of the Input-Output Control System

The **input-output control system** (IOCS) is responsible for processing the I/O requests from the executing process. It does such things as checking to see whether the requested device is available, and it may be responsible for suspending the executing process as necessary. If the requested device is available, the IOCS will transfer control (step (b) in Figure 9.2) to a routine that can communicate with the device. Common names for the routines that talk directly to a device are device driver and I/O handler. (The authors have also seen such names as CAT and SPOT applied whimsically by overworked programmers.)

9.1.4 Overview of Device Drivers

The **device driver** is the part of the OS that directly controls the operation of a device. To do this typically requires that the driver be capable of testing status bits received from the device and setting control bits for the device. Therefore, drivers are usually written in a language suited to such operations, such as assembly language or a system programming language. Depending on the device and the system, the driver may also be responsible for the actual data transfers to or from the device (step (c) in Figure 9.2). It may, however, use special hardware such as DMA or an I/O channel to make the transfers [Mano, 1982; Leibson, 1982b; Gorsline, 1986].

When the I/O transfer is finished, the driver will send a message to the IOCS telling it that the operation has completed (step (d) in Figure 9.2). It will also inform the IOCS of any errors that may have occurred while the data transfer was in progress. Assuming that the read request has been processed without errors, the IOCS will remove the process that made the request from the I/O suspend queue and transfer it to the active queue, where it can again compete for the CPU. Step (e) in Figure 9.2 implies that control is passed directly from the IOCS to the process when the process is removed from the I/O suspend queue. In reality, the IOCS will usually transfer control to the short-term scheduler, which then determines what process will execute next.

9.2 THE INPUT-OUTPUT CONTROL SYSTEM (IOCS)

The IOCS is responsible for checking the availability of devices prior to initiating operations and for checking the status of devices after requests have been satisfied. It also makes sure that the requests are passed on to the correct device driver. In essence, it is a traffic controller. [Mock and Swift, 1959; Allen and Foote, 1964; Ossanna et al., 1965].

9.2.1 Requests for I/O Service

Requests from a process are normally for one of the following:

Data transfer (read or write)
Device status
Device positioning

When a request is made to the IOCS, it may be necessary to do something with the calling process while the request is being satisfied. The SNAIL diagram reproduced in Figure 9.1 shows the transition from execution to the suspend that a process normally takes while waiting for an I/O operation to be completed.

It may be possible to satisfy some I/O requests immediately and not remove the process from the execute queue. If, for instance, the executing process has just requested the status of some device, the IOCS can usually provide such information within a few microseconds. In most cases, it would make no sense to move the process to the suspend state for this short period of time. Therefore, the process remains on the execute queue while the status is found, and then it is allowed to continue executing.

Some read and write requests may also be processed very quickly if the device is buffered [Ferguson, 1960; Ossanna et al., 1965; Watson, 1970]. In this case the device physically transfers an entire block of information for each read or write, rather than a specific record or field requested by the user. With buffering, which is often used with disk-type devices, an I/O request can often be fulfilled by simply moving part of a block from one location in memory to another. If the move is executed by the device driver before returning control to the IOCS, nothing is gained by suspending the calling process.

A request to position a device usually requires that the requesting process be suspended also. Moving a disk head to a different track or spacing a tape drive backwards several records usually takes a relatively long time, and system performance is improved if the process making the request is suspended until the move is complete.

9.2.2 Logical and Physical Devices

One of the responsibilities of the IOCS is to determine which I/O device will be used for each I/O request. This may not be as simple as it first appears. In the sample program statements shown in Section 9.1.1, the source code included a reference to the device to which the I/O operation was directed—input for PASCAL and 5 for

FORTRAN. In most systems, input and 5 are just logical references that the programmer uses and they have no particular relation to the physical devices that will be used. If this is the case, there must be some way to map logical references (devices) to physical devices. The mapping information is usually kept in a table within the operating system; we will call it the logical unit table (LUT). Figure 9.3(a) shows one possible implementation of an LUT. When a request for an I/O operation is made by the executing process, the IOCS uses the logical reference as an index to the LUT. There the IOCS finds the physical device and the address of the device driver that services that device.

In the LUT of Figure 9.3(a) we see that there are some missing numbers in the logical unit number column. This is because the currently executing process has not requested or has been denied access to these units for some reason. The LUT also lists the same physical device and driver address for three different logical unit numbers. The repetition means that in this example three logical devices, 1, 2, and 7, are currently being served by the same physical device, 7. (Maybe the laser printer and the letter-quality printer are being repaired, so that output to them must be directed to the line printer.) We can also see that physical devices 4 and 10 are serviced by the same device driver. This could happen, for instance, if the two devices were identical terminals, and it would be very important if the system has many similar devices (such as 128 terminals all serviced by one driver).

(a)

Logical unit number	Physical device	Driver address
1	7	20420
2	7	20420
3	2	20FOO
4	4	1FC10
6	1	20D02
7	7	20420
21	10	1FC10
22	11	1F120
.	.	
.	.	

(b)

Logical unit number	Physical device	Driver address
1	7	20420
2	7	20420
3	2	20FOO
4	4	1FC10
6	10	1FC10
7	7	20420
21	10	1FC10
22	11	1F120
.	.	
.	.	

Figure 9.3 Logical unit table (LUT) showing relation between the logical unit numbers, physical devices, and the addresses of the associated device driver. (a) Initial LUT. (b) LUT modified to show I/O redirection for logical unit 6.

On single-user systems the conversion from logical to physical device is a fairly simple operation: there is one LUT for the system; and as each process executes, it makes references to devices through that table. The problem becomes more complicated when we move from a single-user system to a multiuser system. Consider, for example, a system with several users, each running a PASCAL program containing a readln statement similar to the one shown in Section 9.1.1. This means that each program, when it is run and becomes a process, will request input from the logical device "input." On our multiuser system, we assume that input for each of the processes will be read from the console device from which the process is initiated. This causes a problem for the system. In one case, "input" may refer to physical device 10, and in another case it may refer to device 21. What can be done to solve the problem, other than outlawing timesharing systems?

One possible solution to the problem is to have a separate LUT for each user. If we choose such an approach, the system will establish a unique LUT for a user each time he or she logs onto the system. Each user may then reference "input" and, through his or her LUT, have it refer to a different physical device. If we want to have a separate LUT for each user, one place to store the LUT would be in the PCB of the process created by that user. But a great deal of wasted space could result if every PCB contained an entire LUT. Therefore, a better solution would be to create an LUT for each user and then have all processes created directly or indirectly by that user have a pointer to that one LUT.

There is an additional benefit to employing a separate LUT for each user. In many applications it may not be desirable to give every user access to all of the I/O resources that are on the system. By having the system create a unique LUT for each user, we may limit the range of devices that a user can access. This serves as a form of protection, since it can in turn limit the capabilities of users. The LUT for a user such as a system programmer could be a copy of the system LUT. This would give that user access to all the devices on the system.

The logical unit table also serves another useful purpose: it makes I/O redirection simple. By **I/O redirection** we mean that the device to which I/O operations are assigned can be changed without changing the original program. As a simple example of this, suppose that you are developing a program and during the development phase you write all output to the terminal to simplify the debugging operation. When you are satisfied with the operation of the program, you will want to execute the program again and have the output sent to the line printer so that you can have a permanent record of the results.

One way to get your output on the printer would be to modify the source code of the program to change all output statements so that they specify the printer rather than the terminal. An easier solution, assuming that the system supports the operation, is to modify an entry in your LUT so that the logical unit that corresponds to the physical terminal will now correspond to the physical printer. Figure 9.3(b) shows the LUT after logical unit 6 has been redirected to physical device 10.

Nearly all modern operating systems allow some form of I/O redirection. On the MS-DOS or PC-DOS system [Van Wolverton, 1984], the ASSIGN command is used this way to redirect disk accesses from one disk device to another, and the MODE command can be used to redirect I/O for nondisk devices. Other systems allow redirection by treating every device as a file. Redirection on UNIX [Ritchie, 1978] is accomplished in this manner by replacing one file designation by another.

9.2.3 Memory Allocation for Data Buffers

When a process requests I/O, it must tell the IOCS the memory address of the data buffer. In the example in Section 9.1.2, "buffer" was used by the PASCAL program to hold the information being read into the program. At first glance, it seems that there are no problems; the IOCS will be able to tell the driver where the data from the device can be stored. But as usual in operating systems, things are seldom as simple as they first appear.

Because we are discussing the design of a multiuser system, we must consider what happens when the system suspends the process requesting I/O and switches execution to a new process. What happens if the new process needs additional memory and asks the system for more? The system may decide that since the suspended process is not in the active state, some or all of its memory can be temporarily reassigned. Such reassignment will cause a problem when the I/O driver writes incoming data into a location that no longer belongs to the process that made the I/O request. Several solutions to this problem are presented below.

The most obvious solution is to prevent the system from taking memory away from a process that is in the middle of an I/O request. On some systems this is referred to as *locking* the process into memory. Although locking solves the problem, it may not be a very efficient solution (in terms of memory utilization), given some forms of memory management. If a large process requests a single item from a terminal, a great deal of memory may be tied up for an extended period of time while the process is waiting for the terminal to respond, especially if the data entry clerk is temporarily distracted. On some systems, typically those using paging or segmentation, it is possible to lock *only* the portion of memory that actually contains the data buffer. Such selective locking can significantly reduce the amount of memory that must be tied up while a process is waiting for I/O.

Another solution to the problem is to have the system itself buffer all data being transferred between processes and devices. For a read, the IOCS would request that information be transferred to an area of memory within the system; and when the transfer was completed, the IOCS would first make sure that the process requesting the input was in memory and would then move the data into the process's memory space. This solves the memory locking problem; however, it can cause another problem. The memory used to buffer the input data must come from that allocated to the system, and there may not be enough of this memory to satisfy all requests for I/O. There is another disadvantage to the method: time is required to transfer the data from the buffer in system memory to the buffer in the calling process. These transfers add to the total overhead of the OS, and on a system that does a great deal of I/O (such as a terminal-oriented system), the performance of the system can suffer.

The third solution is left as an exercise for the student. Please send us a copy of the solution when you find it. It will fit nicely into the future publications.

9.2.4 I/O Suspend Queues

What happens to a process when it is suspended? First, suspension means that the process is removed from the execute state. This implies that the PCB is removed from the linked list of executing processes and moved to a list of suspended processes. Where is the suspend list maintained?

One place to keep the list is in the IOCS; on systems that group all suspended processes into one queue, this is often done. There is another logical location for a list of suspended processes. Since it is the device driver that is responsible for satisfying requests for I/O from any given device, the queue of all processes waiting for the device can be attached to the driver itself. One location within the driver will be a pointer to the head of a queue of PCBs for all processes that are requesting I/O through the driver.

This approach separates suspended processes into groups that are based on what driver they are using and can therefore reduce the time needed to find a particular process when it is time either to move it to another queue or to initiate a request on its behalf.

9.2.5 I/O without Wait

Some systems have a special type of I/O request: READ or WRITE without wait [Beck, 1985]. If this type of request is made, the process making the request is allowed to remain on the execute queue while the I/O request is being satisfied. When a request of this type is made it becomes the responsibility of the requesting process to determine when the operation has been completed.

The following code segment shows how a read without wait could be used to start an input operation long before the data is needed by the process:

```
{This is just a program segment and therefore we do not include all the
 boilerplate needed to make an executable program.                        }

    begin
       no_wait_readline(reader,data);

       processing that does not depend on "data";
       repeat                                     {                }
           flag :=readline_complete(reader)       {   BUSY WAIT    }
       until flag = true;                         {                }

       processing that does depend on "data";
    end.
```

Although this program eliminates the forced suspend that the system imposes on processes that request input, the programmer must assume responsibility for checking to see that the read has been completed before attempting to use the input data. The program may also be expensive to run, since a lot of time could be spent execut-

ing inside the repeat loop and checking the flag. The time wasted testing the flag
could be eliminated if a semaphore were used to coordinate the operation of the process and the I/O driver. The process would execute a wait, and the driver would signal when the operation was completed. However, this just forces the process into the
suspend queue for the semaphore rather than the suspend queue for the I/O device.

```
procedure IOCS(command,logical_unit,buffer_address,count,
               user_error,status,iostatus);

{ This procedure is responsible for processing all I/O requests.  If
  the request is for I/O completion, status is checked and if it is not
  OK and the process does not handle its own error, the process
  termination flag is set.  Control is passed to the short-term
  scheduler along with the pcb of the process whose I/O was completed.

  For other I/O operation, IOCS checks for a valid logical unit in the
  LUT.  Then if the request looks valid, IOCS calls the driver to
  initiate the request. If the request cannot be completed before the
  return to IOCS, the process is placed on the I/O suspend queue by
  the driver.                                                         }

{ Called by          : executing process, DRIVER_COMPLETION
  Procedures called  : SHORT_TERM_SCHEDULER, DRIVER_INITIATOR
  Parameters passed  : command, logical_unit, buffer_address,
                       count, iostatus, user_errors
  Parameters returned: status, status after request processed
  Entry conditions   : I/O request or completion request
  Exit conditions    : Request initiated and process suspended, or
                       request completed and process made active, or
                       process termination flag set                  }

global variables
  execute_queue, active_queue   : pcb_pointer;

local variables
  i/o_suspend_queue : pcb pointer;   {I/O suspend queue for system}
  pcb_done          : pcb pointer    {pointer to pcb that is done}

begin
{ Select the procedure to process the I/O request.                   }

    case command of
       read, write, status, position : INITIATE;
       complete                      : COMPLETE;
       otherwise                     : ERROR_EXIT(invalid_command);
    end;
    return;

  procedure ERROR_EXIT(error);
  { Return to user with error or set user to terminate.              }
    begin
      if user_error = true then return
         else begin
           status := error;
           execute_queue^.termination_flag := true;
           SHORT_TERM_SCHEDULER;
         end;
    end; {ERROR_EXIT}
end; {IOCS}
```

Figure 9.4   Mainline code for a simple IOCS.

9.2.6 A Sample Input-Output Control System

The IOCS we will present in this section is rather basic. It converts requests from
logical reference to physical reference, checks the requests for validity, and suspends
the requesting process when necessary. It does not buffer any data that is being
transferred between processes and devices. Since it transfers control to the driver for
all I/O requests, I/O without wait could be implemented within the device drivers if
that were deemed necessary. Figures 9.4 through 9.6 contain the pseudocode for the
IOCS.

```
procedure COMPLETE;
{ This procedure is defined within the scope of IOCS and therefore has
  access to all of the variables within IOCS.  If the command is for
  completion then get the returned pcb, set the status, and set the
  termination flag if necessary.                                         }

begin
{ If an error occurred, set the process to terminate; if not, have the
  short-term scheduler put the process on the active queue.              }

   status := iostatus;
   REMOVE_PCB(io_suspend_queue,pcb_done,);
   if (iostatus <> good_completion) and user_error = false then
      pcb_done^.termination_flag := true;
   SHORT_TERM_SCHEDULER(pcb_done);
end; {I/O operation complete}
```

Figure 9.5 Completion procedure for the IOCS.

```
procedure INITIATE;
{ This procedure is defined within the scope of IOCS and therefore has
  access to all of the variables within IOCS.  Process a request to
  initiate an I/O.  Get the driver address from the LUT if the logical
  unit is valid.                                                         }

begin
{ Check for a valid logical unit.  If not, take error return.           }

   if logical_unit not in LUT then
      begin
         status := invalid_logical_unit;
         ERROR_EXIT(invalid_logical_unit);
      end; {invalid logical unit}

{ Get the driver address from the LUT and pass it the request.          }

   get driver_initiator address from LUT;
   DRIVER_INITIATOR(command,logical_unit,buffer,length,iostatus);

{ Check for an error and then go to the short-term scheduler.           }

   status := iostatus;
   if (iostatus = error) and (user_error = false) then
         execute_queue^.termination_flag := true
   else MOVE_PCB(execute_queue, suspend_queue,);
   SHORT_TERM_SCHEDULER;

end; {Initiate I/O}
```

Figure 9.6 Command initiator procedure for the IOCS.

9.3 DEVICE DRIVERS

The device driver, or I/O handler, is the low-level system routine that must communicate with the I/O hardware of the system. As is the case with most low-level routines, the driver is usually written in assembly language or a systems programming language, since it must access the hardware via privileged I/O instructions. These instructions, which typically cannot be executed by user processes, are not available in most higher-level languages.

To simplify our discussion of the driver, we will split it into two parts: the initiation section and the continuation section. The **initiator** is responsible for getting an I/O operation started, and the **continuator** is responsible for processing interrupts and transferring data after an operation has been started.

9.3.1 Validating Service Requests

The first function the drive initiation section must perform is to make sure that the operation being requested is one that can be performed by the device. Most systems, for instance, will not let the user read input data from the line printer. If the driver detects a request that is not supported by the hardware to which it is attached, it will return to the IOCS with a parameter that tells the IOCS an error has occurred. The IOCS can then decide to abort the calling process or just inform the process of an I/O error and let it continue.

Some versions of PASCAL (UCSD and Turbo [Softech, 1980; Borland, 1983]) allow the user to test for an error after I/O operations by invoking a compiler option prior to the I/O request and then checking the variable "ioresult" after the request. The following code shows how this feature can be used:

```
write('Key in the name of the input file. ');
readln(file_name);
assign(data_file,file_name);
{$I-} reset(data_file); {$I+}
if ioresult < >0 then
    begin
        writeln('Data File ',filename,' could not be opened!');
        writeln('Request aborted.')
        exit
    end; {end if}
```

If the variable "ioresult" is zero after the operation is performed, it means that the operation has been performed without any problems, and the process continues. If an error is detected, it becomes the user process's responsibility to take corrective actions. In the example, a message is sent to the user and the process is terminated.

Some I/O operations that at first seem ridiculous may actually have a use. On early disk-based operating systems, it was quite common to have the disk driver accept a rewind command. This did not mean that the disk would stop and start spinning in the other direction. The rewind command was included because earlier magnetic tape–based systems often required a rewind command before a file could be read. The rewind command on a disk-based system was used to start a read or a write at the beginning of the file being referenced. Other examples of seemingly incongruous operations that are sometimes allowed are backspace (to another record) on a disk and seek on a sequential device.

9.3.2 Status of the Device

In this section and the next, we will deviate from our philosophy of avoiding specific systems and devices and discuss some of the characteristics of the Intel 8251A communications chip [Intel, 1986]. Since this chip has been used on many different systems, it almost qualifies as a generic example. The 8251A is a 40-pin device that serves as an interface between a processor chip and a serial device. Its primary purpose is to take parallel information from the processor and convert it into serial data for the external device, or vice versa.

The 8251A has several internal registers that are accessible by sending an address to the chip along with a read or write command. The data registers in the 8251A can be loaded or read in parallel from the processor's bus. Data being sent to or received from the external device is shifted into the data registers serially. The chip is capable of operating in either the synchronous or the asynchronous mode and can accept data bytes that are 5, 6, 7, or 8 bits wide. The device driver sets the exact mode of operation by sending control information to the chip.

Before the driver initiates a data transfer on behalf of a process, it must determine the status of the device. This is usually done by loading the contents of the device's status register into the CPU and testing the different bits. The status word format for the 8251A is shown in Figure 9.7. By reading the status word and testing the individual bits, the processor knows whether errors have occurred while data was being received and also when a byte of data has been received and is available.

It is probably obvious that the information in the status word shown is relevant

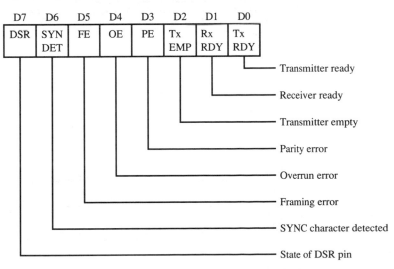

Figure 9.7   The status register format for an Intel 8251A.

only to the 8251A. Almost every device will have its own unique status word. Some devices have multiple status words when the complexity of the device requires it.

The status word or register in a device is accessed by sending a read request with the address of the register. On some processors, reading this register is the same as reading a memory location; but on other processors, there are special instructions that access I/O devices [Stone, 1982]. On many machines, only certain

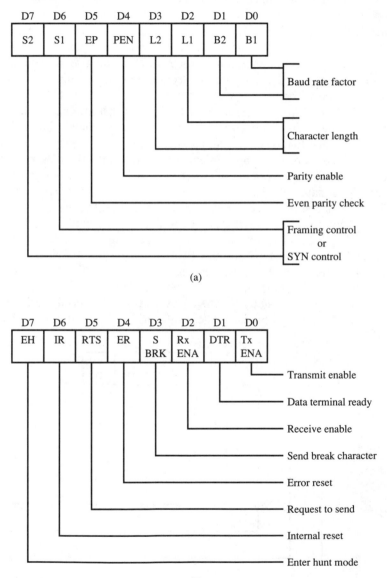

(a)

(b)

Figure 9.8 Intel 8251A register formats. (a) Mode register. (b) Command register.

processes—those that are part of the OS—can execute privileged I/O instructions. This is one way the OS protects itself from mischievous or maladroit users.

On some systems, the status of a device may be sent back to the process that has requested the I/O operation. Often, a generic status word is returned rather than the actual bits from the device's status register. This makes it possible for application programs to be independent of the particular physical device being used. In the previous section, the use of the variable "ioresult" in PASCAL was described to show how status can be read in a high-level language.

9.3.3 Initiating an I/O Request

After the driver has read the status of the device and determined that it is available for use, it will send a command to the device. This is done by writing a control word into the control register of the device. Some complex devices may require multiple control words. Figure 9.8 shows the two control registers in the Intel 8251A that must be set before it can be used to transfer data. The registers, called "command" and "mode," have their own addresses and are loaded independently. The contents of the command register determine whether the 8251A will receive or transmit data and how it will use the external control lines DTR and RTS. It also controls the reset operation on the chip. The mode register controls parity, transmission speed, and character length. In addition, it also specifies how synchronization will be established with the external device.

The operation may or may not require the transfer of data. If the operation is a write, the driver may send a data word to the device after the write command has been sent. If the operation is a read, the driver may wait for the data by loading the status word and testing the data ready bit. The assembly language code to implement a simple read operation with the Intel 8251A is shown in Figure 9.9. On many systems this is called *wait loop I/O*. This type of I/O is very wasteful of CPU time and is typically used only on single-user systems such as Apple II [Apple, 1979]. On multiprogramming systems, after the driver has initiated an operation, it should return control to the IOCS so that the system can do something useful while the device is busy.

Some devices transfer data at a very high rate so that it may not be possible for the CPU to keep up with the device if data transfers are managed by a procedure running on the CPU. In such cases a direct memory access device may be used to actually move data from the device to memory [Leibson 1982b; Mano, 1982]. It is the responsibility of the initiation part of the driver to program the DMA device so that it will perform the data transfer. This usually means that the DMA has to be given the buffer address, number of words to be transferred, and control information such as "read" or "write."

9.3.4 Interrupt Handlers

Waiting for a device to complete an operation can be very wasteful of CPU time. Using the interrupt capability of a CPU to recognize the completion of an operation can save a great deal of processor time. With this method, control is transferred back to the driver when an interrupt is received from the device, and the driver handles the

```
; DATA COMMUNICATIONS PORT DATA INPUT ROUTINE
;
; This routine loads the mode and command registers on the
; 8251A to request a read operation.  It then checks the
; status of the chip to see whether data has been received.
; It remains in a loop testing bit 1 of the status word
; until the bit is set.  When the bit is set, the data is
; read into the CPU and stored in the AL register.
; Control is then passed back to the calling program.
;
;  registers modified : AL, STATUS
;  parameters passed  : none
;  parameters returned: data in AL
;
COMSTAT    EQU    00F5           ;Address of 8251A status register
COMDATA    EQU    00F4           ;Address of 8251A data register
RDYBIT     EQU    0002           ;Mask for receive data ready bit
MODE       EQU    00F0           ;Physical address of mode register
COMM       EQU    00F1           ;Physical address of command register
READCH     EQU    0006           ;READ command for mode register
CONTROL    EQU    004D           ;READ command for command register
;
READ       MOV    MODE,READCH    ;Set mode register
           MOV    COMM,CONTROL   ;Set command register
;
LDCOM      MOV    AL,COMSTAT     ;Load status byte into AL
           AND    AL,RDYBIT      ;Mask off all other status bits
                                 ;in the status register
           JZ     LDCOM          ;If not ready, try status again
;
           MOV    AL,COMDATA     ;Load the data word into AL
           RET                   ;Return to calling program
```

Figure 9.9   Wait loop input routine for communications chip.

interrupt. The driver may have to save the current state of the processor so that the interrupted process can be restarted after the interrupt has been processed.

What do we mean when we say the driver "handles the interrupt"? If the original request was for a read, the interrupt from the device signals that the device has the data ready for the calling process. The driver must load the data into the CPU from the device and store it into a buffer. This is done by executing an instruction that moves data from a device to an internal register or memory location.

After the data has been transferred to the buffer, the pointer showing where the next piece of data is to be stored must be updated and a check must be made to see whether all the requested data has been read. The driver may also check the device status to see whether any errors have occurred during the transfer. When all of these operations have been completed, the control is returned to the process that was temporarily suspended by the interrupt.

9.3.5 Completion of the I/O Request

Eventually, one hopes, all the data requested by the process will be read in from the device. The driver will recognize the situation when the count of remaining transfers reaches zero or when the status from the device shows that an end of input has been found. When this occurs, the driver performs a final check of the status and, rather than returning to the process that was interrupted, passes control to the IOCS.

The IOCS must now do something with the process that made the request for the data. If there were no errors detected during the I/O operation and no resources were preempted from the process during the operation, the IOCS will remove the process from the I/O suspend queue and place it on the active queue. If an error has occurred, the IOCS may have several options: (1) request that the operation be retried, (2) abort the process and send an error message to the operator, or (3) send the status to the process and let it decide what to do about the problem. If a resource was taken from the process while I/O was being performed, the IOCS will move the process to the blocked queue, where it must wait for the resource that was preempted. Figure 9.10 shows these state changes on the SNAIL diagram.

9.3.6 Sharing Drivers between Devices

Because devices require different commands and return different status information, separate drivers are usually required for each type of device. From the description of how a driver operates, you may also think that a separate driver is required for every

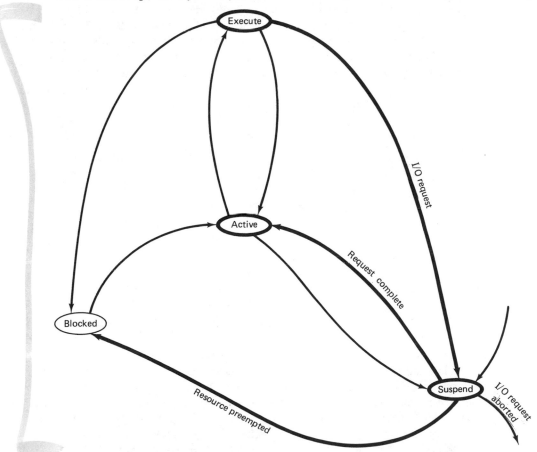

Figure 9.10   The state transitions that can occur after an I/O operation is completed.

physical device on the system. If that were the case, operating systems would be even larger than they are now. Fortunately, on many systems it is possible to share one driver among many devices. A driver that is often shared is the one which controls terminals.

On some machines, sharing a program is almost trivial. If the CPU allows separation of code and data, all that has to be done is to provide a separate data segment for each physical device that must be serviced by the driver.

On CPUs that do not support the separation of code and data, sharing a driver among multiple devices can be a little tricky. One way to solve the problem is to have the IOCS pass to the driver a block of information that will be used by the driver to initiate an I/O request. The block will include the type of operation requested, addresses of any buffers needed, and any other data associated with the request. If the system cannot interrupt the driver while it is initiating a request, this will work. Otherwise the driver might become confused and intermix requests from two or more processes.

The driver continuator is used to take care of interrupts, and this part of the driver must be given access to the block of information that the IOCS has passed to the initiation part of the driver. One way to accomplish proper accessing is to create an interrupt table for the system. The **interrupt table** will map interrupts to blocks of data that are associated with the device that has caused the interrupt. An example of an interrupt table is shown in Figure 9.11. In the example, the physical address of the interrupting device is used to find the address of the data block or information block that will be used by the driver continuator.

Interrupt number	Buffer address
1	2420
2	0
3	462O
4	40F0
5	0
.	.
.	.

Figure 9.11 The interrupt table for a system that vectors interrupts directly to the device driver.

9.3.7 A Sample Device Driver

Figures 9.12 and 9.13 show the pseudocode for a device driver for a terminal. There are additional functions that might need to be included for some systems, but all of the functions described in the paragraphs above are implemented in the example.

The initiator is called to start an I/O operation. It checks the device status; and if there is no problem, it initiates the request. If the request is for a read or a write, the process must be suspended until the operation completes. When an interrupt occurs on the device, the continuator section is called from the system routine that receives all interrupts. After status is checked, data is inputted or outputted depending on the type of interrupt. When all the data has been transferred, the IOCS is called with a completion command, and the process will then be returned to the active state.

```
procedure TERMINAL_INITIATOR(command,device,buffer,length,status);

{ This device driver controls the operation of a simple terminal
  capable of displaying characters on the screen and receiving
  characters from the keyboard.  The driver has two main sections:
  initiator and continuator.  The initiator is called by IOCS when a
  read, write or status call is made to the device. The continuator is
  called by FLIH when the device requests an interrupt              }

{ Called by           : IOCS
  Procedures called   : none
  Parameters passed   : command, device, buffer, length
  Entry conditions    : interrupts disabled, cpu registers saved,
                        write data, if any, in buffer
  Exit conditions     : device status in status, operation initiated   }

local variables
  temp_pcb              : pcb_pointer;

begin
{ Begin processing request by getting the device status.  Next go to
  code for read or write.                                            }

  input status from device;
  case command of
{ Read request. If device is down, return status to IOCS and if it is
  not, start the read operation and suspend the process.             }

    read  :if device_status <> down then
              begin
                output read_command;
                status := operation_initiated;
              end; {if not down}

{ Write request. If device is down, return status to IOCS and if it
  is not, start the write operation and suspend the process.         }

    write :if status <> down then
              begin
                output write_command;
                status := operation_initiated;
              end; {if not down}

{ Status request. Return without suspending calling process.         }

    status: ; {Status was loaded at begining of procedure.}

{ Invalid request for this driver.                                    }

    otherwise: status := invalid_request;
  end; {case}

end; {TERMINAL_INITIATOR}
```

Figure 9.12   The input/output driver initiator.

```
procedure TERMINAL_CONTINUATOR(ptr);

{ Called by           : FLIH
  Procedures called   : IOCS
  Parameters pased    : ptr, which points to an area containing the
                        buffer and other information, such as the count
  Parameters returned: status, buffer
  Entry conditions    : interrupts disabled, cpu registers saved
                      : write data, if any, in buffer
  Exit conditions     : device status in status, read data in buffer    }

begin
{ Get status and check to see if the device has an input character.
  If it does, input the byte and store it into the process's memory.
  If all the bytes have been input, then call IOCS with a completion
  command.                                                               }

    get device_status from device;
    if device_status[RxRDY] = true then
      begin
        input device_data into buffer;
        decrement count;
        if count = 0 then
          begin
            status := device_status + completion_bit;
            IOCS(complete,device#,,,,,status);
          end; {read complete}
      end {if read interrupt}

{ Check to see if the device is ready to accept a byte. If it is,
  output the byte from the process's buffer. If all requested bytes
  have been output, goto IOCS with a completion request.                 }

    else if device_status[TxRDY] = true then
          begin {when the transmit ready bit in status word true}
            output byte from buffer;
            decrement count;
            if count = 0 then
              begin
                status := device_status + completion_bit;
                IOCS(complete,device#,,,,,status);
              end; {write complete}
          end {if write interrupt}

{ If there was neither a read or write ready, then it must have been
  an invalid interrupt so ignore it. (a hardware error or noise)         }

        else send invalid interrupt message to operator and return;

end; {TERMINAL_CONTINUATOR}
```

Figure 9.13   The input/output driver continuator.

9.3.8 Processing an I/O Request

In Figure 9.14, we show the major components of the OS that are involved with I/O operations. The sequence of events that initiate an I/O operation is as follows:

1. Process requests I/O to a logical unit.
2. IOCS uses LUT to convert logical to physical request.
3. IOCS requests that driver initiator start the I/O operation.

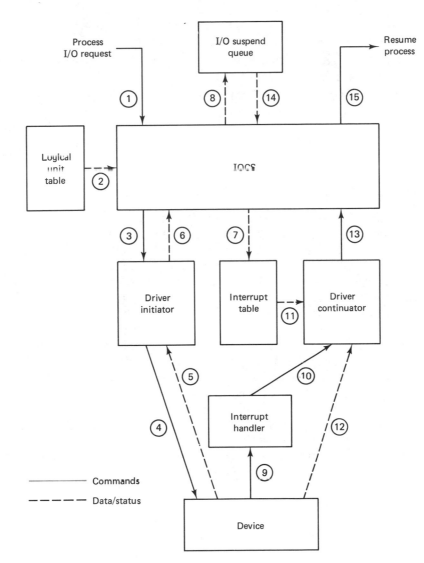

Figure 9.14   Steps in processing an I/O read request.

4. Driver sends command to device.

5. Driver checks device status.

6. Driver returns status to IOCS.

7. IOCS stores information into interrupt table for driver continuator.

8. IOCS places requesting process onto I/O suspend queue.

After the interrupt from the device, the following sequence of events takes place:

9. Completion interrupt occurs.

10. System interrupt handler passes control to driver continuator.

11. Driver continuator gets information about the request from the interrupt table.

12. Driver transfers data and status into process's buffer.

13. Driver requests an I/O completion from IOCS. (This happens after the last data element has been read.)

14. IOCS moves process from I/O suspend to active queue.

15. Process resumes execution (after being selected by the scheduler).

The above sequences do not take into account what happens when errors occur. They are intended to show what typically happens when a read request is made.

9.4 SCHEDULING PROCESSES ON THE SUSPEND QUEUE

The device drivers we have considered so far are rather simple. Although we have not explicitly stated it, we made the assumption that whenever an operation was completed on a device, the next request in line was initiated. In other words, we assumed FCFS scheduling. For most devices this is all that is necessary. Some devices, however, can benefit from a more sophisticated scheduling policy.

The best example of a device that needs something other than FCFS scheduling is the system disk. This is often one of the most heavily used resources on the system, and it is not uncommon to find many requests for I/O pending at any time. Each time a process reads from the disk, it is necessary to position the head over the correct disk track. The time it takes to move the head is related to how far the head must move. Figure 9.15 shows a possible set of tracks that must be read to satisfy the pending set of I/O requests.

Since the time spent moving the disk head is proportional to the total distance traveled, it seems reasonable to look for a way to reduce the total movement and therefore the time spent waiting for the disk. The problem is then to find a way of ordering the pending requests that will reduce the total head movement.

Current disk track = 100

Process	Track	Distance (in tracks)
4	19	81
9	376	357
23	205	171
7	134	71
34	18	116
22	56	38
14	192	136
3	396	204
32	29	367
17	3	26
12	19	16
29	40	21

Total head movement = 1604 tracks

Figure 9.15 Pending FCFS disk I/O requests.

Current disk track = 100

Process	Track	Distance (in tracks)
7	134	34
14	192	58
23	205	13
22	56	149
29	40	16
32	29	11
4	19	10
12	19	0
34	18	1
17	3	15
9	376	373
3	396	20

Total head movement = 700 tracks

Figure 9.16 Pending SSTF disk I/O requests.

The first method we will try is called **shortest seek time first,** or SSTF [Hofri, 1980]. Using this method, any time we are ready to start a new I/O operation on the disk we look at the list of pending requests and pick from that list the request that results in the shortest seek. Figure 9.16 shows the requests from Figure 9.15 rearranged on the basis of SSTF.

When we compare the bottom lines in Figures 9.15 and 9.16, it looks as if we have found a way to greatly reduce disk waits, and it doesn't seem to cost much in terms of overhead. Unfortunately, there is a subtle problem lurking about: starvation. From the example shown it is not obvious how it will occur, since all of the requests are satisfied. Suppose, however, that some time before the request for process 9 (track 376) a stream of requests are received for tracks between 40 and 205. All of these requests will require less movement than that needed to get to track 376; therefore, processes 9 and 3 will never be served. Fortunately there is a simple modification to SSTF that eliminates the problem.

The modification requires that we keep track of the direction the head is moving and not reverse direction until all requests that are between the current position and the edge of the disk toward which we are moving have been satisfied. The set of requests from Figure 9.16 is again duplicated in Figure 9.17. This time the modified SSTF method of scheduling is used.

Again, comparing the bottom lines of the figures, it seems we have found a way to prevent starvation and have also improved performance! But before we break an arm patting ourselves on the back over finding this apparent violation of Murphy's law, we must state that the modified SSTF will not always give better performance than SSTF.

You could argue that starvation is extremely unlikely, since systems typically experience periods of light use when requests for all outer tracks can be satisfied. Even if this is true, there is another distinct disadvantage of SSTF. The worst-case time to satisfy a request when using SSTF can increase dramatically if the track re-

Current disk track = 100   Direction = IN (toward track 0)

Process	Track	Distance (in tracks)	
22	56	44	
29	40	16	
32	29	11	
4	19	10	
12	19	0	
34	18	1	
17	3	15	(Direction = OUT)
7	134	131	
14	192	58	
23	205	13	
9	376	171	
3	396	20	

Total head movement = 490 tracks

Figure 9.17 Pending modified SSTF disk I/O requests.

quested is on either edge of the disk and the queue of disk requests is long. On the other hand, the directional scan will satisfy all requests in one cycle (in and out). This can reduce the variation in time to service a disk request.

Another version of the SSTF is called **circular scan** [Gotlieb and MacEwen, 1973]. Using this method, the innermost track is assumed to be next to the outermost track; a request for track 0 would be satisfied right after a request for track 400. A discussion of the advantages of this method over the previous two is left as an exercise.

On devices that have a head for each track, such as older paging drums and disks, requests were ordered to reduce the time spent waiting for a sector to come under the read/write head [Fuller, 1972; Stone and Fuller, 1973]. This was sometimes done on moving-head disks also, but reductions in memory costs have led to the use of RAM buffers—either in the disk controllers or in the CPU—that store an entire track whenever any sector from a track is read. Buffering entire tracks can also reduce the total number of physical disk accesses that are required.

Now that we have found a way to reduce the time spent waiting for disk I/O, who should be responsible for doing the scheduling? There are two logical places we can place the scheduling function: in the IOCS, or in the disk driver. If we put the scheduler in the IOCS, then we could use the same scheduler for all disks. If we put the scheduler in the driver itself, we could have a different scheduler for each disk and possibly develop a different scheduler to take advantage of the characteristics of each physically different disk. Although the decision is not critical, we recommend doing the scheduling in the driver, to retain the greatest flexibility.

9.5 SUMMARY

In this chapter we have followed the functions which the OS performs when satisfying requests for input and output. We started with a request for input from a user's program and found out what preliminary operations the IOCS performed before passing control to the driver, which is the routine that communicates with the device. We then looked briefly at interrupt processing and saw what happens when an interrupt occurs. In Chapter 12 we will look at interrupt processing in more detail and examine the details of the first-level interrupt handler (FLIH).

We hope that all of this has given the reader an appreciation for the complexity of the I/O portion of an OS. On the other hand, by looking at the details of a simple wait loop input operation, we saw that I/O does not have to be complex.

In the next chapter we will examine the I/O devices that are used for secondary storage on the system. We will look at the organization of data on the devices and the methods used to access this information.

In addition to the other references cited, the following are suggested reading. The description of OS/360 in Rosen [1967; also, IBM, 1967] gives a good overview of the design of a large OS and explains some of the I/O design philosophy. The two articles by Leibson [1982a, 1982b] and the text by Stone discuss I/O as it relates to microcomputers. The paper by Coury [1970] suggests why I/O design is important, and Strollo et al. [1969] discusses the use of a separate I/O processor to improve system performance.

One area of I/O that has been analyzed by many researchers is that of disk or drum scheduling. Besides the specific references cited, there have been numerous others that examine different mechanisms and/or analyze the problem from another approach [Abate and Dubner, 1969; Coffman, 1969; Fuller, 1974; Teorey and Pinkerton, 1972; Wilhelm, 1976].

QUESTIONS AND EXERCISES

1. It is more common to see WRITE requests without wait than READ without wait. Why is this? Write a program segment that makes effective use of WRITE without wait.

2. Some systems support many different types of terminal and each has its own special characteristics. One way to take care of this situation is to have a different device driver for each type of terminal; however, this may be very wasteful. Suggest an alternative. (*Hint:* Look at UNIX termcaps.)

3. Explain why it is more efficient to have separate blocked or suspend queues for each resource.

4. Sometimes the queue(s) of processes waiting for a device are not kept in FCFS order. Why?

5. Suppose the OS or a user wants to know for which resource a process is waiting. How is this information found if the resource is implicitly specified by the queue on which the PCB currently resides?

6. Conceivably, if buffers are kept in a system area of memory, then some I/O requests might be satisfied by going to the buffer rather than physically reading data from the device. For example, a commonly accessed inventory file might be read once into memory and then referenced by many different processes. Do you foresee any problems?

7. Suppose a user process has acquired a device and wants to read some data from it. When the initiator checks the status, it finds that the device is broken. What should be done?

8. Construct a sequence of disk requests that demonstrates how SSTF disk scheduling can give better performance than the modified SSTF scheduler.

9. When we use the modified SSTF that satisfies all requests in one direction before reversing directions, system programs and directories are sometimes stored in the middle of the disk. Why?

10. Compare the performance of circular scan with FCFS, SSTF, and modified SSTF scheduling. What advantage, if any, does this method have over modified SSTF?

11. Why can't the system interrupt the driver while it is initiating a request (Section 9.3.6)?

12. The I/O driver shown in Figures 9.12 and 9.13 is very simple. What additional features or operations would have to be added to it if it were a disk driver that maintained a queue of requests and selected the next one based on a shortest seek first?

13. Modify the sequence of events described in Section 9.3.8 to show the error checks that should be made.

14. Create a diagram similar to Figure 9.11 for a write request.

15. How does track buffering, also called "disk caching," reduce the number of physical disk accesses?

16. Disk buffering can cause problems when files on disk are shared by processes. What are those problems?

PROGRAMMING ASSIGNMENTS

1. It is probably not possible for you to write an I/O driver for your system; however, you can simulate one. For this program you will create an I/O driver using input provided by the system from the "read(input,character)" procedure.

   The I/O driver is the program that controls a device by sending commands to it, reading status from it and, transferring data from and to it. The driver you will develop is for the terminal. To make the assignment more interesting, we will assume that the system has ten terminals and that the driver must be able to communicate with all of them concurrently. To do this, it must be able to recognize interrupts from each terminal. To simulate interrupts from multiple terminals, your driver will look for the characters "$n," where n is 0, 1, . . . , 9, and when it finds these characters in the input stream it will assume that the characters that follow are from terminal number n.

   The actual terminal drivers on the systems you will use will most likely handle some characters in a special manner and not pass them on to the calling procedure. Characters such as "return" and "delete" fall into this group. To enable your driver to experience the joy of a completion interrupt and other fun things, we will redefine some standard keys to have special meaning:

#	Delete previous character, no effect if buffer empty
&	Delete all characters, no effects if buffer empty
!	Carriage return
$	Interrupt request

   The driver will store normal characters from each of the terminals into a buffer in the PCB of the calling process.

   To test the operation of your driver, it is necessary that the driver be called by a process. When your system is started, the initialization routine will create a "logon" process for each terminal. The purpose of the logon process is to accept a request for logon from the terminal and, if the logon is successful, allow the user to access system programs.

The logon process looks for the command "logon name" in the input line. If it finds this command it will create a process control block for the new user and transfer control to the command processor routine with the newly created PCB as the active process. If any message other than a valid logon request is received, it is ignored, an error message is sent to the terminal, and a request for a logon is sent to the terminal.

The command processor requests a read from the terminal driver. When a line is returned in the buffer from the driver, the command processor checks to see whether the command is valid; if it is, control is transferred to the appropriate routine. If it is not, an error message is sent to the terminal and a new command is requested. On this simple system, there are not too many operations the user can perform. The following are all the commands that are supported:

list   List all users currently logged on.

send   Send a one-line message to an active user.

read   Get the first message in the mail queue.

logoff   Terminate the user process.

Since your driver must communicate with ten terminals, it needs a table to keep track of which process is requesting input from which terminal. We will call this the interrupt table. The table is an array of pointers to the process control blocks for the process that called for input from each of the terminals. Upon start-up, the table will be filled with pointers to the logon processes. When the driver receives a line termination (!) from the terminal, it returns control to the calling process and that process can read the input line from the buffer. The calling program will take whatever actions are necessary to process the data in the input buffer.

To make it easier to see what is happening in the system, every time there is an interrupt from a terminal ($n) the driver will display the last line sent to the terminal and the contents of the input buffer so that you can see where you are in the current input line.

An input stream will be supplied for you to run on your multiuser system. To show that your program is operating correctly, a special interrupt ($$) will request the dump of the input and output buffers to the line printer. The name of each user who has requested terminal I/O will also be listed.

2. To determine the effect of different disk scheduling methods on performance, write a simulation that tests the four disk scheduling policies FCFS, SSTF, modified SSTF, and circular scan. Create a stream of 2000 track requests uniformly distributed between 1 and 400 that can be used as input by the four schedulers. Start the simulation with 20 requests pending and add a new request whenever one is satisfied.

For each policy, calculate:

Total track movement

Average track movement

Average wait time

Maximum wait time

For this assignment, wait time means the number of requests that are satisfied while a request is waiting for service. Discuss the results of your simulation.

Variation 1: Assume that the probability density function p_{track}, or the probability that a given track will be requested, is given by the equation

$$P_{track} = \begin{cases} k \times \text{track} & \text{for } 1 \le \text{track} \le 200 \\ k \times (401 - \text{track}) & \text{for } 201 \le \text{track} \le 400 \end{cases}$$

where

$$k = \frac{1}{40{,}200}$$

rather than being uniform. Calculate the statistics described above. Discuss the results of your simulation.

Variation 2: In all the previous examples we assumed that the time required to move the disk head was directly proportional to the distance moved. This is definitely not the case for real devices. The velocity of a disk head is more closely approximated by:

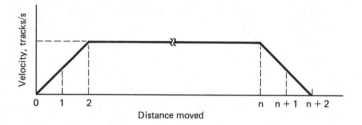

This diagram shows that the head must move some distance (for this example, 2 tracks) before it reaches maximum velocity. It also takes a similar distance to stop.

Use this data on disk head movement and recalculate the statistics described above. Note that in this case average and maximum wait times can be calculated in seconds.

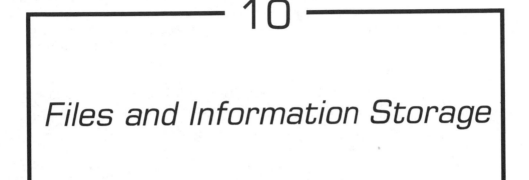

10

Files and Information Storage

There have been many important changes in computers since they first entered the general marketplace. Some of these changes have taken place relatively unnoticed. Some have drastically changed the manner in which we use computers: the ease of using them, and the applications in which we use them. One example of the second case is computer information storage.

On some early systems, card decks were the only means of storage outside main memory. To run a COBOL program, for example, one had to load the card reader with the compiler binary deck. The compiler would then read the COBOL source deck from the reader and would then generate a punched object deck, with any messages going to the console typewriter. One then loaded the reader with the object deck, library routines, and data and then ran the program. Output was normally punched on cards, which were later listed on an off-line device.

The rapid changes in both hardware and software related to files and information storage have had a dramatic effect. We progressed from cards to magnetic tapes, and then to disks and drums. System routines were stored on these devices, and intermediate results such as object code could be passed between them directly rather than on cards. Users could much more conveniently create, modify, and store their programs and data: they could run programs from remote locations; and they could easily save program output for later analysis or for input to other programs.

We continue to see these advances. Optical disks can potentially store billions of bytes of data on line. For about 29 cents you can have a floppy disk the size and weight of a greeting card, and on it you can easily store the same information that used to require thousands of cards. Data-base designers have developed update and query languages close to human (natural) languages, making it almost possible to tell the system in English what to put into a file or what to retrieve from it.

At the heart of this whole scenario is the file. In this chapter we will discuss files, with particular emphasis on how the OS maintains and accesses them. We will keep the discussion generic, so that it does not become burdened with details of particular devices or systems. Also, we will not consider data bases, since in our view they are essentially a level above the basic file system.

The file system is responsible for allocating file space to processes, and therefore it may have to block processes if there is not sufficient space available. Figure 10.1 shows the portions of the SNAIL diagram affected by the file system.

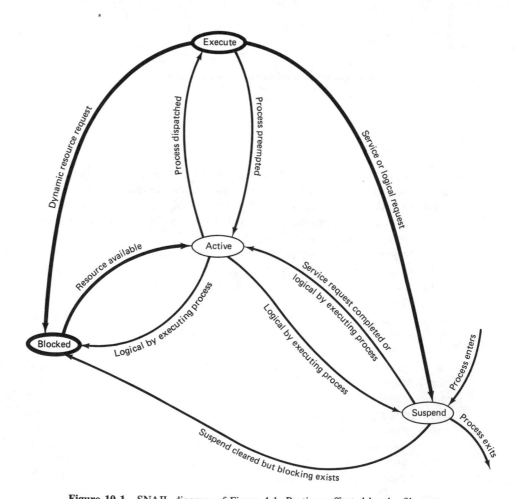

Figure 10.1 SNAIL diagram of Figure 4.1. Portions affected by the file system are drawn bold.

10.1 LOGICAL AND PHYSICAL FILES

In our discussion of memory management and I/O, we explained the idea of a mapping function. The user specifies a logical structure and the system maps it to a physical structure. We have a similar situation with files. The user specifies a logical file design and the system creates a mapping function to the physical hardware on which the file resides.

In most cases we would (ideally) like our OS to make this mapping as transparent as possible. By that we mean that the user should be able to operate strictly on the logical plane without worrying about the physical details. It should be possible to change devices—change from disk to drum, for example, or from one disk to a very different disk—without affecting the user's logical plane. As a matter of fact, it should even be possible to change processors in the same way.

Consider, for a simple counterillustration, a file system that did *not* have this transparent mapping. On one early system, a COBOL user had to give the OS the actual disk address (complete with surface, track, sector, and offset) to access a file from within the program. This system did not separate the logical and physical planes very well, and obviously any change in file structure or physical devices would directly affect the program's ability to access files.

10.2 LEVELS OF OS FILE SUPPORT

Given that the OS maps a user's logical file to some physical representation, an important question arises. At what level should this mapping be done? Should the OS provide sophisticated information management facilities with a variety of possible relationships and access techniques (which the user can then incorporate into logical designs)? Or should the OS provide only a very basic information storage facility and require the user to add any desired features? Phrased in another way, the question is one of structure. How much structure should be furnished by the OS, and how much by the user? [Shub, 1987]

Existing operating systems vary greatly in their answers to this question. Some treat every file as a sequence of bytes, and thus require the user to provide most of the structure. Others have file managers that are in essence data base managers, giving the user a variety of information structures and access techniques. Still others strive for some compromise position; files can be either byte streams or groups of records, with access to records by one of a limited set of standard techniques. Figure 10.2 illustrates the spectrum.

In this chapter we will not focus on any of the approaches individually. Instead we will discuss general aspects which are common to many files and file managers, and also present additional features which some operating systems provide.

10.3 CHARACTERISTICS OF FILES

When we think of a computer file, there are several characteristics which come to mind. Is the file a sequence of bytes, or is it structured in some way such as fields within records? What is the name of the file, and is there a descriptive qualification

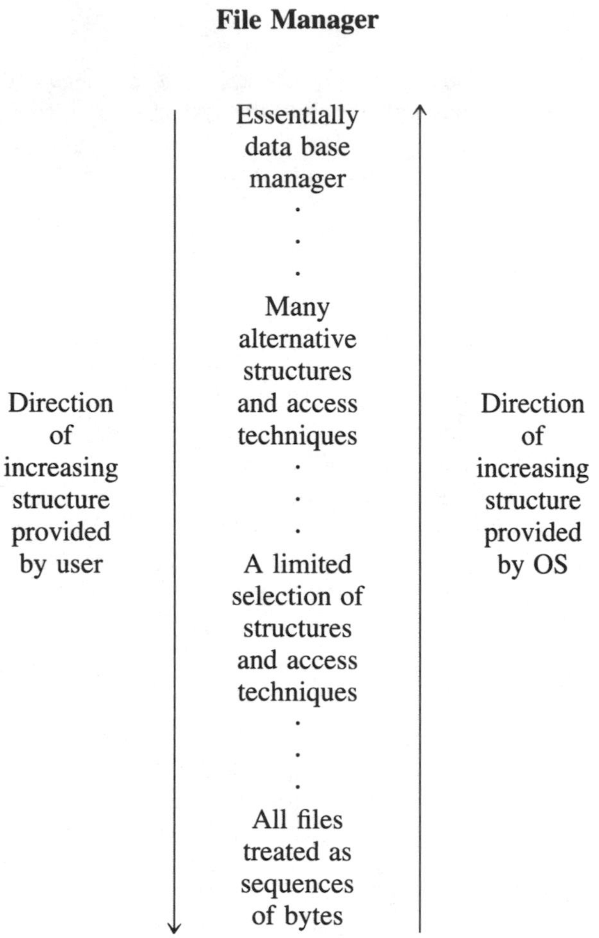

File Manager

Essentially
data base
manager
.

.

.

Many
alternative
structures
and access
techniques

.

.

.

A limited
selection of
structures
and access
techniques

.

.

.

All files
treated as
sequences
of bytes

Direction
of
increasing
structure
provided
by user

Direction
of
increasing
structure
provided
by OS

Figure 10.2 Responsibility spectrum for file structuring.

present? What other attributes does the file have? How will the file be accessed? In this section we will consider these and other characteristics [Madnick and Alsop, 1969; Curtice, 1975; Klein, 1979a; Klein, 1979b].

10.3.1 Structure

As discussed in Section 10.2, all files on a system could be just arbitrary sequences of bits or bytes [Ritchie and Thompson 1974]. Alternatively, the file manager might allow the user to specify some additional structure.

A common structure is to have a file made up of logical units called records. Designers often think of each record as corresponding to some entity in the real world, such as a person, a part, a job, and so forth. These records will be divided into fields, each field giving the value of one descriptor of the entity. Fields are normally considered the smallest unit of access in this type of file structure.

We do not want to stop with just byte sequences or records, however; there are many other common structures for computer files. We could, for instance, have document files from a word processor, structured on the basis of lines and pages. We could have program files, created with an editor, and structured as statements within procedures. As a final example, we could have files generated as output from system routines, such as a compiler, a linkage editor, and a loader; these are typically structured as words with attached information bits, such as relocatable or absolute.

10.3.2 Names

When someone mentions file names, we often think only of a restricted usage of this term. A file name can be much more than a simple character string, such as CHAPTER10, by which we reference a file. In this section we will look at a number of other aspects of file names. We begin with a summary of qualifiers, then consider local versus full names, aliases, and indirect names [Finkel, 1987].

In the following discussion, we refer to the user's "current working area." At any given point in time, the OS will allow each user to access a certain portion of the file system. You might think of it as a default specification assumed by the file manager unless the user states otherwise. We call this the current working area; another common term is the current directory.

Qualifiers are character strings appended to the basic file name to convey some important information about the file. A common syntax is to have the qualifier be three characters separated from the rest of the name by a period (such as CHAPTER10.WDS). Figure 10.3 lists a number of common file qualifiers.

On some systems these qualifiers are purely informational, and are ignored by the OS. On others, every file must have the proper qualifier, and that qualifier information is used by the OS. Finally, some systems recognize and act upon certain qualifiers, but ignore other user-generated qualifiers. (For example, .COM and .EXE are recognized, while .LLW and .JRP are ignored.)

The basic file name together with its qualifier are often called the **local name**. This terminology conveys the idea that we can use such names only for files in our current working area. Files on the same device, but in a different area, might be specified by a **path name** and the local name (such as \BOOK\CHAPTER10.WDS). Files on a different device might be specified by a device designator, path name, and local name (such as A:\BOOK\CHAPTER10.WDS). These more comprehensive file identifiers are often called **full names**.

One might understandably question our introduction of path names without further explanation. However, path names are so dependent on the given system's directory structure that we defer further discussion to Section 10.5.1, which discusses directories.

Those of you who enjoy reading detective stories are probably quite familiar with "aka," or "also known as." This term means that a person is known by another name, an alias. Aliases can also be important in file systems. They allow users to reference the same physical file by different logical names.

For example, suppose that Larry and Jim both want to work on a file called INDEX.WDS. Assume that Larry creates the file, stores it in his current working

DAT   A data file.

FTN ⎫
CBL ⎪   Indicate source code file and specify the language; user can just say
PAS ⎬   COMPGO for "compile and execute," and the system can select the
ASM ⎭   appropriate compiler.

SRC   Indicates source code file; user must specify the language, such as
          PASCALGO.

OBJ   Object code from a compiler.

LNK ⎫
REL ⎬   Output of linkage editor, sometimes designated RELocatable or
BIN ⎭   BINary.

ABS ⎫
COR ⎪   Absolute code, also sometimes called CORe image. Usually re-
COM ⎬   stricted to system routines, since they have to be placed in specific
EXE ⎭   memory areas.

BIN   A different use of BIN, specifying that some data area had been
          dumped to disk in core image, without formats; compact to store
          but difficult to interpret in case of errors.

BAK   Backup of file. Some systems create backups automatically; some
          require the user to make them if wanted.

WDS ⎫
WDP ⎬   Designations of the editor used on a file; sometimes unnecessary
PCW ⎭   because the editor just creates standard character records, some-
          times necessary because the editor uses embedded control charac-
          ters.

PIC   Graphics image.

Figure 10.3   Common file qualifiers.

area, and gives Jim permission to access it. Jim might have to use a long path name to reference this file, since it is in Larry's area. With aliases, Jim can create his own local name for the file, and reference it as though it were a file in his current working area. A sample command might be something like

> AKA \COMPUTER SCIENCE\FACULTY\LARRY\INDEX.WDS, MYINDEX

which allows Jim to use MYINDEX as his local name for the file.

Even a single user can take advantage of aliases. Suppose Jim has large files in several different accounts, and needs to work on all of them. He can enter one working area, create aliases for the files in other areas, and reference them all with just local names.

Aliases do not create additional copies of the file, just additional pointers to one copy. The OS must therefore exercise care in doing file operations (such as DELETE) which could seriously impact other users of the file (see question 12).

Some systems allow another type of file name, similar in certain ways to an alias. It is called an **indirect file name**, and is analogous to indirect addressing in hardware. A user created a file, say NEWNAME.IND, whose only contents is the name of another file. References to NEWNAME.IND are then actually references to the file name that it contains. Question 13 at the end of the chapter asks you to consider differences between aliases and indirect file names.

10.3.3 Other Information

In addition to a name, most operating systems will also keep a variety of other information about a file. These items of information are often called **attributes**; they are usually grouped together into a standard-format descriptor or header associated with every file in the system. This descriptor might be a part of the file itself, or it might be stored as a completely separate entity.

In Figure 10.4 we have listed and briefly described some common file attributes. Some of them have already been introduced or discussed, and some should be obvious. The remainder are discussed in detail later in this chapter. We apologize for the forward references, but it seemed most logical to place the general section on attributes and descriptors here rather than at the end of the chapter.

Systems will not necessarily keep all of these attributes. On the other hand, some might keep even more. Even with a fairly small subset of these attributes, the descriptor could get quite large. Because of this, the OS will probably keep the descriptor with the file itself, not in the directory area. Going through all of this data when trying to locate a file would involve too much overhead, and it is not necessary. Once the OS has located the descriptor, that descriptor can be copied into main memory for subsequent references.

10.3.4 Organization

Sometimes you will see the terms structure and organization used in a way that's just the reverse of our definitions, and sometimes you will see them combined into one attribute. We think it is important to keep the two separate, and we have tried to select the more common usage. Earlier in the chapter we considered structure; now we will look at organization and show you how it is an associated but separate notion.

Structure has to do with how the basic file elements are logically defined, how the basic elements are grouped into other elements, and so on up to the file level. Two of our examples were (1) fields, which formed records, which in turn formed the file; and (2) characters, which formed lines, which in turn formed pages, which in turn formed the file.

Name	Name assigned by user
Identifier	(Could be different from the name in that other qualifiers are added to define a unique, global identifier)
Structure	(For example, lines in pages; machine words with tags)
Type	Whether binary or ASCII
Organization	Whether sequential, random, or other (see Section 10.3.4)
Length of file element	Number of bytes or words in a file element, such as a record
Key field	Field on which sequencing or retrieval is done; usually given as starting location and length
Current file size	Number of elements (such as records) currently in file
Maximum file size	Maximum number of elements allowed in file
Device	Where file is stored
Physical location	Starting location of file on device
Access control	Who can do what
Password(s)	(Used in conjunction with or instead of access control)
Creation time	Time at which file name was first entered into system
Temporary or permanent status	Whether file should be saved after current process is completed, or automatically deleted
Deletion time, if permanent	(Sometimes convenient to have system automatically delete the file at some later time)
Creator	System id of file's creator
Owner	System id of owner, usually the same as the creator although not always (as an example, some data bases make the system the owner)
Last access	Last access of any type
Last modification	(Sometimes need last modification rather than last access; for example, to decide whether recompilation is necessary)
Mode in which file can be opened	(Such as read only)
Exclusive or shared access	Whether file can be opened by more than one process at a time
Number of opens	If shared access, number of processes which currently have this file open
Aliases	Other names for this file

Figure 10.4 Common file attributes.

Organization, on the other hand, refers to the logical level at which the file will be accessed, and the logical manner in which access will be accomplished. In the above examples, we might say that logical access is at the record "level" in the first case and at the line "level" in the second case. Two standard access methods which would be applied to the records or the lines are sequential access and direct (also called random) access [Buchholz, 1963; Cardenas, 1973; Severance and Duhne, 1976].

Sequential access, as the name implies, means that the records are ordered in some manner and we are going to access them in that order, one after another. (Note that the order could, in the simplest case, just be the chronological order in which they were added to the file.) To access record m, we must first go through all the records from 1 to $m - 1$. To next access record $m + n$, we must access $m + 1$ through $m + n - 1$ first. Finally, if we now want to access record $k < m + n$, we must either backspace to k or, more commonly, start the file over again at the beginning (rewind it) and access records 1 through $k - 1$.

Because of their physical structure, some devices (such as magnetic tape) almost mandate the use of sequential files. Sequential files can, however, also be used on direct-access devices such as disks and drums.

A typical example of sequential file processing would be an application in which the data is always processed in a linear order. Consider a payroll system with two sequential input files and one sequential output file. Both input files are ordered on social security number; one is the master employee file, giving information such as pay rate, and the other is the current time card file, giving information such as regular and overtime hours worked. The output file will also be sequential and ordered on social security number. It will contain all of the information necessary to print the checks and check stubs, and to update accounts such as "income taxes withheld."

The key point of this application is, of course, that in its normal flow the process takes records sequentially from both input files and writes records sequentially to the output file. There is no jumping back and forth among records.

There are many applications of sequential files. We have looked at one typical example. A few others are as follows:

Mailings, where labels are generated from sequential address lists

Inputs to a compiler or an assembler

Transaction files in chronological order

Log files, such as logons, logoffs, and files used

History files of many different kinds

Sometimes our application does not lend itself to processing records sequentially. The other standard access method is called **direct access**. Again the name is very descriptive; we can go *directly* to any record in the file without accessing previous records. We can go backwards from our current position without rewinding. The other name for this method, random access, conveys the idea that access will occur in a random order, rather than sequentially.

Earlier we mentioned that magnetic tapes imply sequential files. We should point out here that disks are inherently direct-access devices and hence make implementation of direct access a simple matter.

You can probably think of many instances in which direct access would be convenient. As a simple initial example, consider a shop which manufactures custom-designed pieces of equipment. One of the owners is a computer science student who has designed a tracking system in which part of the customer's order number is also the record number for the order in a direct-access computer file. When a customer calls to inquire about the status of an order, a clerk types in the order number; the system extracts the record number and accesses the customer's record, giving the status of the order. The order number is also on a tag attached to the equipment. As each station in the plant completes its phase of the manufacturing process, that tag is used to update the record. This makes all information up to date.

The key point of this application is that customer inquiries will normally not occur in any regular order. The company would not want the customer waiting for long periods while the system had to scan a large file sequentially.

It is important at this stage to clarify one aspect of direct access. When thinking of examples for this method, you might suggest something such as "Type in Jim's social security number and retrieve his personnel record." Be careful, however. Even at the logical level, we must come up with a *record number*. Direct access does not mean that we can give the system a field value and expect it to go directly to the record with that field value.

If we want to use direct access with a field value, then we normally need to incorporate some form of mapping. In our example, the designer set up an order number in which part of that identifier specified a unique record number in the file. For the social security number suggestion, we might set up a table which gives the record number for each employee's social security number, and use some fast search technique for the look-up. Alternatively, our system might provide some other organization more suitable for our application. We will discuss some other types later in this section.

As with sequential files, there are many applications for direct-access files. The following are two common ones:

Files for routines where record numbers can correspond to some system quantity, like line numbers in a text file

Files where links or chains are used and record number can be similar to a pointer value in a programming language

Before moving on to other methods of organization, we would like to bring up two additional aspects you should keep in mind when considering sequential versus direct organization. First, in some systems, changing a sequential file is difficult. To change file A, one might typically go through the entire file, performing the modifications and writing out the results to a new file, A'. (Unchanged records must also be copied from A to A'.) After this operation is completed, the original file A becomes a backup, and file A' becomes the correct version of file A. The second aspect to consider is that systems often allow sequential files to have variable-length records. (For example, the length of a student's file could depend on the number of classes taken.) Since direct access requires a mapping function, it is usual to require direct-access files to have fixed-length records. Otherwise, to access record n, the mapping function would have to go through every record from 1 to $n - 1$, incorporating the lengths of all those records into its computation. As we implied above, some applications do not fit nicely into sequential or direct-access systems. This encouraged designers to come up with other methods of organization.

Probably the most common alternative type of organization performs the operation we wanted to do in the social security number example—that is, to go directly to a record, but to do it on the basis of a key value rather than a record number. This type of organization is typically called ISAM or KSAM, for **indexed** (or keyed) **sequential access mechanism** [Ghosh and Senko, 1969; IBM, 1974; Klein, 1979b]. The "sequential" is added in the name because most such systems allow us to proceed sequentially through the file once we have located the key value we want.

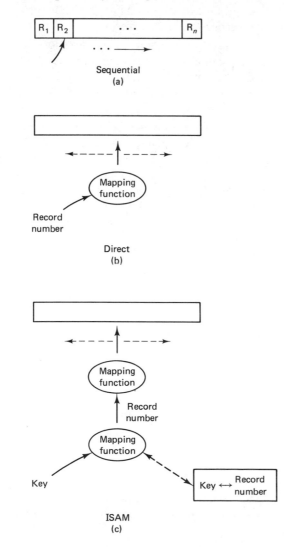

Figure 10.5 File access methods. (a) Sequential. (b) Direct. (c) ISAM access.

ISAM or KSAM files are usually implemented as two files. One contains the key values and the pointers into the other file, which is the actual data. Usually the first file is set up to facilitate fast searching for a desired key.

We have summarized sequential, direct, and ISAM access in Figure 10.5. Note the mapping functions for direct and ISAM methods, and the fact that ISAM uses direct access.

There are many other possible methods of file organization, but those we have discussed are by far the most prevalent. There are three others whose names you might have heard:

Inverted	Sometimes used to imply an ISAM type of organization, but with multiple keys; also used for files with pointers to groups of records based on some field value. For example, student records might be inverted on age, class, major, and home state; hence, we could make requests like "all freshmen."
Multilist	Term sometimes used for methods of organization similar to inverted; however, can also imply a more complex link system to facilitate the determination of intersections, such as "all 19-year-old freshman computer science majors from California."
Tree	Typically implies a structure in which nodes at a given level contain information common to nodes below. For instance, the top level in a student file might give permanent information, such as high school; one of the second levels could give classes taken; a third level under this might list homework, program, and test grades. The advantage is that information in "parent" nodes need not be repeated, but is available at retrieval.

10.4 WORKING WITH FILES

In this section we will look at the various operations which can be done on files. We will then consider the file control block (FCB), a structure attached to a process's PCB to facilitate such operations.

Before going on to the operations themselves, we should raise the crucial question, "Which processes can do which operations on a given file?" This is the file security aspect of our system. We believe that computer security (including file security) is of paramount importance. However, the discussion of security seemed more appropriately treated as a cohesive unit (Chapter 14), rather than as sections in various chapters. Therefore, you should be cognizant of file security, but we will postpone its study for awhile.

10.4.1 Operations

Having specified the structure and organization of a file, our next step is to specify file operations. Although the list in Figure 10.6 is not exhaustive, it contains most of the standard file operations.

create	Sets up the file descriptor and makes the name "known" to the operating system; in some versions this command also allocates all or part of the specified file space.
open	Readies a file for performing operations; usually involves, among other things, copying the descriptor into main memory.
write	Writes a new record into the file at an arbitrary spot.
append	Writes a new record into the file, but adds it at the end of the current file.
read	Reads a record
modify	Writes a new version of a record over the top of the existing one.
copy	Makes a copy of a record or file (original still exists).
move	Moves a record or file (original no longer exists).
delete (erase)	Deletes a record or file.
close	When operations on file are complete, writes out any remaining buffers, updates descriptor and writes it out, etc.
rename	Changes file name.
rewind	Moves current record pointer back to first record in file.
post (flush)	Moves information from system buffer areas to the file.
backspace	Moves one record backward from current position.

Figure 10.6   Common file operations.

The parameters for the commands in Figure 10.6 will vary with the system being used and the organization of the file. On some systems the create command preallocates the space for the entire file, whereas on others that space is allocated dynamically. A read command might have just the file name (for sequential organization), the file name and a record number (for direct-access organization), or the file name and a kcy value (for indexed sequential organization).

One category of file operations—backup and recovery—is not included in Figure 10.4. We discuss them separately here for two reasons: (1) because they are so important, and (2) because they are usually invoked by a periodically-executed OS process or by the computer operator, rather than by standard user commands to the file manager.

Most of us have probably learned the importance of file backups through one or more disastrous experiences. Seeing countless hours of work disappear with the blink of a cursor can leave an indelible mark on one's memory. Many data processing centers use a combination of backup procedures. A **full dump**, as its name implies, means that all of the files on the system are copied. For most installations, this is a very lengthy job, and hence it is usually done infrequently. Between full dumps, the centers typically will do partial (also called incremental) dumps. Such **partial dumps** copy only those files which have changed since the last dump.

As an added safety measure, the center can keep several "generations" of dumps. You might hear these referred to as the great–grandparent, grandparent, and parent of the current file system. Often one or more of these previous generations are kept at a separate location.

Some systems also automatically keep individual file backups within the user's account. Each time a file is changed, the previous version is saved in a corresponding file wtih a BAK qualifier or a time stamp. A few systems even keep several generations of earlier versions, in files with qualifiers such as BAK1, BAK2, and so on.

Of course, a user can always do his or her own supplemental backups. With the low price of storage media such as floppy disks, the cost/benefit ratio is especially attractive.

10.4.2 File Control Block (FCB)

Earlier, we discussed the file descriptor. It contains various attributes of a file and is stored with that file. Whenever a process is using a file, there is a variant of that file descriptor kept in main memory by the OS. This is usually called the **file control block**, or FCB for short.

The FCB is used by the file access routines. It contains most or all of the information in the file descriptor, plus some additional information relating to the current use. In Figure 10.7 we have listed some of the fields which might be kept in an FCB. The first 20 are attributes from the file descriptor and are described in Figure 10.4.

The FCB is usually created when a process issues a "file open" command. The sequence of events might be as follows for the command File_Mgr (open,,,device: filename,fcb_ptr,access_type,disposition,,,,error_status,status)(see Figure 10.8):

Name	Current mode	Type of access for *this* process
Identifier	Current shared	Whether sharing is allowed
Structure	status	during *this* access
Type	Current wait status	If shared access and another
Organization		process is accessing, whether this
Length of record		request should wait or return with
Key field		an appropriate indication
Current file size	Logical unit	Logical unit number used by
Maximum file size		process to reference this file
Device	Current position,	Logical reference to current
Physical location — See Figure 10.4	logical	element
Access control	Element number of	
Password(s)	current element	
Creation time	Current position,	Physical address of current
Temporary or permanent	physical	element
status	Next position,	Physical address of next element
Deletion time, if	physical	
permanent	Buffer size	
Creator	Buffer area	The actual buffer area, with size
Owner		specified by previous field
Last access		
Last modification	Pointer to next	
	FCB	

Figure 10.7 File control block (FCB) information.

1. User process requests file open
2. File manager reads directory information
3. Return status if errors occur
4. Generate new FCB
5. Set information into FCB
6. Update directory information
7. Attach FCB to PCB
8. Return status to user process

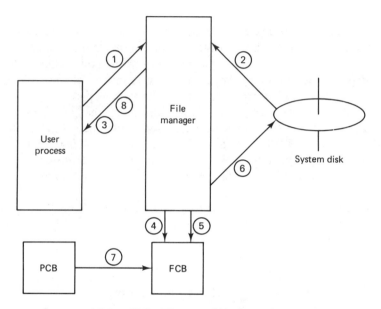

Figure 10.8   File control block creation.

All FCBs for a given process are linked via an FCB pointer in the process control block. Since FCBs often have relatively large data buffers, many systems limit the number of files a process can have open at any one time [Microsoft, 1983].

10.5 LOCATING AND STORING FILES

In this section we describe alternative approaches to the location and storage of files on physical devices. This description includes directories, the management of storage on the device, and the allocation of available storage to files.

10.5.1 Directories

We have already discussed the idea that the OS maps a user's logical file to a system's physical file. Part of this mapping will involve finding the start of that physical file, given the user's logical file name. The data structure used in this operation is the **file directory**, also sometimes called a catalog or table of contents [Klein, 1979a; Hanson, 1980].

Our initial idea for elements in such a directory would probably be simple pairs of items:

logical file name   location of physical file

How should we structure these elements?

A first approach might be a linear list of the paired names and starting points. This method is usually employed only for very small directories, since search time for larger directories structured this way is prohibitive. A common way to decrease search time for those larger directories structured this way is to use hashing [Knuth, 1973]. Even then, one would anticipate a large space requirement to make the hashing efficient and to allow for the anticipated maximum number of files.

The source of difficulty in the previous method is that all files are lumped together into one directory. We could mitigate that problem by having levels in the directory, and thus having more but smaller search spaces.

As a simple example of the impact of this change, suppose that our company has 10 divisions, each division has 20 teams of 5 people, and each person typically saves 50 files. With one large directory, that's 50,000 files! An average search would require examining 25,000 directory entries. If instead we structured our directory in levels corresponding to levels in the company, our search spaces would be

find division	directory of 10 entries
find team in that division	directory of 20 entries
find person in that team	directory of 5 entries
find file for that person	directory of 50 entries

We now have four searches, but at most 50 items in any one of those searches. The average search time for this case would be around 43; this is almost a 600:1 decrease from the previous technique.

The fully qualified file name for this directory structure could then be something like "file.person.team.division." Our directory data elements will have to be modified slightly to accommodate these multiple levels. At the higher levels, the search item would be the name for this level and a pointer to the next level directory, such as:

ACCOUNTING   directory for the accounting division

At the last level, the pointer would be as before—the location of the file:

YTD_SALES   location of YTD_SALES file

This type of directory scheme is often used; typical levels are file, user, group, and account. A sample file reference might be DATA1.JIM.TEACHER.CSCI152; a possible directory structure corresponding to this reference is shown graphically in Figure 10.9.

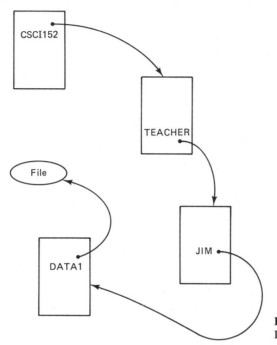

Figure 10.9 Directory structure for DATA1.JIM.TEACHER.CSCI152.

After reading the above description, you might ask why the levels are predefined. Good question! The multilevel directory is actually a tree structure with some restrictions imposed. To expand to a fully general tree directory, we add one bit to our data element. This bit indicates whether the pointer goes to another directory, or to the actual file. Our previous example is redone in Figure 10.10.

With this structure, the user can put in as many levels as desired. The system simply scans directories until it finds an element whose type descriptor indicates that the pointer goes to the target file. Trees are popular directory structures; UNIX, for example, uses a variation of the basic technique described above [Ritchie and Thompson, 1974].

Having looked at the main directory structure, let's make a few observations:

Using a directory element as described makes sharing easy: two or more pointers can go to the same file.

To relieve the user from constantly qualifying file names, we could create a "current" directory and assume that all references are to it, unless otherwise indicated. The specification of this current directory could be extracted from the last qualified reference, or set by a special command (such as CD in UNIX and MS-DOS) [Ritchie and Thompson, 1974; Microsoft, 1983].

Using the idea of a current directory, we could have commands to go up one directory level, go down one, or reset to the highest level.

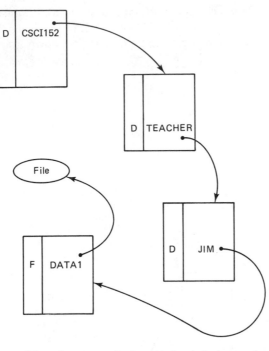

Figure 10.10 Tree directory structure for DATA1.JIM.TEACHER.CSCI152.

To reduce search time and minimize main memory required, it's probably reasonable to keep higher levels of the directory in main memory, and lower levels on the device, along with the files.

We have not specified organization of the directories themselves—the system could use hashing, binary trees, or other techniques.

10.5.2 Storage Management

We have looked at how to find a file once it has been stored. Now we will look at how the file contents themselves are stored. In this section we will consider methods for managing available space, and in the next section, methods for allocating available space for file storage.

First we will establish some constraints. In most current systems the storage media for files are disks or devices that are accessed as disks (such as bulk memory disk emulators). For this reason we will limit our discussion to such devices. Furthermore, most disk systems have a fixed-size unit of allocation, called a **block,** whose size depends primarily on the storage and transfer characteristics of the hardware. We will not consider the use of variable-size blocks.

Given these specifications, our scenario is set. We have a direct-access device which has a fixed number of fixed-size storage blocks. At any time, some of these blocks will be in use and some might be available. We must decide how to

Keep track of which blocks are free and which are available.

Select available blocks to use for a new file.

Maintain a data structure to map the logical file to those newly assigned physical blocks.

Furthermore, note that all of our storage management information must itself be stored in available blocks.

There are many techniques for managing available space on disk. In the remainder of this section we will describe three of the most common: bit maps, linked lists, and index blocks.

A **bit map**, as the name implies, uses a sequence of bits to map out which blocks of disk are free and which blocks are in use. For example, the string 0011101011 could indicate that blocks 0, 1, 5, and 7 are in use while 2,3,4,6,8, and 9 are available. To illustrate numbers you might see in practice, suppose we have a 33.55M-byte disk set up as 65,536 blocks with 512 bytes per block. If we associate one bit with each block, we obviously need 65,536 bits to *map* those blocks. This would require 16 blocks with 4096 bits per block.

Bit maps have an important advantage when one wants to allocate n *adjacent* blocks of disk, rather than n arbitrary blocks. If such a space exists, it will be indicated in the bit map by a sequence of n adjacent "available" bits.

Bit maps could have potential overhead problems as the disk becomes full. The more blocks in use, the more "unavailable" bits we have to scan to find n available blocks. Furthermore, after operating for a while with a nearly full disk, one would expect the blocks of any given file to be scattered over several bit map blocks. This means that deallocation and subsequent allocation could require a significant number of reads and writes of those bit map blocks.

Often in operating systems we use linked lists to keep track of resources, and another method for space management would be to link available disk blocks in a chain. However, to allocate n blocks we would need to do n disk reads to follow the chain. That could cause considerable overhead, especially since we are just allocating the blocks and not doing any useful operations on their contents.

This problem could be partially alleviated if we linked *groups* of blocks rather than individual blocks. The pointer would specify the first block in a sequence of j adjacent available blocks. That first block would contain "j" (the size of the block) and a pointer to the next group. Of course, the improvement in this method is only significant if blocks are normally allocated and deallocated in adjacent groups rather than individual random units.

An alternative idea using lists would be to link together blocks of pointers, rather than the free blocks themselves. Using our previously described disk as an example, we could address any block with two bytes. Hence a block could contain 256 of these 2-byte pointers. The first 255 entries could be pointers to available blocks; the 256th could be a pointer to the next block of pointers. This is a popular method of storage management. The blocks of pointers are known as **index blocks**, and hence the method itself is known as the index block method.

One problem with this method is that keeping track of continuous areas of free space is difficult. Also, at least one of the index blocks will normally be only partially full; hence we need some method to indicate which pointer fields are actual pointers and which are unused.

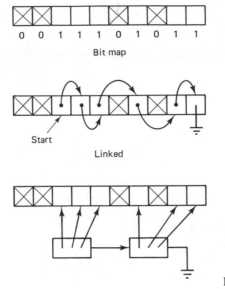

0   0   1   1   1   0   1   0   1   1

Bit map

Start

Linked

Index blocks

Figure 10.11 Managing available space on disk.

We have illustrated the three methods in Figure 10.11. The shaded areas indicate areas in use, and the blanks, areas that are not in use.

10.5.3 Allocating Space to Files

Having discussed storage management, we turn now to techniques for allocating some of the current free space to a new file. There are (again) three common techniques: contiguous allocation, linked allocation, and indexed allocation.

Contiguous allocation means that all of the blocks a file requires are allocated as one contiguous sequence of adjacent available blocks. If the file requires j blocks, then the allocation procedure selects some group of $m = k + j$ adjacent blocks from the free block pool. If $k > 0$, then the k "extra" blocks are returned to the pool. This should remind you of the movable-boundary, variable-size region approach to contiguous memory allocation. To review problems associated with contiguous allocation, it might be helpful to reread Section 7.3.2 at this time.

As with memory management, we can use first fit, best fit, or worst fit to select a sequence from the free block pool. Also, if the disk becomes too fragmented, we can *burp, crunch,* or *pack* it to bring together free blocks.

With contiguous allocation, we have a potential problem of file growth. If the file exceeds its initial allocation and additional adjacent blocks are not available, then in most systems the file must be moved. In some file managers a certain percentage overallocation is automatically built in to allow limited expansion without moving. Also, some systems allow tacking on nonadjacent blocks to a contiguous file. These are called **extents**; they normally involve considerable overhead in directory and random-access operations.

You might ask why growth is such a problem—shouldn't we know pretty well ahead of time how big a data file is going to be? Perhaps, but sometimes data files grow larger than expected, and also remember that we are not always dealing with "data files" in the strict sense of "data." Haven't you seen instances in which version 5 of one of your programming assignments was much bigger than version 1, and much bigger than you thought it would be? Contiguous allocation does have an important strength: there is minimal look-up no matter what access method is used. To perform sequential access, you just go through the blocks one after another. To do direct or indexed access, you can just compute an offset from the starting block.

For the next two allocation techniques, recall our discussion of free-space management. We looked first at linking blocks themselves, and then at linking index blocks. Allocation techniques can be viewed the same way.

To use **linked allocation**, we simply chain together a list of blocks as long as we need for the file. Later growth is no problem, since we can just link in additional blocks to the end of the file. This technique, though simple, does not work well for methods other than sequential access. We have no way to determine the location of block m other than scanning blocks 1 through $m - 1$. Linked allocation was used on early mainframes and is still used on some current minicomputer and microcomputer systems, where disk size is not large.

As an alternative, we turn to index blocks. With free-space allocation, we used the first $n - 1$ block addresses for free blocks and the last as a pointer to the next index block. We probably do not want to use exactly the same technique for allocation, however. For later records in larger files the access time would be prohibitive—we would have to scan too many linked index blocks.

To alleviate this problem we turn to a tree structure for the index blocks. There are many versions of such a structure; we will present a general idea from which you can develop particular variations. In order to show concrete examples we will go back to our 33.55M-byte disk description.

If an index block can reference d data blocks of b bytes each and our file is less than or equal to db bytes in size, then we use just the one index block. This is shown in Figure 10.12. For our example, blocks are 512 bytes and can store 256 pointers. Hence db would be $256 \times 512 = 131,072$ bytes.

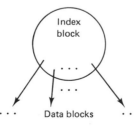

Figure 10.12   Single index block.

If the file is (or grows) larger than db bytes, then we add a second-level index block. This block points to d first-level index blocks, which in turn point to d file blocks. Hence we can access d^2b bytes ($256 \times 256 \times 512 = 33,554,432$ in our example). This two-level structure is shown in Figure 10.13. Normally one does not go beyond three levels of indexes. That would access d^3b bytes, which is 8,589,934,592 for our example. Figure 10.14 shows our final three-level index structure.

Note that the mapping is not difficult. We simply take the offset from the start of the file and break it into components. These components tell us which index to follow at each level.

As we mentioned, there are many variations of this technique. We cannot discuss all of them, but one in particular should be noted. We can reduce average

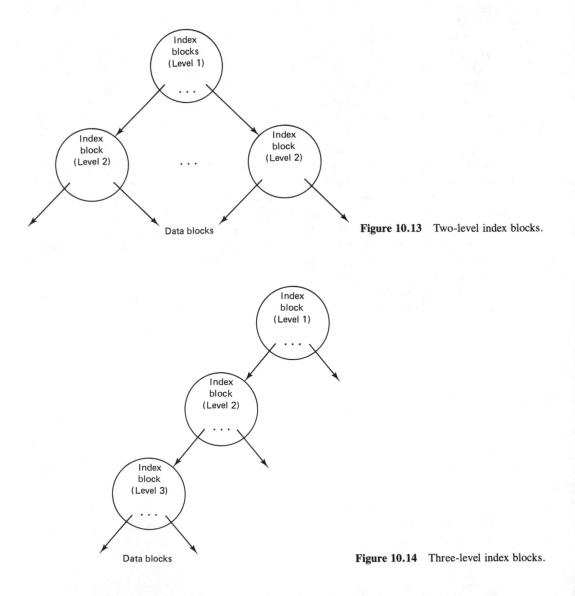

Figure 10.13 Two-level index blocks.

Figure 10.14 Three-level index blocks.

search time by using nodes for both file pointers and directory pointers. If the reference is in a portion of the file indexed by the node itself, we need not go through other levels. UNIX uses such an approach in its file system [Ritchie and Thompson, 1974].

10.6 A SAMPLE FILE MANAGER

In this section we will look at the pseudocode for a simple file manager. In order to convey major concepts without complicating details, we will make a major assumption—the directories for our file devices are kept entirely in main memory. This will avoid the necessity of file reads during directory searches.

There is an associated assumption which is minor in itself, but which can simplify other parts of our OS. Normally, the directory entry for a program file keeps information about the file, but not the program per se. We will assume that the directory in our example includes fields for the program size (as distinct from the file size) and the starting execution address. Since our directories are in main memory, we can thus obtain these two quantities without initiating a disk read.

The pseudocode for our file manager is shown in Figures 10.15 through 10.24. In actual code, sections which access the directory would be going through a monitor; otherwise it would be possible, for example, to have more than one process gain write access to a file. For simplicity we have not shown such monitor calls explicitly.

The "check" command just checks to see whether or not the file is on the device, and if so, whether it can be opened with the stated access. The "search" is similar, except that it is used for a program read and thus it also needs to see whether the file contains an executable program. Furthermore, since a program read is assumed to follow the search, an FCB is generated and attached to the FCB_list of the executing process.

After being allocated memory, a process creating an offspring uses the "prog_read" to load the code for the offspring. An FCB has already been created, and so this command simply loads in the program file. Since the parent would have to do another "search" prior to creating another offspring, the FCB is removed from the parent's list and deleted.

The "open" command first verifies that the file is in the directory and that the calling process can access it with the stated access_type. If there are no errors, then the FCB is generated and attached to the PCB of the calling process.

The "read" and "write" commands follow a similar pattern. They first check for a proper FCB and then see whether data transfers can be done with the buffer already in memory, or whether a transfer between the buffer and the device is required. If the device must be accessed, they call the IOCS.

The last two commands, "close" and "delete," are straightforward. The only thing that might be pointed out is the necessity of writing any modified data in the memory buffer to the device if the file is to be permanent and the data has not yet been written.

```
procedure FILE_MGR(command,buffer,length,device:filename,
                   fcb_ptr,access_type,disposition,file_size,
                   prog_size,start_address,user_error,status)

{ This is the procedure responsible for managing files.  That includes
  modifying and searching the directory, opening and closing files,
  creating and deleting files and reading and writing from or to files.

  Pseudocode for operations which access the directory appears in this
  procedure, for continuity.  However, such operations are actually
  implemented using a monitor.                                          }

{  Called by            : LONG_TERM_SCHEDULER and user processes
   Procedures called    : IOCS
   Parameters passed    : command -- check, search (directory),
                                     open, read, program_read,
                                     write, close, create, delete
                        : buffer, area in user memory
                        : length, of data to be moved
                        : device:filename
                        : fcb_pointer
                        : access_type, read or write
                        : user_error, should user be notified
   Parameters returned  : file_size
                        : prog_size, for program file
                        : start_address, for program file
                        : status, result of operation
   Entry conditions     : none
   Exit conditions      : directory and disk might be changed          }

global variables
     array of directories;

begin

   case command of
      check            :  CHECK_CODE;
      open             :  OPEN_CODE;
      search           :  SEARCH_CODE;
      prog_read        :  PROG_READ_CODE;
      read             :  READ_CODE;
      write            :  WRITE_CODE;
      close            :  CLOSE_CODE;
      delete           :  DELETE_CODE;
      otherwise        :  ERROR_EXIT(invalid_command);
   end;

end;  { file manager }
```

Figure 10.15 A simple file manager.

```
procedure CHECK_CODE;

{ Check command.  Presence in directory and permission to
  access are checked.                                                  }

begin
   if filename not in device directory
     then status := not_found
     else if file cannot be opened for this process/access
            then status := cannot_be_accessed
            else status := ok;
   return;
end;
```

Figure 10.16 Code for the file manager's check command.

```
procedure OPEN_CODE;

{ Open command.  This section checks whether the file is in the
  directory and whether the calling process can access it with
  the specified access_type.  If everything is ok, then the FCB
  is generated and attached to the PCB of the calling process          }

begin
  if filename not in device directory then
    ERROR_EXIT(file_not_found};
  if file cannot be accessed by this process with this
    access_type then ERROR_EXIT(cannot_be_accessed),
  status := ok;
  generate fcb;
  set fcb_ptr;
  attach fcb to fcb_list of pcb in execute_queue;
  update directory;
  return;
end;
```

Figure 10.17   Code for file manager's open command.

```
procedure SEARCH_CODE;

{ Search command.  This section checks whether the file is in the
  directory, whether it is an executable file, and whether the calling
  process can execute it.                                               }

begin
  if filename not in device directory then
    ERROR_EXIT(file_not_found};
  if file not executable then
    ERROR_EXIT(not_program_file);
  if program cannot be executed by this process then
    ERROR_EXIT(cannot_execute_program);
  status := ok;
  generate fcb;
  set fcb_ptr;
  update directory;
  set file_size, prog_size, and start_address;
  return;
end;
```

Figure 10.18   Code for file manager's search command.

```
procedure PROG_READ_CODE;

{ Program read command.  Since an FCB has already been created,
  required checks are minimal.                                          }

begin
  if not proper fcb then ERROR_EXIT(fcb_error);
  get information from fcb;
  IOCS(position,device,,track/sector,false,status,);
  IOCS(read,device,buffer,length,false,status,);
  remove fcb from fcb_list of pcb in execute_queue;
  delete fcb;
  update directory;
  return;
end;
```

Figure 10.19   Code for file manager's program read command.

```
procedure READ_CODE;

{ Read command.  Again, we assume that most checks were done during fcb
  creation.  It is necessary to see whether requested data is already
  in the fcb buffer, or whether an actual read is required.              }

begin
  if not proper fcb then ERROR_EXIT(fcb_error);
  if data already in fcb buffer then
    begin
      move data from fcb buffer to user buffer;
      update fcb;
      return;
    end;
  get information from fcb;
  IOCS(position,device,,track/sector,user_error,status,);

{ If user_error is false and there was an error, IOCS will take
  care of termination.  Therefore, if control comes back here
  with an error, then user_error must be true.                          }

  if status <> ok then return;
  IOCS(read,device,fcb_buffer,length,user_error,status,);
  if status <> ok then return;
  move data from fcb buffer to user buffer;
  update fcb;
  return;
end;
```

Figure 10.20 Code for file manager's read command.

```
procedure WRITE_CODE;

{ Write command.  Comments are analogous to "read."                     }

begin
  if not proper fcb then ERROR_EXIT(fcb_error);
  if data will fit in fcb buffer then
    begin
      move data from user buffer to fcb buffer;
      update fcb;
      return;
    end;
  get information from fcb;
  if there is insufficient space in file then
    begin
      if there is space left on device then
        begin
          allocate block;
          update directory and fcb;
        end
      else ERROR_EXIT(no_more_space_on_device);
    end;

  IOCS(position,device,,track/sector,user_error,status,);
  if status <> ok then return;
  IOCS(write,device,fcb_buffer,length,user_error,status,);
  if status <> ok then return;
  move data from user buffer to fcb buffer;
  update fcb;
  return;
end;
```

Figure 10.21 Code for file manager's write command.

```
procedure CLOSE_CODE;

{ Close command.  A determination must be made to see whether the user
  wants to keep the file or delete it.  If it is to be kept, then any
  unwritten data in the buffer must be written out.                        }

begin
   if not proper fcb then ERROR EXIT(fcb_error);
   if disposition = scratch then
      begin
         delete directory entry;
         deallocate space on device;
         remove fcb from fcb_list of pcb in execute_queue;
         delete fcb;
         return;
      end;
   if unwritten data is still in fcb buffer then
      begin
         if there is insufficient space in file then
            begin
               if there is space left on device then
                  begin
                     allocate block;
                     update directory and fcb;
                  end
               else ERROR_EXIT(no_more_space_on_device);
            end;
         IOCS(position,device,,track/sector,user_error,status,);
         if status <> ok then return;
         IOCS(write,device,fcb_buffer,length,user_error,status,);
         if status <> ok then return;
      end;
   remove fcb from fcb_list of pcb in execute queue;
   delete fcb;
   update directory;
   end;
```

Figure 10.22   Code for file manager's close command.

```
procedure DELETE_CODE;

{ Delete command.  This command necessitates some checks, since
  there is no FCB.                                                          }

begin
   if filename not in device directory then
      ERROR_EXIT(file_not_found);
   if file cannot be deleted by this process then
      ERROR_EXIT(cannot_delete_this_file);
   delete directory entry;
   return space on device;
end;
```

Figure 10.23   Code for file manager's delete command.

```
procedure ERROR_EXIT(error);

{ Error exit for file manager. Parameter indicates cause of error.      }

begin
  if user_error then

{ User is checking for errors.  Set cause and return.                   }

    begin
      status := error;
      return;
    end
  else

{ User is not checking for errors.  Terminate process and go to
  short term scheduler.                                                 }

    begin
      execute_queue^.terminate_flag := true;
      SHORT_TERM_SCHEDULER;
    end;
end;
```

Figure 10.24   Code for file manager's error exit.

10.7 SUMMARY

Files are a crucial component of almost every computer system. In this chapter we discussed a variety of aspects of files and file management. Since most of us are familiar with manual files, we began with them and then progressed to computer files.

The description of computer files started with their structure and organization, their names, and the attributes assigned to them. We then looked at operations on files. To facilitate such operations on a file by a process, many operating systems attach an FCB to the process's PCB, and we next considered possible entries in such an FCB.

Finally, we described alternate approaches to the storage and location of files on physical devices. This description included directories, the management of storage on the device, and the allocation of available storage to files.

The introduction to Part III indicated that we would be discussing necessary extensions to the central components of an operating system. So far we have considered I/O and files, two obviously important aspects. We turn now to spooling, which is used to help balance the widely divergent costs and speeds of various system components.

There are a number of articles which give general introductions, definitions, and discussions related to files. Among these are Daley and Neumann [1965], Barron et al. [1967], Chapin [1969], and Hsiao and Harary [1970]. Three articles already cited in the text are also excellent in this regard: Madnick and Alsop [1969] and Klein [1979a, 1979b].

Books on file design, organization, and processing include Omlor [1981], Hanson [1982], Loomis [1983], and Peterson and Lew [1986]. Omlar discusses experiments in document retrieval. Loomis covers both data structures and data files.

Babad [1977] presents a general model of record and file partitioning and shows how to specialize the model for particular applications. Lum et al. [1971] is a study of eight different key-to-address transformation techniques, a summary of their performances over various conditions, and a discussion of the peculiarities of each technique. A tutorial on selecting record access paths can be found in Severance and Carlis [1977]; this article has an especially good bibliography.

Many of us have discovered through sad experience the potentially disastrous results of hardware or software failure during file processing. Barnett [1978] describes a file system especially designed to tolerate hardware and software failures.

QUESTIONS AND EXERCISES

1. Using some large manual file with which you have worked, illustrate the important terms introduced in this chapter (such as directory, record, field, descriptor, and organization).

2. Using a computer with which you are familiar, evaluate the transparency of its file mapping function.

3. Give advantages and disadvantages of having a file that is an arbitrary sequence of bytes as opposed to a structured entity.

4. Describe one situation in which a file must be opened with exclusive access, and one in which shared access is acceptable.

5. Contrast an FCB and a directory entry.

6. Suppose a process must access a sequential file for a record in a position prior to the current record position. What characteristics of the device or file mapping function might imply that it is better to rewind and reread than to backspace?

7. Describe how you would set up the mapping function to go from a field value to its corresponding record number. Where would you store necessary information permanently, and where would you store it when the file is being accessed?

8. Why would an FCB contain the physical position of the "next record"?

9. In Figure 10.9, why don't the entries need flags to indicate which pointers go to other directories and which go to target files?

10. Describe a technique to facilitate the location of contiguous free blocks in a system which uses the index block method of storage management.

11. The index block method of space allocation to files might be modified so that some of the pointers in level i index blocks went to data, and some to level $i + 1$ index blocks. Why would this be done? Illustrate a possible structure.

12. Describe a method for deleting files in a system which allows aliases.

13. Discuss several important differences between aliases and indirect file names.

PROGRAMMING ASSIGNMENT

Tree-structured directories are found in most newer operating systems. The purpose of this exercise is to create a file system and the part of a command interpreter which provides the user interface to that file system.

The file system you implement will have a hierarchical directory structure. Directories will just be ordinary files, and any directory may contain file entries for files that are themselves directories.

Disk format: The disk may be considered to be a sequence of blocks of size "blksize" (512 bytes per block on UCSD PASCAL systems) numbered from 0 to "nblk" − 1. Block 0 will contain a bit map with one bit corresponding to each of the blocks on the disk. A 1 in the bit map means that the corresponding block on disk is currently not in use. When the disk is initialized, all the bits, except the first two, are set to 1. Block 1 will contain the root directory for the disk, sometimes referred to as a volume. During initialization, the root directory is set to all null characters, and whenever a new directory is created, it is also set to all null characters.

Directory format: The directory will be filled with "ndir" directory entries. Each entry will be a record that includes the following fields:

name	9 characters
type	3 characters, type of file (directory or other)
location	integer, starting block of the file
size	integer, number of blocks in the file.

File format: Each file will contain some number of bytes followed by a CTRL-C, which signifies an end of file. Text files will contain lines of characters; each line will be followed by a carriage return. When a new file is created, an EOF character is inserted in the first position of the file.

File names: Names of directories and other files are specified by giving the entire path name followed by the file name:

```
filename :: = [path:]name
directoryname :: = [path:]name:
path   :: = name:name:..name
name   :: = 1  to 9  characters
```

To show that your file management system operates correctly, the following commands must be implemented:

L	list root directory
L filename	list text in a file
L directoryname	list directory entries
M filename,size	make a file of size number of blocks
M directoryname	make a directory file
D filename	delete the specified file
D directoryname	delete the specified directory, if it is empty
B	list the bit map
A filename	append to a text file (command is terminated by "//" in first two characters of a line)
C filename1,filename2	copy file from 1 to 2 (create new file2 if file2 doesn't exist)

Directory listings should have the following header:

Directory name: (including path if any)
Name   Type   Location   Size

File listings have the following format:

File name: (including path if any)
Line #
00001 (line 1)
00002 (line 2)
EOF

The bit map should be listed as a series of 1s and 0s, with 32 bits per line. The number of lines required will depend on the number of blocks allocated to your disk. If you are using a floppy, this should be an entire diskette.

Some of the error conditions your program will need to check are:

DUPLICATE FILE/DIRECTORY NAME filename
INVALID COMMAND (just display the message; then continue)
INSUFFICIENT SPACE
DIRECTORY EMPTY

Your documentation should list all error conditions that you test.

11

Spooling: Concurrency in Action

Not too long after programmers started using common I/O routines rather than writing their own, they noticed that a great deal of the CPU's time seemed to be spent waiting for cards to be read from the reader or lines to be listed on the printer. Unfortunately, there was little that could be done to solve this problem until hardware designers created a way for I/O devices to signal the CPU that they needed attention. The addition of interrupts to the processor was the key to turn a single-user system into a multiprogramming system.

Spooling [Lynch, 1967; Barron, 1971], the topic of this chapter, has no direct effect on the flow of processes in the SNAIL diagram. The spooler processes and drivers described in this chapter act like application programs; they call on the file system and the I/O system to transfer data. Although these systems may cause processes to be suspended or moved to a different queue, these actions are not taken by the spooler procedures.

Other authors, such as Shaw [1974] discuss spooling immediately after introducing concurrency primitives and emphasize how spooling is a good example of interprocess communication and coordination. We have chosen to place spooling after the chapters on I/O and files because spooling is dependent on I/O and file operations. This is also a good time to review some of the process coordination techniques described earlier.

11.1 THE PROBLEM OF SLOW PERIPHERALS AND FAST, EXPENSIVE CPUs

A reasonable question to ask at this point is, "Why did developers want a complicated multiuser or multiprogramming system?" The answer is not necessarily that all system programmers wanted job security. The true answer can be found by examining Figure 11.1(a), which shows how time was spent executing a process on a simple single-user system. We see that the system first spent some time reading input while the printer was idle and the CPU was spending most of its time in an I/O wait loop; then the CPU processed the information while the printer and reader remained idle; finally, the results were sent to the printer while the reader and the CPU waited.

There would be nothing wrong with this if it were not for the fact that mechanical devices, such as readers and printers, were much, much slower than CPUs and also that these peripherals were much less expensive than the CPUs to which they were attached. These two facts meant that systems had very fast, expensive CPUs waiting on very slow, less expensive input-output devices.

Figure 11.1(b) shows one of the first steps taken to reduce the problem of slow peripherals. Attempts were made to increase the effective speed of readers and printers. One way this was done was to use high-speed magnetic tape drives in place of card readers and printers on mainframe computers. As the figure shows, this increased CPU utilization significantly.

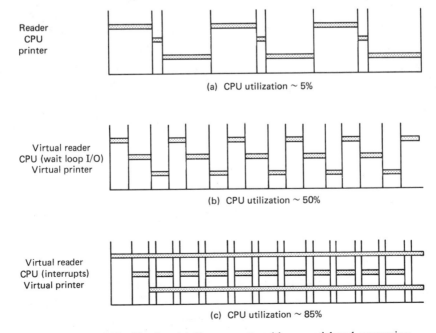

(a) CPU utilization ~ 5%

(b) CPU utilization ~ 50%

(c) CPU utilization ~ 85%

Figure 11.1   CPU utilization. (a) For a program with sequential read, processing, and output. (b) For a system with fast peripherals. (c) For a system with concurrent I/O and program processing.

A better solution to the problem is probably obvious: Have the CPU read input, write output, and process data concurrently. The result of concurrent operations with high-speed peripherals is shown graphically in Figure 11.1(c). For this case CPU utilization has again increased, along with peripheral utilization. These parallel operations were one of the early important applications of concurrency in a computer system.

11.2 REPLACING SLOW DEVICES WITH FAST ONES

The problem of slow peripherals became acute with the large mainframes of the late 1950s, and so a solution had to be found. Question: How do you improve the throughput of a 600 card per minute reader? Obvious answer: Replace it with a 45,000 card per minute reader. Unfortunately, engineers had not figured out how to move paper that fast. However, they had designed magnetic tape devices that could transfer data at a rate equivalent to 45,000 cards per minute. Therefore the solution shown in Figure 11.2 was suggested.

One could purchase inexpensive CPUs that do nothing but transfer information from cards to magnetic tape. Since reels of tape were often referred to as spools, the term **spooling** was used to describe the operation of placing card images onto a spool of tape. The spools of tape were then transferred to the tape reader on the mainframe, and this created a virtual card reader with a transfer rate of

$$(75 \text{ in/s})(800 \text{ char/in})(60 \text{ s/min}) = 360,000 \text{ char/min}$$

(*Note:* We are cheating a little, since the cards had 12 bits per character position and the tape had only 6 bits; however, most card encodings did not make use of the full 12 bits.)

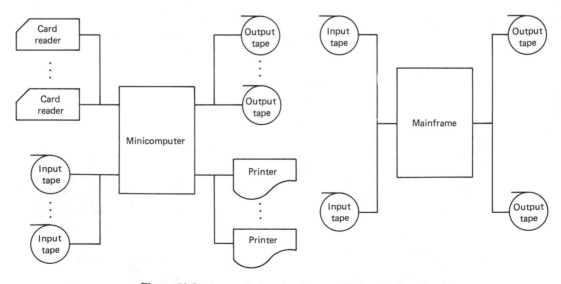

Figure 11.2   System designed to improve CPU utilization of mainframe.

The same operation worked in reverse for output; the mainframe stored its output onto a tape. When the tape was full or the job complete, the tape would be transferred to a drive on the inexpensive CPU and the output would be spooled off to a slow line printer. As Figure 11.2 shows, it took several card readers and line printers (and perhaps several minicomputers) to keep up with the mainframe. The basic idea of first transferring data from a slow peripheral to a faster device and then transferring the data to the very fast CPU is still used on today's systems, but the devices have changed.

On current systems, disk devices have replaced magnetic tapes as spooling devices. The effect of this change in system design on timing can be seen in Figure 11.1(b); the wait time for I/O by the CPU has been greatly reduced. The tape drives that replaced card readers and printers were sometimes referred to as **pseudo-devices.**

11.3 INTERRUPTS TO THE RESCUE

Even with the change shown in Figure 11.1(b), the CPU still had to wait while data was transferred. However, with the addition of interrupts to the CPU, we can initiate an I/O operation and perform another function while the input device is reading. When the data has been read, the device can interrupt the CPU, which will then use that data. This interrupt eliminates wait loop I/O, which wastes a great amount of CPU time.

Figure 11.1(c) shows the effect of fast virtual readers and printers and *concurrent* input, output, and processing. The total time saved by overlapping I/O and processing will depend on the relative speed of the peripherals and the CPU. It will also depend on how a program operates. Some programs read a few pieces of input data, calculate for a long time, and then output a simple answer. Other programs spend very little time actually computing results but a great amount of time reading in data and printing it back out.

11.4 SPOOLING ON LARGE SYSTEMS

Why was it necessary to buy one or more additional computers that did nothing but transfer data from one peripheral to another (Figures 11.1(b) and 11.2)? The answer is that early mainframes did not support interrupts and an I/O structure that would allow it to execute a user's program while transferring data to and from I/O devices. Today's systems do have these features and therefore do not require an additional, external computer to do the transfers. Figure 11.3 shows a current implementation of spooling. One process on the CPU does nothing but read input from slow devices and transfer the data to a high-speed disk. A driverlike procedure intercepts all requests for input and converts them to reads from the disk. The disk has now become our virtual card reader, with a transfer rate of 100,000 characters per second or higher!

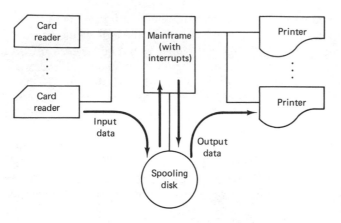

Figure 11.3 System with input and output spooling to and from disk.

Another driver takes output and stores it to disk. Finally, after the user job has completed, another process takes output from the disk and transfers it to the printer as fast as the printer can accept it. The system is now simultaneously transferring input data from peripherals and output data to other peripherals in addition to executing programs. That is, while the CPU is executing job n, it is reading in job $n + 1$ and printing job $n - 1$. This whole conglomeration can now be given an acronym which fits nicely with our spooling concept, Simultaneous Peripheral Operations OnLine.

11.4.1 How a Spooler Gets Started

Spooling is an example of an overhead operation that the system performs in order to improve overall system performance. It is the system's responsibility to initiate the spooling operation. In most systems the initial program loading (or bootstrapping) creates some processes that take care of such system operations; the spooler processes are usually created in this manner.

The code in Figure 11.4 shows how the system will create the processes needed to start spooling. The long-term scheduler (which was described in Chapter 5) is called to start things off. A more detailed description of the start-up procedure will be given in Chapter 13. Given the specified information, the long-term scheduler will create a PCB for the process and see that it is loaded into memory. When this has been accomplished, the process will be available for execution just like any other process in the active state.

11.4.2 Details of the Input Spooler: IN_SPOOL

We can now assume that the input and output spool processes have been created and are ready to execute. In this section we look at the pseudocode for IN_SPOOL. We will assume that we have a simple system with a single input device, the reader. For batch users, all job control statements, programs, and data enter the system through this device.

Figure 11.5 shows the pseudocode for IN_SPOOL. We first observe that IN_SPOOL uses a monitor to communicate with the processes that use the spool

```
procedure START_UP;

{ This is a portion of the system start-up routine.  It is not part of
  any formal process but rather a special section of code; it is used
  only for initiating system processes, and is not called or referenced
  after start-up.                                                        }

{ Called by            : initiated by bootstrap routine
  Procedures called    : LONG_TERM_SCHEDULER
  Parameters passed    : none
  Parameters returned  : none
  Entry conditions     : none
  Exit conditions      : all system processes initiatod               }

begin
            *
            *
            *
  Create UPP;
            *
            *
            *
  Create INITIATOR process and have it wait on "request_pending"
     condition in "WAITING_LIST" monitor;
  Create REMOVAL process and place its pcb on "removal_ptr";
            *
            *
            *
  LONG_TERM_SCHEDULER(create,sys_dev:inspool.exe,inspool,sys_pri,
                     max_cpu,max_lines,nowait,,true,status_inspool);
  LONG_TERM_SCHEDULER(create,sys_dev:outspool.exe,outspool,sys_pri,
                     max_cpu,max_lines,nowait,,true,status_outspool);
            *
            *
            *

{ Note the liberal use of magic dots (*) which will make any program do
  what you want it to do.  Professors are always allowed to use them in
  examples but students are seldom given the same privilege.            }

end; {START_UP}
```

Figure 11.4   A portion of the system START_UP routine.

files. IN_SPOOL must first acquire access to the card reader; it does so by calling the RESOURCE_MGR. Since IN_SPOOL was created when the system was started, we can assume it will request the card reader before any other process has a chance to do so. After initializing a count variable, IN_SPOOL enters a loop which it will repeat until power is turned off, the system is restarted, or the system manager aborts it.

IN_SPOOL looks for an input that declares a new job and dumps anything else into the bit bucket. When it finds a JOB command, it opens a file on disk where it can store the incoming lines. It keeps adding lines to the file until an ENDJOB command is found. When this happens, the file is closed and the INSPOOL_MONITOR is accessed to add the job to the queue of available jobs. At this point, IN_SPOOL starts again looking for another JOB card.

This simple input spooler does not do anything clever when exceptions occur. One might ask, for instance, "What happens if the disk has no more space available?" [Shaw, 1974] You might also wonder how multiple input devices are spooled. These are not trivial questions, and they must be answered before an OS is designed.

```
program IN_SPOOL;

{ This is the code for the process that is responsible for reading
  information from the input device and transferring it to a disk
  file for use by the command interpreter.  It is initiated by the    }
  system start-up routine and runs indefinitely.

{ Called by            : created by START_UP routine
  Procedures called    : FILE_MGR, IOCS, INSPOOL_MONITOR, RESOURCE_MGR
  Parameters passed    : none
  Parameters returned: job_ready monitor variable set each pass
  Entry conditions     : batch_job_queue in system empty
  Exit conditions      : file name added to job_queue each pass         }

local variables
     file_name, line  : string;
     status            : integer;

begin
{ Acquire the system input device and enter infinite loop.              }

   RESOURCE_MGR(acquire,system_input_device,reader,);

   repeat forever
{ Read records until a job record is found.                             }

     PROCEED:
     repeat
       IOCS(read,reader,line,record_length,true,status,);
       if status <> ok then display error message and goto PROCEED;
     until line = 'JOB';

{ Create a unique name for the input spool file and open the file.      }

     file_name := concat('spool',string(job_count));
     FILE_MGR(open,,,file_name,,write,,,,,true,status);

{ Repeat record reads and file writes until an 'ENDJOB' is found.       }

     repeat
       FILE_MGR(write,line,record_length,file_name,,,,,,,true,status);
       if status <>ok then display error message and goto CLOSE_FILE;
       IOCS(read,reader,line,record_length,true,status,)
       if status <> ok then goto CLOSE_FILE;
     until line = 'ENDJOB';

{ Close the spool file and signal the batch command interpreter.        }

     CLOSE_FILE: FILE_MGR(close,,,file_name,,,keep,,true,status);
                 if status = ok then INSPOOL_MONITOR.add(file_name)
                     else display error message;
   end repeat forever;
end; {IN_SPOOL}
```

Figure 11.5   A simple IN_SPOOL routine.

The interested reader can check the references listed in the chapter to see how these problems have been solved on actual systems.

We must mention here what happens to the jobs that have been read in from cards and spooled to disk. From the commands in IN_SPOOL, we see that after a file name is added to the batch_job_queue, the condition job_ready is signaled. The process waiting for this signal is the batch job command interpreter, which was also created by the system start-up routine. When the command interpreter is signaled that a job file is available, it will open the job file and start reading and executing the commands contained therein.

11.4.3 Inspool and Outspool Drivers: Fooling User Programs

How do we convince users that they should read input from spool files and send their output to our output spooler rather than to the line printer? The answer is that we do not! We will add new I/O drivers to the system that, through the logical mapping which the IOCS performs, will replace the standard input and output device drivers for the user processes.

The code for the new input driver is shown in Figure 11.6. It really is not a driver in the normal sense, since it does not actually control any I/O device; hence it

```
procedure IN_SPOOL_DRIVER(command,device,spool_name,buffer,
                          length,status);

{ This procedure is a pseudodriver.  It is not really a device driver
  since it controls no physical device.  When a process requests input
  from the reader on the system, IOCS maps the request to this
  procedure and it reads characters from a disk file rather than the
  physical reader.                                                    }

{ Called by           : IOCS
  Procedures called   : FILE_MGR
  Parameters passed   : command, spool_name
  Parameters returned : buffer,length, status
  Entry conditions    : process requesting input from batch device;
  Exit conditions     : data in buffer and/or status               }

local variables
    iostatus            : error indicator;
begin

  case command of

{ Open command.  Opens a new spool file and returns status to user.   }

    open: begin
            FILE_MGR(open,,,spool_name,,read,,,,,true,iostatus);
            status := iostatus;
          end;

{ Read a line from the input spool file.                              }

    read: begin
            FILE_MGR(read,buffer,length,spool_name,,,,,,,true,iostatus);
            status := iostatus;
            if iostatus = end_of_file then
               FILE_MGR(close,,,spool_name,,scratch,,,,,true,iostatus);
          end;

{ Invalid command for this driver.                                     }

    otherwise: status := command_rejected;

  end; {case}

end; {IN_SPOOL_DRIVER}
```

Figure 11.6   A pseudodevice driver for reading IN_SPOOL files.

is often called a pseudodriver. When the batch job command interpreter has been signaled that an input spool file is available for execution, it calls its standard input driver, which the IOCS has mapped to INSPOOL_DRIVER, with a request to open the spool file. The command interpreter then reads lines from the file by making requests to INSPOOL_DRIVER.

When executing commands from the inspool file, if the command interpreter finds a RUN PROGRAM, it requests creation of a process that will execute, as the batch process, PROGRAM; it then waits for its child process to complete. When the batch process executing PROGRAM requests input data from the default input device, the IOCS will map the reads to INSPOOL_DRIVER. The process will therefore get its input data from the inspool file.

The output driver performs a corresponding function. It is responsible for opening a disk file for a process and then directing all output from the process to the file. When the process terminates, the driver is sent a termination request. This request causes the driver to close the file and signal the output spooler so that it will know that file is ready to be physically sent to the printer. Development of the code for the driver is left as an exercise.

In Figure 11.7 we show the parts of the OS that are associated with input spooling. The individual steps, starting with the acquisition of the card reader and proceeding to closing of the spoolfile are as follows:

1. Input spooler requests input device from resource manager.
2. Input spooler receives input device (these two steps occur when the input spooler is first created).
3. The batch command interpreter waits for a signal indicating that an input spool file is ready from the input spooler.
4. Input spooler requests a read from the input device.
5. Data is transferred from the input device to inspool.
6. Input spooler requests the creation of a new input spool file from the file manager.
7. Input spooler transfers data to the file until an end of job is found.
8. Input spooler closes the input spool file.

At this point a new batch job is ready to be passed to the command interpreter. The input spooler will continue reading from the input device and may create additional batch jobs while the current one is being executed.

9. Input spooler signals that a new spool file is ready.
10. Command interpreter receives signal from input spooler.
11. Command interpreter sends initiate command to input spool driver.
12. Input spool driver opens next input spool file.
13. Input spool driver reads data from file.
14. Input spool transfers data to command interpreter.
15. Command interpreter creates process to execute batch program (when it finds a RUN PROGRAM command).

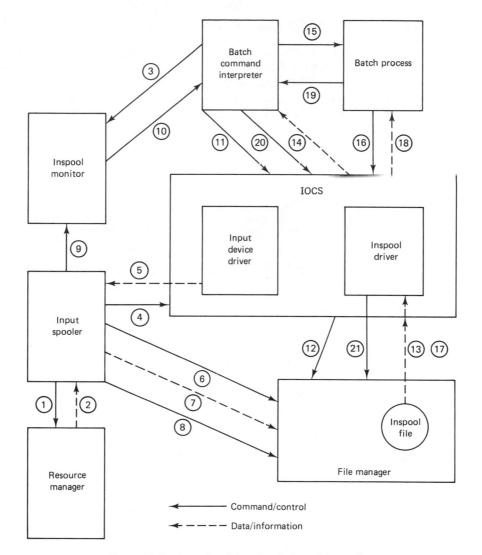

Figure 11.7   Control and data flow in input job spooling.

16. Batch process requests read from input spool driver.

17. Input spool driver reads data from input spool file.

18. Data is transferred to batch process.

19. Batch process terminates.

20. Command interpreter sends termination request to input spool driver.

21. Input spool driver closes and deletes the input spool file.

At this point, a batch job has been executed. The command interpreter will go back and wait for a signal that the next batch job is available.

11.4.4 Details of the Output Spooler (OUT_SPOOL)

The output spooler process is also created at the time the system is started and runs until the system is shut down. OUT_SPOOL communicates with the batch command interpreter via the monitor OUTSPOOL_MONITOR. It waits for a file to be placed on the output spool file queue. When signaled that a file is ready, OUT_SPOOL transfers one line at a time until an end of file is found. If errors occur during the file read or the output to the printer, OUT_SPOOL goes and waits for the next file. Figure 11.8 shows the code for OUT_SPOOL.

```
program OUT_SPOOL;

{ This process is responsible for transferring output spool files from
  disk to the printer.  It is initiated by the system startup routine
  and runs until the system is shut down.  It usually spends a great
  deal of time waiting for a signal from the device driver that is
  accepting output from user processes.                               }

{ Called by           : created by START_UP routine
  Procedures called   : FILE_MGR, IOCS, OUTSPOOL_MONITOR, RESOURCE_MGR
  Parameters passed   : none
  Parameters returned : none
  Entry conditions    : spool file on queue when signaled
  Exit conditions     : file printed and removed from disk each pass   }

local variables
    file_name, line  : string;
    status           : error indicator;

begin
{ Acquire the printer and enter infinite loop.                        }

   RESOURCE_MGR(acquire,line_printer,printer,);

   repeat forever

{ Wait in the monitor until an output spool file is available.  If
  the file cannot be opened, wait for another file.                   }

      PROCEED:
      OUTSPOOL_MONITOR.remove(file_name);
      FILE_MGR(open,,,file_name,,read,,,,,true,status);
      if status <> ok then display error message and goto PROCEED;

{ Repeat spool file reads and printer writes until eof on spool file. }

      repeat
         FILE_MGR(read,line,record_length,file_name,,,,,,,true,status);
         if status <> ok then display error message and goto CLOSE_FILE;
         IOCS(write,printer,line,record_length,true,status,);
         if status <> ok then display error message and goto CLOSE_FILE;
      until status = end_of_file;

{ Close the spool file and go back to wait for another file.          }

      CLOSE_FILE:
      FILE_MGR(close,,,file_name,,,scratch,,,,true,status);
      if status <> ok then display error message;

   end repeat forever;

end; {OUTPUT_SPOOLER}
```

Figure 11.8 A simple OUT_SPOOL routine.

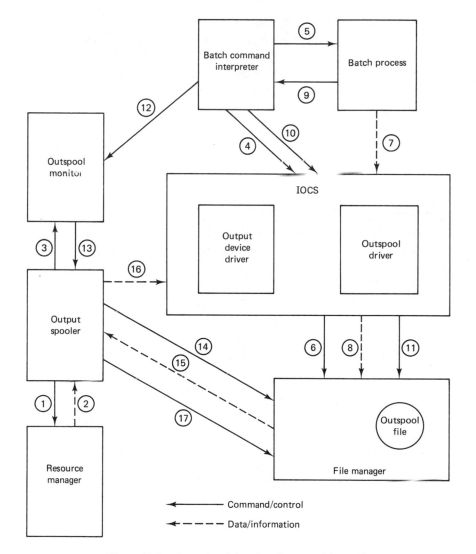

Figure 11.9 Control and data flow in output job spooling.

Depending on what has been going on in the system, there may be several files ready to send to the printer. Our simple OUT_SPOOL outputs files on an FCFS basis. Some systems use the priority of the process that created the spool file to select output spool files in priority order.

In Figure 11.9 we show the important steps that occur in creating and printing an output spool file. Starting with the acquisition of the print device by the output spooler, the steps are:

1. Output spooler requests the output device from the resource manager.
2. Output spooler receives the output device.
3. Output spooler waits for a signal from the command interpreter.

4. Command interpreter sends an initiation request to the output spool driver.
5. The command interpreter creates a batch process (this was explained in Figure 11.7).
6. Output spool driver requests creation of an output spool file.
7. Batch process sends data to output spool driver.
8. Output spool driver sends data to output spool file.
9. Batch process terminates.
10. Command interpreter sends termination request to output spool driver.
11. Output spool driver closes output spool file and puts its name on output queue.
12. Command interpreter signals output spooler that a file is ready to be printed.

At this point a new file has been added to the queue of files that are ready to be printed. The command interpreter will wait for another batch job, and the output spooling of the output spool file can commence as follows:

13. Output spooler receives the signal from the command interpreter.
14. Output spooler opens the next output spool file.
15. Output spooler reads data from output spool file.
16. Output spooler sends data to output device.
17. Output spooler closes and deletes output spool file.

The output spooler is now ready to go back and wait for another signal from the command interpreter.

As we have seen, spooling is not a trivial operation; however, by looking closely at the operations involved, we found that there was no real mystery involved. Device drivers were called, the file system was accessed, and monitors were used to coordinate the spooling activities. You should remember that, as with most of our other implementations, this is only one way to accomplish spooling. References cited elsewhere within the chapter suggest other implementations.

11.5 SPOOLING ON SMALL SYSTEMS

At first it might seem that spooling is a technique that is reasonably applied only to large systems where CPU time is expensive; for a while this was true. As with many concepts in computer science, though, if you do not think an idea is feasible today, wait until tomorrow and things will change.

There are numerous applications of spooling techniques on today's microcomputer systems. First, basic spooling as described above is used on systems' floppy and hard disk drives. A second application is shown as a simple modification of output spooling in Figure 11.10. In this example we take advantage of the fact that main memory is essentially free (at least, very inexpensive). Instead of sending output to a disk, we now send it to an area of main memory that serves as a **virtual disk**, or "RAM disk" [Tanenbaum, 1987]. We still rely on the interrupt features of

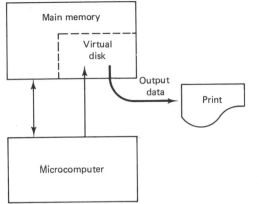

Figure 11.10   Spooling to a virtual disk.

our CPU to enable us to concurrently write output while processing our application program. In essence, what we have done is to create a virtual printer that operates at memory speed!

A variation on this theme replaces the spooler that uses main memory with one that uses RAM in an external box. Two versions of this are shown in Figure 11.11. Figure 11.11(a) shows one computer accessing a printer through the print spooler. What we are typically trying to accomplish with this configuration is to make it appear that the printer is much faster than it actually is. If you have ever sat at a personal computer while waiting for a long paper to print, you can appreciate the advantage of such an arrangement. The feat is accomplished by sending output to the external buffer, which can accept data at a much greater rate than the printer.

A second use of a print spooler is shown in Figure 11.11(b), where four CPUs are sharing one printer. How things have changed! A few years ago our very expensive computers needed many inexpensive printers to create a cost-effective system. Now computers are cheap and we tie several of them together so that we can justify having one expensive laser printer with multiple fonts and graphic printing capability.

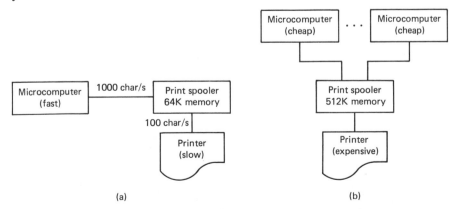

Figure 11.11   Spooling on microprocessors. (a) An external spooler with memory and processor. (b) An external spooler with multiple processor inputs for use with expensive shared printers.

11.6 THE COST OF SPOOLING

In this chapter we have discussed only the advantages of spooling. In the interest of completeness we must list a few of the costs involved. First, we add to the total system overhead the time spent doing system work rather than executing user processes. This is because we have added four extra layers of software between the user process and input-output devices and because passing through these routines takes time. (The devices also take space that might be needed by users.) We have also added another burden to the file system, since it must now manage additional files; and we have increased the number of disk accesses that the I/O system must process.

Spooling can also lead to deadlock [Shaw, 1974]. Deadlock can occur when several processes are writing to output spool files and all of the disk space becomes full. At this point no process can proceed, because each needs an additional resource, more file space. A review of the material in Chapter 8 might suggest ways to get around this problem.

11.7 SPOOLING AS AN APPLICATION OF CONCURRENT PROCESSING

So far, our discussion of spooling has been directed toward how it is implemented and how it can be used in a variety of systems. We now turn our attention to an equally important topic, spooling as an application of concurrency.

In Section 11.4 the programs IN_SPOOL and OUT_SPOOL were described. It is important to note that both are *programs*, not *procedures*. They are different from procedures, such as drivers, schedulers, and resource managers, which make up the bulk of the operating system. When the system is first turned on, these programs exist as executable files on disk. Before they can be executed, they must enter the system and compete for resources as any other program would. The differences are that their execution is requested by the system startup routine rather than a user request, and they execute at the system priority rather than at user priority. In all other ways, they behave as any other process would.

When IN_SPOOL and OUT_SPOOL are executing they go through the same states a user process does. They request I/O and are suspended, waiting for completion; after completion, they are placed on the active queue, where they wait for the CPU. They do not have to wait as long as user processes, however, because they have system level priority.

Since IN_SPOOL and OUT_SPOOL run asynchronously with respect to user processes and other system processes, they contribute to the **degree of multiprogramming** (number of concurrent processes) on the system. Two monitors were described that coordinate the operation of these programs and the remainder of the operating system. In Figure 11.6 we saw that IN_SPOOL uses INSPOOL_MONITOR to signal the command interpreter that a new job is ready. Similarly, OUT_SPOOL_MONITOR is used by the command interpreter to signal OUT_SPOOL that a new output file is ready for printing.

By creating separate processes that are responsible for reading cards and printing output, we have simplified the rest of our operating system and made it more efficient and easier to design and maintain. Like the construction company in Chapter 1, we have subcontracted out parts of the job that can be done more efficiently by others.

11.8 SUMMARY

In this chapter we looked at the problem of price-performance mismatch between CPUs and peripherals. We saw how spooling can reduce the magnitude of the problem and what the drawbacks of spooling are. By breaking down the spooling operation into its basic components, we observed that spooling can be implemented in a straightforward fashion using cooperating processes coordinated by monitors.

We also looked at how an idea, spooling, originated to meet the needs of large mainframe applications where CPU cost and utilization were critical and evolved to suit microcomputer applications where the cost and utilization of the printer are critical. By modifying the implementation and taking advantage of new technology, we have been able to make effective use of the concept over three decades, and we will probably continue to use it in the future.

Finally, we examined spooling as an application of concurrent processing. We used spooling as an example of system processes running concurrently with user processes, both competing for system resources.

In their text on concurrency, Holt et al. [1978] describe the implementation of spooling using concurrent processes. Additional information on spooling can be found in three other texts: Kurzban et al. [1975], Lister [1979], and Turner [1986].

QUESTIONS AND EXERCISES

1. Can deadlock occur when only input spooling is used? If yes, explain how it could happen.
2. Suppose the output spooler runs out of disk space but the line printers are all idle. What would this mean?
3. On some card-based systems it was all too common to have user programs disappear without a trace. Relate this to the first "repeat" loop in the spooler of Figure 11.5.
4. We have discussed spoolers in terms of sequential I/O peripherals. Can you conceive of spooling where the original source or ultimate destination is a nonsequential device? Can you envision a spooling application where the peripheral is not a classic I/O device such as a printer, card reader, or disk?
5. Compare and contrast spooling and I/O buffering.
6. Input spool files are a potential security weakness. Why?
7. Develop the pseudocode for the driver that takes information from user processes and stores it to output spool files.
8. Discuss how spooling could be done with a system that has several input or output devices rather than just one.

9. Why are IN_SPOOL and OUT_SPOOL *processes* rather than *procedures*?

10. What problems would occur with IN_SPOOL if we wanted to have multiple batch jobs executing concurrently?

PROGRAMMING ASSIGNMENTS

1. Write an output spooler. If you have access to a system that allows multiprocessing, create several processes and call the spooler from each one after random delays. The output from each process should be simple, consecutively numbered lines containing the process ID so that you can easily check the operation of your spooler. The processes should all call your pseudodevice driver rather than calling the standard output device (that is, you should replace writeln(..) with sp_write(..) in the processes).

    If you do not have access to a multiprocessing system, you can still have the joy of creating your own spooler! Write a program that randomly selects one of several different procedures that in turn call sp_write(..). As above, have each of the procedures send consecutively numbered lines to the spooler to verify its operation.

    In either case, check to see that all files are printed correctly with no missing or added lines. Also make sure that all the files are deleted after they have been processed.

2. Write one of the spoolers described above and then, by carefully selecting the size and output characteristics, force a deadlock situation. Eliminate the deadlock so that the system can proceed. *Note:* Be considerate of other system users and do not force the entire system into a deadlock.

PART 4
System Structure, Security and Performance

In the final part of the book we first describe the heart of the system, the kernel, which coordinates the activities of all the other parts of the system. The three primary functions that are performed by the kernel—process dispatching, process synchronization and coordination, and interrupt processing—are examined in Chapter 12.

As a way of putting all the pieces of a system together, we will look at a layered approach to the design of complicated systems. We will apply this layering structure, described in Chapter 13, to the individual components described in earlier chapters. In this chapter we will also examine all the steps that take place within the system when a user process executes.

After putting all the pieces together, we will look at two topics that should be a concern at all levels of the operating system: security and performance. Chapter 14 introduces the reader to the basic concepts of computer system security. Topics such as data encryption and passwords are described and applied to various levels of the system.

In the final chapter, we will look at system performance. We will investigate ways of measuring performance and ways to model system performance. We will also see how when designing a system one can make trade-offs to improve performance.

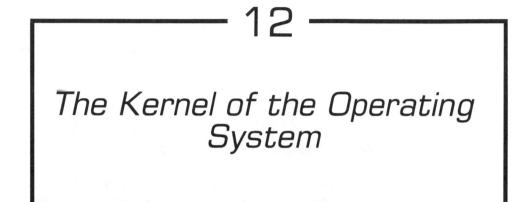

12

The Kernel of the Operating System

Back in the Introduction we described the operating system as being a number of procedures and concurrent processes. In Part II of the text we examined many of the procedures and processes in detail to see how each performed its function. In this chapter we will look at the low-level part of the system, the kernel. The **kernel** is responsible for coordinating the operations of the processes that make up the operating system.

Each system seems to have different functions embedded in the kernel. The kernel of UNIX [Thompson, 1978; Johnson and Ritchie, 1978] contains most of the basic features of the OS, whereas the kernel described by Lister [1979] performs only three basic functions. For our purposes, we will break the kernel into three parts similar to those Lister defined:

The dispatcher, which is responsible for placing processes into execution

The monitor_control, which controls access to monitors

The first-level interrupt handler (FLIH), which analyzes all interrupts and activates the appropriate handler

The kernel is one of the few parts of the system that are still often written in assembler language. There are three main reasons:

The dispatcher is invoked each time a process is placed into execution; it must be short and efficient, since it operates with the interrupts disabled and may have to execute privileged memory mapping instructions.

The FLIH must execute privileged I/O instructions and must therefore also be fast.

The monitor controller must be fast, since it may have to operate with interrupts disabled.

The part of the UNIX kernel that is written in assembly language is approximately 1000 lines of code, which is less than 10% of the total. The assembly code performs functions similar to the ones defined in our kernel. Since it is the part of the OS that is most machine-dependent, it has been most responsible for bugs when UNIX is transported to different CPUs [Johnson and Ritchie, 1978].

12.1 THE PROCESS DISPATCHER AND THE IDLE PROCESS

In Chapter 6 we described the difference between dispatching and scheduling. As stated there, the dispatcher has a relatively simple job; it places a process into the execution state. To do this, it must load the CPU's environment, which includes the registers and status, with the values stored in the process's PCB.

The first problem the dispatcher must solve is where to find the PCB for the process that it will dispatch. If the system has a single active queue, the problem is trivial: take the process at the head of the active queue. If the active queue is more complex, as is the one with several priority queues that is described in Chapter 6, the dispatcher will have to start at the highest priority level and search down until it finds a process at some level. A pertinent question at this point is, "What happens if there is *no* process on any of the active queues?"

There are several things that can be done when the system has no process to execute. The first that comes to mind is to have the dispatcher go into a loop looking at the active queues until a process is moved onto one of the queues. When a process is found, it is dispatched. This solution has problems which are left to the student as an exercise.

An alternative is to create an idle process which runs at the lowest priority on the system. This **idle process**, which can never have its priority increased by an aging operation, is created when the system is started up and is always available to execute. What does this process do when it executes? The answer: It simply doesn't matter.

On some systems, we have seen rather interesting idle processes. A common one on earlier systems caused the display register to blink in a distinctive fashion. Besides giving the operator a hypnotic pattern to lull him to sleep, the rate at which the pattern changed gave the operator a gauge of how busy the CPU was. (If the lights stopped moving completely, the company was really getting its money's worth out of the CPU.) On other systems, the idle process is used to perform some operation that might not be worth the cost of required CPU time, but that is potentially useful to someone. Calculating the next prime number by some esoteric method or calculating π to 100,000 digits might be an example of these types of processes.

(Another name given to such processes that run when there is nothing else to do is ghost processes.)

Because not everyone is content with flashing lights or prime numbers, system designers have tried to come up with useful work that can be done by the idle process. Two common examples of this are the running of diagnostics and the archiving of files to a backup device. There are many diagnostics that can be run on both the hardware and the system software to check for potential failures. On systems that

```
procedure DISPATCHER;

{ This procedure is responsible for placing the highest priority
  process currently in the active state into execution. It first
  searches the active queues for a pcb and then restores the CPU's
  registers from the pcb. It then enables interrupts and loads the
  program counter with the address from the pcb.                     }

{ Called by            : SHORT_TERM_SCHEDULER
  Procedures called    : none
  Parameters passed    : none
  Parameters returned: none
  Entry conditions     : interrupts disabled
  Exit conditions      : interrupts enabled and process executing    }

global variables
     system_queue, user_hipri_queue, user_rr_queue     : pcb_pointer;
     user_longrr_queue, user_batch_queue, idle_queue   : pcb_pointer;
     execute_queue                                     : pcb_pointer;

local variables
     temp_pointer       : pcb_pointer;

begin
{ Find the process in the active state with the highest priority
  by searching the system_queue, user_hipri_queue, user_rr_queue,
  user_longrr_queue, and user_batch_queue in order.                  }

  if system_queue <> nil then
    move first pcb from system_queue to temp_pointer
    else if user_hipri_queue <> nil then
      move first pcb from user_hipri_queue to temp_pointer
      else if user_rr_queue <> nil then
        move first pcb from user_rr_queue to temp_pointer
        else if user_longrr_queue <> nil then
          move first pcb from user_longrr_queue to temp_pointer
          else if user_batch_queue <> nil then
            move first pcb from user_batch_queue to temp_pointer

{ If all else fails get the idle process.                            }

            else move idle process pcb to temp_pointer;

{ Move the selected process to the execute state and restore all of
  the CPU's registers and enable the interrupts before starting.     }

  move temp_pointer to execute_queue;
  restore cpu registers from temp_pointer pcb;

  { The following must be one uninterruptible operation: }
  enable interrupts and load program counter from pcb on execute queue;

end; {DISPATCHER}
```

Figure 12.1   The dispatcher.

have backup storage for disk files, typically magnetic tape, files that have been modified since they were last saved to magnetic tape are rewritten to provide current backups. Doing this can provide an inexpensive way to guarantee that user files are backed up in the event of some type of system failure. This use of the idle process could cause serious problems. In Question 8 at the end of the chapter, you are asked to examine this problem and its solution. For our system we will assume that there is an idle process, residing on the active queue at level 5 (lowest priority). Therefore the dispatcher will always have a process to place into execution.

Figure 12.1 shows the code for the DISPATCHER. Although we have used a high-level pseudocode to describe the DISPATCHER, remember that the actual implementation would probably be done in assembly language. Since there will always be at least one process on the active queue, the design is simplified and the DISPATCHER is short and fast.

The DISPATCHER starts by looking for a process in one of the six active queues, starting with the highest-priority queue, the system process queue. When it finds one, it removes the process from the queue and places the PCB for the selected process onto the execute queue. After moving the PCB to the execute queue, it restores the CPU's environment from the PCB. It then enables interrupts and transfers control to the next executable instruction in the process.

12.2 PROCESS SYNCHRONIZATION AND COMMUNICATION

Next we will look at the related operations of process synchronization and communication. For our system, we will assume that monitors are used to provide these functions. Our kernel will therefore include a procedure that controls access to monitors.

There are several ways that monitors can be implemented. On some systems the microcode for the CPU provides special instructions to enter, signal, wait, and exit from a monitor. On other systems, semaphores are provided by the hardware or microcode and they are then used to create monitor functions. On some systems interrupts are disabled during the entire time a process is in the monitor, to guarantee mutually exclusive access to the code and data. The implementation we present in this section does not depend on any particular method of implementation. It could be used with any of those described above.

Our kernel will contain the procedure MONITOR_CONTROL to regulate access to monitors. The procedure, shown in Figures 12.2 through 12.6, accepts four commands: enter, signal, wait, and exit. The system will require another procedure that creates a monitor, but the code for this procedure is left as an exercise. The monitor access and creation procedures can only be entered by making a system request which temporarily disables interrupts. This guarantees the integrity of the monitor structures and prevents accidental modification.

After a monitor has been created, a process uses it by requesting entry with a procedure call such as

```
message.producer(filename);
```

where "message" is the name of the monitor, "producer" is the name of the gate that

```
procedure MONITOR_CONTROL(monitor_name,operation,queue);

{ This procedure is called by any process that wants to access a
  monitor.  To use the facilities of a monitor, a process makes a
  request to enter the monitor at one of the entry gates.  When a
  process has been granted entry, it can access any resources being
  protected by the monitor.  The process that has been given access
  to the monitor may also signal a condition, wait on a condition
  or exit the monitor.                                              }

{ Called by           : executing process
  Procedures called   : SHORT_TERM_SCHEDULER
  Parameters passed   : monitor_name, operation, queue
  Parameters returned : none
  Entry conditions    : interrupts disabled
  Exit conditions     : process executing or scheduler executing,
                        interrupts enabled                         }

global variables
     execute_queue    : pcb_pointer;
     monitor_list;    : monitor_pointer;

local variables
     temp_pointer     : pcb_pointer;

begin
{ If the monitor name and commands are valid then execute the specified
  request.  Otherwise terminate the calling process.               }

   if monitor_name in monitor_list then
     begin
       case operation of
         entry   : ENTRY_CONTROL;
         wait, exit, signal :
             if monitor_name.owner <> execute_queue.name then ERROR_EXIT
               else if operation = wait then WAIT_CONTROL
                 else if operation = exit then EXIT_CONTROL
                   else if operation = signal then SIGNAL_CONTROL;
         otherwise: ERROR_EXIT;
       end;
       return;
     end
   else ERROR_EXIT;

procedure ERROR_EXIT;

  begin
  { Set termination bit in the PCB and go to the short-term scheduler. }

    log error message and set termination_flag in executing pcb to true;
    SHORT_TERM_SCHEDULER;
  end; {ERROR_EXIT}

end; {MONITOR_CONTROL}
```

Figure 12.2 Mainline code for monitor control.

will be entered, and "filename" is a parameter that will be used within the monitor code. The compiler converts this into the following calls:

```
call MONITOR_CONTROL(message,enter,producer);
call message(producer,filename);
call MONITOR_CONTROL(message,exit);
```

```
procedure ENTRY_CONTROL;
{ This procedure is declared within the scope of MONITOR_CONTROL and
  has access to all of its variables.                              }

begin
{ If the monitor is busy, block the calling process.  If the monitor
  is free, let the process continue and set the monitor busy flag.  }

    if monitor_name.busy then
      begin
        MOVE_PCB(execute_queue,monitor_name.entry_queue[queue],);
        SHORT_TERM_SCHEDULER;
      end {if monitor busy}
    else
      begin
        monitor_name.busy := true;
        monitor_name.owner := execute_queue.name
      end; {monitor free}
end; {ENTRY_CONTROL}
```

Figure 12.3   Entry request for monitor control.

```
procedure SIGNAL_CONTROL;
{ This procedure is declared within the scope of MONITOR_CONTROL and
  has access to all of its variables.                              }

begin
{ If the condition queue is empty return to the signaler and if not,
  block the signaler and activate the waiter.                      }

    if monitor_name.condition_queue[queue] <> nil then
      begin
        MOVE_PCB(execute_queue,monitor_name.waiting_signaler_queue,);
        MOVE_PCB(monitor_name.condition_queue[queue],active_queue,);
        change monitor owner to new active process;
        SHORT_TERM_SCHEDULER;
      end; {process waiting on condition}

end; {SIGNAL_CONTROL}
```

Figure 12.4   Signal request for monitor control.

The MONITOR_CONTROL procedure first checks to see whether the monitor requested has been created. If it has not, the requesting process is aborted. If the monitor exists, the busy flag for the monitor is checked to see whether the monitor is in use. If it is in use, the calling process is placed on the entry queue specified in the request. If the monitor is not busy, its flag is set to busy and the process is allowed to continue. Note that MONITOR_CONTROL does not have to know anything about the code associated with the monitor; it just controls access to the monitor.

Once a process has been granted access to the monitor, it may access the resources protected by the monitor as it chooses. It may also wait or signal any condition that has been defined for the monitor. And when it is through, it must exit the monitor.

When a process requests a signal on a condition, the MONITOR_CONTROL procedure first checks to see whether the process making the request is the one that is currently in the monitor. If it is not the current process, it is terminated. If it is the current process, the queue for the specified condition is checked. If there is a process waiting for the condition to be signaled, the signaling process is placed on

```
procedure WAIT_CONTROL;
{ This procedure is declared within the scope of MONITOR_CONTROL and
  has access to all of its variables.                              }

begin
{ Move process to the condition queue and set monitor to not busy.   }

   MOVE_PCB(execute_queue,condition_queue[queue],);

{ Check to see if there are any processes waiting at entry gates.  If
  there are then move one to active and make it the monitor owner.   }

   if any processes are on entry queues then
     begin
       MOVE_PCB(monitor_name.entry_queue[selected_one],active_queue,);
       change monitor owner to new active process;
     end {process waiting to enter}
   else

{ Check to see if there are waiting signalers.  If there are, move a
  signaler to the active queue.                                      }

     begin
       if any processes are on signaler queue then
         begin
           MOVE_PCB(monitor_name.signaler_queue,active_queue,);
           change monitor owner to new active process;
         end {if waiting signaler}

{ If no process is waiting anywhere then move all the processes from
  the exit_queue to the active queue.                                }

       else
         begin
           while monitor_name.exit_queue <> nil do
                 MOVE_PCB(monitor_name.exit_queue,active_queue,);
           monitor_name.busy := false;
         end; {no waiting signalers}

   SHORT_TERM_SCHEDULER;

end; {WAIT_CONTROL}
```

Figure 12.5 Wait request for monitor control.

the waiting signaler's queue and the process that has been waiting is moved to the active state. If no process is waiting for the signal, the signaling process is allowed to continue.

When a process requests a wait for a condition, we first check to see whether it is the process currently accessing the monitor. If it is the current process, it is placed on the end of the wait queue for that condition. If it is not the current process, it is aborted.

The exit operation must be requested when a process has completed all its work in the monitor. If there are no processes currently on an entry queue or on the signaler's queue, then the calling process is allowed to continue executing (now outside the monitor, of course).

If there are other processes trying to enter the monitor, the process trying to exit is placed on the exit queue. This guarantees that waiting processes will not suffer from indefinite postponement.

```
procedure EXIT_CONTROL;
{ This procedure is declared within the scope of MONITOR_CONTROL and
  has access to all of its variables.                                    }

begin

   MOVE_PCB(execute_queue,monitor_name.exit_queue,);

{ Check to see if there are processes at entry gates.  If there are,
  block the process trying to exit and move one trying to enter to
  the active queue.                                                      }

   if any processes are on entry queues then
     begin
       MOVE_PCB(entry_queue[selected_one],active_queue,);
       change monitor owner to new active process;
     end {process waiting to enter}
   else

{ Check to see if there are waiting signalers.  If there are, block
  the one trying to exit and move a signaler to the active queue.        }

     begin
       if any processes are on signaler queue then
         begin
           MOVE_PCB(monitor_name.signaler_queue,active_queue,);
           change monitor owner to new active process;
         end {if waiting signaler}

{ If no process is waiting anywhere then move all the processes from
  the exit_queue to the active queue.                                    }

       else
         begin
           while monitor_name.exit_queue <> nil do
                 MOVE_PCB(monitor_name.exit_queue,active_queue,);
           monitor_name.busy := false;
         end; {no waiting signalers}

   SHORT_TERM_SCHEDULER;

end; {EXIT_CONTROL}
```

Figure 12.6 Exit request for monitor control.

There may be processes that have signaled a condition and because another process was waiting for that signal have been forced to wait on the waiting signalers' queue. If there is a waiting signaler, it is allowed to proceed and the process trying to exit is also forced to wait on the exit queue.

Finally, it is possible that there are several processes queued up trying to exit the monitor. If this happens, all of the processes trying to exit are moved from the exit queue to the system active queue. Subsequently the scheduler will decide which one is allowed to execute.

There are other features that can be put into monitors, causing them to function differently. Some implementations of monitors will save the status of a condition, so that the monitor condition variable is like a semaphore in that respect. One of the questions at the end of the chapter requires that you modify the code of MONITOR_CONTROL so that it will save signals on a condition.

12.3 THE FIRST-LEVEL INTERRUPT HANDLER (FLIH)

In several earlier chapters we made mention of the FLIH. This is the system routine that executes each time a hardware or software interrupt is acknowledged. The exact operations of the FLIH are dependent in part on the way the interrupt hardware is designed.

The structure of the interrupt system may determine whether a first-level interrupt handler separate from the driver is needed. If all interrupts cause control to be transferred to one routine, then an FLIH is appropriate. On systems that can transfer control to a different routine for each possible interrupt, the functions of the FLIH may be embedded in the individual interrupt handler. (For a discussion of interrupts, review the material in the Introduction and Chapter 9.)

12.3.1 Context Swapping

There are two primary functions that the FLIH performs. The first is to save the status of the interrupted process and transfer control to a new process. This operation, context swapping, [Lampson, 1968] was described in Chapter 6. Depending on the hardware of the machine, this may be short and simple or it may require many instructions and considerable time.

The hardware in some CPUs may push all or nearly all of the information regarding the currently executing process onto an interrupt stack and change the instruction pointer to the FLIH when the interrupt occurs. If this is the case, context swapping is essentially done in hardware (or microcode) before the FLIH starts.

On other CPUs the interrupt may just cause the instruction pointer to be saved; the FLIH is then responsible for saving all of the other registers in the CPU that will be modified during the processing of the interrupt. One reason for having the FLIH separate from the interrupt handler is that the context swapping can be put into one routine and not duplicated in each of the interrupt handlers.

12.3.2 Selecting the Appropriate Routine

The second function of the FLIH is to determine which routine will handle the interrupt, and then call it. How does it find the correct routine? One way is to put the address of the routine into the interrupt table. Figure 12.7 shows an interrupt table

Interrupt number	Interrupt handler address	Buffer address
1	1F120	2420
2	20420	0
3	20420	462O
4	21D02	40F0
5	22080	0
.	.	.
.	.	.

Figure 12.7 The interrupt table for a system that vectors all interrupts to FLIH.

where the routine address is included along with the interrupt number and the current buffer address. (Refer to Chapter 9 for a discussion of the buffer address field.)

Figure 12.8 shows a sample first-level interrupt handler. For this FLIH it was assumed that the hardware only saves the instruction pointer of the interrupted process before transferring control to the FLIH. The FLIH first disables interrupts and saves the state of the CPU. The hardware on some systems disables the interrupt system when an interrupt is acknowledged; in this case, the FLIH can immediately save the state of the CPU.

```
procedure FLIH;

{ This procedure is entered as soon as the hardware acknowledges an
  interrupt.  Its functions are to save the status of the hardware
  and to transfer control to the routine that will process the
  interrupt.  It uses the system interrupt table to determine which
  routine will process the interrupt.                                    }

{ Called by            : hardware interrupt
  Procedures called    : interrupt processor
  Parameters passed    : none
  Parameters returned: none
  Entry conditions     : interrupts disabled, instruction pointer saved
                             on interrupt stack
  Exit conditions      : cpu registers restored

global variables
  interrupt_table      : table of interrupt numbers, driver addresses,
                             and buffer addresses
  local variables
    count              : integer; {remaining character count}
    pointer            : integer; {pointer to next buffer character}
    buffer             : integer; {address of data buffer}

begin
{ Save the status of the machine.  Get the interrupt number and
  check interrupt table to find a driver continuator or other
  interrupt processor address.                                           }

  disable interrupts;               {this may have been done by hardware}
  push registers on interrupt stack;
  obtain interrupt_number;
  search interrupt table for match with interrupt_number;

{ Get the necessary information from the interrupt table and go to
  the driver continuator section.                                        }

  if interrupt_number found then
    begin
      vector := driver_address;
      count  := buffer_address;
      pointer:= buffer_address + 1;
      buffer := buffer_address + 2;
      vector(count,pointer,buffer);
    end {interrupt_number was in table}
  else send illegal interrupt message to operator;

{ Return here if this was not a completion interrupt.                    }

  pop registers from interrupt stack;
  enable interrupts;
end; {FLIH}
```

Figure 12.8 The FLIH.

The interrupt number is then compared with the valid interrupts in the interrupt table to see whether the interrupt is valid. If it is a valid interrupt, the interrupt processing routine (the driver continuator for I/O interrupts) is called. For our system, the driver continuator address is passed in the buffer information from the interrupt table so that a driver can service multiple devices.

If the interrupt number is not found in the interrupt table, an "illegal interrupt" message is sent to the operator. An illegal interrupt might result from a hardware failure or an electrical transient caused by turning on the power to a device.

After the routine has processed the interrupt, it passes control back to the FLIH if the interrupt has not caused any change in the active queue. If the interrupt has caused a process to be added to the active queue, the driver will not return to the FLIH; it will make a completion call to the IOCS. If control is passed back to the FLIH, it restores the state of the CPU from the stack and passes control to the process that was interrupted.

12.4 SUMMARY

The operations performed by the kernel are quite limited: dispatching processes, synchronizing processes, and deciding what to do when an interrupt occurs. From the pseudocode shown for these three functions, we saw that each is a relatively simple and distinct operation.

In the next chapter we will discuss how the various parts of the system are tied together. We will also see how a system can be built as successive layers of programs and how these layers communicate with each other.

A simple, but interesting and complete, kernel is described and coded in Holt et al. [1978]. Brinch Hansen provides us with two other kernel descriptions that are informative reading [Brinch Hansen, 1970; 1976]. The paper by Crowley [1981] describes an alternative kernel for UNIX that, although slow, is worth examining. The design of the kernel for HYDRA [Wulf et al., 1974] provides us with an approach to the design of a multiprocessor system. The kernel that Popek and Kline [1978] propose emphasizes security considerations in kernel construction.

QUESTIONS AND EXERCISES

1. Why might there be problems if the DISPATCHER stays in a loop looking for a process to place into execution when it finds the active queue empty? (*Hint:* What is the state of the interrupt system when the kernel is executing?)

2. What type of hardware and software diagnostics can be executed while the system is running? What problems can occur when running diagnostics on line?

3. How is the "load program counter" operation in the process DISPATCHER accomplished in assembly language?

4. Write the pseudocode for the procedure monitor_create.

5. The FLIH disables interrupts while it processes one. What happens if a very fast device wants to interrupt because it has data ready and the data will be lost if the interrupt is not handled immediately?

6. There is a potential problem with the DISPATCHER shown in Figure 12.1; it involves the last two lines. What is the problem? How can it be overcome?

7. Revise our monitor control so that a condition variable "remembers" if it was signaled when no processes were waiting.

8. In Section 12.1 we stated that the idle process can do archiving rather than just blinking lights. This can cause a problem. What is the problem? How can it be solved?

9. In Section 12.2 the description of the signal operation states that the signaling process is placed on a waiting signalers' queue. Why not just move the waiting process to the active queue and allow the signaler to proceed (which is done in some implementations of monitors)?

10. Is it possible that a process trying to exit a monitor will be forced to wait indefinitely? Explain your answer.

─── 13 ───

Structure and Flow
in a Layered Operating
System

The main purpose of this chapter is to show how the various parts of an OS that have been described in Chapters 5 through 12 can all be connected to form a system. To accomplish this, we will start with a description of a *layered* approach for the structure of the OS.

After showing how all the pieces can be put together, we follow the execution of a process from its creation, through its use of system facilities, and to its termination. Finally, we will see how the parts of the system can be loaded into memory and how system processes can be initiated.

13.1 A LAYERED ORGANIZATION FOR OPERATING SYSTEMS

In order to effectively integrate the components of our OS, we will put the pieces together as a series of layers, each new one on top of the preceding one. Layering has become popular in both hardware and software. For example, the International Standards Organization (ISO) standard network interface has seven layers, going from 1 to 7 [Martin, 1981]. The layered structure for OS construction has been used on several systems [Dijkstra, 1968; Brinch Hansen, 1970]. The popularity and portability of UNIX [Thompson, 1978] has also contributed to the belief that a layered OS is superior to other design approaches. An excellent reference to layered operating systems can be found in Lister [1979].

The base of our layered structure (which, following the ISO approach, we will show pictorially as a straticulate column) is the kernel. As described in the previous chapter, it contains the first-level interrupt handler, the dispatcher, and facilities for process synchronization. This base for our column is shown in Figure 13.1. It is a very hardware-dependent part of the system and can be thought of as the first layer of software covering the system hardware.

Hardware

Figure 13.1   Foundation layer of column: the kernel.

The next layer is the memory manager. Since it must work with the paging hardware, it is also somewhat hardware-dependent. It uses some of the services provided by the kernel to accomplish its operations. Page fault interrupts, memory address violation interrupts, and memory error interrupts are detected by the kernel software and passed to the appropriate routines within the memory manager for resolution. Figure 13.2 shows the structure with the memory manager software added.

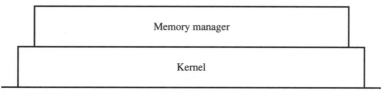

Hardware

Figure 13.2   Adding the memory manager to the system.

The third layer of the system is the IOCS. Again, some of this software is very much hardware-dependent. Input-output drivers must work directly with the hardware features of the machine. The I/O layer is also dependent on the kernel to process interrupts and pass control to the correct driver routines. It may also need the services of the memory manager to acquire I/O buffer space. The system with the I/O layer is shown in Figure 13.3.

Layers 1, 2, and 3 are the parts of the OS that are most dependent on the underlying hardware. Some of the software in these layers will probably be written in assembly language or a system's programming language because of the need to access special hardware features and the need to build a fast, efficient system. As we progress to the layers beyond layer 3, we will find that the software becomes less and less dependent on the hardware.

The file manager is our next layer, and in many cases it can be written with little regard to the physical hardware that will be used to support it. It is possible that some characteristics of the disk drives will affect the performance of the file man-

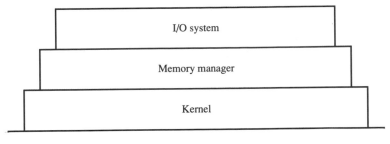

Figure 13.3   Adding the IOCS layer to the system.

ager, but most of the file management techniques described in Chapter 10 can be applied to any hardware we have available.

The file manager can be independent of the hardware because the I/O system, memory manager, and kernel isolate it from the actual hardware. The file manager does not need to be concerned with how interrupts from the disk will be processed or how the driver gets the status of the disk. All it needs to know is how to use these services provided by the lower layers of the system.

This leads us to an important characteristic and feature of layered systems. Layered systems must be designed so that each layer has a precise set of rules that tell outer layers how to access it. This set of rules is usually called the **interface requirement**. As long as the interface requirement is strictly followed, it is possible to completely change one of the layers of the system without affecting the code in any of the other layers. For instance, suppose after working on our system for some time we decide to change the disk space allocation scheme from one based on contiguous allocation to one based on indexed blocks. As long as the new file manager accepts the same requests and returns the same information, the outer layers need not even know a change has occurred.

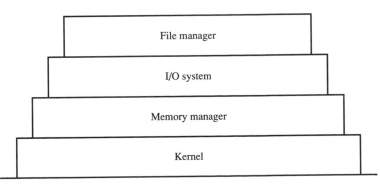

Figure 13.4   Adding the file manager to the system.

Since the outer layers of the OS are not dependent on the hardware characteristics, they are often written in languages that facilitate development of sophisticated data structures and are easy to maintain. Languages currently popular for this type of software include C, Modula-2, PASCAL, and systems programming languages. The layered system with the file manager added is shown in Figure 13.4.

The next layer we will add is not at all dependent on the hardware. The short-term scheduler is responsible for maintaining the active queue on the system. When it is activated, it orders the ready queue and then calls the dispatcher within the kernel to place the highest-priority process into execution. The short-term scheduler is shown as layer 5 in Figure 13.5.

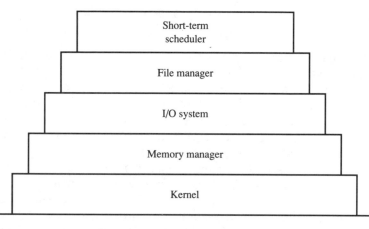

Hardware

Figure 13.5 Adding the short-term scheduler to the system.

The short-term scheduler is responsible for managing one resource, the CPU. Since our system has many other resources, we must find a place for the manager of these additional resources. We will place the resource manager at layer 6. One could make a good argument for swapping the short-term scheduler and the resource manager based on the fact that processes may need the resource manager after the short-term scheduler has provided its service. This would be the case when dynamic resource allocation is used. Therefore, even though we show the resource manager as layer 6 in Figure 13.6, some systems might have it as layer 5.

We have been working our way from the lower, hardware-dependent layers of the system toward the outer layers, the ones with which the user most often interacts. Layer 7, which is shown in Figure 13.7, is the long-term scheduler. This layer controls the process mix on the system and is responsible for creating and terminating processes. It uses the capabilities of all of the lower layers to complete its operations. For example, it calls the file manager to find program files; it calls the memory manager to find space for new processes, and it uses the IOCS to read in programs. The IOCS in turn uses the kernel to handle interrupts.

The last system layer on the operating system provides the system with its personality. This outer cap, or **shell**, is the part of the system the user interacts with di-

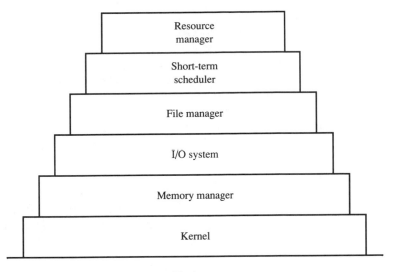

Figure 13.6   Adding the resource manager to the system.

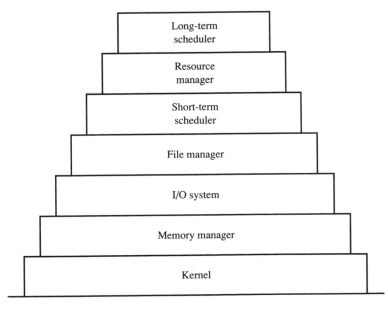

Figure 13.7   Adding the long-term scheduler to the system.

rectly and often determines how well users like the system. The generic name for this layer is the *command interpreter*. When a user logs onto a system, it is usually the command interpreter that sends the prompt to the screen and is responsible for analyzing user requests and calling on the proper system routines to satisfy these requests. Several well-known command interpreters have been designed for the UNIX system, including the Bourne shell [Bourne, 1978].

Because of the growing popularity of menus on microcomputer systems, several companies have developed shells that run on MS-DOS or PC-DOS [Central Point Software, 1987; Peter Norton, 1987b]. They are designed to hide the details of DOS from the user. Instead of typing DOS commands, the user selects the commands from a series of menus by moving the cursor to the appropriate location on the screen, using cursor keys or a mouse. This type of shell is increasingly popular with users who are poor typists or who do not use the system often enough to memorize the DOS commands. Figure 13.8 shows the command interpreter layer.

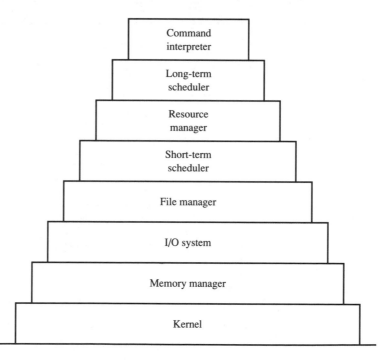

Figure 13.8   Adding the command interpreter to the system.

The last layer, then, is the user layer. This is also sometimes called the application layer, since it contains the applications programs for our system. Sometimes the shells described in the previous paragraph are in reality just application-level programs that give a more friendly user interface to the basic command interpreter. A complete diagram of the straticulate column is shown in Figure 13.9.

If you look at layered descriptions of other systems, don't be surprised to see systems with more layers than we have shown [Brown and Denning, 1984]. A com-

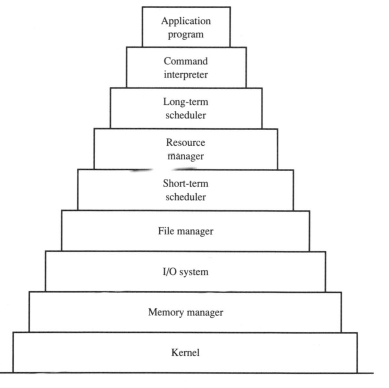

Figure 13.9 Final layered system as a straticulate column.

mon layer that is added to many systems is a data-base management package. Other systems will add layers that just provide a remote terminal interface to some special application program. Layering is an important and useful tool in developing large, complicated systems, and its use and acceptance are growing.

A logical extension of the layering concept is to create a *virtual machine* for each user. This method essentially wraps one or more layers around the vendor-supplied system, thus creating the *illusion* that a certain set of capabilities are available to the user. Probably the most well-known implementation of this design approach is one that can be found on the IBM 370: the VM370 operating system [Goldberg, 1974].

Now that we have put the pieces of the system together, in the next section we will follow the execution of a user command through the layers of that system.

13.2 A SAMPLE PROCESS LIFE CYCLE

To better understand the interactions of the layers of the operating system, we will follow the execution of an application program which executes as a process at layer 9. The relevant code for the process is shown in Figure 13.10. The statements

```
        program(paycheck,std_out);
                    *
1.      open(mag_tape as data1);
                    *
                    *
2.      read(data1,line);
                    *
                    *
3.      open(c:employee as data2);
                    *
                    *
4.      write(data2,line2);
                    *
                    *
5.      open(std_out);
                    *
                    *
6.      write(line3);
                    *
                    *
7.      close(data2);
                    *
                    *
8.      close(data1);
                    *
9.      end;
```

Figure 13.10 Portions of a sample application program.

within the program that require OS services are labeled with numbers so that we may follow their execution.

Before the program can execute, it is necessary to create a process for it. The user causes this to happen by typing in the following in response to the command interpreter prompt:

```
>run paycheck, 2
```

The command interpreter parses the command and finds "run," which tells it that a process must be created and added to the list of processes trying to enter the system. It finds the name of the executable file, "paycheck.exe," and calls the long-term scheduler with the following statement:

```
LONG_TERM_SCHEDULER(create,paycheck.exe,2,def_lines,def_time,
              wait,,,);
```

where the parameters are as follows:

create	request for a new process
paycheck.exe	name of the disk file
2	priority the new process will have
def_time	default CPU time
def_lines	default number of lines of output
wait	specification that the parent process (in this case, the command interpreter) will wait for the child to terminate before continuing

The long-term scheduler is responsible for ordering the requests for new processes. It is also responsible for creating the process which the system will use to execute the program. It first checks to see whether the program file exists by calling the FILE_MGR with the following statement:

```
FILE_MGR(search,,,payroll.exe,,file_size,prog_size,
         start_address,,status);
```

where the parameters are as follows:

search	command to the file manager to do a directory search
file_size	size of the file
prog_size	size of the program
start_address	starting execution address
status	result of the directory search
payroll.exe	name of the program file

Assuming that the file is found, the next step is to place the request for the process on the creation queue. To do this the long-term scheduler accesses the process request monitor with the following code:

```
WAITING_LIST.add_request(prog_size,def_time,def_lines,
         mem_address);
```

where the first three parameters are as defined above and

mem_address	starting memory address of the process (assigned after selection)

The long-term scheduler will try to select a process creation request whenever such a request is made or when resources are released by some other process. Again, the process request monitor is accessed, this time to see whether a process can be created; the code is:

```
WAITING_LIST.select_request;
```

As part of the selection sequence of events, the long-term scheduler must acquire memory on behalf of the process from the memory manager with the following request:

```
MEMORY_MGR(allocate,prog_size,load_address,status);
```

where the parameters are as follows:

allocate	memory manager command
prog_size	value returned by the file manager

| load_address | memory location of the block allocated |
| status | error indicator if the request was larger than the largest block available |

The long-term scheduler calls the file manager to load the executable file into memory with the following:

```
FILE_MGR(prog_read,load_address,file_size,payroll.exe,,,,,
         true,status);
```

where the parameters are as follows:

| prog_read | file manager command to load a program file |
| true | specification that errors should be returned to the long-term scheduler |

After the file has been read into the memory, the PCB for the new process will be moved to the active queue. The program will be in memory and the starting address of the program will be stored in the restart address of the PCB. After the process has worked its way to the head of the active queue, it will be dispatched and start executing.

The code for the program, which is now executing as a process, will at some time need operating system services to continue. We assume that the compiler has converted statement 1 into the following code:

```
RESOURCE_MGR(allocate,mag_tape,device ,status);
```

where the parameters are as follows:

allocate	request for a new device
mag_tape	class of device requested
data1	logical unit reference number for the device
status	result of operation

The resource manager will check to see whether any resources of type mag_tape are available. If there is one available (and whatever allocation scheme we are using confirms that it can be allocated without creating a potential deadlock), then it will be allocated to "paycheck" by attaching an RCB to the process's PCB. If there is no mag tape that can be assigned, the process will be placed on the blocked queue until one becomes available. An entry will also be made in the user's LUT so that the process can access the tape with future I/O requests.

Later, after the process has successfully acquired the right to access a mag tape, statement 2 will be executed. The object code generated for this statement will be:

```
IOCS(read,data1,line,length,errors,status);
```

where the parameters are as follows:

read	I/O command
data1	logical unit number for the tape unit assigned to the process by the resource manager
input_buffer	address of the data buffer
length	number of characters to read
errors	indicator to IOCS that the user process does not want to be responsible for handling I/O errors
status	result of the operation

For this example, since the process has specified that it will not be responsible for dealing with I/O errors, the process will be terminated should an error occur. The IOCS will examine the request to verify the logical unit number and the command and then call the appropriate device driver with the following:

```
DRIVER_INITIATOR(read,device ,line,length,status);
```

where all the parameters are defined as above.

When control passes back to the IOCS with the status of the specified I/O initiation, the PCB of the process making the request will have moved from execute to I/O suspend, where it will remain until the read operation on the mag tape is completed.

When the data has all been transferred from tape to memory, a completion interrupt will be requested by the mag tape controller. The FLIH will be activated and will save the status of the machine and then go to the interrupt table to find the address of the driver continuator that is responsible for acknowledging the interrupt; it will then call that continuator.

The driver continuator section will check status and perform all of its necessary housekeeping. It will then call the IOCS with a completion request with the following:

```
IOCS(completion,device ,,,,status);
```

where the parameters are as follows:

completion	indicators to IOCS that an I/O operation has completed
device	device number
status	result of operation

When the IOCS determines that the data transfer has taken place without error, it will remove the process from the I/O suspend queue and pass its PCB to the short-term scheduler with:

```
SHORT_TERM_SCHED(pcb_pointer);
```

where

    pcb_pointer   pointer to the PCB for the process that has just completed its
                      I/O request

The short-term scheduler will put the PCB passed to it onto the appropriate active queue and then order the queues. Once the queues have been ordered, it is time to call the dispatcher with

```
DISPATCHER;
```

The dispatcher requires no parameters; it simply takes the PCB at the head of the highest-priority nonempty active queue and places that PCB into the execution queue.

The next statement that requires system intervention is the open statement 3. The following code will have been generated for this statement:

```
FILE_MGR(open, , , c: employee, data2, read, , , errors, status);
```

where the parameters are as follows:

    open   file operation requested
    c:employee   disk drive and name of the file
    data2   pointer to the FCB the process will use to reference the file
    read   type of access requested
    errors   indicator whose value is false
    status   result of the request

Again, since "errors" is false, the process will be terminated if there is an error opening the file,.

Statement 4 is a request to the system to write a line of data to the disk file. The code for the statement will be

```
FILE_MGR(write, output_buffer, length, data2, , , , errors, status);
```

where the parameters are as follows:

    write   file manager command
    output_buffer   pointer to the data buffer
    length   number of bytes that will be transferred
    data2   pointer to the FCB opened
    errors   indicator whose value is false
    status   result of the request

The file manager will try to complete the request by transferring information from the user's buffer to the data area in the FCB. If there is sufficient room in the FCB, no call will be made to the IOCS to physically write the FCB buffer area to disk, and it will not be necessary to suspend the process. If the buffer area is full, the process will be suspended while a disk write takes place.

Since the process accesses the standard output device, std_out, that device must also be opened. We will assume that the standard output is a spool file that will be printed after the process completes. The open statement might not appear in the actual program but might rather be generated as a result of the program statement (which referenced std_out). Whether it is called implicitly or explicitly by the program in a statement such as 5, the following code will be generated:

```
FILE_MGR(open,,,outspool,std_out,write,,,errors,status);
```

where the parameters are similar to those used in the previous file open statement.

All further writes that do not specify a device will be directed to the std_out device. Therefore statement 6 will be converted to the following by the compiler:

```
IOCS(write,std_out,line3,120,errors,status);
```

where again the parameters are similar to those in previous IOCS commands.

After the program has finished with the I/O devices, the close commands in statements 7 and 8 are executed to close the files and return the resources to the system. The code generated for statement 7 is:

```
FILE_MGR(close,keep,,,data2,,,,errors,status);
```

where the parameters are as follows:

close   file manager command

keep   specification that the file is to be made permanent rather than temporary

The code for statement 8 is:

```
RESOURCE_MGR(return,mag_tape,device,status);
```

where return is the resource manager command.

The final statement of the program causes the following code to be generated:

```
LONG_TERM_SCHEDULER(exit,,,,,,,,,);
```

where exit requests termination of the executing process.

This brings us full circle in our trip through a typical process life cycle. Sometimes people are truly amazed that all of these things can actually work. They do, and we hope that with the ideas of modularity, layers, and concurrency you can comprehend and appreciate how such a complex activity can be designed and implemented as a large set of small, understandable components.

In this section we have looked at the creation, execution, and termination of a user process. We saw how the user program code was converted to calls to the OS when system services were required and followed these calls from the layer 9 process down through the other layers of the system. In the next section we will examine how the system is first loaded into memory and how it starts execution.

13.3 SYSTEM START-UP: BOOTSTRAPPING THE SYSTEM

The questions we now want to address are "What happens when we turn the system on in the morning?" and "How do you get all of those pieces going?" Since no two systems start up in exactly the same way, we will again give generic answers to these related questions.

For any computer to start executing, it must have some instructions to execute. Most systems today have some nonvolatile memory which stores a program that can run when the system is turned on. Often this is some form of read-only memory that cannot be accidentally destroyed by the user. On older machines, when power was first turned on, it was the operator's responsibility to (1) halt the machine, (2) load the address of the start-up program into the memory address register, and (3) press RUN. Most current machines use an interrupt that is activated when the power is turned on or when the RESET switch is depressed.

The start-up program, or **bootstrap**, will begin loading the system routines into memory. Creating an entire operating system from a set of disk files is not necessarily a trivial task, and the space in read-only memory is often quite limited. For these reasons, starting up the system is usually a multistep operation. The ROM resident part of the bootstrap program usually only reads the first few sectors from track 0 of the system disk drive before it transfers control to this second, disk-resident part of the bootstrap program. This program continues the operation of constructing the OS. Since the second part of the bootstrap program resides on a relatively inexpensive and large medium, it can be made as large and complex as necessary to load in the remainder of the OS.

There is another function which is performed by most start-up programs on modern systems. The start-up program is usually responsible for running some diagnostic checks on the processor and main memory. If it detects any failures, it tries to report them to the operator and then halts the computer. Assuming there have been no failures, we can get on with building the operating system.

The system loader will first bring in the kernel, the memory manager, and the I/O system from disk files. It will then build some of the tables necessary for the system such as the interrupt table, logical unit table, and page tables. The loader will work its way out through the layers of the system from the memory manager to the long-term scheduler.

At this point, the loader has created a system that is capable of executing processes. The loader is now ready to create the processes that are a necessary part of the operating system. A quick review of a process control block shows that every process has a pointer to its parent. That being the case, a process must be created that can be the parent of all other processes; we will call this process UPP, for uni-

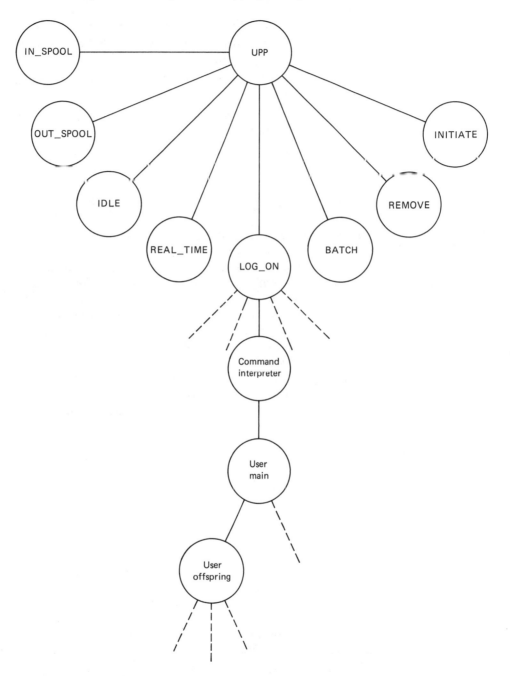

Figure 13.11 Family tree of processes on the system.

versal progenitor process. After this process is created, it will use the system facilities to create the required system processes.

The parent process UPP is responsible for creating the following system processes:

IN_SPOOL	Process that reads jobs from input spool device
OUT_SPOOL	Process that dumps output spool files to the printer
IDLE	The idle process
REMOVE	The process responsible for removing terminated processes
INITIATE	Process that selects requests from the process creation request queue
BATCH	Command interpreter process for batch processes
LOGON	Process that creates command interpreter processes for terminals
REAL_TIME	Process that starts real-time processes for the system

The family tree of processes within the system is shown in Figure 13.11. As can be seen, all processes in the system have a parent except UPP.

To enable users to access the system from terminals, a command interpreter process is created for each terminal by the LOGON process after a successful logon. Each of these command interpreters sends a prompt to the terminal to which it is attached. This may sound like a waste of memory, but that does not have to be the case if the system's memory management scheme supports code sharing. Once his or her command interpreter has been created, a terminal user can then access the system through that process.

When a user logs off the system, the LOGON process will be notified that one of its children, the command interpreter, has terminated. The LOGON process will wait for another LOGON request, and the cycle will start over again.

13.4 SUMMARY

At the beginning of this text we emphasized the idea of an operating system designed as a central nucleus (kernel) controlling a set of concurrent processes. In this chapter we have presented a detailed organization for such an operating system. That organization is based on layering. The kernel forms the bottom layer, and successive layers provide increasing capabilities: memory management, I/O, files, scheduling, resource allocation, command interpretation, and user interfacing.

Operations within the layered structure were illustrated with a sample user request. We followed the request through the system, looking at the functions performed in various layers and the interfaces between the layers.

Finally, we took a look at how the system starts operation. The operation of the bootstrap program was described, and we saw how processes were created to service the various users of the system including batch, real-time, and terminal.

In Chapter 12 we looked at the kernel, and in this chapter we have described and illustrated a layered OS with the kernel as its basis. We turn now to a topic which has received considerable attention recently: techniques to improve the security of our OS.

Another good reference to a layered OS can be found in Liskov [1972]. In this paper Liskov describes the Venus operating system and provides some interesting historical information about OS design. Hall et al. [1980] describes how a UNIX-like virtual machine was created so that people would not have to be retrained to use a new system.

QUESTIONS AND EXERCISES

1. Describe problems which might occur if the order of the layering were changed.

2. Could any of the components we have in the kernel be moved to an outer layer?

3. Are there any components in outer layers which you might want to put in the kernel?

4. How can layering help facilitate the creation of virtual machines for different users?

5. Why are REMOVE and INITIATE implemented as *processes* and not as *procedures*?

6. In Section 13.1 we stated that changing a layer, such as the memory manager, will not affect any of the layers outside of it. Will such a change affect any of the layers inside of it?

7. Show how Figure 13.11 could be modified so that we could create a way for a system manager to access the system without going through the standard logon.

8. Assuming we have created a manager for the system (see Exercise 7), how could the manager easily get rid of all terminal users?

9. Most systems allow the system manager (or user, for a single-user system) to create a set of operations that are automatically executed when the system is started up. How is this implemented on your system?

10. Draw a diagram that shows the flow of events described in Section 13.2, A Sample Process Life Cycle.

11. Modify the diagram described in Exercise 10 to show the flow of events if the system uses demand paging.

12. How can the bootstrap loader bring in anything before the kernel, drivers, and so forth, arc available?

PROGRAMMING ASSIGNMENT

In Section 13.1 we described how a shell could be placed on top of the command interpreter to "hide" the features of the system from the user. Write a menu-oriented shell that gives the user access to the command interpreter. Your shell should be able to accept requests to:

    List files on the disk
    Copy a file to another device
    Display the current date and time
    Change the current working directory
    Execute a word processor
    Compile a program

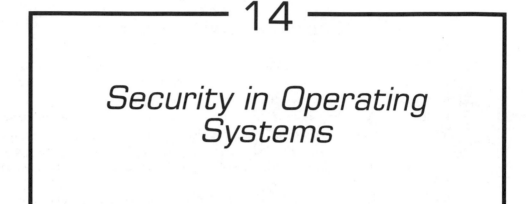

14

Security in Operating Systems

Security and privacy have become two of *the* most important and complex issues in computer science. In addition to the technical aspects, there are myriad moral and legal considerations which the system designer must consider [Hoffman, 1977].

In some respects computer security is similar to other familiar kinds of security. Essentially, we want to control access to resources. A lock on the door of a house controls access to the house; a lock on a terminal controls access to that terminal. However, there are many more facets to security on a computer system. A sampling of topics often covered in a security class or seminar shown in Figure 14.1.

To illustrate the diversity of problems that are encountered when dealing with computer system security, consider the following things that people have done to or done with computer systems to breach the system's security [Parker 1976]:

Flooding a computer center by placing a garden hose through a mail slot

Removing labels from all of the hundreds of tape reels in a tape library

Creating phony resources via altered software

Using the computer to find financial accounts that have not been used for a long time, and stealing from them

Using modified deposit slips to put everyone's deposits into a single account

Intercepting and rerouting a large trans-Atlantic monetary transfer

Stealing passwords and data via wiretapping

Type	Examples	Some purposes
Physical	Locks Guards Badges	Prevent vandalism; protect valuable equipment against theft; protect data from theft by physical means, such as stealing tapes
Environmental	Smoke detectors Humidity sensors Fire extinguishers	Protect personnel and equipment
Insurance	Loss of data or computing time Liability	Provide monetary reimbursements for losses
Backup data storage	Copies at other sites Special storage facilities	Prevent loss of valuable date
Backup computing facilities	Second system Contract with a timeshare company	Provide means to do computing if main site goes down
Identification at logon	Passwords Physical attributes	Restrict access to system
Authorization	Matrix C-Lists	Restrict users to doing only what they are authorized to do
Statistical	Noise Gaps	Prevent manipulation of statistical data base to get individual information
Data base	Encryption Passwords	Regulate accesses to data base
Communication	Encryption Call-back	Prevent theft of information or computer usage via tampering with remote terminal hookups

Figure 14.1   Some aspects of computer security.

Disrupting a business by using a computer to constantly call and tie up a company's phone lines

Placing a "trapdoor" into a system so that the programmer could get back into the system later for devious purposes

Placing a "Trojan horse" into a system, so that at some later time resources could be moved to a special account and all records which might be used to trace the transfer could be destroyed

Modifying software so checks continued to be sent to deceased people, but at a special set of addresses

Modifying a racetrack computer system so portions of purses could be stolen by creating winning tickets after the race, and adjusting payoffs accordingly

In this chapter we can look at security only with respect to operating systems. Even then, we can touch on only a fraction of the aspects. We will restrict our investigations to the areas of identification, authorization, and encryption.

14.1 IDENTIFICATION

One of the first security considerations in any transaction is for both parties to *identify* each other. In computer security we do not limit the discussion to having the operating system identifying the user. With the increasing popularity of networks and remote access, it is often equally important for the user to identify what he or she is talking to. Some classic security breaches have occurred when a person or another system fooled users into thinking that they were on a certain system when they really were not [Hoffman, 1977].

For example, suppose someone has gained access to lines coming into a company's timesharing system. When a logon request from a remote terminal is detected, the intruder temporarily breaks the connection. He connects his own computer to the remote terminal and sends a logoff message to the company computer. The user at the remote terminal transmits large amounts of valuable data, all to be stored on the intruder's computer. After the session is completed, the intruder reconnects the remote line to the company's timesharing system and leaves.

Part of the identification procedure can involve physical location. A common implementation of location checks is call-back; if Jim (or someone claiming to be Jim) calls up system XYZ, the system might not accept the logon directly—instead it calls back a prespecified number for Jim, assuming that if the person is at the given number then there is support for the claim that he is Jim. Another example of this approach is to have hard-wired terminals whose locations have some security ramifications, such as being in a locked room accessible only by certain programmers.

Often we do not have such physical location constraints, or we want to go beyond them. Then, for identification of a system we use something it "knows," and for identification of a person something he or she "is," "has," or "knows."

One of the "knows" categories most of us have used is passwords. We can use passwords in both directions—system identifying user and user identifying system. An important security consideration is the selection of the passwords. Much research has gone into this area [Wood, 1977], and we cannot review it all here. Suffice it to say that the system designer wants to keep away from both ends of the difficulty spectrum. Common passwords, such as initials and name variations, are too easy to guess. Totally random computer-generated combinations are often so difficult to remember that they are written down, which defeats the purpose of having a secure system.

As a little illustration of breaking into a system which uses unregulated single passwords for protection, we experimented with the accounts of a large computer science class. We knew a few of the students fairly well, but most were just casual acquaintances. With approval of both the students and the system administrator, we made a few attempts to log onto each account. The success rate was about 8 percent, a surprising figure considering the small number of simple guesses for each account.

One interesting technique which has been developed for password generation is to use a large set of syllables and combine them randomly, but under certain phonetic restrictions [Wood, 1977]. The results are essentially "pronounceable nonsense," easier to remember than randomly generated character sequences but hard to guess! As an example, consider syllables drawn randomly from a dictionary, as shown in Figure 14.2. We could generate passwords such as dacerdle, kiniscri, kerchada, lacenton, ondemas, permasot, and so on.

on	cent	ar	cer	cha
cri	de	da	ot	dle
mas	mak	dor	ker	kin
is	kin	la	per	com

Figure 14.2   Set of randomly selected syllables.

Passwords can be used by the operating system at levels other than logon. In Chapter 10, on files, we indicated that a password or passwords could be kept in the file descriptor, and access rights to the file could be determined by reference to the password entry.

Sometimes the operating system forces users to change passwords periodically. In the extreme case, passwords could be used only once; however, this again implies written lists. There could be potential coordination problems, such as what to do if a transmission error occurred when a password was being sent. On the other hand, the necessary coordination provides added security; if the next password does not work, it could be an indication that an intruder has logged on.

Things a person knows need not be passwords. Some systems ask questions from personnel files, trivia questions a user supplies, or combinations of the two [Hoffman, 1977]. Other systems use little formulas that are functions of variant parameters, such as the time of logon and the terminal number; these have the advantage that someone who sees or intercepts a value now probably could not use it again later. For instance, a user might have the formula "square the last digit of the time and add the product of the second digit in the session number and the first digit in the terminal number." If the user requested logon and the system included in its response

TIME 09:35:27   SESSION 236   TERMINAL 12

then the password would be $7^2 + 3 \times 1 = 52$. Someone who saw the "52" might try it later, but it is unlikely that the time, session, and terminal numbers would give the same result.

One final comment should be made regarding passwords. Security is greatly increased if the passwords are not stored directly, but rather as the value of a *one-way* (trapdoor) *function* [D. E. Denning, 1982]. For example, if Larry's password is some string A, then we store string X = trapdoor(A). When someone claiming to be Larry logs on and enters string B, we compute Y = trapdoor(B) and compare X and Y. That way, someone who penetrates the system password file will get X— which isn't much help in breaking into the system! As an example of the importance of this safeguard, consider various types of automated financial systems; if passwords or identification numbers are stored in plain text, then it becomes much easier for an employee of the financial institution to steal them.

Earlier in this section we mentioned two other identification possibilities, something a person is or has. The "is" part usually refers to some definitive personal characteristic. Work is being done on such things as voiceprints, fingerprints, hand geometry, and signature analysis [Hoffman, 1977]. The "has" part usually refers to something a user has in his or her possession. Keys and identification cards are standard examples.

One generally true principle is that if each of several individual techniques has a certain security level, then higher levels of security would be implied by combining techniques. A typical example is a banking computer system in which a card (user has) and a secret identification number, PIN (user knows), are combined.

This has been a brief introduction to identification. We now turn to the question of authorization, which is controlling what the identified person can do.

14.2 AUTHORIZATION

Once identification has been verified, the next phase is usually authorization. Simply put, we are satisfied we know who is trying to use the system, and now we want to decide what that user will be allowed to do.

The prototypical solution to this problem is the authorization matrix [Conway et al., 1972]. One axis has the users (or more generally the subjects or actors), and the other axis has the objects, such as files. The intersection of a given subject and a given object contains the corresponding authorization, such as "Jim can only read file LARRY.DAT." Figure 14.3 shows a sample matrix, with R, W, E, and M specifying read, write, execute, and modify, and an empty cell specifying no access.

	F1	F2	INF	P1	P2	A	B	C	D
Larry			R	E		M		R	
Sam	W		R			W			
Joe	M					M			R
System	W	W	W	E	E	W	W	W	W
Tom			R		E	M			
Pam	R			E	E		W	W	

Figure 14.3 Authorization matrix.

Unfortunately, the number of subjects and objects normally makes the size of such a matrix unmanageable. Most elements are empty, so sparse matrix techniques could be used to store the information [Amsbury, 1985]. However, the usual approach is to store information along one axis or the other: (1) for each subject keep a list of all objects that subject can access, with the list entry for a given object containing the specific rights the subject has to it, or (2) for each object keep a list of all subjects that can access it, with the list entry for a given subject containing the specific rights the subject has to the object.

You can probably see the search problems with either method. If we store by object then a file used by all of the OS classes might have hundreds of subjects, and hence long search times. Also, consider the problem of making modifications to the list: What happens if an object changes and we have to check and perhaps modify every subject list, or a subject changes and we have to check and perhaps modify every object list?

Some systems cut down on the size of the access matrix by grouping elements instead of considering them individually. For example, we could limit execution of a certain file to:

Only the owner
Everyone on the owner's team
Everyone in the owner's division
The "world"

In the last three cases we do not list individuals, but rather groups.

Another interesting idea for authorization is to use an analogy with tickets to some event [Linden, 1976; D. E. Denning and P. J. Denning, 1979]. A given object is considered to have a set of tickets associated with it, and these tickets can be given to various subjects. Each ticket specifies a certain access right, and hence a subject having a ticket to an object has the right to that object specified on the ticket. The set of tickets a subject has at any given time can be kept on a list, and attempted operations are verified via the ticket list. Since the tickets give the subject a capability to access the object, the list (and the method itself) are called **capability lists,** or C-Lists for short.

A well-known and frequently used approach to the limitation of access capabilities is the *ring* approach employed by systems such as Multics [Schroeder and Saltzer, 1972]. The kernel forms the central circle, and other elements are viewed as members of concentric rings going out from this center. The farther from the center a given ring is, the lower its capabilities. In order to get into the next inner ring, a process must go through a specific gate; this allows the system to carefully check all such transitions.

In the previous sections we have looked at specific security topics—identification and authorization. We turn now to a general topic with broad applications.

14.3 ENCRYPTION

Most of us are acquainted with the idea of taking ordinary text and changing it into some form of secret writing, that is, **encrypting** the text. Many aspects of operating system security depend on encryption, and so we will look briefly at this fascinating topic. For a thorough, informative, and very readable discussion of encryption, see Kahn [1967].

The usual goal of encryption is to take something like a message that anyone can read if he or she can access it and change it to some form in which only selected individuals can understand it, regardless of who gains access to it. Put another way, we take *cleartext* and encode it to produce *ciphertext*.

Usually we want to perform this transformation on the basis of a special value called a *key*. Hence we might view the process pictorially as shown in Figure 14.4. Later, we will probably want to do the reverse—take the ciphertext and produce the cleartext, as shown in Figure 14.5.

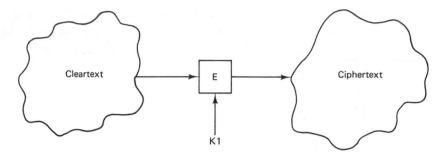

Figure 14.4 Encryption using key K1.

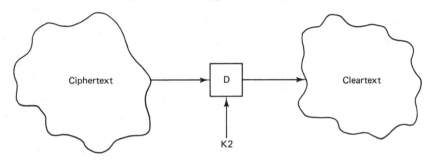

Figure 14.5 Decryption using key K2.

In the description above, we have specified two keys, K1 and K2. If these keys are actually different, then our system is called a **two-key system.** If they are the same, or if they can be easily derived from each other, the system is called a **one-key** or **classic system** [D. E. Denning, 1982].

There are two standard approaches to encryption. One relies on substituting ciphertext characters for cleartext characters; the other transposes existing cleartext to produce ciphertext [Lempel, 1979; Meyer and Matyas, 1982].

A simple substitution could be accomplished by adding an offset to the numeric encoding of each cleartext character and taking the result modulo the alphabet size to give the numeric encoding of the corresponding ciphertext character. Offsetting our standard alphabet by 3 would give

$$\text{COMPUTER} \longrightarrow \text{FRPSXWHU}$$

In this case, the encryption key would be 3. The decryption key would be -3, or equivalently 23 in addition modulo 26.

A simple transposition would be to take blocks of characters and permute the characters by some pattern, such as 71265843 for an 8-character block. This implies that character 1 in cleartext goes to position 7 in ciphertext, and so on. Using our previous cleartext,

$$\text{COMPUTER SCIENCE} \longrightarrow \text{OMREUPCTC SNEEIC}$$

The encryption key is then the pattern of replacements. The decryption key is just the inverse of the permutation.

As we mentioned earlier, security can often be increased by combining techniques. Hence we might use both the offset and the permutation when encrypting a file.

These examples are simple, and not very secure, methods of encrypting information. They are just for illustration. Current commercial methods are much more complex, although they still rely on the basic ideas of substitution and transposition.

Today's best-known one-key system is the Data Encryption Standard, or DES [NBS, 1977]. It uses a complex pattern of cascaded substitutions and transpositions, based on a 64-bit key.

Probably the major two-key system is the RSA algorithm [Rivest et al., 1978], which uses exponentiation over a large-modulus field. One exponent is used to encrypt and a different exponent to decrypt. In order to obtain either exponent from the other you need to know the prime factors used to generate the modulus, and the modulus is so large (typically 200 decimal digits) that current approaches to factoring cannot be applied in any reasonable amount of time. Hence one exponent and the modulus can be made public, while the other exponent serves as the user's secret key. In the next section we will see how this can be applied to secure communications among many individuals.

14.4 SOME APPLICATIONS OF ENCRYPTION

There are many ways in which an operating system can use encryption. We will describe only a few.

The DES system is often used for encrypting files. Hence, if someone penetrates the file system, or steals a tape or disk, the information is still protected at another level. We can use DES with a system master key to store our passwords. This gives us a protected password file, and the ability to have the operating system decipher and use the password for other applications, such as the enciphering key for a file. The DES system can also be used for communications among a trusted group of individuals. We use the term "trusted" because everyone in the group must have the key.

Manufacturers have implemented DES directly in hardware chips [Hoffman, 1977]. This greatly increases encryption and decryption rates, and therefore broadens the scope of applications because we aren't slowing things down so much during large data transfers.

Although DES has many advantages, a problem arises when we want to establish secure communications between pairs of individuals from a large group of size n. Using a one-key system such as DES, we would need to establish $n(n - 1)$ trusted groups of two people each. This would imply maintenance of $n(n - 1)$ keys, a difficult task.

This was a major impetus to development of two-key systems for use in computer-oriented communications. Since in such an application one of the keys is available to the entire group of n individuals, that is, the "public," you will probably hear these two-key systems referenced as **public key systems** [Rivest et al., 1978].

With the RSA algorithm we introduced earlier, each user has a key and a modulus available in a public file. Then, for example, Larry can contact Jim by encrypting a message with Jim's public information (the key and the modulus). It is important to stress, however, that this is a two-key system. A snooper could not decode the message using that same public information which Larry used to encode it. (This is illustrated in an example below.) Only Jim, we can hope, would have his secret key with which to decode the message.

It is easy to show the process pictorially, especially if we make one further observation. The encryption and decryption algorithms are the same; only the key information changes. Therefore, instead of using EJPub for *E*ncryption with *J*im's *Pub*lic information and DJSec for *D*ecryption with *J*im's *Sec*ret key, let's just use F for the algorithm and talk about applying F with Jim's public key (resulting in FJPub) or Jim's secret key (FJSec).

Then, to send a message to Jim, Larry would use

$$C = FJPub(message)$$

Jim would get the message and apply

$$FJSec(C) = FJSec(FJPub(message)) = message$$

but a snooper who tried a one-key approach would get

$$FJPub(C) = FJPub(FJPub(message)) = JUNK$$

These transformations are shown pictorially in Figure 14.6.

The fact that the functions in the RSA technique can be applied in either order has another advantage. Suppose Larry wants to sign the message he sends to Jim. He generates a cleartext *signature* consisting of his name and some other time-variant information such as the message number and the system clock. For example,

$$S = Larry \ \#1234 \ 1330:8/1/86$$

He then encrypts this signature using his secret key:

$$S' = FLSec(S)$$

Finally, he writes the message, appends both S and S' to it, and encrypts the whole thing with Jim's public key

$$C = FJPub(Dear \ Jim, \ how \ are \ you, \ I \ am \ fine \ . \ . \ . \ S \ S')$$

Jim decrypts the message using his secret key. He gets everything in cleartext *except* S', which is meaningless because it was S encrypted using Larry's secret key. Now he applies

$$T = FLPub(S')$$

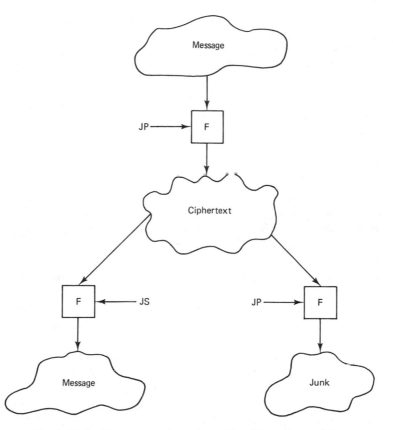

Figure 14.6   Message transformations with public and secret keys.

If Larry did send the message, then

$$T = FLPub(S') = FLPub(FLSec(S)) = S$$

since the operations are commutative. Furthermore, since only Larry is supposed to know Larry's secret key, this implies a form of signature in the validation sense.

This notion has even been used internally by an operating system. Certain highly privileged processes can be run only if the request includes such a digital signature, which the operating system decrypts and compares against its authorization list.

14.5 SUMMARY

Computer security is an important and fascinating subject. In this chapter we have introduced three OS security topics: identification, authorization, and encryption. We have looked at various types of identification procedures, based on the ideas of "is," "has," and "knows." We considered two general types of authorization, one using authorization matrices or vectors, the other using capability lists. The discussion of encryption included a summary of general techniques, and sample applications in areas such as data storage and communications.

This concludes our chapter on security. We hope you will continue to study the subject in advanced OS classes, and other classes such as those on data bases and networks, where the need for security becomes paramount.

Two books are imperative reading for anyone interested in computer security. Kahn's book on cryptography [1967] is an acknowledged classic in the field. It traces cryptography from ancient Egypt through the mid 1960's, and is perhaps best described as fascinating and captivating. D. E. Denning's book [1982] achieves the lofty goal of technical completeness, precision, and accuracy presented in an understandable and very readable style. Discussions include not only techniques and applications, but also mathematical foundations, analyses, and algorithms.

Two works presenting the need for privacy and protection are Hoffman [1969] and Popek [1974]. Both of these articles have excellent bibliographies.

Branstad [1973], Graham [1968], and Harrison et al. [1976] look specifically at protection in operating systems. Multics has been a focal point of operating systems security for many years; a classic paper on protection and control in this system is Saltzer [1974].

A superb general article on passwords is Wood [1977]. For a good overview of password techniques, and a history of their use in one particular system, see Morris and Thompson [1979].

We have already discussed recommended books on cryptography. Two comprehensive articles on the subject are Diffie and Hellman [1979] and Simmons [1979].

Capability-based addressing and language constructs for expressing protection are OS security topics that have received much attention. Fabry [1974] and Ekanadham and Bernstein [1979] discuss the former; Morris [1973] and Jones and Liskov [1978] discuss the latter.

QUESTIONS AND EXERCISES

1. List two methods other than those named in this chapter that have been used to circumvent computer system security.
2. One method that was used on early timesharing systems to "steal" data was to declare a large array within a program (or a large file on disk) and read the area before ever storing anything into it. What methods can be used to prevent this?
3. How does your timesharing system reduce the risk of having passwords stolen?
4. For your timesharing system, describe how access to shared files is regulated.
5. Nowadays it is common to see an office computer system consisting of a set of personal computers rather than a single CPU timeshared via terminals. What security ramifications do you see in this change?
6. There is considerable current effort in the area of "certifying" that an OS is secure at various levels. Try to find some information on what is involved in such certification.
7. WKLVCLVCIDLUOACHDVA
8. JRQFXDWULDWOCQVRVKLWHRQCCLVCGDUKCUCH

15

Operating System Performance

Including a final chapter on performance caused us mixed emotions. On the one hand, how can we present a survey of operating systems without some discussion of how to measure the performance of such systems? On the other hand, it is difficult to cover the subject in a book, much less a chapter.

In keeping with the rest of the text, we will try to give you a practical, applied introduction to performance measurement and analysis. First, we will describe some situations in which people might want to look at the performance of an OS. Next, we will consider the many facets of performance, focusing on those we consider immediately applicable to our discussion. Section 15.3 will give some metrics appropriate to operating systems, and Section 15.4, some ways to determine them. Tuning [Ferrari, 1978] is a common term used by system programmers and operators; in Section 15.5 we will show some of the ways a system's operators might tune an OS. In Section 15.6, we present ways application programmers can structure their programs to improve the performance of those programs.

15.1 REASONS FOR EXAMINING SYSTEM PERFORMANCE

One of the most important times for evaluating the performance of a system—and probably also your first—is when you are planning to purchase a new computer system. The system might be **bundled**, which means that the vendor sells you a combined hardware and software package. Even with bundled systems you will still have a choice of versions of a given OS and other options that may significantly affect performance. Nowadays, though, it is not uncommon to purchase the system **unbundled**, meaning that you can purchase hardware from one vendor and shop around for the software to run on that hardware. Most likely you will also want to compare the performance of similar systems from different vendors. In either case, you will want to evaluate the performance of the total system.

Builders of operating systems must also be concerned about the performance of their products. Suppose that you work for a computer manufacturer and need to specify an OS for your new machine. It is conceivable that you would design an entirely new OS, but now it is more likely that you will select an existing OS, perhaps modifying it for special applications or special hardware characteristics. Recently many manufacturers have chosen to implement some version of UNIX on their new computer systems rather than incur the expense of writing their own proprietary operating systems. Whether you create a new system or **port** [Johnson and Ritchie, 1978] an existing OS to the hardware (move existing software to a new hardware configuration), it is desirable to be able to predict how your system will perform on your hardware.

If you were a computer center manager you would have a slightly different view of performance. Since you must plan for the growth of use of the system over time, you are interested in the available capacity of a system. Capacity planning [Lazowska et al., 1984] becomes an important topic for you as a computer center manager.

Finally, it might be that you are an operations manager and are moderately happy with the existing OS but would like to change certain characteristics such as CPU utilization, throughput, turnaround, or response time. For instance, one set of your users might not be happy with the time it takes to run their large data-base updates, or another group might not be pleased with the time required to compile and link programs. Quite often, improving performance for one group of users will have a negative effect on another group of users. When you make an adjustment to the system intended to improve performance for one group of users, you need to know if it will have a negative affect on other users.

5.2 THE MANY ASPECTS OF PERFORMANCE

In the previous section we tried to gently introduce you to one of the problems in the study of performance: There are many different evaluative scales on which people try to judge the elusive quantity system performance. The way performance is evaluated will depend on whom one is trying to please. Also, the techniques used to evaluate or measure the system's performance will depend on one's point of view. In this section we will discuss several performance indices that are useful and some methods that are used to calculate system performance.

To the EDP manager, performance might be a quantitative metric based on throughput. He or she will want to know such things as these:

Number of batch jobs completed per day
Unused CPU time

Remaining I/O channel capacity

Number of timesharing users logged onto the system

Total system idle time

The systems programmer has a different view of performance and would probably want to know more detailed information about the system. Some of the metrics in which this person would be interested include the following:

Resource utilization

CPU time spent running the idle process

The fraction of CPU time for context switching

The ratio of time spent in head movement to time spent in actual data transfer on the system disk

Time spent swapping pages

Not even users have the same view of performance. To some, the important metrics might be these:

Turnaround time

Time to update a large data base

Time to run the payroll program

To other users, the following might be the important metrics:

Terminal response time

Time to access an item in a data base

Time to print a report

In addition to all of these quantitative measures of performance we must add some qualitative measures. We would expect the EDP manager to be concerned with "user satisfaction." He or she might also consider how "good" the accounting information and utilization reports are. The system manager worries about how "easy" it is to tune the system, and the system programmer wants to know how "complete" the utilization figures are. Users will probably want a system that is "user-friendly."

Although such qualitative aspects are certainly important, we cannot consider them in depth here. We will look only at those parameters which we can measure quantitatively. For example, in Chapter 6 we looked at the response and wait times for different types of short-term schedulers; in this chapter we want to examine methods that will allow us to select a scheduler that optimizes some measure of system performance rather than trying to find one that users consider "good."

Given our primary focus on quantitative metrics, you might think measurements and evaluations are fairly cut and dried. As usual, things might not be as straightforward as they seem. When trying to measure the performance of a system, we often run into one or more of the following problems:

The tool used to take the measurement affects the parameter being measured.

The tool needed to make the measurement does not exist.

The system we want to evaluate is not available for test or perhaps not even in existence.

Terms like "response time" may mean different things to different people.

To illustrate the first problem, suppose you install a device in your car which gives you a continuously updated display of your car's miles per gallon. That device uses energy, and therefore it will lower the quantity it is measuring—the miles per gallon. You may snicker at this example because the effect would probably be minimal. However, consider the case where you run a program every second to check how long the active queue is. In this case, the measurement device, the program, can have a significant effect on the memory being used and the available CPU time and therefore on the parameter it is trying to measure.

The point of this discussion is simply to warn you that care must be taken when you select a technique to measure an OS performance metric. If you have a complex procedure which repeatedly computes priorities for every node in a queue, then adding a few lines of code to the procedure to count and record the number of nodes might have little relative effect. If, on the other hand, you are measuring performance of a context swapping procedure in a FLIH, where speed is of utmost concern, a few lines of code could seriously affect the parameter being measured. Before using any tool, you should know how it will affect the system being measured.

A problem that often confronts those who wish to analyze the performance of a system is that the tool they need to take the measurement does not exist. One can always take the position that if it does not exist, we can build it. However, this can be an expensive, time-consuming effort. Many mature systems have been around long enough that a comprehensive set of tools have been built to monitor their performance. Some manufacturers have even developed a set of tools that can be moved to new systems without too much work. There are still, unfortunately, many situations when the cost of developing a tool cannot be justified in terms of what will be gained from using that tool. It is the responsibility of the designer to recognize this and look for acceptable alternatives.

As long as we have the correct tool and are careful how we take our measurements, we can obtain many metrics about an OS. We will look more at measurement techniques for existing systems in Sections 15.3 and 15.4. However, suppose we are evaluating something not yet in use on our system, such as a new long-term scheduler which the developer of our OS is offering. To complicate matters further, suppose that the software itself does not yet exist. This could happen if we were considering implementing a new algorithm for static resource allocation in our system.

If the software exists, it might be possible to just try it out for a few weeks to see how it performs. One must be very, very careful when doing this. Trying a new PASCAL compiler or other application program in layer 9 of the OS is one thing; trying something in one of the inner layers, such as a short-term scheduler, could cause a major disruption of service to the users.

An interesting approach to performance evaluation, regardless of whether the system is in the code or the algorithm stage, is the closed-form analytic model. One develops a mathematical model of the system, as a function of certain parameters that are descriptive of the application. When the parameters for a given system are specified, the model is "solved" and the theoretical value of the performance metric is determined [Kleinrock, 1975; Lavenberg, 1983; Lazowska et al., 1984].

Suppose we want to analyze a simple batch system that has a single CPU and a stream of incoming jobs, as shown in Figure 15.1. For this system, we might want to know:

What is the expected length of the job queue?
What is the expected wait time for a job?
What is the expected CPU utilization?
Other parameters.

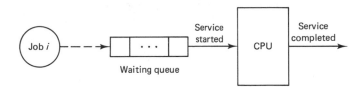

Figure 15.1   Single-server queueing system.

(*Note*: In most of our discussions we mention only expected or average values of the parameters of interest. In reality, we would most likely also want to know the variance and possibly the complete distribution.) To analyze the system, we need to be able to write equations that describe the system and then solve those equations.

Assume that we want to know how the job queue for the system in Figure 15.1 varies with time. The length l of the queue will be:

$$\text{queue length} = \text{initial number} + \text{number added} - \text{number removed} \qquad (15.1)$$

If we knew the three numbers in Equation (15.1), we could describe the queue length. There are several ways we could attempt to find these numbers. The first might be to measure the numbers for some real system and thereby determine:

$$\text{initial number} = k \qquad\qquad (15.2)$$

$$\text{number added} = \text{function1(time)} \qquad (15.3)$$

$$\text{number removed} = \text{function2(time)} \qquad (15.4)$$

With these substitutions the equation for the queue length becomes:

$$\text{queue length(time)} = k + \text{function1(time)}$$
$$- \text{function2(time)} \qquad (15.5)$$

Knowing what function1 and function2 are, we can calculate the desired statistics for queue length. However, the functions are usually available only as distributions.

Another approach is to hope that the functions in which we are interested can be approximated by some function that we can analyze. Two simple distribution functions that are often used to describe the arrival time of new jobs at the system queue and service times for jobs running on the CPU are the Poisson (or exponential) and uniform distributions [Coffman and Wood, 1966]. For those interested in the analytic solution to problems such as the one described above, we suggest the texts by Frieberger [1972], Lazowska et al. [1984], Kleinrock [1975; 1976], and Lavenberg [1983].

The single-queue, single-server system shown in Figure 15.1 is not unique to computer systems. It is descriptive of a wide variety of systems that have a line of customers waiting for a single server. Examples that most often come to mind are a street vendor selling hotdogs, the dentist office, and the checkout counter in the cafeteria at the student union during the lunch hour.

A slight modification to the system, shown in Figure 15.2, adds additional CPUs. The system becomes a single-queue, multiple-server system in this case. This type of system is also common in many noncomputer applications. Because the types of systems described are so universally applicable, they have been analyzed extensively for many years.

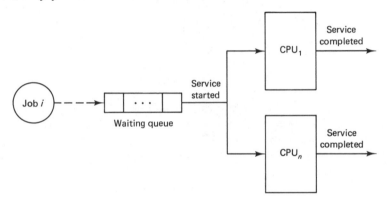

Figure 15.2   Multiple-server queueing system.

There has been a great deal of research in this area, and some of the results have been very useful. Solutions have been found for a wide variety of arrival time and service time distribution functions (number added(time) and number removed (time)). Some of these results are reported in the references listed above. We state again that not all performance analysis problems are amenable to such analytic methods.

A different approach to modeling is to simulate the system [Nielson, 1967; Ferrari, 1978; Lavenberg, 1983]. As you might have gathered from our assignments in earlier chapters, we consider simulation a very useful and viable technique. Using this method you can investigate the behavior of a certain component without actually modifying the existing OS. Depending on the method you use, you will often not even need a fully coded version of the element you want to measure; just important behavioral characteristics are required. Usually it is easy to change these characteristics and rerun the simulation to study different variations. In most cases it is also easy to change the characteristics of the application and see how the different variations in usage patterns (workload) affect performance.

As an example, let's go back to the version of our long-term scheduler which included static resource allocation. You could set up a model of this scheduler and then try different variations by changing the relative importance of wait time k and/or the normalizing values, such as OC $\times$ 200. Furthermore, you could test these variations with different process request populations; such populations might differ in average, mean, range, and standard deviation of (1) CPU time, (2) memory, (3) lines of output, and (4) non–serially reusable resources required.

Our fourth, and final, problem had to do with comparing apples and oranges, and it manifests itself in two ways. First, even if we are dealing with quantitative metrics, we must somehow *subjectively* assign them some relative importance. The reason is that we are seldom able to make a modification with positive effects on everything. Improving one metric, such as response time for short processes, usually has an adverse effect on another metric, such as turnaround time for long processes. Because of this interaction, we must use these subjective judgments to determine a compromise between the two demands.

The second problem associated with comparing metrics occurs because the same parameter on two machines might have different meanings [Calingaert, 1967]. Suppose we are comparing the interrupt response time for two machines and find that machine A has a time of 1 μs and the other has a time of 20 μs. Our initial reaction is to say that machine A is much faster. We might find out, however that machine A saves only the program counter before transferring to the FLIH whereas machine B saves the entire machine status and moves the executing process to the active queue before transferring to the FLIH. In such a case, machine B might be much faster than machine A. We must be certain that we are comparing apples and apples before making any decisions.

15.3 SOME USEFUL PERFORMANCE METRICS

There are a great many metrics which you will hear mentioned in discussions of performance. In this section we will discuss throughput, turnaround, response, and utilization plus some other metrics which could be important to you as a systems programmer.

Throughput is usually defined as (work done)/(unit time); the major problem is defining work done. For batch systems work is often defined as the number of jobs completed, and (jobs_completed)/(unit_time) is often a useful metric. However, for interactive systems, such as an airline reservation system or an automated banking system, work must be redefined. On the latter systems, the number of transactions processed per unit time is a better measure of throughput. In timesharing systems used for program development, neither of these metrics is of much use. For development systems you might define throughput as the number of compiles per day. All three of these metrics are forms of throughput and can be useful.

Turnaround is typically defined as the elapsed time between submission and completion of a job. Again, "job" implies a batch-oriented system. In order to make turnaround a meaningful metric for on-line systems, we could define turnaround to mean the time necessary to process a transaction. For the timesharing system it might mean the time required to compile a program or more generally, respond to any command. In each of the above, turnaround is related to the time needed to complete an operation, and this index can also be a useful metric if we know how to interpret the results.

Response time in the context of performance is usually not the same as response time in short-term scheduling. As a matter of fact, it even has multiple meanings with respect to performance. Some use it for the time required to get any kind of feedback from the system after the ENTER key has been pressed. Others consider it to mean the time to respond to some simple command, such as "What is today's date?" or "What is my session number?" Still others develop some benchmark they consider typical of their users' commands and measure **response time** as the time to complete that benchmark.

Utilization refers to the percentage of the time a resource is doing useful work. Utilization can be applied to any resource, including terminals, communication lines, the CPU, memory, channels, disks, printers, and plotters. The main problem associated with this term is what constitutes useful work. If an I/O channel is bringing in a new channel program for the next data transfer, should that be considered useful work or system overhead? Should the time the CPU spends performing context switches be considered useful work or overhead?

One must be careful when answering these questions. If system overhead, such as context switching, is included in useful work, then a system totally bogged down switching from user to user might have some resources 100 percent utilized even though users are getting essentially 0 percent of the CPU time for their processes. On the other hand, if a system is running beautifully, at full capacity, with 50 happy timesharing users and close to 100 percent utilization of major resources, is it fair to say the system is only $(100 - x)$ percent utilized, because x percent goes to context switching? Isn't that overhead part of the requirement to keep those users happy and productive? Unfortunately, there are no simple answers to these somewhat philosophical questions.

Besides these four common performance metrics, as a systems programmer you might be interested in some internal metrics. Some examples are:

Length of the long-term scheduler's waiting list

Time each process creation request spends in the long-term scheduler's waiting list

Number of processes in the short-term scheduler's queue

Response, wait, and completion time in the short-term scheduler sense

Length of the I/O suspend queue

Percentage of time an I/O request actually goes to a device versus the time it is satisfied from a buffer area

Average disk seek distance

The percentage of memory accesses that are found in cache memory, or the hit ratio

Length of the blocked queue

> Average number of pages per process
> Number of page or segment faults per unit time
> Number of FCBs per process
> I/O buffer sizes

Some of these metrics might be useful by themselves, and some must be used in conjunction with others (such as time in waiting list as a function of resources required).

Now that we have defined a number of possible performance metrics, it is time to describe how they can be determined.

15.4 MEASUREMENT TECHNIQUES

In this section we will discuss methods that can be used to measure the performance of an existing system. The three methods we will examine are software monitors, hardware monitors, and benchmark programs. Each has its area of application and can give the analyst useful information when applied correctly.

15.4.1 Benchmark Programs

Benchmark programs are probably the oldest method used to evaluate the performance of different systems. In order to use a **benchmark program,** you must begin by acquiring a program that has the characteristics of the application programs you will be running. This is not necessarily an easy task! If you choose to write the benchmark, you must first choose a language for the program that can be compiled and run on all the machines that will be evaluated. After the program has been written, it is executed on the different systems and parameters such as execution time, response time, and memory usage are measured. If all goes well, the results are compared and the best system is selected.

Unfortunately, it is not easy to develop good benchmark programs. Because of this, some analysts have used "standard" benchmarks rather than develop their own. One of the more famous benchmark programs is the Whetstone benchmark program [Lazowska et al., 1984]. It has been used for many years to measure the execution times of mathematical operations on many different machines. In a recent publication "MC68020 vs. 80386," Motorola [1987] described how one has to be careful interpreting published benchmark results. The article also has listings of several common benchmarks, and has a table comparing the performance of many different computers based on the "DHRYSTONE 1.1 Benchmark" [Motorola, 1987]. The problem with this type of benchmark is that it usually does not reflect the actual use in which the system will be placed.

Benchmark programs may not be perfect, but they are pervasive. They are used to measure the performance of every type of system from the largest mainframe to the smallest personal computers. At least one personal computer publication, *Creative Computing*, often published a very simple benchmark program along with the execution times for numerous CPUs [Ahl, 1983]. In current advertisements for

IBM-compatible PCs, it is common to see phrases such as "Runs the NORTON SI at 7.1." The company is claiming that its machine runs at 7.1 times the speed of a standard IBM PC based on a benchmark program from Peter Norton Computing [Peter Norton Computing, 1987a].

We should make a distinction here between using the benchmark to measure a particular performance parameter, such as execution time, and using the benchmark program to provide a known load for the system. In the latter case the benchmark program is not responsible for taking any performance data; all it does is provide a workload for the system [Ferrari, 1978]. Because of the need to generate different types of workloads, some companies have written **artificial workload generators.** These are programs that generate benchmark programs.

An analyst who wishes to create a new benchmark program using an artificial workload generator will run the generator and specify the characteristics of the desired workload. These parameters might include:

Distribution of program sizes

Terminal requests per unit time

Disk requests per unit time

System service requests per unit time

Type of computation—floating-point, string manipulation, or array processing

After analyzing the parameters, the generator will create a sequence of programs that have the desired characteristics.

Another approach used to create an artificial workload is to first sample the real workload and then build an artificial workload based on the sample [Ferrari et al., 1983]. This method seems attractive since it eliminates the need to estimate or guess what the real workload is.

There are two basic methods used to gather data about the workload: time-sampling and one-out-of-n sampling. In the first case, the running system is sampled at some intervals and data about the state of the systems is recorded. In the second case, one out of every n components executed on the system is sampled. One of the questions at the end of the chapter asks you to estimate the bias associated with each of these methods of sampling. With either method it is important that the number of samples be large enough to guarantee that the artificial workload is statistically close to the real workload.

A final note should be made about benchmark programs. The benchmark is worthless if the person creating it has not closely predicted the type of application that would ultimately be run on the system. Many horror stories start out, "But the benchmark ran great!"

15.4.2 Software Performance Monitors

Software performance monitors [Lucas, 1971; Ferrari et al., 1983], not to be confused with process synchronization monitors, are also programs written to measure the performance of a system. Unlike benchmark programs, however, they operate in the background and just gather statistics rather than trying to simulate the operations of an application program. They are also different in that they must be system-dependent. This is necessary because the monitors must have access to data that is embedded in the operating system.

The monitors can collect all of the information described in Section 15.3. For large operating systems, such as those for the IBM 360/370 computers, many monitors have been developed [Sedgewick et al., 1970]. Some of these monitors have been written to gather statistics on just one part of the system. Since the performance of the secondary storage subsystems often has a very dramatic effect on the performance of the entire system, monitors have been developed just to measure this one portion of the system

Two companies that have developed products that collect performance metrics on disk systems are BGS Systems and Boole and Babbage [NCCMG, 1986]. These monitors have been designed to measure such details as length of time the disk is connected to the I/O channel, the ratio of reads to writes, the hit ratio for disk cache memory, and software overhead times. These products were developed to help users make decisions about upgrading their systems. By showing how much time is saved by upgrading the disk subsystem, the user can determine whether an upgrade is cost-effective. This is one of the tools often used by capacity planners.

Other companies have developed special-purpose software monitors that measure the response time through a communications network to a host computer and back to the terminal. These monitors can measure the performance of the hardware involved and the communication hardware and software. The list of special-purpose monitors continues to grow as systems become more complex.

Another type of software monitor that has proved useful for improving performance of system and application programs is the activity profiler. A **profiler** is a program that monitors the execution of a program and can display information such as how many times procedures are called and how much time is spent executing the various procedures within a program. We will take a more detailed look at profilers in Section 15.6.

Developers of software monitors have to be particularly careful to make sure their monitors do not significantly affect the performance metrics of the system they are measuring. Sometimes it is possible to determine how the monitor affects the performance of the system and subtract its effects from the measured metric and therefore produce the correct result. In other cases one cannot accurately estimate how much the monitor has contributed to a measured quantity, or the monitor's execution may alter performance so drastically that the monitor cannot be used. In cases like this it is necessary to find a technique that can measure the desired metric without affecting it. This need led to the development of hardware devices that monitored the performance of systems.

15.4.3 Hardware Monitors

Hardware monitors [Svobodova, 1976] offer two primary advantages over software monitors. They can measure metrics without significantly affecting the parameters they are measuring, and they can be used to collect data that is not available to a software monitor. Some parameters, such as the time between an interrupt request and the CPU response to the request, or how long it takes the FLIH to execute, probably cannot be measured directly with just software. These types of measurements can be taken quite easily with a hardware monitor.

The major disadvantage of hardware monitors is that they are usually expensive. Since they are implemented in hardware rather than software, they are also harder to modify as new versions of computers are developed. Another problem with using hardware monitors is that it is sometimes difficult to correlate measured hardware events with what caused them. For instance, when the hardware monitor detects an increase in page fault rate, is it because too many application processes were running or because OS overhead was too high? (A possible solution to this problem is to use a hybrid software and hardware monitor to record both system load and detailed performance indices.) In spite of these potential problems, hardware monitors remain an important tool for the system designer and user.

There are two general approaches that have been taken to the design of **hardware monitors.** The first approach is to develop a hardware box that can be attached to a specific computer so that it will measure some set of metrics that are accessible on that computer [Estrin et al., 1967]. The other approach is to develop a general-purpose analyzer that can be attached to the address, data, and control lines of any computer [Hewlett-Packard, 1976].

We will look more closely at the general-purpose monitors, since they are now becoming standard development tools for computer engineers. Logic-state analyzers were the first versions of these products. They were designed to monitor address, data, and control lines on a digital machine and display information the designer of either the hardware or the software found useful. They were a vast improvement over the oscilloscope.

The next step in the evolution of these monitors occurred when someone decided to build into the monitor the ability to convert bit patterns on data lines back into assembly language mnemonics. This allowed the designer to more easily interpret the data from the monitor and observe the performance of the system being monitored.

Another enhancement of these monitors came about when the **in-circuit-emulator** (ICE) was developed. This device allowed the designer to substitute the monitor for the actual CPU chip in a microcomputer-based system. By doing this, the designer could halt the CPU when some combination of events occurred or when a particular memory location was accessed. The ICE made it possible to make very detailed measurements of both hardware and software [Hewlett-Packard, 1980; Tektronix, 1982].

The hardware monitors described above have revolutionized the development of microcomputer-based hardware and software. There are many companies that now make these types of monitors. Microcomputer manufacturers such as Motorola and Intel [1982] now sell development systems that give users the capabilities described above. Even companies that do not sell microcomputer chips, such as Hewlett-Packard and Tektronix, have marketed development systems for many of the popular microcomputers.

The special needs of one segment of the system have led to development of special purpose hardware monitors. A good example of this is the **protocol ana-**

lyzer. This is a tool that has been developed to analyze communication lines used in distributed or networked systems. The protocol analyzer is attached to the communication line and monitors all traffic on the line. It can be used to study loads and to find errors in the communication protocol. Several companies, including Hewlett-Packard, have developed protocol analyzers that are now standard tools in the communication industry.

We would be remiss if we did not mention one of the major problems that can arise when using either hardware or software monitors to collect performance data: voluminous amounts of data. Care must be taken when collecting data to try to ensure that only relevant data are recorded. With the tools available today, it is at times too easy to collect data. It may, however, not be easy to find the relevant performance information buried in reams of data, if one does have a plan to analyze that data.

The first step in reducing the problem is to try to eliminate unwanted or useless data. This can often be done by carefully analyzing the problem before gathering data and placing conditions on when the data will actually be recorded. Most hardware and software monitors give the user the capability to sample data and start recording only when an event or condition of interest has occurred. If you have ever been presented with a memory dump of your entire program when an error occurred in a small routine somewhere in the middle of that program, then you have seen the problem of too much data and not enough information.

Both hardware and software monitors will continue to play an important part in the development and analysis of computer systems. Each type has its use, but it is up to the designer or analyst to make sure the correct tool is applied to the problem.

15.5 TUNING A SYSTEM FOR OPTIMUM PERFORMANCE

In the previous section we discussed several ways to measure the performance of a computer system. We were interested in measuring parameters so that we could design a system that would perform well and so that we could make decisions about choosing new system components. There is a third reason for measuring system performance: in many cases we want to adjust some parameter in the system so that we can improve the performance. This adjustment is usually called tuning.

Tuning normally refers not to major modification of a component, such as rewriting the long-term scheduler, but rather to adjusting some of the parameters built into a system component. Since these can vary so much depending on the particular system, we will not attempt an exhaustive discussion. Here are a few possibilities:

The parameters in the long-term scheduler's priority computations

The weighting values the long-term scheduler applies to various factors in deciding when to allow another process into the system

The a and b slopes in a modified round robin short-term scheduler

The manner in which time slices are modified on repeated passes through the short-term scheduler's queue or queues

The number of pages a process can have in main memory

Parameters in the page replacement algorithm

Number and size of I/O buffers

Number of terminals that can log on

Size of RAM disk

Examining the list of tunable parameters, you will see that we have already discussed tuning even though we did not use that term explicitly. In Chapters 5 and 6, for instance, we discussed the parameters related to scheduling. In Chapter 7 the parameters affecting paging and the memory management system were analyzed. When we tune the system, we modify some of these parameters in order to improve the performance of the system as measured by one or more of the metrics described in Section 15.3.

Good questions to ask at this time are "Who tunes the system?" and "How is it done?" Although users may be able to specify some parameters such as priority or buffer size, it is usually the system manager who is responsible for tuning the system. We do not want individual programmers going around changing system parameters unless anarchy is our goal.

There are at least two mechanisms commonly used to enable the manager to tune the system. When the system is booted, the operator can usually set some of the parameters that affect system performance. If the parameters need adjustment while the system is running, the system manager can run a program which will allow him or her to change the parameters and thereby tune the system. The normal procedure is to run a software or hardware monitor and find out which metric is not at its optimum level and then run the tuning program to change an associated parameter. This procedure is repeated until the desired level of performance is reached.

There has been some work done to create programs that automatically tune the system while it is running, particularly in the network routing area. However, some of the decisions that are made are more subjective than objective, and these are difficult to include in a program. In the future you might see expert systems techniques applied to the tuning problem.

Tuning is something the system manager does to improve the performance of the system. In the next section we will look at what application programmers can do to improve the performance of their programs.

15.6 A SIMPLE PERFORMANCE CASE STUDY

In this section we will present an approach that can be used to examine the performance of a sample system, and also suggest ways to improve that sample system. The approach presented is an iterative one:

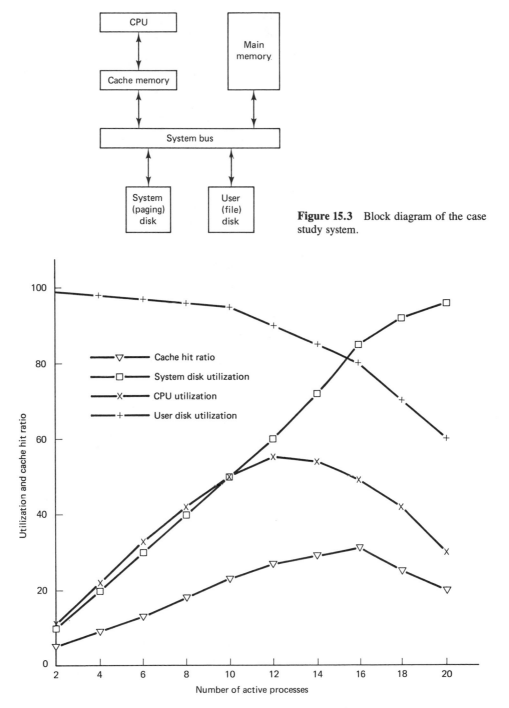

Figure 15.3 Block diagram of the case study system.

Figure 15.4 Utilization percentages and cache hit ratio.

```
repeat
    measure performance metrics
    analyze data
    implement changes if necessary
until metrics are satisfactory
```

For our case study we must first define the system that we will be studying. A block diagram of the system is shown in Figure 15.3. It consists of a CPU, main memory, cache memory, system disk, and user disk.

The next step is to measure the performance of our system. Any or all of the techniques described earlier in the chapter may be used. If the system is operational, we can use hardware or software monitors to gather real data. If the system is just in the design phase, we can simulate it and collect simulation data. Whatever method we choose, after gathering the data we need to analyze it.

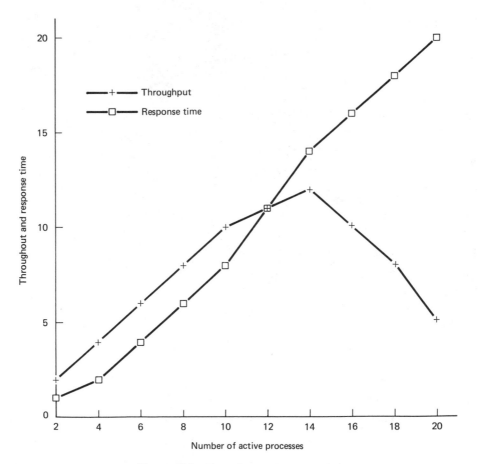

Figure 15.5 Throughput and response time.

Figures 15.4 and 15.5 show the type of data that would typically be collected. The first figure shows the utilization of the major components of the system, and the second shows how throughput and response time vary with the number of active processes on the system. The data in the figures has been exaggerated to emphasize the problems. The data shows that two components of the system seem to be limiting performance: the system disk and the cache memory.

The next step in the procedure described earlier is to modify the system and try again. The results of two separate modifications of the system are shown in Figures 15.6 and 15.7. The first figure shows how throughput is improved when more cache memory is added to the system, and the second shows the result of adding a faster system disk. For this simple analysis we concentrated on throughput. In other cases we would probably want to also investigate other metrics such as response time or resource utilization.

As we stated at the beginning of the section, we can keep making changes and

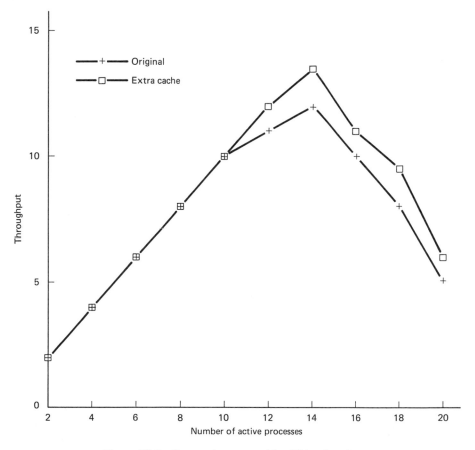

Figure 15.6 Case study system with additional cache memory.

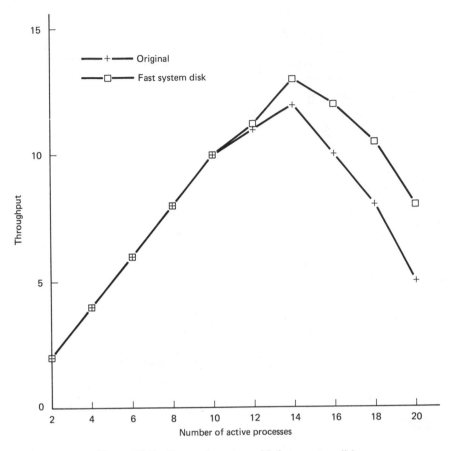

Figure 15.7   Case study system with faster system disk.

measuring the system until we are satisfied with the results or we run out of time or money. At this point, you can probably see the advantage of working with a simulation model rather than an actual system. It is usually much easier and faster to change a model than a real system.

15.7 PERFORMANCE AND THE APPLICATIONS PROGRAMMER

Programs such as transaction processors and inventory programs can place a heavy demand on system resources, and therefore application programmers should also be interested in performance. Although they have no control over the scheduling and paging, they do have control over the way their application is constructed.

There are numerous trade-offs that can be made in developing an application. The number of physical I/O operations can be reduced if large memory buffers are allocated. In other cases, it will be possible to trade off CPU time for memory space.

Table 15.1 [Soderstrom, 1986] shows the "cost" of several different operations that might be included in an application.

From the table, we can see that a system call requires approximately 100 times as much CPU time as executing a complex IF test. The table also shows that starting up a communications line requires 5 times as much I/O activity as opening a file. Although the information shown in Table 15.1 is applicable only for a Hewlett-Packard 3000, numbers such as those shown can be found for other systems. Given information of this type, it is possible to analyze an application and make intelligent design decisions that will improve performance.

TABLE 15.1   PROGRAM COST IN TERMS OF CPU-SECONDS AND I/O TRANSACTIONS

Group	Approximate cost	Operations
Group 1	(0.000003 CPU)	Add two binary numbers; one simple IF statement
Group 2	(0.00003 CPU)	A complicated IF test; a static COBOL procedure call
Group 3	(0.0003 CPU)	A system call
Group 4	(0.003 CPU)	A medium-sized logic loop; an in-memory sort of 100 items; a memory cache read or write; a read or write to a disk buffer
Group 5	(0.03 CPU, 1 I/O)	A dynamic COBOL procedure call; a disk read or write; a terminal read or write
Group 6	(0.1 CPU, 5 I/O)	A data-base transaction; read edit and redisplay a single field on terminal; a write across a communication line; a full screen update
Group 7	(0.5 CPU, 10 I/O)	Opening a file; an interprocess transfer; a simple system command; starting up a new program
Group 8	(2 CPU, 50 I/O)	Starting up a communication line; running a short program; logging onto the system

As a last example of how intelligent design can improve performance, recall the example cited in the Introduction. We showed two segments of code that summed the elements of a large array; one summed by rows and the other by columns. By finding out how the compiler stores array data, we can determine which method will cause the fewest page faults when executed. Reducing the number of page faults will in turn reduce the time the process waits for disk I/O and therefore decrease its total time in the system.

UNIX is a system noted for its wide variety of programmers' tools. One of its tools collects program activity information. Figure 15.8 shows a simple C program that includes several functions, stuff1, stuff2 and stuff3. Table 15.2 shows the activity profile generated for the program.

The information in Table 15.2 can be used to determine the areas of the program in which the most time is being spent. The first column shows the percentage of time spent in each of the routines listed in the Name column. You should observe that many of the routines shown are system library routines and their names do not appear within the program itself.

```c
#include <stdio.h>

main()
{
    int exp, lower, i, j, upper, step, printstep;
    double power(), raised;
    int data1, data2, data3, stuff1(), stuff2(), stuff3();

    printf("enter lower, upper, step, power, printstep ==>");
    scanf("%d %d %d %d %d", &lower, &upper, &step, &exp, &printstep );
    printf("\n\n%d %d %d %d %d\n\n", lower, upper, step, exp, printstep);

    printf("number power\n");

    i = lower; j = 0;
    while ( i <= upper)  {
        j++;
        raised = power( i, exp );
        if ( i <= upper / 3) {data1 = stuff1(i-1); }
        if ( i >  upper / 3) {data2 = stuff2(i+1); }
        data3 = stuff3(3*i);
        if ( j == printstep ) {
            j = 0, printf( "%-6d  %-12.1f \n", i, raised );
        }
        i = i + step;
    }
}

double power( num, exp )
int num, exp;
{
    int i=1;
    double fnum, p=1;
    fnum = (double) num;
    for ( ; i <= exp; ++i )  p = p * fnum;
    return( p );
}

int stuff1( a )
int a;
{  return( 2 * a ); }

int stuff2( a )
int a;
{  return( 2 * a ); }

int stuff3( a )
int a;
{  return( 2 * a ); }
```

Figure 15.8   A sample C program.

Once we know where a program is spending its time, we can see where we should expend effort trying to improve its performance. We may look for alternate ways to perform calculations or we may decide to rewrite parts of the program in a more efficient language. Sometimes rewriting a small portion of an application in assembly language can have a significant affect on performance. The same technique has also been used to decide which parts of the OS should be written in microcode when time is extremely critical.

In this section we have tried to show a few of the characteristics of a program that the programmer can control in order to increase the performance of an applica-

TABLE 15.2   ACTIVITY PROFILE FOR THE PROGRAM IN FIGURE 15.8.

% Time	Seconds	Cumsecs	#Calls	msec/call	Name
93.6	0.44	0.44	153	2.88	fptrap
4.3	0.02	0.46	6	3.	write
2.1	0.01	0.47	1	10.	main
0.0	0.00	0.47	50	0.0	stuff3
0.0	0.00	0.47	17	0.0	stuff1
0.0	0.00	0.47	2	0.	monitor
0.0	0.00	0.47	1	0.	creat
0.0	0.00	0.47	5	0.	printf
0.0	0.00	0.47	2	0.	profil
0.0	0.00	0.47	1	0.	scanf
0.0	0.00	0.47	1	0.	_doscan
0.0	0.00	0.47	1	0.	_filbuf
0.0	0.00	0.47	5	0.	_doprnt
0.0	0.00	0.47	2	0.	fcvt
0.0	0.00	0.47	2	0.	_dtop
0.0	0.00	0.47	2	0.	_ltostr
0.0	0.00	0.47	1	0.	memchr
0.0	0.00	0.47	50	0.0	power
0.0	0.00	0.47	1	0.	getenv
0.0	0.00	0.47	2	0.	fflush
0.0	0.00	0.47	5	0.	_xflsbuf
0.0	0.00	0.47	1	0.	_wrtchk
0.0	0.00	0.47	2	0.	_findbuf
0.0	0.00	0.47	1	0.	memcpy
0.0	0.00	0.47	2	0.	isatty
0.0	0.00	0.47	2	0.	ioctl
0.0	0.00	0.47	1	0.	read
0.0	0.00	0.47	1	0.	strcpy
0.0	0.00	0.47	14	0.0	ungetc
0.0	0.00	0.47	33	0.0	stuff2

tion. Combining good programming practices with knowledgeable selection of system components and tuning the system will usually lead to improved performance of a computer system.

15.8 THE FINAL SUMMARY

This chapter has introduced you to some of the important concepts of operating system performance. We have discussed ways to gauge the performance of a system and also ways to measure performance metrics. It is very likely that performance will continue to be an important consideration for both system designers and users, whether they are involved with microcomputer systems or large mainframe systems.

The list of potential references for this chapter is nearly overwhelming. We include only enough here to give the interested reader a start. The paper by Lynch [1972] has a good bibliography and discusses how performance and system structure are related. We also recommend the texts by Drummond [1973] and Hellerman and Conroy [1975] as good introductions to performance analysis. The book by Ferrari et al. [1983] provides a broad overview of measurement and performance and includes some good practical material.

Throughout this text we have tried to teach both how operating systems are designed and why alternative approaches are needed for different systems. We have gone from basic concepts of concurrency to the components of an OS, to a layered structure for the design of an entire OS. We hope that, armed with this knowledge, you will be more productive than the group who are trying to reach new heights by standing on each other's feet.

QUESTIONS AND EXERCISES

1. What are some additional performance metrics that an EDP manager could use?
2. What are some additional performance metrics that a system programmer could use?
3. What are some additional performance metrics that would be important to users?
4. List the advantages of using software monitors over hardware monitors.
5. List the advantages of using hardware monitors over software monitors.
6. Give examples where simulation would be a better tool for studying performance than analytic methods.
7. Are benchmark programs a useful tool in comparing the performance of different systems? Why?
8. What are some additional parameters that can be tuned?
9. Discuss how the groups described in Table 15.1 would be used on a system that was (1) I/O-bound or (2) CPU bound.
10. How do you think the information in Table 15.1 was gathered?
11. Create a function that allows you to compare the cost of running application programs based on I/O operations, on CPU time, on memory space used, and on data-base accesses. State any assumptions you have made.
12. When using either simulation or analytic models, it is imperative that you verify that the model gives the same results as the actual system. This is called model verification. Suggest several ways in which this could be done.
13. Give examples that show how improving one performance metric reduces another one.
14. Two sampling methods, time-sampling and one-out-of-n sampling, were described in Section 15.4. How is each of these biased in terms of events with long and short execution times?

PROGRAMMING ASSIGNMENTS

1. Write a benchmark program that will evaluate the performance of several computers to which you have access (perhaps some personal computers, a minicomputer, and a mainframe). With this benchmark, determine the execution times for the following operations:

| integer | add, subtract, multiply, and divide |
| floating-point | add, subtract, multiply, and divide |

When making your measurements, be sure to eliminate the effects of your measurement tool on the results.

Turn in the following:

Your benchmark program
The timing measurements
An analysis of the result

It possible, your analysis should include a comparison between the observed timings and the timings given by the manufacturer of the processor.

2. If you have access to a multiprogramming system that supports virtual memory, write the two programs for accessing a large array that were listed in the Introduction and measure the wall clock time required to execute them. Are the results what you expected?

APPENDIX

Loading, Linking and Relocation

In this appendix we will consider three problems: loading programs into memory, linking separately compiled routines into an executable program, and relocating modules from one region of memory to another. The first problem is a relatively simple one to solve, but the second and third will require considerable effort.

In some curricula, the material in this appendix is covered in a systems programming course. We have chosen to include it in our text for those who have not been introduced to loaders and linkers. This material provides useful background material for Chapter 7, Memory Management.

A. 1 LOADING EXECUTABLE FILES FROM SECONDARY STORAGE

Loaders are a kind of program that has been around as long as there has been some form of secondary storage on computers. One form of loader, the "bootstrap" loader, is a program that some of us can remember in our sleep.

The basic program loader was such an important part of the system that some computers, such as the Hewlett-Packard 2116 [Hewlett-Packard, 1969], stored it in a special section of memory that could be protected by a toggle switch. (Inexpensive read-only memory was not readily available on machines of the early 1960s.) The bootstrap loader on this machine was used every time the system was restarted from paper tape, magnetic tape, or a disk. The program was stored in the main memory of the computer, and since memory in those days was very expensive, the program

314

had to be short. For the HP 2116, it was 64 words. To restart the computer, you would halt the machine, put the system restart tape into the standard input device, enable the memory that contained the bootstrap program, set the program counter to the starting address of the bootstrap, and press RESET and RUN.

When all went well, the bootstrap loader would read the system in from the secondary storage and halt with a 102077 in the display register. You would then disable the memory containing the bootstrap before loading the starting address of the system into the program counter and pressing RUN. If you forgot to do this and the program that was loaded accidentally stored data into the memory used for the bootstrap, you had to reload the bootstrap program from the switch register. This happened so often to those of us who were forgetful that we actually had to carry a copy of the bootstrap loader in our wallets. (What we really carried was a paper-tape version of the program that could be read into memory by a 12-instruction program that we all knew by heart.) One of the authors can still toggle that sequence of instructions into the computer even though it has been more than ten years since he last forgot the enable switch and was forced to do so.

The object of the personal recollection in the preceding paragraph was to show both how simple a loader program can be and how often it is used. On the HP 21XX family of computers it was possible to write a program that would load another program in from secondary storage with just 12 instructions. Since this is the case, you are probably wondering why it was necessary to have a 64-word program in protected memory to do the same job. To answer this we need to look at the information that is typically stored with an executable program on secondary storage.

A sample format of a file that contains an executable program is shown in Figure A.1. In addition to the instructions and data, the file has the location in memory at which the program is to be loaded, the length, the starting address, and some data that is used to verify that the correct information has been loaded. The length word is used to determine how much information should be read from secondary storage and also to verify that the program will fit into memory. The starting address is the address that is placed into the PCB to show where the program is to begin executing the next time it is dispatched.

```
LOAD ADDRESS
CHECKSUM WORD
PROGRAM LENGTH
STARTING ADDRESS
      *
      *
instructions
      *
      *
   data
      *
      *
```

Figure A.1 Typical format for an executable program file.

On systems that used relatively unreliable secondary storage devices such as paper tape and magnetic tape, it was common to include a checksum character or word with the data. When the file was created, the **checksum** word was calculated by adding all of the instructions and data together (modulo word length) and storing the value either at the beginning or end of the file. When the file was read from tape, the checksum was recalculated and compared with the value stored at the time the file was created. If the two didn't compare, the deadly HALT 02 error was displayed and you had to rewind the tape and try again. On more modern devices, verifying that the data read is correct is often done by the hardware, and there might be no need for checksum words as part of the file.

The argument above should have you convinced that loading a program from secondary storage need not be a very complex operation. The code shown in Figure A.2 is the 12-instruction program that was used to load the bootstrap program into memory. This simple program does not read the starting address from the file or check for any error conditions. It only reads characters and stores them into consecutive memory locations. The other operations were performed by the more complex loader that was stored in protected memory.

Now that you have seen how simple loading is, it is time to see how one creates the executable file that can be placed into memory by the loader.

```
I/O  -->  LOOP STC  12B,C     START THE READER & CLEAR ITS READY FLAG
Wait  |        SFS  12B       SKIP NEXT INSTRUCTION IF READY FLAG SET
Loop -->       JMP  *-1       GOTO TEST IF NOT READY
            *

               LIA  12B       LOAD 8 BITS INTO A REG (LOWER 8 BITS
                                UPPER 8 BITS GET 0'S
               ALF,ALF        SHIFT A LEFT 4, SHIFT A LEFT 4
            *

I/O  -->       STC  12B,C     START THE READER & CLEAR READY FLAG
Wait  |        SFS  12B       SKIP NEXT INSTRUCTION IF READY FLAG SET
Loop -->       JMP  *-1       GOTO TEST IF NOT READY
            *

               MIA  12B       MERGE 8 BITS INTO A REG (LOWER 8 BITS)
               STA  B,I       STORE A USING B REG AS INDIRECT ADDRESS
               INB            INCREMENT THE STORAGE ADDRESS
               JMP  LOOP      GO START NEXT READ

            *   B register is loaded with starting address
            *   before program is executed
            *   12B is the octal address of the reader
```

Figure A.2   Simple example of a program loader—HP 2116.

A.2 BINDING LOGICAL ADDRESSES TO PHYSICAL ADDRESSES

Before proceeding, we need to review the definitions of logical and physical addresses. A physical address refers to the actual location of an object in memory. When a programmer includes the instruction

```
          STORE     7,100
```

in a program, he or she is specifying the physical address of a register, 7, and the physical address in memory, 100. When the programmer writes the instruction as

```
          STORE     R7,DATA1
```

he or she is using the logical names or addresses for the register and memory location. When the first instruction is used, it could be executed without having to translate the addresses. When the second form of the instruction is used it is necessary to assign physical addresses to R7 and DATA1 before the instruction can be executed. Assigning physical addresses to logical addresses is called **binding** [Cheatham and Leonard, 1967; Aho and Ullman, 1977].

Binding can occur at several different stages in the coding, compilation, loading, or execution of a program. When the programmer specifies the address directly as part of the instruction, he or she is performing the binding in the coding phase. When the compiler (or assembler) performs the conversion, binding occurs at the compilation phase. When the loader makes the conversion, we say that binding occurs at load time. The last time at which binding can occur is the instant the instruction is executed

As we will see in later sections, it is better to delay binding as long as possible in multiprogramming systems. By delaying binding we make it possible to reload a program into any available region in physical memory, not just the one into which it was first loaded.

A.3 LINKING SEPARATELY COMPILED ROUTINES

In the Introduction we poked fun at some of the mistakes programmers made over the years and described how they often failed to take advantage of their predecessors' work. We must now acknowledge that a good programming technique, using program libraries, was developed early and used by many programmers. In order to make effective use of program libraries, it was necessary to develop ways to link together routines that were compiled or assembled at different times [Kurzban et al., 1975; McCarthy et al., 1963].

Before getting into the details of linkage editing, a quick overview of the operation is in order. Figure A.3 shows graphically what we are trying to accomplish. For this example, assume that three object modules have previously been created: MAIN, SUB1, and SUB2.

The **linkage editor** reads the information from the object modules and builds an executable program file. While building the executable program, the linkage editor will create a symbol table [Presser and White, 1972] that it will use in much the same way an assembler or compiler does. The linkage editor will also create a map showing where the information from the object modules is stored in the executable program. The symbol table is used primarily by the linkage editor itself, but the load map can usually be printed out for use by the programmer during program debugging. With this brief overview of the linkage editor operation, we are ready to proceed.

A.3.1 What the Compiler or Assembler Generates

On most systems the output of a compiler or assembler, which we will call **object code,** is not code that can be executed directly [Barron, 1969]. Typically, object code must first be linked with other routines, as shown in Figure A.4, to produce an executable module. The linkage editor relies on information passed to it in the object modules to perform the linkage.

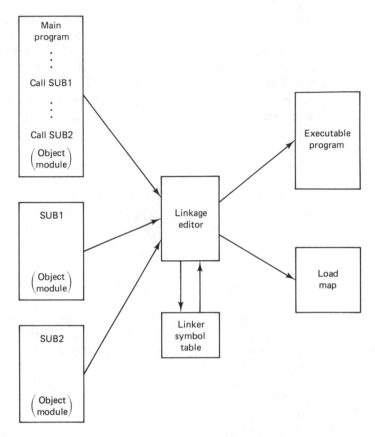

Figure A.3   The linkage editing operations.

To see what information is passed in the object module, look at the sample generic assembly language program shown in Figure A.4. Line 01 defines the name of the module, and on some systems it will also define the primary entry point to the module. If the name is also the primary entry point into the module, then this information must be passed on to the linkage editor. Our assembler will generate the following record of information for the linkage editor, or linker for short, based in part on the NAME pseudoinstruction:

        NAME MAIN 32

where 32 is the length of the MAIN module including its code and data.

Lines 03 and 04 will both cause information to be passed on to the linker. Line 03, ENTRY, defines the labels within this module that will be accessible to separately assembled routines. The assembler will pass along the name of the label and its relative address within this module. This will enable the linker to calculate the address of the label so that other modules can reference it. The EXTERNAL statement, line 04, tells the assembler that the labels listed on that line are not labels within the current module but that they exist in other modules. If this statement were not present, all instructions referencing these labels would result in an

```
stmt   rel
  #    addr
----   ----


  01                        NAME       MAIN
  02
  03                        ENTRY      DATA1, LOCATE
  04                        EXTERNAL   SUB1, SUB2, DATA2, EXIT
  05          ONE           EQUATE     1
  06
  07                        GLOBAL     DATA3  MYPCB
  08
  09   0000   MASK          BYTE       00000111B
  10   0001   DATA1         BYTE       "A"
  11
  12   0002   MAIN          MOVE       DATA1,R1
  13   0005                 AND        MASK,R1
  14   0008                 MOVE       R1,DATA2
  15   0011                 JSB        SUB1
  16   0014                 MOVE       #ONE,R2
  17   0017                 MOVE       DATA3,R3
  18   0020   LOCATE        JSB        SUB2
  19   0023                 PUSH       MYPCB
  20   0026                 PUSH       #"N"
  21   0029                 JUMP       EXIT
  22
  23                        END        MAIN
```

Figure A.4   Sample assembly language program.

"undefined label" error message from the assembler. The assembler passes on information about entry points and external labels in the following manner:

```
ENTRY        DATA1   0001     { Addresses relative to       }
             LOCATE  0020     { start of the object module  }
EXTERNAL     SUB1    (1)
             SUB2    (2)
             DATA2   (3)
             EXIT    (4)
```

The numbers following the labels in the external statement give a simple way in which the externals can be referenced within the object module.

The EQUATE statement in line 05 only provides information to the assembler. It does not directly cause any data to be passed to the linker.

Line 07 informs the assembler that the variables DATA3 and MYPCB are stored in an area where all modules linked with this one can reference them. Global variables are sometimes stored in an area separate from other data and code. Sometimes the user can specify where globals should be stored. To inform the linker that a global variable will be referenced, the following record is created:

```
GLOBAL       DATA3   0     { Addresses relative to the }
             MYPCB   1     { start of the global area  }
```

where the relative address is the relative location of DATA3 and MYPCB within the global area referenced by this module. (As an example, FORTRAN uses the COMMON statement to create global variables.)

The two variables MASK and DATA1 are defined by lines 09 and 10. Since DATA1 was defined as an entry point, its location within MAIN will be passed to the linker along with its name.

The code portion of the module begins at line 12, which is labeled MAIN. Lines 12 through 18 all have mnemonics for machine-executable instructions. The assembler will pass along the bit patterns for the machine instructions together with the available address information for the operands. Line 12 will cause the op-code for the MOVE instruction to be generated; it will be followed by the addresses for DATA1 and R1. The address for R1, which we will assume is one of the general-purpose registers within the CPU, will probably be included as part of the instruction op-code. The assembler can also tell the linker where the address of DATA1 is within the current module. As a result of all this the assembler will generate an instruction that might look like the following:

```
opcode     (R) 0001      {address of DATA1}
```

where (R) indicates that the address that follows is relative to the beginning of the current module. Line 13 results in the generation of a similar instruction:

```
opcode     (R) 0000      {address of MASK}
```

Lines 14 and 15 both reference external labels and therefore cause the following similar instructions to be generated:

```
opcode     (X) 3
opcode     (X) 1
```

where (X) states that the address that follows is external and 3 and 1 refer to the labels found in the EXTERNAL pseudoinstruction from line 04. Note that these are not really addresses but rather pointers to one of the labels in the EXTERNAL statement.

The instruction at line 16 is different from all the previous instructions. The symbol # before ONE indicates that the instruction is an immediate type and therefore the operand is part of the instruction. Because of this, the assembler can generate the entire instruction that will be executed without any help from the linker. This is often referred to as an absolute instruction, and its format is:

```
opcode     (A) 1
```

where the (A) states that the information, a 1 in this case, that follows is absolute and requires no adjusting.

The variable DATA3, referenced in line 17, is found in the global data area. The instruction that references it is

```
opcode     (G) 0
```

where (G) indicates that the following address is within the global area. The 0 means that the first location of the global area is the location being referenced.

Lines 18 and 21 again reference external addresses. Line 19 pushes the global variable MYPCB on the stack and line 20 pushes an immediate value, an ASCII character N, onto the stack. The format of these instructions is:

```
opcode    (X) 2
opcode    (G) 1
opcode    (A) "N"
opcode    (X) 4
```

where (X) indicates an external label number.

The final instruction of the assembly language program is the pseudoinstruction END. In addition to specifying that this is the last instruction of the module MAIN, this instruction is used to tell the linker (and subsequently the loader) where control should transfer to start execution of the module. The instruction generates

```
END  (R) address of MAIN
```

where, in this case, MAIN refers to line 12 of the program.

The complete assembler object code is shown in Figure A.5. There are a few additional points that need to be made about the object code. First, note that although the address of MASK is passed in the object code, the label itself does not appear in the code. This is because the label is a local one and can only be referenced within the module MAIN. The label ONE, which is equated to 1 in the assembler symbol table, is also a local label and is not passed on for the same reason.

The example used above is from a somewhat generic assembler. A compiler for the same machine would produce similar output, but it was easier to show the equivalence between assembler instructions and object code generated. In the next section we will see how the linker processes the object code we have generated.

```
NAME        MAIN 32
ENTRY       DATA1    0001
            LOCATE   0020
EXTERNAL    SUB1     (1)
            SUB2     (2)
            DATA2    (3)
            EXIT     (4)
GLOBAL      DATA3  0
            MYPCB  1
            (A) 7
            (A) 65
opcode      (R) 0001
opcode      (R) 0000
opcode      (X) 3
opcode      (X) 1
opcode      (A) 1
opcode      (G) 0
opcode      (X) 2
opcode      (G) 1
opcode      (A) "N"
opcode      (X) 4
END         (R) 0002
```

Figure A.5 Complete assembler object code.

A.3.2 The Linker Symbol Table

We assume that you are familiar with the operation of a two-pass assembler, although we will not rely too heavily on that knowledge. In a two-pass assembler, the assembler creates a symbol table on the first pass; information about all the labels referenced within the program is collected into this table. During the second pass, the symbol table information is used to create the object code.

The linker must also create a symbol table, which it uses to solve addressing problems. The assembler creates its table by noting the addresses of all labels found in a program and also by gathering information on all external and global references. Since the linker does not have access to the source code, it must create its table just from the information passed in the object code. The linker receives information about labels from the NAME, ENTRY, EXTERNAL, GLOBAL, and END records.

There are numerous ways to construct the linker symbol table. The method we present here requires only one pass through the object code, and we will call this a one-pass linker. The format for the linker symbol table is shown in Figure A.6.

LINKER SYMBOL TABLE

Module name _____		Module length _____
Starting address _____		Global address _____
Execution address _____		Global length _____
LABEL	ADDRESS	LINK PATH	EXTERNAL #
_____	_____	_____	_____

Figure A.6 Linker symbol table format.

In Figure A.7(a) through (e) we show how the table is modified after the records in the object code for the module MAIN are processed. We have made some assumptions in creating the symbol table in Figure A.6:

Machine-executable instructions are all 3 bytes.

Addresses are all in decimal.

The starting address for the program is 2000.

The GLOBAL area starts at 8000.

The linker knows the addresses of OS routines (such as EXIT).

U means undefined or unused.

LINKER SYMBOL TABLE

Module name MAIN___		Module length 32_____
Starting address 2000___		Global address _____
Execution address _____		Global length _____
LABEL	ADDRESS	LINK PATH	EXTERNAL #
_____	_____	_____	_____

(a)

Figure A.7 Linker Symbol Table after processing records. (a) NAME record processed. (b) ENTRY record processed. (c) EXTERNAL record processed. (d) GLOBAL record processed. (e) END record processed.

LINKER SYMBOL TABLE

Module name	MAIN			Module length	32
Starting address	2000			Global address	
Execution address				Global length	
LABEL	ADDRESS		LINK PATH		EXTERNAL #
DATA1	2001		U		U
LOCATE	2020		U		U

(b)

LINKER SYMBOL TABLE

Module name	MAIN			Module length	32
Starting address	2000			Global address	
Execution address				Global length	
LABEL	ADDRESS		LINK PATH		EXTERNAL #
DATA1	2001		U		U
LOCATE	2020		U		U
SUB1	U		U		1
SUB2	U		U		2
DATA2	U		U		3
EXIT	1100		U		4

(c)

LINKER SYMBOL TABLE

Module name	MAIN			Module length	32
Starting address	2000			Global address	8000
Execution address				Global length	2
LABEL	ADDRESS		LINK PATH		EXTERNAL #
DATA1	2001		U		U
LOCATE	2020		U		U
SUB1	U		U		1
SUB2	U		U		2
DATA2	U		U		3
EXIT	1100		U		4

(d)

LINKER SYMBOL TABLE

Module name	MAIN			Module length	32
Starting address	2000			Global address	8000
Execution address	2002			Global length	2
LABEL	ADDRESS		LINK PATH		EXTERNAL #
DATA1	2001		U		U
LOCATE	2020		U		U
SUB1	U		2012		1
SUB2	U		2021		2
DATA2	U		2009		3
EXIT	1100		U		4

(e)

Figure A.7 *(cont.)*

In the table, LABEL refers to the labels transmitted in the ENTRY and EXTERNAL records. The address field for labels in ENTRY records can be calculated immediately, since the starting address of the module is known and the relative address of the label is known. Labels from EXTERNAL records require two additional entries: LINK PATH and EXTERNAL #. The LINK PATH is used to create a linked list of all locations that must have an address inserted before the instruction can be executed. The EXTERNAL # is used as an index into the symbol table. From the table we find the address of the external, which we then insert into the instruction in the object code.

A few observations should be made now concerning the symbol table and the code that has been produced. Note that MASK and ONE do not appear in the table, since, as was pointed out earlier, they were local variables within MAIN. The code that has been produced to this point, which is shown in Figure A.8, is not executable. No addresses have been supplied for the external references SUB1, SUB2, and DATA2. The locations that should have these addresses are presently used as links to other locations that need the same addresses. For the example shown, all of the additional links are zero because each external was referenced only once.

The linker's problem of undefined external references, which is similar to the forward reference problem [Aho and Ullman, 1977], has been with programmers for a long time. Compiler and assembler writers have had to deal with it, and now we find the same problem when creating a linker. In the next section we will look briefly at some alternative solutions to the problem.

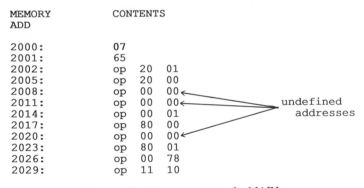

Figure A.8 Memory contents for MAIN.

A.3.3 The Forward Reference Problem

In the previous section we solved the forward reference problem by creating a linked list of all locations which needed a particular address that was not yet known. When the address is finally found, we simply trace all the locations in the linked list and fill in the correct address. One advantage to this is that we have to read the object code only once. A possible disadvantage occurs when the executable code is stored on disk and one has to search a linked list of blocks on the disk to fill in all of the addresses. This can be a very slow process.

An alternative method that also requires only one pass through the object code relies on the use of indirect addresses for all forward references. The column in the linker symbol table labeled LINK PATH is replaced by one called INDIRECT LINK. With this method, when an instruction in the object code references a label that has not yet been defined, the instruction is changed to the indirect form of the instruction and the operand address is replaced by the address of a location that will eventually contain the address of the label. The following shows how this would be accomplished:

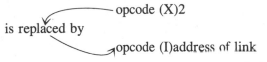

is replaced by

opcode (X)2

opcode (I)address of link

where again (X) is an external reference and now (I) means indirect addressing is applied to the instruction. Figure A.9 illustrates graphically how this method works.

This method has both advantages and disadvantages compared to the linked-list method. The primary advantage is that it is no longer necessary to follow a linked list to insert the correct address into every instruction. It is necessary only to store the correct address in the link word. Unfortunately, that also brings us to the primary disadvantage: the linker must make room for the link word in the program space. A second disadvantage is that an extra memory reference will be needed at execution time to resolve the indirect address. Finally, this method will work only if the hardware supports multiple levels of indirect addressing and all memory reference instructions allow the indirect addressing mode.

A third method that is often used is the same one used in two-pass assemblers. The object code is processed twice. On the first pass the linker symbol table is created, and on the second pass the executable code is created (if, of course, all of the externals have been resolved on the first pass). This method eliminates the problems associated with one-pass methods but requires two passes through the object code.

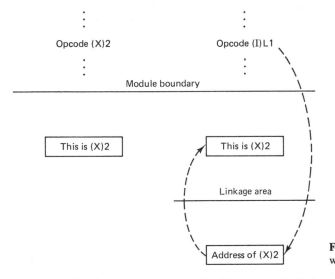

Figure A.9   Indirect addressing for forward references.

In the next section we look at what the linker does when it has linked all of the modules that have been specified and still has undefined externals. Usually the linker will try to find the missing labels within one of the library files on the system.

A.3.4 Linking with Library Routines

Most programs we write, especially those written in high-level languages, will reference routines that we seldom consider. For instance, if you include the following statement in your PASCAL program:

```
x_side := hypotenuse*sin(angle);
```

it is usually not necessary to declare that "sin" is an external function. The compiler will recognize that "sin" is a routine supplied by the system and is an implied external to the user program. It is probably not so obvious that "sin" itself may also reference an external function, such as a function that calculates the Tchebycheff approximation for a sine series. It is obviously possible for the Tchebycheff function in turn to call additional functions. This process can go on for many levels, and the linker must be prepared to cope with the problem. How does it do this?

When you request that the linkage editor link together your main routine and several subroutines, you specify the names of the files that contain the object code for the modules. When all of the specified modules have been linked together, the linker checks the linker symbol table to see whether every label listed in the first column has an address in the second column. If not, it may ask you whether there are additional files you want linked to the program. If you indicate that there are no additional files to include, the linker might ask whether you want to search the system library to try to resolve the undefined externals. You would normally answer yes to this question.

On some systems, you may have a choice of which system library you wish to have searched. Suppose, for example, that you have made a call to a routine named PLOT. One library might have a PLOT routine that outputs to the pen plotter, and another library might have a different routine named PLOT that outputs to a color terminal. By selecting one library or the other the user specifies which plotting device will be used.

Once the correct library file has been selected, the linker starts reading the library. It looks for modules that include labels which are still undefined in the program it is currently trying to link. Each time it finds such a label, it links the object code for that module to the program. This might add more externals to the symbol table. When the linker reaches the end of the library file, the externals should by now all be resolved. If so, the linker has produced an executable code module. What can be done when the externals have not been resolved is left as a question at the end of the appendix.

A.3.5 The Executable Code Module

To complete the linking operation for the module MAIN, we need to come up with another module that has as entries the externals specified in MAIN. Consider the module SUBS shown in Figure A.10. It has SUB1, SUB2, and DATA2 as entry points; these match the externals from MAIN. Unfortunately, it has an additional external, CONVT, which is not in MAIN. The result of linking MAIN and SUBS together is shown in Figure A.11. Note that there is one undefined label, CONVT, in both the symbol table and the code modules.

```
stmt   rel
 #     addr
----   ----
 01                    NAME       SUBS
 02
 03                    ENTRY      SUB1, SUB2, DATA2
 04                    EXTERNAL   DATA1, CONVT
 05
 06    0000  MASK      BYTE       01110111B
 07    0001  DATA2     BYTE       11110000B
 08
 09    0002  SUB1      MOVE       DATA1,R3
 10    0005            AND        MASK,R3
 11    0008            MOVE       R3,DATA1
 12    0011            RETURN
 13
 14    0012  SUB2      AND        MASK,R3
 15    0015            JSB        CONVT
 16    0018            RETURN
 17
 18                    END
```

Figure A.10 Subroutine module referenced by MAIN.

LINKER SYMBOL TABLE

Module name	SUBS		Module length	19
Staring address	3000		Global address	8000
Execution address	2002		Global length	0

LABEL	ADDRESS	LINK PATH	EXTERNAL #
DATA1	2001	U	1
LOCATE	2020	U	U
SUB1	3002	U	U
SUB2	3012	U	U
DATA2	3001	U	U
EXIT	1100	U	U
CONVT	U	3016	2

(a)

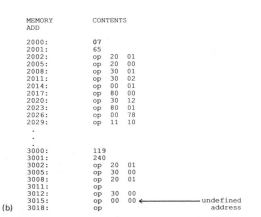

```
MEMORY      CONTENTS
ADD

2000:       07
2001:       65
2002:       op   20   01
2005:       op   20   00
2008:       op   30   01
2011:       op   30   02
2014:       op   00   01
2017:       op   80   00
2020:       op   30   12
2023:       op   80   01
2026:       op   00   78
2029:       op   11   10
  .
  .
3000:       119
3001:       240
3002:       op   20   01
3005:       op   30   00
3008:       op   20   01
3011:       op
3012:       op   30   00
3015:       op   00   00  ←————————— undefined
3018:       op                       address
```
(b)

Figure A.11 Linker output. (a) Symbol table after linking SUBS. (b) Memory contents for MAIN and SUBS.

The symbol table in Figure A.11(a) shows that the execution address has not changed. The table also shows the length of SUBS and the fact that it declares no global variables. The code module in Figure A.11(b) shows that SUBS was loaded into memory starting at location 3000. The assumption was made that the RETURN instructions in SUBS memory addresses 3011 and 3018 require only one byte rather than three.

The last operation that the linker will perform for this program is to link it to the system library routine which contains the label CONVT. The memory contents after this linkage occurs are shown in Figure A.12. We have assumed that the module containing CONVT is loaded starting at location 4000. The creation of the corresponding linker symbol table is left as an exercise.

There is one additional question that might well be asked at this point: "What does the linker do with the executable code?" There are at least two possible answers. On many older systems, the executable code was actually in memory at the completion of the linkage operation. In this case, the next step would probably be to transfer control to the execution address and let the program run.

On many current systems, the executable code is not all in memory at the completion of the linkage process; it is in a temporary disk file. When this is the case, the normal procedure is to write any remaining memory resident part of the module out to disk and create a permanent file containing the executable code. Any

	MEMORY ADD	CONTENTS		
	2000:	07		
	2001:	65		
	2002:	op	20	01
	2005:	op	20	00
	2008:	op	30	01
MAIN	2011:	op	30	02
	2014:	op	00	01
	2017:	op	80	00
	2020:	op	30	12
	2023:	op	80	01
	2026:	op	00	78
	2029:	op	11	10
	.			
	.			
	3000:	119		
	3001:	240		
	3002:	op	20	01
	3005:	op	30	00
SUBS	3008:	op	20	01
	3011:	op		
	3012:	op	30	00
	3015:	op	40	00
	3018:	op		
	.			
	.			
	4000:	op	40	10
	4003:	op	40	11
CONVT	4006:	op	80	00
	4009:	op		
	.			
	.			
GLOBALS	8000	00		
	8001	00		

Figure A.12 Memory contents for MAIN, SUBS, and CONVERT.

time the user wishes to run the program that has been linked, a process will be created and the file will be loaded and executed as described in Chapter 5.

In the final sections of this appendix, we will examine a problem that was glossed over in the discussion on linking. This is the problem of relocation. When we were talking about linking, we assumed that modules could arbitrarily be moved wherever the linker chose to place them. How and when this can be done will now be considered.

A.4 STATIC AND DYNAMIC RELOCATION

Relocation is the operation of moving a program or module from one location to another. Your first question might be "Why is this necessary?" To answer this, look at the output from an assembler. The assembler typically assumes that all programs will start at the same location, and this is most often address 0. If we assemble a main program and several subroutines separately, the assembler will generate object code for each assuming that it will be loaded starting at location 0. Obviously only one module can be loaded starting at location 0; all other modules will have to be loaded somewhere else. Moving these modules to other locations is the process of relocation.

On many older computers relocation and linking were combined together into one operation performed by the relocating linkage editor. On these older machines relocation was done one time; when the programmer requested that several modules be linked with any required system routines, a region of memory was selected and the modules were linked into that region. All of the addresses of the instructions referencing memory were adjusted so that they pointed to the correct address within the selected region (binding occurred at linkage time). The resulting executable code was tied directly to that one region of memory. This approach, which was called **static relocation,** caused problems when it was applied in multiprogramming systems.

Multiprogramming systems rely on the ability to move processes out of memory when they are not being used and some other process needs memory space. This in itself causes no problem; however, when the system needs to bring the process back into memory there may be problems. When static relocation is used, a process being loaded back into memory must be loaded into exactly the same region it occupied when it was first relocated and linked. The reason is that at relocation time absolute addresses were stored into all memory reference instructions. If the original region of memory is being used by some other process, the one trying to return must wait even if all of the rest of memory is free! This leads to low utilization of the CPU and memory.

To solve the problem, we need some mechanism that will allow a process to be reloaded into a different region each time it is brought back into memory. After a brief look at the problem, you might suggest that we use the relocating linkage editor each time we reload a process. In some cases this might work; however, it would result in a very, very slow system.

Fortunately for us, the hardware designers came to the rescue. All that was needed was one additional register and an adder to sum the contents of the register and the address field of an instruction. The added register was called a base or **relocation register.** The mechanism was as follows: relocate and link a program assuming that the program would be loaded starting at location 0. At load time, place the module into any available region and load the starting address of that region into the relocation register. Each time an address is generated by the program, add that address to the relocation register and use that as the *effective memory address* (binding occurred at execution time). Figure A.13 shows graphically how dynamic relocation is implemented with a relocation register.

This method, which allowed the executable module to be moved to any memory location, was called **dynamic relocation.** It proved to be inexpensive to implement and added very little to the overhead of the system. The advantage was that processes could be loaded into any available memory region and this in turn gave better utilization of the CPU and memory. Nearly all systems now use some form of dynamic relocation. The paging and segmentation mechanisms described in Chapter 7 are other examples of ways to achieve dynamic relocation.

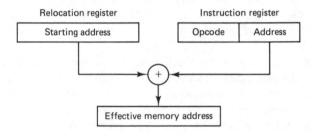

Figure A.13   Dynamic relocation with a base register.

A.5 AN EXAMPLE OF RELOCATION AND LINKING

In this section we will look again at the executable code generated for the modules MAIN and SUBS. What we will do this time is relocate the modules assuming that the starting address for MAIN is 0. We will then relocate SUBS into the area immediately following MAIN and finally relocate the system routine CONVERT into memory following SUBS. Figure A.14 shows the memory image for the executable module.

Comparing the memory image in Figure A.14 with that in Figure A.11, we note several differences. First, the GLOBAL area was moved to the first two locations in the block. Next, the modules MAIN, SUBS, and CONVERT have all been squeezed together with no spaces in between. By doing this, we have created an executable module that can be loaded into one contiguous region of memory. This is the format that we assume existed back in Chapter 4 when we discussed loading the code to start a process.

We must point out here that machines which separate code and data segments would have to create two memory images: one for code and one for data. Furthermore, a system with paging or segmentation will not necessarily load the entire program contiguously.

	MEMORY ADD	CONTENTS		
GLOBALS	0000:	00		
	0001:	00		
	0002:	07		
	0003:	65		
	0004:	op	00	03
	0007:	op	00	02
	0010:	op	00	35
MAIN	0013:	op	00	36
	0016:	op	00	01
	0019:	op	00	00
	0022:	op	00	47
	0025:	op	00	01
	0028:	op	00	78
	0031:	op	11	10
	0034:	119		
	0035:	240		
	0036:	op	00	03
	0039:	op	00	34
SUBS	0042:	op	00	03
	0045:	op		
	0046:	op	00	34
	0049:	op	00	53
	0052:	op		
	0053:	op	00	63
	0056:	op	00	64
CONVT	0059:	op	00	00
	0062:	op		
	0063:	60		
	0064:	20		

Figure A.14 Memory contents for MAIN, SUBS, and CONVERT after being linked into contiguous memory locations.

A.6 SUMMARY

Loading, relocation, and linking are operations that must be performed before any process can execute. Dynamic relocation is a highly desirable, if not essential, feature of a multiprogramming system. It is so important that special hardware was created to ease the operation and reduce the associated overhead. Finally, linking and relocation make possible the use of libraries, which have simplified life for both systems and application programmers.

Linking and relocation operations have been around for a long time. A good description is available in McCarthy et al. [1963]. The text by Barron [1969] is one of the few that have much information on linking and loading. A more recent text by Pfleeger [1982] has some additional material on the subject.

QUESTIONS AND EXERCISES

1. Why are external symbol numbers used rather than the labels themselves in the object code records? (For example, opcode (X)3.)

2. Show where each instruction in the object code for MAIN maps into the memory listing shown in Figure A.8.

3. In Section A.3.3 it was stated that the indirect link method would work only if the CPU used supported multiple levels of indirect addressing. Why?

4. Can you think of any reasons why the linker would still have undefined externals after it has made a pass through the library file? What should be done in each case?

5. Why didn't the execution address change (symbol table, Figure A.11(a)) after SUBS was loaded?

6. Create the linker symbol table that would exist after CONVERT was linked to MAIN and SUBS. State any assumption you had to make.

7. In Section A.4 we suggested that relocation could be performed each time a process was reloaded into memory. What is wrong with this method other than just the fact that it is slow?

8. Which operands in the memory image of Figure A.14 are *not* added to the base register before they are used?

9. When we place the globals before the code and data, we must make an assumption about the GLOBAL area used by the remaining programs that will be loaded. What is that assumption? How can the problem be avoided?

10. Create the linker symbol table that would have been built by the loader when generating the memory image of Figure A.14.

11. Symbolic debugging requires that the debugger have access to the symbols defined in the source program. How would the assembler (compiler) and linker have to be modified to accommodate this operation?

12. How does PASCAL support global variables?

PROGRAMMING ASSIGNMENT

Write a relocating linkage editor for a hypothetical machine whose compilers and assemblers generate the following form of object module:

module name	8 characters
number of entry points	3-digit integer
first entry point name	8 characters
relative displacement of first entry point	5-digit integer
second entry point name	8 characters
relative displacement of second entry point	5-digit integer
(same for remaining entry points)	
number of externals	3-digit integer
first external name	8 characters
relative displacement of first reference to this external	5-digit integer
second external name	8 characters
relative displacement of first reference to this external	5-digit integer
(same for remaining external references)	

number of instructions	5-digit integer
first instruction	
address type:	1 character
r relocatable	
a absolute	
e external	
s skip storage	
op code, registers,	3 digits
etc.	
address	5 digits

(same for remaining instructions)

Each of these components is on one line, separated by a space. For example, an external reference would be of the form

```
XXXXXXXX  DDDDD
TANGENT    00104
```

and an instruction would be of the form

```
X  DDD  DDDDD
e  103  23456
```

The input to the linkage editor, then, consists of two lines followed by a sequence of object modules:

number of modules	3-digit integer
starting point for execution	5-digit integer
module 1 (as described)	
module 2 (as described)	
etc.	

Output of your linkage editor should be a linked relocatable load module, ready to be loaded into main memory. Each line in this module will simply be

address type	1 character
r relocatable	
a absolute	
instruction	8-digit integer

Note that during linkage editing there could be errors. In this case no load module would be generated.

Bibliography

ABATE AND DUBNER [1969]: J. Abate and H. Dubner, "Optimizing the Performance of a Drumlike Storage," *IEEE Trans. Computers,* Vol. c-18, No. 11, pp. 992–996 (November).

ABELL ET AL. [1970]: V. A. Abell, S. Rosen, and R. E. Wagner, "Scheduling in a General Purpose Operating System," *AFIPS FJCC,* Vol. 37, pp. 89–96.

ACM [1978]: "ACM Curriculum 1978," *Comm. ACM,* Vol. 33, No. 3, pp. 147–165 (March).

AHL [1983]: D. H. Ahl, "Benchmark Comparison Test," *Creative Computing,* Vol. 9, No. 11, pp. 259–260 (November).

AHO ET AL. [1971]: A. V. Aho, P. J. Denning, and J. D. Ullman, "Principles of Optimal Page Replacement," *ACM,* Vol. 18, No. 1, pp. 80–93 (January).

AHO AND ULLMAN [1977]: A. V. Aho and J. D. Ullman, *Principles of Compiler Design,* Addison-Wesley, Reading, Mass.

ALDERSON ET AL. [1972]: A. Alderson, W. C. Lynch, and B. Randell, "Thrashing in a Multiprogrammed Paging System," in Hoare and Perrott [1972].

ALLEN AND FOOTE [1964]: T. R. Allen and J. E. Foote, "Input/Output Software Capability for a Man-Machine Communication and Image Processing System," *AFIPS FJCC,* Vol. 26, Pt. 1, pp. 387–396.

AMSBURY [1985]: W. Amsbury, *Data Structures: from Arrays to Priority Queues,* Wadsworth, Belmont, Calif.

APPLE [1979]: *Apple II+ Reference Manual,* Apple Computer, Inc., Cupertino, Calif.

334

ATWOOD [1976]: J. W. Atwood, "Concurrency in Operating Systems," *IEEE Computer*, Vol. 9, No. 9, pp. 18–26 (October).

BABAD [1977]: J. M. Babad, "A Record and File Partitioning Model," *Comm. ACM*, Vol. 20, No. 1, pp. 23–31, (January).

BAILEY AND LUNDGAARD [1983]: T. E. Bailey and K. Lundgaard, *Program Design with Pseudocode*, Brooks/Cole, Monterey, Calif.

BARNETT [1978]: J. K. R. Barnett, "A Highly Reliable File System Which Supports Multiprocessing," *Software—Practice and Experience*, Vol. 8, No. 6, pp. 645–667 (November–December).

BARRON [1969]: D. W. Barron, *Assemblers and Loaders*, MacDonald, London, and American Elsevier, New York.

BARRON [1971]: D. W. Barron, *Computer Operating Systems*, Chapman & Hall, London.

BARRON ET AL. [1967]: D. W. Barron, A. G. Fraser, D. F. Hartley, B. Landy, and R. M. Needham, "File Handling at Cambridge University," *AFIPS SJCC*, Vol. 30, pp. 163–167.

BARTLETT [1978]: F. Bartlett, "A 'NonStop' Operating System," *Proc. 11th Hawaii Int. Conf. System Sci.* pp. 103–117.

BATSON ET AL. [1970]: A. P. Batson, S. Ju, and D. Wood, "Measurements of Segment Size," *Comm. ACM*, Vol. 13, No. 3, pp. 155–159 (March).

BAYS [1977]: C. Bays, "A Comparison of Next-Fit, First-Fit, and Best-Fit," *Comm. ACM*, Vol. 20, No. 3, pp. 191–192 (March).

BECK [1982]: L. L. Beck, "A Dynamic Storage Allocation Technique Based on Memory Residence Time," *Comm. ACM*, Vol. 25, No. 10, pp. 714–724 (October).

BECK [1985]: L. L. Beck, *An Introduction to Systems Programming*, Addison-Wesley, Reading, Mass.

BELADY ET AL. [1969]: L. A. Belady, R. A. Nelson, and G. S. Shedler, "An Anomaly in Space-Time Characteristics of Certain Programs Running in a Paging Machine," *Comm. ACM*, Vol. 12, No. 6 (June).

BEN-ARI [1982]: M. Ben-Ari, *Principles of Concurrent Programming*, Prentice-Hall, Englewood Cliffs, N. J.

BENSOUSSAN ET AL. [1972]: A. Bensoussan, C. T. Clingen, and R. C. Daley, "The Multics Virtual Memory: Concepts and Design," *Comm. ACM*, Vol. 15, No. 5, pp. 308–318 (May).

BOARDMAN [1977]: T. L. Boardman, Jr., "A Microprocessor Architecture for Digital Device Implementation," *AFIPS NCC*, Vol. 46, pp. 201–205.

BORLAND [1983]: *Turbo Pascal*, Borland, Int. Inc., Scotts Valley, Calif.

BOURNE [1978]: S. R. Bourne, "The UNIX Shell," *Bell Sys. Tech. J.*, Vol. 57, No. 6, Pt. 2, pp. 1971–2020 (July–August).

BRANSTAD [1973]: D. K. Branstad, "Privacy and Protection in Operating Systems," *IEEE Computer*, Vol. 6, No. 1, pp. 43–46 (January).

BRINCH HANSEN [1970]: P. Brinch Hansen, "The Nucleus of a Multiprogramming System," *Comm. ACM*, Vol. 13, No. 4 (April).

BRINCH HANSEN [1971]: P. Brinch Hansen, "An Analysis of Response Ratio Scheduling," *Proc. IFIP Cong. 71*.

BRINCH HANSEN [1972]: P. Brinch Hansen, "Structured Multiprogramming Concepts," *Comm. ACM*, Vol. 15, No. 7, pp. 574–578 (July).

BRINCH HANSEN [1973a]: P. Brinch Hansen, *Operating System Principles,* Prentice-Hall, Englewood Cliffs, N. J.

BRINCH HANSEN [1973b]: P. Brinch Hansen, "Concurrent Programming Concepts," *ACM Computing Surveys,* Vol. 5, No. 4, pp. 223–245 (December).

BRINCH HANSEN [1975]: P. Brinch Hansen, "The Programming Language Concurrent Pascal," *IEEE Trans. Software Eng.,* Vol. SE-1, No. 2, pp. 199–207 (June).

BRINCH HANSEN [1976]: P. Brinch Hansen, "The SOLD Operating System: A Concurrent Pascal Program," *Software—Practice and Experience,* Vol. 6, pp. 141–149.

BRINCH HANSEN [1978]: P. Brinch Hansen, "Distributed Processes: A Concurrent Programming Concept," *Comm. ACM,* Vol. 21, No. 11, pp. 934–941 (November).

BROOKS [1982]: F. P. Brooks, *The Mythical Man-Month,* Addison-Wesley, Reading, Mass.

BROWN AND DENNING [1984]: R. L. Brown and P. J. Denning, "Advanced Operating Systems," *IEEE Computer,* Vol. 17, No. 10, pp. 173–190 (October).

BUCHHOLZ [1963]: W. Buchholz, "File Organization and Addressing," *IBM Sys. J.* Vol 2, pp. 86–111 (June).

BUNT [1976]: R. B. Bunt, "Scheduling Techniques for Operating Systems," *Computer,* Vol. 9, No. 10, pp. 10–17 (October).

BURNS [1978]: J. E. Burns, "Mutual Exclusion with Linear Waiting Using Binary Shared Variables," *SIGACT News,* Vol. 10, No. 2 (Summer).

CALINGAERT [1967]: P. Calingaert, "System Performance Evaluation: Survey and Appraisal," *Comm. ACM,* Vol. 10, No. 1, pp. 12–18 (January).

CALINGAERT [1979]: P. Calingaert, *Assemblers, Compilers, and Program Translation,* Computer Science Press, Rockville, Md.

CALINGAERT [1982]: P. Calingaert, *Operating System Elements,* Prentice-Hall, Englewood Cliffs, N. J.

CARDENAS [1973]: A. F. Cardenas, "Evaluation and Selection of File Organization in a Model and System," *Comm. ACM,* Vol. 16, No. 9, pp. 540–548 (September).

CENTRAL POINT SOFTWARE [1987]: *PC Tools, Central Point Software,* Portland, Ore.

CHAPIN [1969]: N. Chapin, "Common File Organization Techniques Compared," *AFIPS FJCC,* Vol. 35, pp. 413–422.

CHEATHAM AND LEONARD [1967]: T. E. Cheatham, Jr., and G. F. Leonard, "An Introduction to the CL-II Programming System," in Rosen [1967].

COFFMAN [1968]: E. G. Coffman, "Analysis of Two Time-Sharing Algorithms Designed for Limited Swapping," *J. ACM,* Vol. 15, No. 3, pp. 341–353 (July).

COFFMAN [1969]: E. G. Coffman, "Analysis of a Drum Input/Output Queue under Scheduling Operation in a Paged Computer System," *J. ACM,* Vol. 16, No. 1, pp. 73–90 (January).

COFFMAN AND DENNING [1973]: E. G. Coffman, Jr. and P. J. Denning, *Operating Systems Theory,* Prentice-Hall, Englewood Cliffs, N. J., (1973).

COFFMAN ET AL. [1971]: E. G. Coffman, M. J. Elphick, and A. Shoshani, "System Deadlocks," *ACM Computing Surveys,* Vol. 3, No. 3, pp. 67–78 (June).

COFFMAN AND KLEINROCK [1968]: E. G. Coffman and L. Kleinrock, "Feedback Queueing Models for Time-Shared Systems," *J. ACM,* Vol. 15, No. 4, pp. 549–576 (October).

COFFMAN AND RYAN [1972]: E. G. Coffman and T. A. Ryan, "A Study of Storage Partitioning Using a Mathematical Model of Locality," *Comm. ACM,* Vol. 15, No. 3, pp. 185–190 (March).

COFFMAN AND VARIAN [1968]: E. G. Coffman and L. C. Varian, "Further Experimental Data on the Behavior of Programs in a Paging Environment," *Comm. ACM,* Vol. 11, No. 7, pp. 471–474 (July).

COFFMAN AND WOOD [1966]: E. G. Coffman and R. C. Wood, "Interarrival Statistics for Time-Sharing Systems," *Comm. ACM,* Vol. 9, No. 7, pp. 500–503 (July).

CONTI ET AL. [1968]: C. J. Conti, D. H. Gibson, and S. H. Pitkowsky, "Structural Aspects of the System/360 Model 85," *IBM Sys. J.* Vol. 7, No. 1, pp. 2–14.

CONWAY ET AL. [1967]: R. W. Conway, W. L. Maxwell, and L. W. Miller, *Theory of Scheduling,* Addison-Wesley, Reading, Mass.

CONWAY ET AL. [1972]: R. W. Conway, W. L. Maxwell, and H. L. Morgan, "On the Implementation of Security Measures in Information Systems," *Comm. ACM,* Vol. 15, No. 4, pp. 211–220.

CORBATO AND VYSSOTSKY [1967]: F. J. Corbato and V. A. Vyssotsky, "Introduction and Overview of the Multics System," in Rosen [1967].

COURTOIS ET AL. [1971]: P. J. Courtois, F. Heymans, and D. L. Parnas, "Concurrent Control with 'Readers' and 'Writers,'" *Comm. ACM,* Vol. 14, No. 10, pp. 667–668 (October).

COURY [1970]: F. F. Coury, "A Systems Approach to Minicomputer I/O," *AFIPS SJCC,* Vol. 36, pp. 677–681.

CROWLEY [1981]: C. Crowley, "The Design and Implementation of a New UNIX Kernel," *AFIPS NCC,* Vol. 50, pp. 1079–1086.

CURTICE [1975]: R. M. Curtice, "Access Mechanisms and Data Structure Support in DBMS," *QED*. Information Sciences, Wellesley, Mass.

DALEY AND DENNIS [1968]: R. C. Daley and J. B. Dennis, "Virtual Memory, Processes and Sharing in Multics," *Comm. ACM,* Vol. 11, No. 5, pp. 306–312 (May).

DALEY AND NEUMANN [1965]: R. C. Daley and P. G. Neumann, "A General-Purpose File System for Secondary Storage," *AFIPS FJCC,* Vol. 27, pp. 213–229.

DEBRUIJN [1967]: N. G. deBruijn, "Additional Comments on a Problem in Concurrent Programming and Control," *Comm. ACM,* Vol. 10, No. 3, pp. 137–138 (March).

DEITEL [1984]: H. M. Deitel, *An Introduction to Operating Systems,* Addison-Wesley, Reading, Mass.

DEMARCO [1979]: T. DeMarco, *Structured Analysis and System Specification,* Prentice-Hall, Englewood Cliffs, N. J.

DENNING, D. E. [1982]: D. E. Denning, *Cryptography and Data Security,* Addison-Wesley, Reading, Mass.

DENNING, D. E. AND DENNING [1979]: D. E. Denning and P. J. Denning, "Data Security," *ACM Computer Surveys,* Vol. 11, No. 3, pp. 227–243 (September).

DENNING, P. J. [1968]: P. J. Denning, "The Working Set Model for Program Behavior," *Comm. ACM,* Vol. 11, No. 5, pp. 323–333 (May).

DENNING, P. J. [1970]: P. J. Denning, "Virtual Memory," *ACM Computing Surveys,* Vol. 2, No. 3, pp. 153–189 (September).

DENNING, P. J. [1972]: P. J. Denning, "A Note on Paging Drum Efficiency," *ACM Computing Surveys,* Vol. 4, No. 1, pp. 1–3 (September).

DENNING, P. J. [1980]: P. J. Denning, "Working Sets Past and Present," *IEEE Trans. Soft-Eng.,* Vol SE-6, No. 1, pp. 64–84 (January).

DENNING, P. J. [1982]: P. J. Denning, "Are Operating Systems Obsolete?" *Comm. ACM,* Vol. 25, No. 4, pp. 225–227 (April).

DENNING, P. J., AND SCHWARTZ [1972]: P. J. Denning and S. C. Schwartz, "Properties of the Working Set Model," *Comm. ACM,* Vol. 15, No. 3, (March).

DENNIS [1965]: J. B. Dennis, "Segmentation and the Design of Multiprogrammed Computer Systems," *J. ACM,* Vol. 12, No. 4, pp. 589–602 (October).

DEVILLERS [1977]: R. Devillers, "Game Interpretation of the Deadlock Avoidance Problem," *Comm. ACM,* Vol. 20, No. 10, pp. 741–745 (October).

DIFFIE AND HELLMAN [1979]: W. Diffie and M. E. Hellman, "Privacy and Authentication," *Proc. IEEE,* Vol. 67, No. 3, pp. 397–427 (March).

DIJKSTRA [1965a]: E. W. Dijkstra, "Solution of a Problem in Concurrent Programming," *Comm. ACM,* Vol. 8, No. 9, p. 569 (September).

DIJKSTRA [1965b]: E. W. Dijkstra, "Cooperating Sequential Processes," EWD123, Mathematics Department, Technological University, Eindhoven, Netherlands, September. Reprinted in F. Genuys (ed.), *Programming Languages,* Academic Press, London (1968).

DIJKSTRA [1968]: E. W. Dijkstra, "The Structure of the 'THE' Multiprogramming System," *Comm. ACM,* Vol. 18, No. 8, pp. 341–346 (May).

DOHERTY [1970]: W. J. Doherty, "Scheduling TDD/360 for Responsiveness," *AFIPS FJCC,* Vol. 37, pp. 97–111.

DORAN [1976]: R. W. Doran, "Virtual Memory," *IEEE Computer,* Vol. 9, No. 10, pp. 27–37 (October).

DRUMMOND [1973]: M. E. Drummond, Jr., *Evaluation and Measurement Techniques for Digital Computer Systems,* Prentice-Hall, Englewood Cliffs, N. J.

EKANADHAM AND BERNSTEIN [1979]: K. Ekanadham and A. J. Bernstein, "Conditional Capabilities," *IEEE Trans. Software Eng.* Vol. SE-5, No. 5, pp. 458–464 (September).

ERWIN AND JENSEN [1970]: J. D. Erwin and E. D. Jensen, "Interrupt Processing with Queued Content-Addressable Memories," *AFIPS FJCC,* Vol. 37, pp. 621–627.

ESTRIN ET AL. [1967]: G. Estrin, D. Hopkins, B. Cooper, and S. D. Crocker, "SNUPER COMPUTER—A Computer in Instrumentation Automation," *AFIPS SJCC,* Vol. 30, pp. 645–656.

FABRY [1974]: R. S. Fabry, "Capability-Based Addressing," *Comm. ACM,* Vol. 17, No. 7, pp. 403–412 (July).

FERGUSON [1960]: D. E. Ferguson, "Input-Output Buffering and FORTRAN," *J. ACM,* Vol. 7, No. 1, pp. 1–9, (January).

FERRARI [1978]: D. Ferrari, *Computer Systems Performance Evaluation,* Prentice-Hall, Englewood Cliffs, N. J.

FERRARI ET AL. [1983]: Domenico Ferrari, Giuseppe Serazzi, and Alessandro Zeigner, *Measurement and Tuning of Computer Systems,* Prentice-Hall, Englewood Cliffs, New Jersey, (1978).

FOTHERINGHAM [1961]: J. Fotheringham, "Dynamic Storage Allocation in the Atlas Computer Including an Automatic Use of a Backing Store," *Comm. ACM,* Vol. 4, No. 10, pp. 435–436 (October).

FRAILEY [1973]: D. J. Frailey, "A Practical Approach to Managing Resources and Avoiding Deadlock," *Comm. ACM,* Vol. 16, No. 5, pp. 323–329 (May).

FRIEBERGER [1972]: W. Frieberger (ed.), *Statistical Computer Performance Evaluation,* Academic Press, New York.

FULLER [1972]: S. H. Fuller, "An Optimal Drum Scheduling Algorithm," *IEEE Trans. Computers,* Vol. C-21, No. 11, pp. 1153–1165 (November).

FULLER [1974]: S. H. Fuller, "Minimal-Total-Processing-Time Drum and Disk Scheduling Disciplines," *Comm. ACM,* Vol. 17, No. 7, pp. 376–381 (July).

GHOSH AND SENKO [1969]: S. P. Ghosh and M. E. Senko, "File Organization on the Selection of Random Access Index Points for Sequential Files," *J. ACM,* Vol. 16, No. 4, pp. 569–579 (October).

GOLDBERG [1974]: R. P. Goldberg, "Survey of Virtual Machine Research," *IEEE Computer,* Vol. 3, No. 6, pp. 34–43 (June).

GORSLINE [1986]: G. W. Gorsline, *Computer Organization,* Prentice-Hall, Englewood Cliffs, N. J.

GOTLIEB AND MACEWEN [1973]: C. C. Gotlieb and G. H. MacEwen, "Performance of Movable-Head Disk Scheduling Disciplines," *J. ACM,* Vol. 20, No. 4, pp. 604–623 (October).

GRAHAM [1968]: R. M. Graham, "Protection in an Information Processing Utility," *Comm. ACM,* Vol. 11, No. 5, pp. 365–369 (May).

HABERMANN [1969]: A. N. Habermann, "Prevention of System Deadlocks," *Comm. ACM,* Vol. 12, No. 7, pp. 373–377 (July).

HABERMANN [1972]: A. N. Habermann, "Synchronization of Communicating Processes," *Comm. ACM,* Vol. 15, No. 3, pp. 171–176 (March).

HABERMANN [1976]: A. N. Habermann, *Introduction to Operating System Design,* Science Research Associates, Palo Alto, Calif.

HALL ET AL. [1980]: D. E. Hall, D. K. Scherrer, and J. S. Sventek, "A Virtual Operating System," *Comm. ACM,* Vol. 23, No. 9, pp. 495–502 (September).

HANSON [1980]: D. R. Hanson, "A Portable File Directory System," *Software—Practice and Experience,* Vol. 10, No. 8, pp. 623–634 (August).

HANSON [1982]: O. Hanson, *Design of Computer Data Files,* Computer Science Press, Rockville, Md.

HARLAND [1986]: D. M. Harland, *Concurrency and Programming Languages,* Ellis Horwood, Chichester, England.

HARRISON ET AL. [1976]: M. A. Harrison, W. L. Ruzzo, and J. D. Ullman, "Protection in Operating Systems," *Comm. ACM,* Vol. 19, No. 8, pp. 461–471 (August).

HATCH AND GEYER [1968]: T. F. Hatch, Jr., and J. B. Geyer, "Hardware/Software Interaction on the Honeywell Model 8200," *AFIPS FJCC,* Vol. 33, Pt. 1, pp. 891–901.

HAVENDER [1968]: J. W. Havender, "Avoiding Deadlock in Multitasking Systems," *IBM Sys. J.,* Vol. 7, No. 2, pp. 74–84.

HELLERMAN AND CONROY [1975]: H. Hellerman and T. F. Conroy, *Computer System Performance,* McGraw-Hill, New York.

HENDERSON AND ZALCSTEIN [1980]: P. Henderson and Y. Zalcstein, "Synchronization Problems Solvable by Generalized PV Systems," *J. ACM,* Vol. 27, No. 1, pp. 60–71 (January).

HEWLETT-PACKARD [1969]: *A Pocket Guide to the 2116 Computer,* Hewlett-Packard Co., Palo Alto, Calif.

HEWLETT-PACKARD [1976]: *Hewlett-Packard 1610 Logic Analyzer,* Hewlett-Packard Co., Colorado Springs, Colo.

HEWLETT-PACKARD [1980]: *Hewlett-Packard 64000 System Overview Manual,* Hewlett-Packard Co., Colorado Springs, Colo.

HEWLETT-PACKARD [1984]: *HP 3000 Computer Systems General Information Manual,* Hewlett-Packard Co., Cupertino, Calif.

HOARE [1974]: C. A. R. Hoare, "Monitors: An Operating System Structuring Concept," *Comm. ACM,* Vol. 17, No. 10, pp. 549–557 (October); erratum in *Comm. ACM,* Vol. 18, No. 2, p. 95 (February 1975).

HOARE [1978]: C. A. R. Hoare, "Communicating Sequential Processes," *Comm. ACM,* Vol. 21, No. 8, pp. 666–677 (August).

HOARE AND PERROTT [1972]: C. A. R. Hoare and R. H. Perrott (eds.), *Operating System Techniques,* Academic Press, London.

HOFFMAN [1969]: L. J. Hoffman, "Computers and Privacy: A Survey," *ACM Computing Surveys,* Vol. 1, No. 2, pp. 85–103 (June).

HOFFMAN [1977]: L. J. Hoffman, *Modern Methods for Computer Security and Privacy,* Prentice-Hall, Englewood Cliffs, N. J.

HOFRI [1980]: M. Hofri, "Disk Scheduling: FCFS vs. SSTF Revisited," *Comm. ACM,* Vol. 23, No. 11, pp. 181–198 (November).

HOLT [1971]: R. C. Holt, "Comments on Prevention of System Deadlocks," *Comm. ACM,* Vol. 14, No. 1, pp. 36–38 (January).

HOLT [1972]: R. C. Holt, "Some Deadlock Properties of Computer Systems," *ACM Computing Surveys,* Vol. 4, No. 3, pp. 179–196 (September).

HOLT ET AL. [1978]: R. C. Holt, G. S. Graham, E. D. Lazowska, and M. A. Scott, *Structured Concurrent Programming with Operating System Applications,* Addison-Wesley, Reading, Mass.

HOWARD [1973]: J. H. Howard, "Mixed Solutions for the Deadlock Problem," *Comm. ACM,* Vol. 16, No. 7, pp. 427–430 (July).

HOWARD [1976]: J. H. Howard, "Providing Monitors," *Comm. ACM,* Vol. 19, No. 5, pp. 273–279 (July).

HOWARTH ET AL. [1961]: D. J. Howarth, R. B. Payne, and F. H. Sumner, "The Manchester University Atlas Operating System, Part II: User's Description," *Computer J.* Vol. 4, No. 3, pp. 226–229 (October).

HSIAO AND HARARY [1970]: D. Hsiao and F. Harary, "A Formal System for Information Retrieval from Files," *Comm. ACM,* Vol. 13, No. 2, pp. 67–73 (February).

HYMAN [1966]: H. Hyman, "Comments on a Concurrent Programming Control," *Comm. ACM,* Vol. 9, No. 1, p. 45 (January).

IBM [1967]: *IBM Operating System/360 Concepts and Facilities* (excerpts), in Rosen [1967].

IBM [1974]: *Introduction to IBM/360 Direct Access Storage Devices and Organization Methods,* GC20-1649-8, IBM Data Processing Division. Endicott, N.Y.

IEEE [1983]: "The Model Program in Computer Science and Engineering," *IEEE Computer Soc.*

INTEL [1981]: *Introduction to the iAPX 432 Architecture,* Intel Corp., Santa Clara, Calif.

INTEL [1982]: *Intel Development Systems,* Intel Corp., Santa Clara, Calif.

INTEL [1986]: *System Data Catalog,* Intel Corp., Santa Clara, Calif.

IRONS [1965]: E. T. Irons, "A Rapid Turnaround Multiprogramming System," *Comm. ACM,* Vol. 8, No. 3, pp. 152–157 (March).

ISLOOR AND MARSLAND [1980]: S. S. Isloor ad T. A. Marsland, "The Deadlock Problem: An Overview," *IEEE Computer,* Vol. 13, No. 9, pp. 58–78 (September).

JOHNSON AND RITCHIE [1978]: K. Johnson and D. M. Ritchie, "Portability of C Programs and the UNIX System," *Bell Sys. Tech. J.,* Vol. 57, No. 6, Pt. 2, pp. 2021–2048 (July–August).

JONES AND LISKOV [1978]: A. K. Jones and B. H. Liskov, "A Language Extension for Expressing Constraints on Data Access," *Comm. ACM,* Vol. 21, No. 5, pp. 358–367 (May).

KAHN [1967]: D. Kahn, *The Codebreakers: The Story of Secret Writing,* Macmillan, New York.

KAMEDA [1980]: T. Kameda, "Testing Deadlock-Freedom of Computer Systems," *J. ACM,* Vo. 27, No. 2, pp. 270–280 (April).

KARP [1983]: R. A. Karp, *Proving Operating Systems Correct,* UMI Research Press, Ann Arbor, Mich.

KESSELS [1977]: J. L. Kessels, "An Alternative to Event Queues for Synchronization in Monitors," *Comm. ACM,* Vol. 20, No. 7, pp. 500–503 (July).

KIEBURTZ AND SILBERSCHATZ [1978]: R. B. Kieburtz and A. Silberschatz, "Capability Managers," *IEEE Trans. Software Eng.* Vol. SE-4, No. 6, pp. 467–477 (November).

KILBURN ET AL. [1961a]: T. Kilburn, D. J. Howarth, R. B. Payne, and F. H. Sumner, "The Manchester University Atlas Operating System, Part 1: Internal Organization," *Computer J.,* Vol. 4, No. 3, pp 222–225 (October).

KILBURN ET AL. [1961b]: T. Kilburn, R. B. Payne, and D. J. Howarth, "The Atlas Supervisor," *Proc. Eastern Joint Computer Conf.,* AFIPS, Vol. 20; reprinted in Rosen [1967].

KILBURN ET AL. [1962]: T. Kilburn, D. B. G. Edwards, M. J. Lanigan, and F. H. Sumner, "One-Level Storage System," *IEEE Trans. Electronic Computers,* Vol. EC-11, No. 2 (April).

KLEIN [1979a]: M. Klein, "Files on Parade, I: Types of Files," *Byte,* Vol. 4, No. 2 (February).

KLEIN [1979b]: M. Klein, "Files on Parade, II: Using Files," *Byte,* Vol. 4, No. 3 (March).

KLEINROCK [1967]: L. Kleinrock, "Time-Shared Systems: A Theoretical Treatment," *J. ACM,* Vol. 14, No. 2, pp. 242–261 (April).

KLEINROCK [1970]: L. Kleinrock, "A Continuum of Scheduling Policies," *Proc. AFIPS SJCC,* Vol. 36, pp. 453–458.

KLEINROCK [1975]: L. Kleinrock, *Queueing Systems,* Vol. I, Wiley-Interscience, New York.

KLEINROCK [1976]: L. Kleinrock, *Queueing Systems,* Vol. II, Wiley-Interscience, New York.

KNUTH [1966]: D. E. Knuth, "Additional Comments on a Problem in Concurrent Programming Control," *Comm. ACM,* Vol. 9, No. 5, pp. 3221–3222 (May).

KNUTH [1973]: D. E. Knuth, *The Art of Computer Programming,* Vol. 3: *Sorting and Searching,* Addison-Wesley, Reading, Mass.

KURZBAN ET AL. [1975]: S. Kurzban, T. S. Heines, and A. P. Sayers, *Operating Systems,* Petrocelli/Charter, New York.

LAMBERT [1984]: G. N. Lambert, "A comparative study of system response time on program developer productivity," *IBM System Journal,* Vol. 23, No. 1, pp. 36–43 (1984).

LAMPORT [1974]: L. Lamport, "A New Solution of Dijkstra's Concurrent Programming Problem," *Comm. ACM,* Vol. 17, No. 8, pp. 453–455 (August).

LAMPSON [1968]: B. W. Lampson, "A Scheduling Philosophy for Multiprocessing System," *Comm. ACM,* Vol. 11, No. 5, pp. 347–360.

LAMPSON AND REDELL [1980]: B. W. Lampson and D. D. Redell, "Experience with Processes and Monitors in MESA," *Comm. ACM,* Vol. 23, No. 2, pp. 105–117 (February).

LAUESEN [1975]: S. Lauesen, "A Large Semaphore Based Operating System," *Comm. ACM,* Vol. 18, No. 7, pp. 377–389 (July).

LAVENBERG [1983]: S. S. Lavenberg (ed.), *Computer Performance Modeling Handbook,* Academic Press, New York.

LAZOWSKA ET AL. [1984]: E. D. Lazowska, J. Zahorjan, G. S. Graham, and K. C. Sevcik, *Quantitative System Performance: Computer System Analysis Using Queueing Network Models,* Prentice-Hall, Englewood Cliffs, N. J.

LEIBSON [1982a]: S. Leibson, "The Input/Output Primer, Part 1: What Is I/O?" *Byte,* Vol. 7, No. 2 (January).

LEIBSON [1982b]: S. Leibson, "The Input/Output Primer, Part 2: Interrupts and Direct Memory Access," *Byte,* Vol. 7, No. 3, (February).

LEMPEL [1979]: A. Lempel, "Cryptology in Transition," *ACM Computing Surveys,* Vol. 11, No. 4, pp. 286–303 (December).

LINDEN [1976]: T. A. Linden, "Operating System Structures to Support Security and Reliable Software," *ACM Computing Surveys,* Vol. 8, No. 4, pp. 409–445 (December).

LISKOV [1972]: B. H. Liskov, "The Design of the Venus Operating System," *Comm. ACM,* Vol. 15, No. 3, pp. 144–149 (March).

LISTER [1979]: A. M. Lister, *Fundamentals of Operating Systems,* Macmillan, London; Springer-Verlag, New York.

LOMET [1980]: D. Lomet, "Subsystems of Processes with Deadlock Avoidance," *IEEE Trans. Software Eng.,* Vol. SE-6, No. 3, pp. 297–303 (May).

LOOMIS [1983]: M. Loomis, *Data Management and File Processing,* Prentice-Hall, Englewood Cliffs, N. J.

LUCAS [1971]: H. C. Lucas, "Performance Evaluation and Monitoring," *ACM Computing Surveys,* Vol. 3, No. 3, pp. 79–91 (September).

LUM ET AL. [1971]: V. Y. Lum, P. S. T. Yuen, and M. Dodd, "Key to Address Transformation Techniques: A Fundamental Performance Study on Large Existing Formatted Files," *Comm. ACM,* Vol. 14, No. 4, pp. 228–239 (April).

LYNCH [1967]: W. C. Lynch, "Description of a High Capacity Fast Turnaround University Computing Center," *Proc. ACM Nat. Mtg.* (August).

LYNCH [1972]: W. C. Lynch, "Operating System Performance," *Comm. ACM,* Vol. 15, No. 7, pp. 579–586 (July).

MADNICK AND ALSOP [1969]: S. E. Madnick and J. W. Alsop II, "A Modular Approach to File System Design," *AFIPS SJCC,* Vol. 34, pp. 1–13.

MADNICK AND DONOVAN [1974]: S. E. Madnick and J. J. Donovan, *Operating Systems,* McGraw-Hill, New York.

MANO [1982]: M. M. Mano, *Computer System Architecture,* 2nd ed., Prentice-Hall, Englewood Cliffs, N. J.

MARTIN [1981]: J. Martin, *Computer Networks and Distributed Processing,* Prentice-Hall, Englewood Cliffs, N. J.

McCARTHY ET AL. [1963]: J. McCarthy, F. T. Corbato, and M. M. Daggett, "The Linking Segment Subprogram and Linking Loader," *Comm. ACM,* Vol. 6 (July); also in Rosen [1967].

McGRAW AND ANDREWS [1979]: J. R. McGraw and G. R. Andrews, "Access Control in Parallel Programs," *IEEE Trans. Software Eng.,* Vol. SE-5, No. 1, pp. 1–9 (January).

McKELL ET AL. [1979]: L. J. McKell, J. V. Hansen, and L. E. Heitger, "Charging for Computer Resources," *Computing Surveys,* Vol. 11, No. 2, pp. 105–120 (June).

McKELLAR AND COFFMAN [1969]: A. McKellar and E. G. Coffman, "The Organization of

Matricies and Matrix Operations in a Paged Multiprogramming Environment," *Comm. ACM,* Vol. 12, No. 3, pp. 153–165 (March).

McKinney [1969]: J. M. McKinney, "A Survey of Analytical Time-Sharing Models," *ACM Computing Surveys,* Vol. 1, No. 2, pp. 105–116 (June).

Meyer and Matyas [1982]: C. H. Meyer and S. M. Matyas, *Cryptography: A New Dimension in Computer Data Security,* John Wiley, New York.

Microsoft [1983]: *MS-DOS User Reference Manual,* Microsoft Corp., Bellevue, Wash.

Minoura [1982]: T. Minoura, "Deadlock Avoidance Revisited," *J. ACM,* Vol. 29, No. 4, pp. 1023–1048 (October).

Mock and Swift [1959]: O. Mock and C. J. Swift, "The Share 709 System: Programmed Input-Output Buffering," *J. ACM,* Vol. 6, No. 2, pp. 145–151.

Morris [1973]: J. H. Morris, "Protection in Programming Languages," *Comm. ACM,* Vol. 16, No. 1, pp. 15–21 (January).

Morris [1968]: R. Morris, "Scatter Storage Techniques," *Comm. ACM,* Vol. 11, No. 1, pp. 38–44 (January).

Morris and Thompson [1979]: R. Morris and K. Thompson, "Password Security: A Case History," *Comm. ACM,* Vol. 22, No. 11, pp. 594–597 (November).

Motorola [1986]: *MC68020 vs. 80386,* Motorola Co., Phoenix, AZ.

NBS [1977]: "Data Encryption Standard," *FIPS* Pub. 46, National Bureau of Standards, Washington, D.C. (January).

Nehmer [1975]: J. Nehmer, "Dispatching Primitives for the Construction of Operating System Kernels," *Acta Informatica,* Vol. 5, pp. 237–255.

Nielson [1967]: N. R. Nielson, "The Simulation of Time-Sharing Systems," *Comm. ACM,* Vol. 10, No. 7, pp. 397–412 (July).

Northern California Computer Measurement Group (NCCMG) [1985]: Meeting discussion (November, 1985).

Omlor [1981]: J. D. Omlor, *Efficiency Analysis of File Organization and Information Retrieval,* UMI Research Press, Ann Arbor, Mich.

Oppenheimer and Weizer [1968]: G. Oppenheimer and N. Weizer, "Resource Management for a Medium-Scale Time-Sharing Operating System," *Comm. ACM,* Vol. 11, No. 5, pp. 313–322 (May).

Organick [1972]: E. I. Organick, *The Multics System: An Examination of Its Structure,* MIT Press, Cambridge, Mass.

Organick [1973]: E. I. Organick, *Computer System Organization: The B57000/B67000 Series,* Academic Press, New York.

Ossanna et al. [1965]: J. F. Ossanna, L. E. Mikus, and S. D. Dunten, "Communications and Input/Output Switching in a Multiplex Computing System," *AFIPS FJCC,* Vol. 27, Pt. 1, pp. 231–241.

Padegs [1968]: A. Padegs, "Structural Aspects of the System/360 Model 85: The Cache," *IBM Sys. J.,* Vol. 7, No. 1, pp. 15–22.

Parker [1977]: D. B. Parker, *Crime by Computer,* Scribner's, New York.

Parnas [1972a]: D. L. Parnas, "A Technique for Software Module Specification with Examples," *Comm. ACM,* Vol. 15, No. 12, pp. 1053–1058 (December).

Parnas [1972b]: D. L. Parnas, "On the Criteria to Be Used in Decomposing Systems into Modules," *Comm. ACM,* Vol. 15, No. 5, pp. 330–336 (May).

PARNAS AND HABERMANN [1972]: D. L. Parnas and A. N. Habermann, "Comment on Deadlock Prevention Method," *Comm. ACM,* Vol. 15, No. 9, pp. 840–841 (September).

PETER NORTON COMPUTING [1987a]: *Norton Utilities,* Peter Norton Computing, Santa Monica, Calif.

PETER NORTON COMPUTING [1987b]: *The Commander,* Peter Norton Computing, Santa Monica, Calif.

PETERSON [1981]: G. L. Peterson, "Myths about the Mutual Exclusion Problem," *Information Processing Letters,* Vol. 12, No. 3, pp. 115–116 (June).

PETERSON AND LEW [1986]: W. W. Peterson and A. Lew, *File Design and Programming,* John Wiley, New York.

PETERSON AND SILBERSCHATZ [1983]: J. L. Peterson and A. Silberschatz, *Operating System Concepts,* Addison-Wesley, Reading, Mass.

PFLEEGER [1982]: C. P. Pfleeger, *Machine Organization: An Introduction to the Structure of Computer Systems,* John Wiley, New York.

POPEK [1974]: G. J. Popek, "Protection Structures," *IEEE Computer,* Vol. 7, No. 6, pp. 22–23 (June).

POPEK AND KLINE [1978]: G. J. Popek and C. S. Kline, "Issues in Kernel Design," *AFIPS NCC,* Vol. 47, pp. 1079–1086.

PRESSER [1975]: L. Presser, "Multiprogramming Coordination," *ACM Computing Surveys,* Vol. 7, No. 1, pp. 21–44 (March).

PRESSER AND WHITE [1972]: L. Presser and J. R. White, "Linkers and Loaders," *ACM Computing Surveys,* Vol. 4, No. 3, pp. 149–167 (September).

PRESSMAN [1982]: R. S. Pressman, *Software Engineering: A Practitioner's Approach,* McGraw-Hill, New York.

PRIEVE AND FABRY [1976]: B. G. Prieve and R. S. Fabry, "VMIN—An Optimal Variable-Space Page Replacement Algorithm," *Comm. ACM,* Vol. 19, No. 5, pp. 295–297 (May).

RANDELL [1969]: B. Randell, "A Note on Storage Fragmentation and Program Segmentation," *Comm. ACM,* Vol. 12, No. 7, pp. 365–372 (July).

RANDELL AND KUEHNER [1968]: B. Randell and C. J. Kuehner, "Dynamic Storage Allocation Systems," *Comm. ACM,* Vol. 11, No. 5, pp. 297–304 (May).

REED AND KANODIA [1979]: D. P. Reed and R. K. Kanodia, "Synchronization with Event-counts and Sequences," *Comm. ACM,* Vol. 22, No. 2, pp. 115–123 (February).

RITCHIE [1978]: D. M. Ritchie, "A Retrospective," *Bell Sys. Tech. J.,* Vol. 57, No. 6, Pt. 2, pp. 1947–1969 (July–August).

RITCHIE AND THOMPSON [1974]: D. M. Ritchie and K. Thompson, "The UNIX Time Sharing System," *Comm. ACM,* Vol. 17, No. 7, (July). Reprinted in *Bell Sys. Tech. J.,* Vol. 57, No. 6, Pt. 2, pp. 1909–1929 (July–August 1978).

RIVEST ET AL. [1978]: R. L. Rivest, A. Shamir, and L. Adleman, "On Digital Signatures and Public Key Cryptosystems," *Comm. ACM,* Vol. 21, No. 2, pp. 120–126 (February).

ROSEN [1967]: S. Rosen (ed.), *Programming Systems and Languages,* McGraw-Hill, New York.

ROSEN [1968]: S. Rosen, "Hardware Design Reflecting Software Requirements," *AFIPS FJCC,* Vol. 33, pp. 1443–1449.

RUSCHITZKA AND FABRY [1977]: M. Ruschitzka and R. S. Fabry, "A Unifying Approach to Scheduling," *Comm. ACM,* Vol. 20, No. 7, pp. 469–477 (July).

SALTZER [1974]: J. H. Saltzer, "Protection and the Control of Information Sharing in Multics," *Comm. ACM,* Vol. 17, No. 7, pp. 388–402 (July).

SALTZER AND SCHROEDER [1975]: J. H. Saltzer and M. D. Schroeder, "The Protection of Information in Computer Systems," *Proc. IEEE,* Vol. 63, No. 9, pp. 1278–1308.

SCHMID [1976]: H. A. Schmid, "On the Efficient Implementation of Conditional Critical Regions and the Construction of Monitors," *Acta Informatica,* Vol. 6, No. 3, pp. 227–279.

SCHROEDER AND SALTZER [1972]: M. D. Schroeder and J. H. Saltzer, "A Hardware Architecture for Implementing Protection Rings," *Comm. ACM,* pp. 157– 170 (March).

SEDGEWICK ET AL. [1970]: R. Sedgewick, R. Stone, and J. W. McDonald, "SPY—A Program to Monitor OS/360," *AFIPS FJCC,* Vol. 37, pp. 119–128.

SEVERANCE AND CARLIS [1977]: D. G. Severance and J. V. Carlis, "Selecting Record Access Paths," *ACM Computing Surveys,* Vol. 9, No. 4, pp. 259–272 (December).

SEVERANCE AND DUHNE [1976]: D. G. Severance and R. Duhne, "A Practitioner's Guide to Addressing Algebra," *Comm. ACM,* Vol. 19, No. 6, pp. 314–326 (June).

SHAW [1974]: A. C. Shaw, *The Logical Design of Operating Systems,* Prentice-Hall, Englewood Cliffs, N.J.

SHEMER [1967]: J. E. Shemer, "Some Mathematical Considerations of Time-Sharing Scheduling Algorithms," *J. ACM,* Vol. 14, No. 2, pp. 262–272 (April).

SHORE [1975]: J. E. Shore, "On the External Storage Fragmentation Produced by First-Fit and Best-Fit Allocation Strategies," *Comm. ACM,* Vol. 18, No. 8 (August).

SHUB [1987]: C. Shub, Personal communications, (September 1987).

SIMMONS [1979]: G. J. Simmons, "Symmetric and Asymmetric Encryption," *ACM Computing Surveys,* Vol. 11, No. 4, pp. 304–330 (December).

SMITH [1943]: L. D. Smith, *Cryptography: The Science of Secret Writing,* W. W. Norton Company, New York.

SODERSTROM [1986]: R. Soderstrom, "Better Performance, II," *The HP Chronicle,* Vol. 3, No. 9, pp. 24–26 (August).

SOFTECH [1983]: *UCSD Pascal Reference Manual,* SofTech, Microsystems, Inc., San Diego, Calif.

SOMMERVILLE [1985]: I. Sommerville, *Software Engineering,* 2nd ed., Addison-Wesley, Reading, Mass.

STONE [1982]: H. S. Stone, *Microcomputer Interfacing,* Addison-Wesley, Reading, Mass.

STONE AND FULLER [1973]: H. S. Stone and S. H. Fuller, "On the Near Optimality of the Shortest-Latency-Time-First Drum Scheduling Discipline," *Comm. ACM,* Vol. 16, No. 6, pp. 352–353 (June).

STROLLO ET AL. [1969]: T. R. Strollo, R. S. Tomlinson, and E. R. Fiala, "A Time-Shared I/O Processor for Real-Time Hybrid Computation," *AFIPS FJCC,* Vol. 35, pp. 781–788.

SVOBODOVA [1976]: L. Svobodova, *Computer Performance Measurement and Evaluation Methods: Analysis and Applications,* Elsevier, New York.

TANENBAUM [1987]: A. S. Tanenbaum, *Operating Systems Design and Implementation,* Prentice-Hall, Englewood Cliffs, N.J.

TEOREY AND PINKERTON [1972]: T. J. Teorey and T. B. Pinkerton, "A Comparative Analysis of Disk Scheduling Policies," *Comm. ACM,* Vol. 15, No. 3, pp. 177–184 (March).

TEKTRONIX [1982]: *Tektronix 8500 Series Development Systems,* Tektronix Corp., Beaverton, Oreg.

THADHANI [1981]: A. J. Thadhani, "Interactive user productivity," *IBM Systems Journal,* Vol. 20, No. 4, pp. 407–423.

THADHANI [1984]: A. J. Thadhani, "Factors affecting programmer program productivity during application development," *IBM Systems Journal,* Vol. 23, No. 1, pp. 19–35.

THOMPSON [1978]: K. Thompson, "UNIX Implementation," *Bell Sys. Tech. J.,* Vol. 57, No. 6, Pt. 2, pp. 1931–1946 (July–August).

TSICHRITZIS AND BERNSTEIN [1974]: D. C. Tsichritzis and P. A. Bernstein, *Operating Systems,* Academic Press, New York.

TURNER [1986]: R. W. Turner, *Operating Systems: Design and Implementation,* Macmillan, New York.

WATSON [1970]: R. W. Watson, *Timesharing System Design Concepts,* McGraw-Hill, New York.

WILHELM [1976]: N. C. Wilhelm, "An Anomoly in Disk Scheduling: A Comparison of FCFS and SSTF Seek Scheduling Using an Empirical Model for Disk Accesses," *Comm. ACM,* Vol. 19, No. 1 (January).

WILKES [1972]: M. V. Wilkes, *Time-Sharing Computer Systems,* 2nd ed., MacDonald, London, and American Elsevier, New York.

WILKES [1973]: M. V. Wilkes, "The Dynamics of Paging," *Computer J.,* Vol. 16, pp. 4–9 (February).

WITT [1985]: B. I. Witt, "Communicating Modules: A Software Design Model for Concurrent Distributed Systems," *IEEE Computer,* Vol. 18, No. 1, pp. 67–77 (January).

WOLVERTON [1984]: V. Wolverton, *Running MS DOS,* Microsoft Press, Bellevue, Washington.

WOOD [1977]: H. M. Wood, *The Use of Passwords for Controlled Access to Computer Resources,* National Bureau of Standards, Special Publication 500-9, Washington, D.C. (May).

WULF ET AL. [1974]: W. A. Wulf, E. S. Cohen, W. M. Corwin, A. K. Jones, R. Levin, C. Pierson, and F. J. Pollack, "HYDRA: The Kernel of a Multiprocessor Operating System," *Comm. ACM,* Vol. 17, No. 6, pp. 337–345 (June).

Index